COOPERATION AND CONFLICT
IN OCCUPATIONAL SAFETY
AND HEALTH

COOPERATION AND CONFLICT IN OCCUPATIONAL SAFETY AND HEALTH

A MULTINATION STUDY OF THE AUTOMOTIVE INDUSTRY

RICHARD E. WOKUTCH

New York
Westport, Connecticut
London

Library of Congress Cataloging-in-Publication Data

Wokutch, Richard E.
  Cooperation and conflict in occupational safety and health : a
multination study of the automotive industry / Richard E. Wokutch.
      p.   cm.
  Includes bibliographical references.
  ISBN 0-275-93530-2 (alk. paper)
  1. Automobile industry and trade—Safety measures.   2. Automobile
industry and trade—Health aspects.   I. Title.
HD7269.A8W65   1990
363.11'96292—dc20   89-77106

British Library Cataloguing in Publication Data is available.

Library of Congress Catalog Card Number: 89-77106
ISBN: 0-275-93530-2

First published in 1990

Praeger Publishers, One Madison Avenue, New York, NY 10010
An imprint of Greenwood Publishing Group, Inc.

Printed in the United States of America

The paper used in this book complies with the
Permanent Paper Standard issued by the National
Information Standards Organization (Z39.48-1984).

10 9 8 7 6 5 4 3 2 1

To Andreas and Mary Ellen

CONTENTS

ABBREVIATIONS

ANSI	American National Standards Institute
ASiG	Arbeitssicherheitsgesetz
ASV	see NBOSH
BDI	Federation of German Industry
BLS	Bureau of Labor Statistics
COTU	Central Organization of Trade Unions
DBA	Confederation of German Employers
DGB	German Federation of Trade Unions
FKE	Federation of Kenyan Employers
GDP	gross domestic product
GNP	gross national product
HSW Act	Health and Safety at Work Act
KANU	Kenyan African National Union
LDP	Liberal Democratic Party
LO	Landsorganisationen or Swedish Confederation of Trade Unions
MNC	multinational corporation
MIOSHA	Michigan OSHA
NBOSH	National Board of Occupational Safety and Health (sometimes designated as ASV)
NIOSH	National Institute of Occupational Safety and Health

OECD	Organization for Economic Cooperation and Development
OSH Act	Occupational Safety and Health Act
OSHA	Occupational Safety and Health Administration
QWL	quality of work life
SACO/SR	Swedish Confederation of Professional Organizations
SAF	Svenska Arbetsgivareföreningen or Swedish Employers' Confederation
SSI	Supplemental Security Income
TCA	Trade Cooperative Association
TCO	Tjanstemannens Central Organization or Swedish Federation of Salaried Employees in Industry and Service
UAW	United Auto Workers Union
YI	Yrkesinspektionen or Factory Inspectorate

ACKNOWLEDGMENTS

This book represents a figurative and literal intellectual odyssey, that would not have been possible without the assistance of a great many people and substantial institutional support. The research for this book took over eight years and covered over 60,000 miles in seven countries. On numerous occasions along the way I found myself lost (both literally and figuratively). I am indebted to the colleagues whose advice helped steer my thinking on this project in the right direction. This included directing me through the maze of local customs and protocols surrounding the arrangement of interviews and company visits and the release of frequently sensitive data.

I was particularly fortunate to receive two Fulbright Research Fellowships in support of this project. This research would not have been possible without the financial and logistical support provided by these fellowships. The Fulbright Program staffs, current Fulbright recipients, and Fulbright alumni formed a type of extended family that was immensely valuable to me in my research. I would especially like to acknowledge the support provided by the German Fulbright Kommission, and Ulrich Littmann and Reiner Rohr in particular; and by the Japan-United States Educational Commission (Fulbright Program), and Caroline Mantano Yang, Kazuko Kamimura, Atsuko Ozawa, and Mizuho Iwata in particular.

I am equally indebted to my host institutions in Germany and Japan: the Science Center Berlin (Wissenschaftszentrum Berlin) and Hiroshima Institute of Technology (Hiroshima Kogyo Daigaku). Attempting to get settled in and to do substantive work during an all too brief visit can impose difficulties on both the visitor and his hosts. Nevertheless, colleagues and support staff at both of these institutions made my stays at them both pleasant and productive. I would like to acknowledge especially the assistance of Meinolf Dierkes and Ariane Berthoin Antal at the Science Center Berlin and that of Toshiro Kobayashi, Tsuyoshi Ishida, and Bob McWilliams at Hiroshima Institute of Technology. Other German and Japanese colleagues for whose assistance I am indebted include Freidrich Hauss and Rolf Rosenbrock, Koji Matsuda, Michio Nitta, and Yanosuke Mafune.

I wish to acknowledge the support of several other institutions. Virginia Tech and The R. B. Pamplin College of Business provided numerous forms, including travel support and released time from teaching and committee responsibilities, which were picked up by my colleagues. The Barringer Center of Industrial Relations in the Department of Management at Virginia Tech also supported this research. The U.S. embassies in West Germany, Kenya, and Japan and the West German, Swedish, British, Kenyan, and Japanese embassies in the United States provided valuable information and assistance. The Commonwealth of Virginia Trade Center in Tokyo, the Japan Institute of Labour, and the British Fulbright Commission provided important assistance in arranging numerous interviews. Obviously the individual companies that I visited for this research provided invaluable assistance, but confidentiality considerations prohibit me from naming them or thanking individuals within these companies. By the same token, I cannot identify company unions or individuals within these organizations. I do, however, wish to acknowledge the cooperation of the United Auto Workers Union.

My colleagues at Virginia Tech assisted me a great deal with my research by reading early drafts of this manuscript and providing me with feedback and encouragement. These include Dow Scott, Larry Alexander, Al Schick, Kent Murrmann, Jon Shepard, Arnold Schuetz, Konrad Kubin, and Bob Litschert. I would especially like to acknowledge the support and encouragement of Bob Litschert, my department head during most of this project who never lost faith in it despite the "light at the end of the tunnel" predictions he heard from me over a several-year time period.

I would also like to acknowledge the helpful comments on earlier drafts of this manuscript made by Kenneth Thomas of the Naval Postgraduate School.

An undertaking of this nature could not be accomplished without an enormous amount of secretarial assistance. Due to the longevity of this project (and perhaps also due to the unpleasantness of the secretarial tasks associated with it), there have been a great many secretaries who have provided assistance. These include Alice LoMascolo, Sandy Crigger, Frank Smith, Dinah Akers, Anna LoMascolo, Angie Beane, Melissa Kessinger, Allison Taylor, Sarah Wall, and Adair Hocking.

A similarly large number of graduate assistants have been involved in this project during its creation. I would especially like to acknowledge the assistance of Josetta McLaughlin with Chapter 5, Liz McKinney with the bibliography, and Suzanne Rosenthal with editing early drafts of the manuscript. Other graduate assistants who have helped with this project include John Meyer, Martin Rexroad, Bong-Gyu Park, Terry Fletcher, Jim Fluri, Kannan Ramaswamy, Brian Methvin, and Scott Lyman. An undergraduate work-study student, Deborah Cregger, also assisted on this project.

I would like to give special thanks to my parents, Charles and Annette Wokutch, who instilled in me the desire to learn at an early age and who, at considerable personal sacrifice, provided me with the educational opportunities without which this book would not have been possible.

Most of all, I would like to thank my wife, Mary Ellen, and my son, Andreas, for providing me with the time and the incentive to pursue my research. When I started this project Andreas had not yet been conceived and when it is finally published he will be able to read it. (Although whether he will want to is another matter altogether.) Their support and understanding through prolonged international separations and long work weeks enabled me to make this book a reality.

COOPERATION AND CONFLICT
IN OCCUPATIONAL SAFETY
AND HEALTH

1

INTRODUCTION

In recent years, U.S. industry has been confronted with a host of problems, including declining productivity growth, loss of market share in numerous industries to foreign competitors, and frequently acrimonious relations with various corporate "stakeholder" groups (e.g., employees, stockholders, consumers, and environmentalists). These problems were especially severe during the 1981-83 recession, when the U.S. economy suffered through bankruptcy rates second only to those of the Great Depression. Although economic growth has resumed since then, the record trade deficits of the mid and late 1980s indicate that serious underlying problems remain.

These problems and stakeholder confrontations led many firms to reevaluate established business practices. Some observers have called for a comprehensive reformulation of the established set of institutional relationships among business, government, labor, and other important groups in society. In calling for changes, these commentators have frequently cited the managerial practices and institutional arrangements of our successful trading partners, notably Japan, West Germany, and Sweden, as having features worth emulating in the United States (Abegglen, 1984; *Business Week*, 1987; Cohen, 1985; Freund and Epstein, 1984; Magaziner and Reich, 1983; Otsubo, 1986; Ouchi, 1981; Pascale and Athos, 1981; Schonberger, 1982; Taylor, 1979; *Time*, 1981; Vogel, 1986). In particular, some have argued that there is a need to develop a "new social contract" involving cooperative relationships among business, government, labor, and other important groups to replace the traditional social contract characterized by confrontational relationships among these groups.

This research is one effort to assess the viability of this suggestion. It is a multinational study that investigates the regulation and management of occupational safety and health, a work issue that would seem ideally suited for cooperation among the involved parties. This volume describes the results of an eight-year study of occupational safety and health in the automotive industries of several countries. This research has examined and compared management practices and institutional relationships pertaining to occupational safety and health policies and activities in the United States, Sweden, West Germany, the United Kingdom, Japan, and in one developing country, Kenya. It considers these in the context of U.S. firms operating both in the United States and abroad and of foreign firms operating in their home markets and in the United States.

Principal attention is devoted in this study to considering how national legal, political, and structural arrangements pertaining to occupational safety and health affect performance at the national, industrial, corporate, and plant levels. Thus, the broad social, economic, political, and legal environments that shape these arrangements are examined as they relate to occupational safety and health activities and outcomes. It is argued that these factors dictate to a great extent what can and cannot be done in the field of occupational safety and health, therefore suggesting a considerable degree of environmental determinism in this area of management.

Nevertheless, within these national contexts, the considerable variances in occupational safety and health performance among industries, firms, and plants indicate that organizational efforts to address these issues can make a difference. Thus, this study also lends support to the strategic choice perspective (Child, 1972) of the strategic management field as it pertains to occupational safety and health. This suggests that individual managers and their strategic choices can have a considerable impact upon performance. It also means that the potential exists for improvements in safety and health performance to be derived from learning about the relative effectiveness of different approaches. To facilitate such understanding, this research compares and contrasts various national and corporate mechanisms for promoting occupational safety and health. Moreover, it explicitly considers the issue of the potential transferability of safety and health approaches between firms and between countries.

A related focus of this research is on cooperation and conflict among the involved parties in the handling of occupational safety and health in different countries and companies. Cooperation and conflict regarding occupational safety and health are considered both in terms of their causal origins in these environmental factors and their effects on safety and health performance. Based on the findings of this research, a contingency theory of labor-management-government cooperation and conflict is presented. Specifically, it is argued that cooperation is beneficial to promoting occupational safety and health only when each of the parties (labor, management, and government) have some minimum level of power and assertiveness. When this condition is not met, numerous problems arise. This contingency theory sheds new light on debates about the need for and possibility of developing more cooperative labor-management-government relations in the United States consistent with the notion of a new social contract.

Occupational safety and health is a complex issue, and its complexity is multiplied manifold when this issue is considered in an international environment. What becomes clear very early in the study of occupational safety and health is that one cannot look simply at managerial aspects of safety and health without considering regulatory issues. By the same token, regulatory considerations make much more sense when viewed in conjunction with their managerial implications.

This volume is organized in the following manner. The remainder of this chapter contains further discussion of the significance of the issues studied in this research; definitions of key concepts and an overview of the research design are also provided. Chapter 2 provides a historical overview of occupational safety and health in the United States, with special attention devoted to issues of current concern regarding activities of the Occupational Safety and Health Administration (OSHA). This overview is provided to ensure that the reader who is not knowledgeable about occupational safety and health issues in the United States has sufficient background to appreciate the comparisons made later with how these issues are handled in other countries. Chapter 3 describes occupational safety and health activities and relationships in the U.S. automotive industry, the focal industry of this study. Chapter 4 describes and contrasts the handling of occupational safety and health in five countries: the United Kingdom, West Germany, Sweden, Japan, and Kenya. National safety and health systems are described within the context of the social, economic, political, and legal environments in which they operate. Comparisons on several relevant dimensions are made among these five countries and the United States. Chapter 5 provides a multinational comparison of aggregate national statistics of occupational injury rates. Various factors that hamper such comparisons are identified and these are shown to derive from the unique national social, economic, political, and legal environments. In an attempt to take these factors into account, long-term trends in injury rates within countries are considered and national manufacturing-sector occupational fatality rates are compared. Chapters 6 through 8 shift to firm-level and plant-level analyses. Chapter 6 contains an overview and analysis of occupational safety and health activities of one U.S.-based automotive firm, Company X, focusing on three plants--one in the United States, one in Germany, and one in Kenya. Chapter 7 describes and analyzes occupational safety and health activities of another U.S.-based automotive firm, Company Y, concentrating on one U.S. plant and one British plant. Chapter 8 compares the occupational safety and health activities of two plants of Company Z, a Swedish-based automotive firm. One of these plants is located in Sweden and the other is located in the United States. Chapter 9 discusses the conclusions and implications of this research and provides certain recommendations for the handling of occupational safety and health derived from this study.

THE DECLINING U.S. COMPETITIVE POSITION

The evidence of the decline of the United States' competitive position in world markets is inescapable. This country's balance of payments deficit exceeded $100 billion in 1988 for the fifth straight year. The international debt needed to finance the recent deficits has erased all the net foreign investment the United States had accumulated throughout the balance of this century, during much of which this country was the undisputed dominant world economic power. In mid-1985 the United States became a net debtor nation, and by 1987 the United States had amassed the world's largest net foreign debt.

There is little doubt that declining competitiveness of U.S. industries, particularly manufacturing industries, is responsible for much of this deficit problem. Data compiled by the U.S. Bureau of Labor Statistics indicate that U.S. manufacturing output per hour worked increased at an average annual rate of 3.2 percent from 1960 to 1973, but then increased at only a 2.2 percent rate from 1973 to 1985 (Neef, 1986). Not surprisingly, this productivity performance compares unfavorably with the productivity gains of many other industrialized nations. For instance, Japan posted average annual manufacturing productivity gains of 10.3 percent and 5.6 percent, respectively, for these two time periods. Germany (5.8 percent, 3.7 percent), Sweden (6.4 percent, 3.0 percent), and even the United Kingdom (4.3 percent, 2.7 percent) had productivity gains that exceeded those of the United States in both time periods.

One explanation for the decline of the United States' competitive position is the adversarial nature of relationships among management, labor, government, and other corporate stakeholders. While it is true that adversarial relations with corporate stakeholder groups have confronted management for much of our nation's history, it is also true that since the 1960s management's confrontations with labor, consumers, stockholders, environmentalists, minorities, and the various governmental regulatory agencies that have promoted their concerns appear to have become more numerous and more bitter. These developments have attracted the attention of business observers because they have been accompanied by an erosion of the competitive position of the United States in world markets. Moreover, many have argued that these confrontations have actually *caused* this erosion.

One piece of evidence suggesting that the labor-management relations in the United States are in fact more confrontational than those of many of our important competitor countries is provided by comparing industrial dispute rates. Table 1-1 shows the total work days lost due to industrial disputes per 1,000 workers in recent years in the United States, Germany, Sweden, the United Kingdom, Japan, and Kenya. Although there are important differences in the methods of recording and calculating industrial dispute rates in these countries,

TABLE 1-1
TOTAL WORKDAYS LOST DUE TO INDUSTRIAL DISPUTES
PER 1,000 WORKERS

Year	United States	West Germany	Sweden	United Kingdom	Japan	Kenya
1972	329.45[1]	2.53	2.72	995.38	100.40[1]	58.99
1973	328.55[1]	21.49	3.04	292.44	87.54	55.49
1974	905.08[1]	40.37	14.55	596.82	184.51	154.85
1975	204.58	2.72	89.98	243.34	153.47	10.60
1976	269.98	21.30	6.05	134.08	61.73	30.61
1977	231.02	0.95	21.26	413.59	28.43	10.22
1978	247.52	167.60	9.02	381.06	25.10	20.54
1979	483.08	18.94	6.85	1,176.09	16.98	N.A.
1980	209.90	4.98	1,058.24	478.89	18.09	N.A.
1981	168.41	2.28	49.50	177.83	9.92	39.30
1982	91.04	0.60	0.42	225.41	9.54	25.68
1983	173.16	1.65	8.74	161.33	8.84	16.94
1984	80.93	227.90	7.35	1,147.02	6.14	35.18
Average	215.96	39.48	98.29	494.10	50.86	41.67

N.A. = not available

Sources: International Labour Office. 1982 Year Book of Labour Statistics. Geneva, Switzerland, 1982; International Labour Office. 1985 Year Book of Labour Statistics. Geneva, Switzerland, 1985.
[1] These figures are not comparable with other years because of changes in reporting methods used by the country. Hence they have not been included in calculating averages.

these statistics still provide some general insight into the relative frequency of industrial disputes. The average U.S. rate for the time period covered of 216 days per 1,000 workers was much higher than the rates for Germany (39), Sweden (98), Japan (51), and Kenya (42). The United States also fares worse than these countries using data derived from a new method of reporting U.S. strikes begun in 1979, which exclude strikes involving less than 1,000 workers. These new data result in a 201-day average for the 1979-84 time period. Only the United Kingdom, which until recently served as a classic example of a national industrial failure, exceeded the United States with an average of 494 days lost due to industrial disputes. Although there were some improvements in both U.S. productivity growth and work stoppages during the early 1980s in the United States. (*Business Week*, 1984; Perl, 1985a), concern about these issues remains strong. Alarmingly, in 1986, there was zero growth in corporate productivity.

OCCUPATIONAL SAFETY AND HEALTH

The field of occupational safety and health provides an intriguing arena in which to examine relations among labor, management, and government. It is an issue that has been accorded increased importance in recent years. It is also an issue that would appear to be ideal for eliciting labor-management cooperation due to shared interests in reducing occupational injuries and illnesses. Nevertheless, occupational safety and health has proven to be the focus of bitter conflicts over the years.

The reasons for workers' interest in promoting occupational safety and health are obvious, as workers are the ones who may become injured or ill. Management's interest in promoting safety and health is almost as obvious: injuries and illnesses are costly to industry because of potential expenses associated with lost production, increased medical and insurance payments, uninsured compensation to workers, damage to equipment, injury reporting and investigation costs, costs of retraining injured workers or training new workers, legal expenses, and government fines. In 1986 alone, the National Safety Council estimated that there were 1.8 million disabling work injuries that occurred in the United States resulting in a total cost of over $35 billion (National Safety Council, 1987).[1] Estimates of the number of workdays lost due to occupational injuries range from 36.4 million to 70 million days annually (Office of Technology Assessment, 1985). Even using the lower estimates of lost workdays due to injuries, these have exceeded the number of workdays lost due to industrial disputes in the United States for most recent years. In addition, an estimated 100,000 deaths annually result from occupational diseases (President, 1972).

At the firm level, the impact of costs associated with occupational safety and health is just as significant. For example, Roger Smith (1983) estimated that General Motors paid $2.2 billion for health-care insurance in 1983. He also noted that all health-care costs combined added $480 to the cost of each vehicle GM produced in the United States in 1982. Undoubtedly, costs have risen substantially since then, both for General Motors and other firms.

Despite the mutual advantages to management and workers of a safe and healthy work environment, occupational safety and health nevertheless has been a highly controversial issue in labor-management-government relations in the United States and overseas. Recent events have illustrated just how contentious occupational safety and health can be. One was the disaster in Bhopal, India, when toxic gasses escaped from the Union Carbide plant, resulting in the deaths of several thousand people. Closer to home, gas leaks from Union Carbide's operations at Institute, West Virginia, along with OSHA penalties of $1.4 million levied against the company produced added controversy. Also controversial were fines in the hundreds of thousands of dollars levied against such firms as Ford, General Motors, Chrysler, and IBP for underrecording work injuries. Moreover, in a highly publicized case, several managers at an Illinois film reprocessing plant were convicted of murdering a worker from whom they withheld information about workplace hazards (i.e., that he was working with cyanide).

Various authors have criticized business and government in the United States for lack of sufficient concern about safety and health (Gersuny, 1981; Page and O'Brien, 1973; Simon, 1983; Wallick, 1972). Others have criticized OSHA for allegedly excessive and unnecessary regulations (Arthur Andersen and Company, 1979; *Business Week*, 1980; Viscusi, 1983; Weidenbaum, 1981). OSHA has even been the target of ridicule and scorn by both Democrats and Republicans during recent national political campaigns, particularly the 1976, 1980, and 1984 presidential campaigns.

The costs of OSHA regulations have no doubt been responsible for much of this criticism. Bacow (1980) estimated that the capital costs of OSHA compliance in the 1970s exceeded $3 billion annually. Other organizational expenses related to general administration and knowledge of regulations, and materials handling and storage, were also significant (Arthur Andersen and Company, 1979). It is clear that at some point the economic costs of safety and health practices *can* exceed the economic benefits of these practices. At issue in the controversy surrounding OSHA is whether or not this is currently the case in the United States, with respect to the overall regulatory regime and/or specific regulations. Similarly, controversies can and do arise in individual companies and plants over the appropriate level of concern for safety and health. Related controversies have also developed in recent years over whether or not other issues, in addition to economic costs and benefits, should be considered in the regulation and management of safety and health. For example, in a landmark 1981 decision, the Supreme Court ruled that a worker has a basic right to a safe and healthy work environment and that this right should not be subjected to cost-benefit analysis *(American Textile Manufacturers Institute v. Donovan,* 1981).

One important finding of this research is that some degree of conflict pertaining to occupational safety and health may be both unavoidable and even desirable in terms of improving safety and health performance. This is because certain beneficial safety and health activities are unprofitable from the firm's financial perspective and others are unpopular from the workers' comfort or convenience perspective. Thus, assertiveness by labor, management, and government in coping with certain conflicts can reduce industrial injuries and illnesses.

Much of the research to date on occupational worker safety and health has focused on the issue at a national level (Ashford, 1976; Mendeloff, 1979) or at a plant or company level (Bacow, 1980; Blake, Frederick, and Myers, 1976; Kochan, Dyer, and Lypsky, 1977; Rinefort, 1977; Wokutch, 1979). Where international comparisons have been made, these have been concerned with national policies on worker safety and health (Ashford, 1976; Badaracco, 1985; Barth, 1980; Brickman, Jasanoff, and Ilgen, 1985; Hauss and Rosenbrock, 1982; Kelman, 1981). With few exceptions (notably Grunberg, 1983, 1984, and the International Labour Office, 1984b), researchers have not studied occupational safety and health by making plant-to-plant and company-to-company comparisons across countries. This book seeks to help fill that gap by comparing safety and health practices and experiences of company plants operating in different countries in light of national circumstances. Differences between companies headquartered in different countries are also noted. Analysis at the national and industrial levels is provided to supply a context in which to appreciate these comparisons.

In this study, greater attention is focused on occupational safety rather than on occupational health due to the lesser degree of difficulty involved in making international comparisons of safety issues. The statistics on work-related injuries, although also difficult to compare, are more directly comparable than statistics on occupational illnesses. Still, many of the organizational structures designed to promote occupational safety also are used to promote occupational health; and those involved in this field often use the terms "safety" and "safety and health" interchangeably. On occasion this term safety is used in this broader sense in this book, but the meaning should be clear from the context.

THE AUTOMOTIVE INDUSTRY

The automotive industry provides an important and interesting industrial context for this study. The fortunes of this industry have served as a bellwether of the fortunes of the U.S. economy in general. Still, probably no other industry has been confronted by so many economic and social crises, nor has there ever been such an obvious need for cooperation among labor, management, and government. In 1960, U.S. manufacturers produced 48 percent of the world's 16 million cars and trucks, and Japanese manufacturers produced 4 percent. By 1983, the United States held only 24 percent of the world market, while Japan held 28 percent. Studies in the early 1980s placed the Japanese production cost advantage for building a typical small car in Japan at approximately $1,400 to $2,000 per car (Altshuler et al., 1984; National Research Council, 1982). Even adding approximately $400 per vehicle for transportation expenses to the United States (National Research Council, 1982) left Japanese producers with a considerable competitive advantage. Only the substantial exchange rate changes since these studies were conducted have managed to erode some of this Japanese cost advantage.

Japanese exports of automobiles to the United States have been a source of friction in deteriorating trade relations between these two countries. In response to U.S. pressures, all the major Japanese automotive companies either have already set up operations in the United States or will have done so by the early 1990s. As these firms begin production, competitive pressures are bound to intensify. Both U.S. and foreign-based firms will be under increasing pressure to decrease costs and increase production flexibility and product quality. Although improved performance in the safety and health arena is, in many ways, consistent with these other objectives, it is likely that managers and workers will be sorely tempted to sacrifice safety and health in pursuit of such goals.

In addition to foreign competition, a variety of internal problems and external threats have confronted the U.S. auto industry. Since 1965, when Ralph Nader's book *Unsafe at Any Speed* was published, the U.S. auto industry has been a favorite target of social critics and corporate activists. Consumer advocates, labor unions, minority groups, stockholder activists, environmentalists, and the governmental agencies representing these interests have pressed various (and frequently conflicting) demands on automotive firms. The two "oil shocks" of 1973 and 1979 had a great impact on the industry and even threatened the survival of major auto industry employers, including Chrysler, Ford, and American Motors. These oil shocks and competitive pressures later required the major automotive firms to invest an estimated $55 to $80 billion from 1980 to 1984 to overhaul the design of vehicles and production processes.

Competitive pressures also produced fundamental changes in institutional relationships within the industry and in industry relations with government. These changes included the appointment of UAW presidents Douglas Fraser and Owen Bieber to Chrysler's Board of Directors, government-guaranteed loans to Chrysler, wage concessions by workers, reductions of white-collar work forces, profit-sharing plans, employee involvement programs, negotiated restrictions on Japanese imports, and the Reagan administration's efforts to lessen the cost of government regulations. Although many of these changes were quite controversial at the time they were taken, together they may represent important steps in the development of more effective relationships among labor, management, and government.

DEFINITIONS

This study will utilize a number of key concepts to examine the occupational safety and health activities in the automotive industries of the various locations considered. This section provides operational definitions of these key concepts.

Corporate Social Responsibility, Enlightened Self-Interest, and Altruism

Occupational safety and health is typically considered a realm in which firms have social impacts and for which firms are said to have social responsibilities. Many conflicting definitions of the term "corporate social responsibility" have been provided in the literature. Schick, Wokutch, and Conners (1985) identified over 60 definitions of this term, but there are many nuances in these about which we need not be concerned here. A composite definition compiled by the author for teaching purposes will be sufficient for our present needs:

> Corporate social responsibility is decision makers taking morally permissible actions which protect and improve the welfare of society as a whole along with their own interests, but sometimes at the expense of their own interests, even in the long run.

Several distinctions made in this definition are relevant to considerations of occupational safety and health. First, socially responsible activities may benefit the firm in either the short run or the long run. Corporate safety and health officials frequently cite such benefits to the firm in justifying safety and health activities. For example, certain expenditures to increase the safety of production processes or worker awareness of safety could produce short-run financial benefits for the firm. These might result from decreased accident-related costs, such as medical expenses, absenteeism, compensation to injured workers, equipment damage, and lost production.

There are also potential long-run benefits of other safety and health activities. These might result from reduced costs associated with occupational illnesses that are diagnosed years later, or from avoiding long-term increases in contributions to workers' compensation. Safe and healthy working conditions may improve the morale of workers and lead to greater productivity. Also, occupational safety and health conditions have been cited in UAW drives to organize nonunion plants in the United States. A firm hoping to avoid unionization for financial or other reasons might find it in its long-run interest to provide a margin of safety and health in the plant over and above that required by law. Long-run benefits may also result from the public-relations value of a firm's activities. The firm might find it easier to attract qualified workers if it has a reputation for being concerned about its workers. There may even be some consumers who purchase products they would otherwise not have purchased if the firm had a very poor reputation on this dimension.

Activities which promote the interests of society along with the long-run interests of the corporation are said to be in a firm's "enlightened self-interest." Firms that operate this way are also described as pursuing a goal of "long-run profit maximization." The expression "safety pays," which is frequently used by management and labor officials involved in safety and health activities, suggests that safety and health activities are in a firm's enlightened self-interest and that undertaking them will maximize the firm's profits in the long run.

Implicit in the above definition of corporate social responsibility is the possibility that firms will undertake activities that benefit society but are actually detrimental to the firm from a financial standpoint, even in the long run. Such activities would be described as altruistic in an economic or financial sense. The definition of altruism to be used here is the following: promoting the interests of others, that is, society, employees, consumers, etc., without any profit incentive or expectation of profit. Altruism would occur in a firm's occupational safety and health activities if the cost of some measure voluntarily undertaken to promote safety and health exceeded all short-run and long-run benefits of this measure.

These concepts relate to two important questions regarding occupational safety and health: (1) Are firms doing everything they can with respect to occupational safety and health that is in their own enlightened self-interest (or long-run profit interests)? and (2) Are firms undertaking some such activities for altruistic purposes? While the long-run profit implications of activities that are undertaken, or of potential activities not undertaken, are extremely difficult or impossible to ascertain precisely, we will attempt to shed some light on these matters in this book. In doing so, we will address both of these questions.

Conflict and Cooperation

There is no one generally accepted definition of the term "conflict" in the literature. Pondy (1967) and Fink (1968) reviewed and categorized a wide range of definitions and conceptualizations of conflict that existed in the literature, and an even greater diversity of views appears to exist today. Pondy (1967), Fink (1968), and Thomas (1976) each suggested the use of a broad definition of conflict that would encompass most of the different conceptions of this term. One such definition was offered by Thomas: "Conflict is the process which begins when one party perceives that the other has frustrated or is about to frustrate some concern of his" (1976, p. 891). This is a general *situational* definition of the term. That is, conflict is regarded as a kind of situation in which various types of behaviors, emotions, and tactics may result (Thomas, 1979).

In contrast, Schmidt and Kochan provide a narrower, *behavioral* definition of conflict: "overt behavior arising out of a process in which one unit seeks the advancement of its own interests in its relationships with the others. This advancement must result from determined action, not fortuitous circumstance" (1972, p. 363).

This behavioral definition is closer to the popular usage of the term and the sense in which it is used in the title of this book. That is, conflict is seen as a specific kind of behavior (adversarial), which one can use to deal with the kinds of situations mentioned above. Both situational and behavioral views of conflict are utilized in this study, but it should be clear from the context which is being used at the time.

The concerns (or interests) relative to occupational safety and health that may be frustrated are numerous. These include such management concerns as the cost and effectiveness of different approaches to reduce or eliminate hazards in the workplace. Related concerns are compliance with safety and health regulations and containment of the costs of injuries. Workers share concerns about the effectiveness of safety and health measures but are also likely to be very concerned with the convenience to them of various alternative measures. Federal and state safety and health regulators take account of both labor and management concerns and relevant political considerations in guiding their own activities. Another less obvious safety and health-related concern of management, workers, and safety and health regulators is the question of who should control the work environment.

There appears to be less serious dispute in the literature over the meaning of "cooperation." Cooperation or a cooperative situation is defined by Deutsch as "one in which the goals of the participants are so linked that any participant can attain his goal if, and only if, the others with whom he is linked can attain their goals" (1973, p. 20). The term "goals" in this definition for our purposes can be taken to refer to the safety and health concerns specified above.

The traditional lay view of conflict and cooperation is that these are on opposite ends of one behavioral continuum; conflict is viewed as being undesirable and cooperation as being desirable. Alternative views, however, have emerged in the literature in recent years. Negative features of conflict that are assumed to exist according to this traditional view are the lack of recognition of shared goals and the resulting inability to achieve them, the disaffection of the losing party in zero-sum situations, and the potential for conflict to degenerate into disruptive and destructive relations producing physical or emotional harm.

However, scholars have noted that there are positive features of conflict. Deutsch (1973) argues that conflict tends to stabilize and integrate relationships, that it can revitalize existing norms and establish new ones in the relevant group or organization, and that it can help sort out the leadership in organizations. Other benefits include increased motivation, interest, and creativity; higher-quality ideas and solutions; and, in the case of external conflict, increased internal cohesiveness (Deutsch, 1973; Thomas, 1976).

Positive features of cooperation that are suggested by the traditional view include the enhancement of a group or organization's ability to achieve a common or shared goal. Cooperation is also typically believed to enhance the quality of the personal relationships within the group.

There are, however, some who contend that, just as there are positive features of conflict, there are negative features of cooperation. Deutsch (1973) argues that cooperation often leads to specialization and associated negative consequences, such as provincialism and the inability to see the "whole picture." "Group-think" decision making that does not challenge crucial but questionable assumptions can also result. Finally, the enhanced personal relationships can lead to nepotism, strained relationships with others, and, ultimately, lower levels of goal attainment.

In addition to the good/bad view of cooperation and conflict being questioned, others dispute their unidimensionality. Ruble and Thomas (1976) and Thomas (1976) suggested, instead, a two-dimensional model of conflict behavior (see Figure 1-1). This model refers to the behavior of one party toward another party in a conflict situation. Assertiveness (i.e., the emphasis on satisfying one's own concerns) is plotted on the Y-axis; cooperativeness (i.e., emphasis on satisfying others' concerns) is plotted on the X-axis. Ruble and Thomas labeled five regions on the figure as follows: competing (high assertiveness, low cooperativeness); avoiding (low assertiveness, low cooperativeness); compromising (intermediate in both assertiveness and cooperativeness); accommodating (low assertiveness, high cooperativeness); and collaborating (high assertiveness, high cooperativeness). Competing behavior as defined by Ruble and Thomas (1976) corresponds to the popular behavioral view of conflict specified by Schmidt and Kochan (1972). The terms "confrontational" or "adversarial" are also used in this sense in this book.

Conflict behaviors of the type characterized by each of the five regions are appropriate for different situations. Thomas (1979, p. 161) contends that collaborating, for example, is the most appropriate conflict behavior for the following situations:

1. To find an integrative solution when both sets of concerns are too important to be compromised

2. When your objective is to learn

3.   To merge insights from people with different perspectives

4.   To gain commitment by incorporating concerns into a consensus

5.   To work through feelings which have interfered with a relationship

As we will see, many of these situations exist in occupational safety and health relationships and collaborative behavior appears to be an effective way to deal with them.

    These notions of conflict and cooperation, along with avoidance, accommodation, compromise, competition, and collaboration, will be referred to in subsequent chapters to explain relations among labor, management, and government pertaining to occupational safety and health. Figure 1-1 will be particularly useful for describing changes in the relationships over time in the United States and comparing these relationships with those in other countries. In referring to Figure 1-1, management's behavior toward labor and government will be the perspective used.

FIGURE 1-1
TWO-DIMENSIONAL MODEL OF CONFLICT-COPING BEHAVIOR

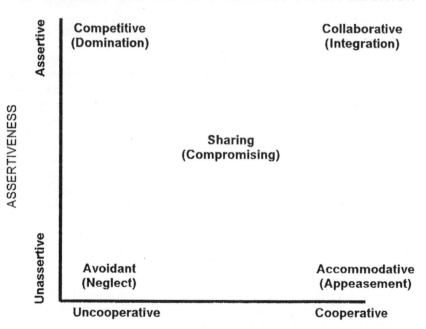

COOPERATIVENESS

Source: Adapted from Ruble, T. L. and Thomas, K. W. "Support for a Two-Dimensional Model of Conflict Behavior." *Organization Behavior and Human Performance*. 16(1), 1976, p. 145.

New Social Contract

As noted earlier, there have been frequent calls in the literature for the development of a "new social contract" governing the relations among business (management), government, and labor. The more general term "social contract" is defined as "a working relationship between society and its institutions that sets the interconnections between the institution and society as a whole and among institutions" (Steiner and Steiner, 1980, p. 12).

Many observers have noted that the relationships among important institutions and groups in the United States have been characterized by confrontational and adversarial behavior in recent years. These adversarial relations frequently have been blamed for the decline in the competitive position of U.S. industries in world markets. *Business Week* (1980) argued that restoration of the competitive position of U.S. industries required nothing short of a rewriting of the social contract in the United States. According to this view, the confrontational relationships among labor, management, and government and other groups would need to be replaced with a set of more cooperative relationships akin to those presumed to exist in Japan, Sweden, and Germany.

The new social contract suggested by *Business Week* (1980) includes several elements: (1) management's emphasis on long-run rather than short-run profits; (2) agreement among leaders of labor, business, government, and interest groups who accurately reflect the interests of their constituencies; (3) labor-management negotiations that take account of the difficult competitive position of U.S. industry and that lead to productivity improvement and cost control; and (4) the elimination of unnecessary governmental regulation of business activities and the replacement of specific regulations with more flexible regulations that achieve the same goals.

Elements of this new social contract are relevant to efforts to improve the management and regulation of occupational safety and health. In particular, greater cooperation among labor, management, and government is likely to promote these efforts. Nevertheless, some degree of conflict in these relationships and assertiveness in dealing with them is not only unavoidable but it is also likely to be beneficial.

This research provides evidence that the reworking of labor-management-government relations in the field of occupational safety and health has implications for other aspects of their relationships. Improved working relationships among these parties and resulting safety and health benefits can pave the way for more effective handling of other work issues of mutual concern.

Injuries, Illnesses, and Accidents

The primary distinction between injuries and illnesses for record-keeping purposes is whether the condition arises from a single or multiple exposure to a hazard. The U.S. Department of Labor, Bureau of Labor Statistics defines an occupational injury as "any injury such as a cut, fracture, sprain or amputation, etc., which results from a work accident or from exposure involving a single incident in the work environment" (1987, p. 1).

The same source defines an occupational illness as "any abnormal condition or disorder, other than one resulting from an occupational injury, caused by exposure to environmental factors associated with employment. It includes acute and chronic illnesses or diseases which may be caused by inhalation, absorption, ingestion, or direct contact" (1987 p. 1).

The single exposure criterion makes injuries more readily identifiable than illnesses and less subject to question about the true cause of the condition. Still, disputes do often arise over where and how a reported injury occurred, especially whether or not it occurred at work. Also, it is sometimes difficult to determine whether a particular condition (e.g., a sore back or shoulder) resulted from a single event or cumulative work stress. In the United States sore backs are one exception to the general rule about single versus multiple exposure. Regardless of whether or not the condition is believed to have resulted from a single exposure, sore backs in the United States are supposed to be recorded as injuries. As we will see, there are different injury-recording conventions in different countries.

The above injury definition suggests that injuries result from accidents. However, not every accident causes an injury, and some accidents cause multiple injuries. The National Safety Council defines an accident as "that occurrence in a sequence of events which usually produces unintended injury, death or property damage" (1982, p. 97).

Unfortunately, the terms "accident" and "injury" are used interchangeably by many companies and even by national safety and health bodies (at least in the English language translation of their publications). In this book, we will attempt to use these terms in a manner consistent with their true meanings.

Safety Needs

Maslow (1968) postulated a hierarchy of needs motivating human behavior. These needs are ordered lexicographically, that is, a lower-level need must be satisfied before the next higher-level need can operate as a motivator. Satisfied needs no longer motivate behavior. The lowest level needs are physiological, including the needs for food, water, sleep, and sex. The next level in Maslow's hierarchy consists of safety needs. This refers to a sense of well-being and protection from physical dangers and threats. Safety needs are followed in order by love needs, esteem needs, and the need for self-actualization. It is argued here that from a psychological or motivational standpoint, safety needs related to occupational safety and health are largely satisfied needs in most of the industrial settings considered. This is by no means meant to suggest that there are no safety and health hazards. Rather, it means that the psychology of the typical worker is such that in most cases he/she assesses the likelihood of being injured or getting sick as low enough that the existing hazards do not constitute motivationally important threats. This assessment by the workers, though perhaps not accurate or desirable, is important to consider when trying to improve occupational safety and health.

RESEARCH DESIGN

The research design employs a combination of methods or approaches. An experimental research approach, with certain similarities to that utilized by cultural anthropologists, is employed. So too are structured interviews, commonly associated with field research in other social sciences. Additionally, archival data related to occupational injuries and governmental regulatory activities are analyzed. Each of these methods individually has certain weaknesses and limitations. However, the multiple operationism afforded by taking these approaches together provides greater confidence in the results (Webb et al., 1966).

In addition to utilizing multiple research techniques, this research analyzes the regulation and management of occupational safety and health on several levels: the national level, industrial level, corporate level, and plant level. Again, the purpose is to gain a fuller understanding of the phenomena considered and to account for the limitations of analysis on only one level. This multilevel analysis requires some effort on the part of the reader to shift gears as he/she moves from chapter to chapter. In the concluding chapter we attempt to draw out the implications from the various types and levels of analysis and to pull these together.

The plant-level analysis reported here is based on research in a total of 12 plants of 5 companies that were visited: Company G headquartered in West Germany--one plant in the United States and one plant in West Germany; Company J headquartered in Japan--one plant in the United States; Company X headquartered in the United States--one plant in the United States, one plant in West Germany, and one plant in Kenya; Company Y headquartered in the United States--two plants in the United States, one plant in England, and one plant in Belgium;[2] and Company Z headquartered in Sweden--one plant in the United States and one plant in Sweden. In continuing research, which is still underway, safety and health activities of Japanese operations of 6 Japanese auto companies and the U.S. operations of 4 of these were also studied. Comparisons are made of the structure, operation, and results of safety and health activities among plants in the different countries of operation of these companies. In this way, some understanding can be gained of the effects of the national environments in which the plants operate.

In-depth structured interviews were conducted with company personnel involved with the issues and programs under study. Data pertaining to inputs, outputs, and operationalization of the programs were collected in each plant. However, the extent of such data made available to the researcher varied considerably from company to company and even plant to plant. Interviews were also conducted with a wide range of individuals from government, labor unions, industry, and academia who had involvement in or knowledge about the handling of these issues at plant, company, industrial and national levels. Here too, there were disparities in the quality and quantity of information that could be secured. As we will see in Chapter 5, many of the differences in the availability and meaning of national occupational safety and health data do not occur by chance. They are, in fact, reflections of national social, economic, political, and legal conditions. If not intentional, they are, in many cases, unavoidable.

This research should be considered exploratory in nature due to the significant limitations that are present. Many of these limitations stem from the sheer scope and complexity of the study and the practical impossibility for any one researcher to become an expert on all the countries, companies, and issues considered in this study.

Certain limitations deriving from the international orientation of the research tell us a great deal about the nature of such research undertakings. The lessons derived from this may be of considerable benefit to those undertaking future international research efforts. Many of these factors that present difficulties in comparing safety and health activities in one nation with those of another, such as widely varying work injury definitions and different legal requirements, also present difficulties to corporations that attempt to manage their safety and health activities across national boundaries. Further discussion of the research design and limitations is contained in the final chapter. So too are implications and recommendations for labor, management, and government.

NOTES

1. Using Bureau of Labor Statistics data, which are compiled differently than National Safety Council data, the Office of Technology Assessment (1985) provides a considerably lower estimate of 6,000 annual deaths due to occupational injuries. However, the Office of Technology Assessment's estimates of the number and cost of occupational injuries are roughly in agreement with those of the National Safety Council.

2. The Belgian plant of Company Y was run by the West German Headquarters of Company Y.

2

WORKER SAFETY AND HEALTH IN THE UNITED STATES

This chapter provides a broad overview of occupational safety and health in the United States, focusing primarily on regulatory aspects. It will come as no surprise to the reader that occupational safety and health is a contentious issue here. This chapter offers a historical context in which to understand how and why this contentiousness arose. It also provides relatively straightforward examples of the effects of assorted social, legal, political, and economic factors on the development of occupational safety and health policies and the disputes that surround them. This background should prove useful for understanding developments within the U.S. auto industry and the operation of occupational safety and health systems in other countries in both their regulatory and managerial aspects. Nevertheless, the reader who is familiar with occupational safety and health regulation and the related controversies may choose to proceed directly to the next chapter.

Controversy surrounding occupational safety and health in the United States is nothing new; it dates back to the earliest days of their regulation. In many ways, disputes were even more intense at these earlier stages of regulation. One reason for this is the nature of working conditions back then.

Despite the questionable accuracy of injury statistics from early in this century, it is obvious that working conditions in the United States in the early 1900s were extremely hazardous compared with conditions today. There is a wide range of estimates of worker fatality rates cited in the literature for this time period due to the relatively primitive data collection techniques at that time. Still, even the lowest of these estimates far exceeds the fatality rates of today. The National Safety Council (1982) estimates that there were between 18,000 and 21,000 workplace fatalities in 1912. In comparison, the National Safety Council estimates that there were 12,300 worker fatalities in 1981 in a work force between two and three times the size of the 1912 work force. This suggests that the 1912 worker fatality rate was at least four times as great as the 1981 rate.

Berman (1978) cites estimates developed by the Bureau of Labor Statistics (BLS) in 1907 and by organized labor in 1904 that placed the annual number of workplace deaths at between 15,000 to 17,500, and 27,000, respectively, from a work force of 26 million persons. In contrast, the Office of Technology Assessment (1985), using Bureau of Labor Statistics data, estimates that there were an average of 6,000 workplace fatalities annually resulting from accidents from 1979 to 1983. During this time period, the labor force was approximately 100 million workers. Comparing these fatality estimates with the earlier Bureau of Labor Statistics estimates suggests that the worker fatality rate was almost ten times as high in 1907 as in the 1979-83 period.

The hazardous conditions that produced these high worker fatality rates early in this century became the focus of much concern, particularly among workers. As a result, labor pursued improvements in working conditions related to safety and health in the legislative and regulatory arenas and directly from management.

WORKERS' COMPENSATION

Most of the early safety and health legislation was enacted at the state level. The most important of these were workman's compensation laws (hereafter referred to as workers' compensation laws). These laws in their present forms were passed by various states, starting with Wisconsin in 1911. (Several states had passed workers' compensation laws a few years earlier, but these had been declared unconstitutional and new laws were required.) Even the earliest state workers' compensation laws were enacted many years after similar legislation had been passed in Europe. Mississippi, the last state to enact workers' compensation legislation, did not do so until 1948.

There is considerable variation among the workers' compensation laws of the states regarding such factors as wage replacement benefits, coverage of specific occupations and categories of employers, and work definitions and requirements for determining work-relatedness of illnesses and injuries. There are, however, some generalizations that can be made about these laws.

The existing workers' compensation laws reflect compromises between labor and management. Workers who are unable to work due to a workplace injury or illness receive part of their lost wages according to a fixed formula, along with coverage of their medical expenses. The employer provides this compensation either through contributions to a state or private insurance fund or directly through self-insurance. As is the case with the earlier European workers' compensation laws, workers do not have to prove negligence on the part of the employer to collect. In exchange for this compensation scheme, workers relinquish their rights in most cases to sue their employers regarding the workplace conditions that may have caused the injury or illness. This protects the employer from very large liability settlements.

Prior to the enactment of workers' compensation laws, injured workers could sue employers for compensation under common law or employer liability laws. The injured worker, however, had to prove negligence on the part of the employer. In addition to contesting the negligence claim, the employer had several other lines of defense

(Gersuny, 1981). These were the principle of contributory negligence, the assumption of risk doctrine, and the fellow servant rule. Thus, employers could defend themselves by showing that the employee's own negligence caused or contributed to the injury; that the injured employee knew that the job was dangerous and assumed responsibility for the risks associated with it upon taking the job; or that another employee's negligence had caused or contributed to the injury.

Because of the need for proving employer negligence and overcoming these various defenses, few injured workers or their survivors received more than token compensation. Prosser (1971) estimates that before workers' compensation, only 6 percent to 30 percent of industrial injuries were compensated. Also, there were often long delays and sizable legal fees facing employees seeking compensation (Gersuny, 1981).

The favorable position of employers relative to injury compensation deteriorated as industrial injury rates increased in the United States in concert with the rapid industrialization that occurred at the beginning of this century. Stone (1984) argues that juries and judges became more sympathetic to injured workers and that the employers' three lines of defense cited previously began to weaken. As a result, employers faced an increased likelihood of paying out large liability awards. This led employers to be more receptive to the workers' compensation programs that were being considered at this time. Similar developments led to the earlier passage of workers' compensation programs in the United Kingdom and Germany.

Stone (1984) also argues that, with the change in compensation for injuries that took place during this time period, there came a change in the thinking about the causes of industrial injuries. Neither workers nor employers were blamed; work injuries were viewed as the inevitable result of industrialization.

Presently several points of disagreement frequently arise between employees and their employers or the employers' insurance carriers, and these disagreements often need to be resolved in court. There are often conflicting views pertaining to whether a given condition is the result of a work-related injury or illness. For example, did an injury really occur or does an illness really exist, and is it work related? The work-relatedness of illnesses is particularly controversial because a given illness is likely to stem from a multiplicity of factors, both work related and nonwork related (Barth, 1980). Disagreements also arise over the extent of the disability. For example, can the injured/sick employee work and, if so, at what sort of job? Such controversies have a bearing on the operation of safety and health programs in the companies considered in this book.

In recent years, the payouts of workers' compensation systems have been increasing throughout the United States and in other industrialized countries (Stone, 1984). Much of this can be attributed to increased compensation for industrial illnesses. Most significant has been a dramatic increase in compensated cases of a range of maladies known collectively as "cumulative trauma disorders." The painful conditions associated with these disorders result from the stress placed on the body from performing the same task over and over again everyday. The BLS occupational illness category "disorders associated with repeated trauma" comprised 47 percent of manufacturing sector occupational illnesses in 1986 compared with just 20 percent in 1976 (U.S. Department of Labor, Bureau of Labor Statistics, 1979, 1988). Overall, so-called "soft tissue disorders," which include motion and back injury and hearing loss, were accounting for 30 percent of workers' compensation claims for the entire private sector as of 1988 (Mallory and Bradford, 1989).

It is, however, not clear that such illnesses are occurring at any greater rate than previously. It is likely that a higher percentage of illnesses are now being compensated. This is the case, for example, with asbestos-related diseases and cumulative trauma disorders such as carpal tunnel syndrome that have only begun to be diagnosed and compensated in recent years.

With the exception of workers' compensation, few laws were passed aimed at improving the safety and health conditions in this nation's workplaces during the first three decades of this century. Even workers' compensation was directed *primarily* at providing financial protection for disabled workers rather than injury/illness prevention. Workers' compensation provided protection for disabled workers against the disruption of income and it provided coverage for their medical expenses.

Secondarily, workers' compensation was intended to have some hazard-reduction effect by way of the relationship between employers' workers' compensation costs and their companies' injury/illness experience. The correlation between the two is greatest where the employer utilizes self-insurance. With state and private workers' compensation, employers with a greater than average number and severity of injuries and illnesses may be required to pay higher premiums. However, the amount of extra premiums varies from one state to another and from one private insurance carrier to another. Other factors that insurance companies use to determine premiums are the wages of the employees, the number of employees, the industry covered, and the rated risk of the jobs performed.

Critics contend that the relationship between injury/illness experience and premiums is not strong enough to provide an incentive for hazard reduction. Evidence to support this view was uncovered in this research. Most safety and health managers did not even know the extent to which the plant's workers' compensation premiums varied with their plant's injury/illness experience. Thus, it is highly unlikely that this unknown factor would have much impact upon performance.

A different view of the hazard-reduction aspect of workers' compensation is provided by Ledvinka (1982). He contends that workers' compensation might actually diminish employers' hazard-reduction incentives. As an insurance program, it is designed to reduce the financial risks to the firm associated with injuries and illnesses. Employers pay fairly predictable amounts into the workers' compensation system even when they have injuries. Also, it shifts some of the costs of the injuries to other parties, including workers whose compensation is typically less than their regular wages and who cannot sue to receive compensation for pain and suffering. Society also bears some of the costs of injuries and illnesses through social security and other welfare program benefits.

Given its importance and the relative scarcity of solid empirical evidence with which to make judgments, it would seem that the issue of injury prevention incentives of different workers' compensation schemes needs additional exploration.

OTHER HEALTH AND SAFETY INITIATIVES

Prior to the enactment of the Occupational Safety and Health Act (OSH Act) in 1970, there were only a few federal regulations pertaining to safety. These were industry specific and directed at such hazardous industries as coal mining and longshoring. Teplow (1976) suggests that a number of factors probably contributed to the relative lack of early safety and health legislation (other than workers' compensation) at both the state and federal levels, despite well-publicized industrial catastrophes of the nineteenth and early twentieth centuries:

(1) the assumption, shared by employers and employees, that hazard was inherent on the job; (2) pride in being able to work in the face of known hazards; (3) the assumption that the constitutional provision of federated states under a central government of limited powers barred federal action, so that when government action appeared to be desirable, it was considered appropriate for the states to act; and (4) the normal diversity of interests and increasing demands on state budgets made the states reluctant to act until major catastrophes galvanized enough public support to make state legislation possible. (Teplow, 1976, p. 210)

Later in the twentieth century, the individual states passed numerous occupational safety and health laws in addition to workers' compensation. The OSH Act was the first comprehensive safety and health legislation passed at the national level.

Prior to the passage of the OSH Act, certain corporations--some voluntarily and some under pressure from labor--undertook considerable efforts to promote safety. The United States Steel Corporation and Du Pont developed early safety programs due to management's initiative. Labor could negotiate with management over safety conditions in the early part of this century, but workers' rights to participate in such negotiations were both affirmed and strengthened with the passage of the National Labor Relations Act (Wagner Act) of 1935. This led to significant improvements in company safety and health programs.

Several private organizations devoted specifically to safety (and in some cases to occupational health as well) played major roles in the development of occupational safety and health practices in this country. For example, the American National Standards Institute (ANSI) and the National Fire Protection Association set voluntary workplace safety standards. Many of these voluntary standards were later incorporated into law with the enactment of the OSH Act. These organizations participate in the development of so-called "consensus standards" regarding safety and health that frequently are adopted by OSHA.

Probably the most important voluntary organization for promoting safety and occupational health has been the National Safety Council. It is a nongovernmental, nonprofit organization that undertakes a wide range of safety and health-related activities. It provides safety training, programs and materials, and record keeping and research pertaining to safety and health. The National Safety Council, was established in 1913, one year after the Association of Iron and Steel Electrical Engineers held the first national work safety conference. In recognition of its work in the safety arena, the National Safety Council was chartered through an act of Congress in 1953.

THE OCCUPATIONAL SAFETY AND HEALTH ACT

The Occupational Safety and Health Act (OSH Act) was passed in 1970 with a great deal of bipartisan support, as reflected by the nearly unanimous votes in both houses of Congress. A description of some of the OSH Act's major provisions and a discussion of the subsequent controversy surrounding this act are presented below.

Much of the impetus for the OSH Act came from the increase in occupational injuries during the years immediately preceding the bill's passage. Although the overall number and rate of work injuries and fatalities decreased dramatically during most of this century, the *number* of work-related deaths and disabling injuries increased during the 1960s, according to National Safety Council statistics. This occurred although the work fatality *rate* continued to decline slightly during this time period. Some sources contended that even the injury *rate* rose during the 1960s. During the hearings on the OSH Act, testimony was introduced indicating that the industrial injury *rate* rose 29 percent from 1961 to 1970 (Ashford, 1976). Others, however, have argued that this apparent rise in the industrial injury rate was a statistical artifact and that injury rates continued to decline during the 1960s (Viscusi, 1983). This confusion over injury experience trends can be attributed to the inadequate injury record-keeping system that existed prior to the passage of the OSH Act.

Probably more significant than the overall number or rate of injuries to the passage of the OSH Act was one highly publicized accident. This was the 1968 mine disaster in Farmington, West Virginia, in which 78 miners died. Public attention was focused on occupational safety and health, making it easier for supporters of increased safety and health regulation to garner political support.

The increase in injuries during the 1960s convinced many that individual states were not doing enough to promote worker safety. Some critics contended that the states were actually trying to attract industry by maintaining lax and less expensive safety standards. To reduce or eliminate this undesirable competition among states, national legislation was seen as necessary. Even those less critical of the states' role in safety and health regulation also supported increased federal involvement, and an effective national consensus emerged on this issue.

The OSH Act set minimum federal standards for the safety and health of working conditions. States were permitted to exceed these standards. States which wished to do so could petition to have jurisdiction for regulation of occupational safety and health activities within their borders assigned to state OSHA departments. As of 1987 there were 25 OSHA plans that had achieved at least initial approval.

The OSH Act established the Occupational Safety and Health Administration (OSHA) to carry out the provisions of this legislation. Despite the nearly unanimous support for the OSH Act, OSHA soon became one of the most controversial federal agencies. Reasons for this development are explored below. In keeping with the thrust of this research, both the cooperative and conflictual aspects of relations among labor, management, and government regarding occupational safety and health are considered. It is shown that, despite large areas of mutual interest regarding safety and health among these parties, occupational safety and health issues are dealt with in a predominantly adversarial fashion in the United States.

COOPERATION IN SAFETY AND HEALTH RELATIONSHIPS

Cooperation occurs when the goals of concerned parties are in common or are positively linked. There is, in fact, a common interest among labor, management, and government in reducing injuries and illnesses. Workers are the most directly affected by injuries and illnesses through physical and mental suffering, possible early death and disability, reduced income, and potential nonreimbursed medical expenses. Workers' reasons for being concerned with safety and health are so obvious that one might wonder why individual workers do not place even a higher priority on their personal safety and health concerns than is the case.

To the extent that union members are concerned with safety and health issues, one would expect to find their union representatives reflecting that viewpoint in their various activities. This would be displayed in union negotiations with management on safety and health conditions, in their support of workers who file grievances regarding these conditions, and in the union's legislative activities. In fact, this research has indicated that union staff members who regularly deal specifically with safety and health matters are much more concerned with these issues than are the rank-and-file members. Safety and health are easy to forget about if there is no pressing problem or recent accident and if one has no specific responsibility.

Similarly, management has considerable incentive for improving safety and health conditions in their operations. There are significant costs of injuries and illnesses related to such factors as medical expenses, workers' compensation costs, lost production, hiring and retraining costs, equipment damage, record-keeping expenses, and lower morale.

Various governmental institutions at the federal and state levels exist for the express purpose of promoting occupational safety and health. These include OSHA and state OSHA plans, the National Institute of Occupational Safety and Health (NIOSH), state workers' compensation agencies (which may be part of the state OSHA plans), and legislative committees concerned with safety and health at the state and federal levels. The commitment of members of these institutions to promoting safety and health, though questioned by some critics, is readily apparent. Their commitment to promoting these concerns comes from their own goals and values that initially motivated them to become involved with safety and health and/or is the result of acculturation to institutional goals and values over time.

In addition to these more or less intrinsic factors, several extrinsic motivations are relevant. All other things being equal, these institutions and their members are regarded more favorably by other governmental institutions (e.g., funding bodies), labor, industry, and the voting public when they are relatively more successful in promoting occupational safety and health in a cost-effective way. Looking at this issue from another perspective, poor performance poses threats to these institutions and their members in the form of reduced funding, job loss, lessened prestige (or, in the case of OSHA, public ridicule), and reduced political support. Politicians may not wish to support such poor-performing institutions due to the political cost of doing so.

CONFLICTS IN SAFETY AND HEALTH RELATIONSHIPS

Despite common or positively linked goals regarding safety and health among labor, management, and government, it is far easier to find examples of conflicts regarding safety and health than of cooperation. To understand why this has been the case, it is useful to place the enactment of the OSH Act in its historical perspective. The OSH Act resulted in a fundamental restructuring of power relationships in the workplace. It gave federal inspectors the right to enter workplaces and penalize employers for any variances from OSHA-mandated working conditions. This represented a major erosion of managerial decision-making authority. Further eroding managerial authority were the provisions in the OSH Act that allowed individual workers to request workplace inspections and that provided for labor to be represented during OSHA inspections.

The matter of control over working conditions in plants is one that lends itself readily to conflict among labor, management, and government representatives. Also likely to provoke conflict among these parties are competing views on the costs and benefits of alternative means to promote safety and health in the workplace. Even more fundamental are conflicts between safety and health goals and other goals of these actors. Thus, managers' production and cost-control goals may at times conflict (or at least appear to conflict) with safety and health concerns. Workers' concerns with convenience and maintaining or increasing production may produce conflicts. And a wide array of political concerns may conflict with the mandates to promote safety and health of various governmental institutions. The remainder of this chapter details the emergence of governmental and political conflicts regarding occupational safety and health, with special attention focused on OSHA, which has been at the center of these conflicts.

It is useful to remember that the passage of the OSH Act in 1970 during the first Nixon administration coincided with the peak of various anti-establishment movements. These included the civil rights, women's, environmental, and anti-Vietnam War movements, all of which had reformist, and, in some cases, revolutionary objectives. Some have suggested that early OSHA inspectors may have gotten carried away by the spirit of the times. According to this view, at least some inspectors felt that the nation's workplaces were inherently unsafe and that their mission was to find the hazards, eliminate them, and in the process punish those responsible.

Almost immediately following passage of the OSHA legislation, the agency became a political football. Labor sought to strengthen the agency by supporting increased funding levels, stricter enforcement of existing regulations, and the imposition of new and more stringent regulations. Industry representatives generally opposed labor on these issues. They wanted reduced funding levels, less strict enforcement or elimination of certain existing regulations, and they opposed the enactment of new regulations.

Political appointees to top level positions at OSHA, like any other political appointee, are subject to the changing political pressures over time. Moreover, the individuals who are appointed to these positions are likely to reflect the dominant national political orientation at the time of their appointment. In the early years of OSHA, industry officials criticized these political appointees and the agency as a whole for reflecting what they perceived to be a bias against business. In recent years, labor officials have criticized political appointees as having goals and values that conflict with those of the agency and those of the career civil servants who staff it.

OSHA's performance came under criticism, among other reasons, because of an increase in the reported injury rates during the 1970s. This increase was partially attributable to a conflict between two of OSHA's goals: reduction of work injuries and improvement in the collection of injury statistics. Diagram 2-1 shows that the lost-workday injury rates (number of lost-workday injury cases per 100 full-time workers) increased for every year during the 1970s, except 1975. Statistics prior to the establishment of OSHA are not comparable due to changes in record keeping practices. While some portion of this apparent increase may be authentic, it is reasonable to assume that part of it was also due simply to refinement of the new injury statistics collection procedures. In the first few years, employers were learning the new record-keeping system and may not have known to record all the injuries that they should have recorded. Over time, these misunderstandings were likely to have been corrected, resulting in more accurate but higher *recorded* injury statistics.

Since the establishment of OSHA there has been, however, an overall decline in the number and rate of fatalities due to occupational injuries, as shown in Table 2-1. (Note that the figures in Table 2-1 are for private-sector employers with 11 or more employees. The numbers of fatalities shown here are considerably lower than the National Safety Council estimates cited in Chapter 1 that come from a self-selected sample of employers of all sizes.) The number of fatalities declined from 4,970 in 1974 to an all-time low of 3,100 in 1983, a 38 percent decline. From 1974 to 1983, the incidence rate of fatalities per 100,000 full-time workers declined from 9.8 to another all-time low, 5.6, representing a 43 percent drop. As noted above, the number and rate of occupational fatalities have been declining throughout this century. Also, 1982 and 1983 were recession years, when the number and rate of injuries tend to decline due to a slower work pace. The effect of the recession on the number and rate of fatalities is demonstrated by a resurgence of both of these in 1984, a year of economic recovery. The 1983 to 1984 increase in the number of fatalities, from 3,100 to 3,740, represented a 21 percent increase; and the increase in the fatality rate, from 5.6 to 6.4, in this time period was 14 percent. Since that time, both the number and rate of fatalities have declined. These stood at 3,610 and 5.9, respectively, in 1986. Overall, there has been a decline of 27 percent in the number of fatalities and a decline of 40 percent in the rate of fatalities over the entire 1974 to 1986 time period.

Bacow (1980) reviews studies by Di Pietro (1976), Mendeloff (1976), Smith (n.d.), and Viscusi (1979) that attempt to evaluate the impact of OSHA on occupational injury rates. Collectively, they show little evidence that injury rates are any lower than they would have been had OSHA not been established. Still, the authors concede that

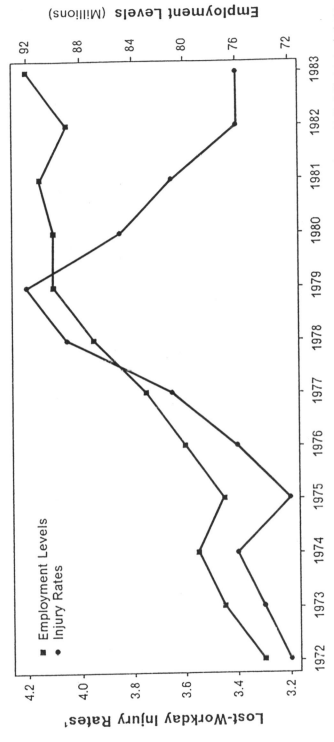

DIAGRAM 2-1
LOST-WORKDAY INJURY RATES/ EMPLOYMENT LEVELS

Employment Levels (Millions)

Lost-Workday Injury Rates[1]

■ Employment Levels
● Injury Rates

Sources: United States Department of Labor, Bureau of Labor Statistics, Occupational Injuries and Illnesses in the United States by Industry, 1983. Washington, D.C.: U.S. Government Printing Office, 1985; and U.S. Department of Labor, Bureau of Labor Statistics, Vol. 31, No. 3, Employment and Earnings. Washington, D.C.: U.S. Government Printing Office, March 1984.
[1] Number of lost-workday injury cases per 100 full-time workers.

such determinations are difficult to make with any confidence because of the problems of comparing data between years. Bacow (1980) reasons that the results are ambiguous enough to allow one to draw either of two conclusions: (1) the effect of OSHA on injury rates is unknown; or (2) the effect of OSHA on injury rates is nonexistent. Due to the ambiguity, both supporters and opponents of OSHA have found it easy to cite evidence to support their preconceptions about the agency.

TABLE 2-1
OCCUPATIONAL INJURY AND ILLNESS
FATALITIES IN U.S. INDUSTRY[1]

	Number of Fatalities	Incidence Rate per 100,000 Full-Time Workers
1973	5,340	N.A.
1974	4,970	9.8
1975	4,570	9.4
1976	3,940	7.9
1977	4,760	9.1
1978	4,590	8.2
1979	4,950	8.6
1980	4,400	7.7
1981	4,370	7.6
1982	4,090	7.4
1983	3,100	5.6
1984	3,740	6.4
1985	3,750	6.2
1986	3,610	5.9

N.A. = not available
Sources: U.S. Department of Labor, Bureau of Labor Statistics. *Occupational Injuries and Illnesses in the United States by Industry.* Washington, D.C.: U.S. Government Printing Office, 1975-1986 editions; and Occupational Safety and Health Administration Public Information Office.
[1] Data apply to all private sector establishments with 11 or more employees.

The effects of political considerations are readily seen by examining the resources devoted to OSHA and the enforcement policies of the agency over time. During the 1970s OSHA grew quite rapidly in terms of budget allocations and number of funded positions. Table 2-2 shows that OSHA's budget grew from approximately $36 million in the fiscal year 1972, its first full year of operation, to approximately $186 million in the fiscal year 1980, the last fiscal year under the Carter administration budget. The number of funded positions increased from 1,696 to 3,086 during the same time period. As discussed below, much attention has been focused on OSHA funding and staffing levels under the Reagan administration. It is, however, interesting to note that during the last year of the Carter administration, there was only a small increase in funding and a decrease in the number of funded positions.

The observation that OSHA's growth stopped before Reagan took office is confirmed by reference to deflated dollar budget figures, that is, those that factor out the effects of inflation on budget allocations. These are also included in Table 2-2. The budget allocations were converted to 1971 dollars by using U.S. Department of Commerce budget deflator factors. As these figures show, the OSHA budget grew in real terms from the agency's inception in 1971 until 1977, with only a slight downturn in 1974. The OSHA budget allocation in real dollars for 1978 was slightly less than that for 1977, but there was a large jump in real dollars from 1978 to 1979. The budget remained fairly stable in real terms for the remainder of the Carter administration and for the transition year, 1981. (This budget year started in October 1980, during the Carter administration, and ended in September 1981, during the Reagan administration.) The Reagan administration's first budget of its own making in 1982 contained a $12 million (or 12 percent) decrease in real dollars for OSHA. Since then, the OSHA budget has been almost constant in real terms. Thus, in real terms, OSHA funding growth virtually ended with the 1979 budget under the Carter administration. However, contraction of the agency's allocations in real terms did not begin until the 1982 Reagan budget.

Similar patterns of growth and decline are seen in the inspection and enforcement experience of OSHA. Tables 2-3, 2-4, and 2-5 show several interesting trends in the number of inspections conducted, the percentages of initial inspections with citations and violations, and the number and types of citations/penalties issued during OSHA's existence. When considered in conjunction with political trends over this time period, these data are quite revealing.

Table 2-3 shows a very rapid increase in the number of inspections from 1972 to 1975. Since the 88,754 inspections in the peak year of 1975, the number of inspections fell to 55,156 in 1978 and since then have tended slightly upward. Two reasons for the decline in the number of inspections during the Carter administration stemmed from policy changes initiated under the Ford administration (Samuels, 1986). First was the retraining of inspectors. This required them to

TABLE 2-2
OSHA FUNDING AND STAFFING LEVELS[1]

Year	Budget Allocation	Budget Allocation[2] (1971 Dollars)	Funded Positions[3]	Authorized	Inspectors on Board at End of Fiscal Year
1971 (April–June)	$15,189,000	$15,189,000	970	N.A.	N.A.
1972	35,884,000	34,216,191	1,696	N.A.	N.A.
1973	69,373,000	63,173,961	1,699	N.A.	N.A.
1974	70,408,000	59,517,868	1,830	N.A.	N.A.
1975	102,000,000	78,111,000	2,471	N.A.	N.A.
1976	117,180,000	84,258,000	2,804	N.A.	N.A.
1977	130,333,000	87,439,000	2,717	N.A.	N.A.
1978	139,070,000	87,376,000	2,817	N.A.	N.A.
1979	173,034,000	100,220,000	3,086	N.A.	N.A.
1980	186,394,000	98,481,000	2,925	1,693	1,387
1981	209,376,000	101,080,000	2,922	1,686	1,221
1982	195,465,000	88,883,000	2,354	1,200	1,055
1983	206,649,000	90,302,000	2,354	1,200	1,210
1984	212,560,000	88,940,000	2,355	1,200	N.A.

N.A. = not available

[1] Source: Occupational Safety and Health Administration, Public Information Office

[2] Budget deflator factors were obtained from the U.S. Department of Commerce. These are also available in the U.S. Office of Management and Budget. *Budget of the United States Government.* Washington, D.C.: U.S. Government Printing Office, successive years.

[3] Funded positions refers to the number of positions authorized by the budget allocation. Not all of these positions are likely to be full at any point in time.

TABLE 2-3
OSHA INSPECTIONS

Year	Total Inspections		Record Inspections	Inspections, Excluding Record Inspections	
1972 (July-Dec.)	17,114		0	17,114	
1973	67,290 ⎫		0	67,290	
1974	79,441 ⎬ 78,029		0	79,441	
1975	88,754 ⎪ (1973-1976	0	88,754	
1976	76,632 ⎭ Average)		0	76,632	
1977	60,910 ⎫		0	60,910	
1978	55,156 ⎬ 59,844		0	55,156	
1979	58,421 ⎪ (1977-1980	0	58,421	
1980	64,888 ⎭ Average)		1	64,887	
1981	55,597 ⎫		1,446	54,151 ⎫	55,816
1982	63,852 ⎬ 62,831	9,612	54,240 ⎬ (1981-1983	
1983	69,045 ⎭ (1981-1983 Average)	9,989	59,056 ⎭ Average)	

Source: U.S. Occupational Safety and Health Administration

be temporarily withdrawn from the field and made them unavailable for inspections. Second was the increased comprehensiveness of inspections deriving from greater emphasis on occupational health concerns. This required more staff and more time per inspection. Thus, not all of the decline in inspections after 1975 could not be attributed to regulatory restraint.

In the last few years, there has been an increasing number of "records inspections." Inspectors now target workplaces for inspection based upon their industry's injury rate and the workplace's own injury history. Records inspections occur when the inspector determines, upon examining the workplace's injury log, that no further inspection is necessary because of the workplace's below-average number of injuries. There is debate over whether or not these records inspections are, in fact, true inspections and should be counted with other inspections. When we exclude records inspections, the number of inspections hit a historical low in 1981 (excluding the start-up partial year of 1972). It has, however, risen slightly since then. A fuller discussion of the controversy surrounding inspection targeting is provided below.

It is interesting to consider the trends in the number of inspections during the time periods corresponding to the terms of office of the four U.S. presidents since OSHA was established. The relationships between these trends and presidential politics clearly show the presence of a political influence on OSHA inspection activities. Again, the partial start-up year of 1972 is excluded from these comparisons.

The growth years of 1973 to 1975 correspond to the first three years of the Nixon/Ford presidency (Gerald Ford replaced Richard Nixon in August 1974). The solid bipartisan political majority that supported the OSH Act made this increase in OSHA's activities politically acceptable. The first decline in the number of inspections occurred in 1976. During the entire 1973-76 time period the average number of inspections was 78,029.

During the first two years of the Carter administration, the number of inspections declined significantly, and then increased moderately during the last two years. During the entire Carter administration, the average number of inspections was 59,844. This was a 23 percent decrease from the previous four-year period under Republican presidents.

Depending on whether or not one counts records inspections, one can draw different conclusions regarding changes in the number of OSHA inspections under the Reagan administration. Virtually all of the records inspections occurred during the Reagan administration. When total inspections, including records inspections, are considered, the average number of inspections during the first three years of the Reagan administration was 62,831, reflecting a slight (5%) increase over the 59,844 average during the Carter administration. When records inspections are excluded, the average number of inspections conducted during the Reagan administration becomes 55,815, representing a slight (7%) decline from the average number conducted during the Carter administration.

Not only are the numbers of inspections indicative of the regulatory climate, but so too are the results of those inspections. Table 2-4 shows the percentages of initial inspections that resulted in penalties or citations in the 1972-83 time period. The trends indicated here are similar to the trends in the numbers of inspections over the years. As Table 2-4 indicates, the percentage of firms receiving a citation or a penalty based upon their initial inspections increased during the 1972-75 time period and fell thereafter. Initial inspections with citations increased from 60 percent of inspections in 1972 to 79 percent in 1975. Since then, they decreased every year from 1975 to 1982, when they hit a historical low of 51 percent. In 1983, there was a slight increase to 52 percent. Initial inspections with penalties increased from 46 percent of inspections in 1972 to 57 percent in 1975; however, they dropped to 23 percent in 1983.

TABLE 2-4
PERCENT OSHA INITIAL INSPECTIONS
WITH CITATIONS AND PENALTIES

Year	Percent of Initial Inspections With Citation		Percent of Initial Inspections With Penalty	
1972 (July-Dec.)	60%		46%	
1973	67%	74.3%	51%	53.0%
1974	74%	(1973-1976	54%	(1973-1976
1975	79%	Average)	57%	Average)
1976	77%		50%	
1977	70%	66.5%	30%	35.3%
1978	67%	(1977-1980	37%	(1977-1980
1979	65%	Average)	38%	Average)
1980	64%		36%	
1981	60%	54.3%	29%	24.3%
1982	51%	(1981-1983	21%	(1981-1983
1983	52%	Average)	23%	Average)

Source: U.S. Occupational Safety and Health Administration.

Looking at OSHA statistics by administrations, there are declines from each administration to the next in the percentages of initial inspections with a citation and percentages of initial inspections with a penalty. During the 1973-76 Nixon/Ford administration, 74.3 percent of the initial inspections resulted in citations, and 53.0 percent resulted in penalties. During the 1977-80 Carter administration, 66.5 percent of the initial inspections resulted in citations, and 35.3 percent resulted in penalties. During the 1981-83 Reagan administration, 54.3 percent of the initial inspections resulted in citations, and 24.3 percent resulted in penalties.

Table 2-5 provides historical data on the total number of violations, and the percentages and numbers for different categories of violations. Corresponding to the increases in the total number of inspections and the percentages of initial inspections with citations and penalties, there was a great increase in the total number of violations issued during the 1972-75 time period. There was a slight decline from 1975 to 1976, followed by a precipitous drop in 1977, the first year of the Carter administration. There was a moderate decline in the number of violations from 1977 to 1980, the remainder of the Carter years. Overall, the average number of total violations in the 1977-80 Carter years was 140,629, representing a 54 percent decline from the average of 308,833 during the 1973-76 Nixon/Ford years.

There was a substantial decline in the number of violations from the last year of the Carter administration to the first year of the Reagan administration. Thereafter, under the Reagan administration, there were modest fluctuations in the number of violations. Overall, during the Reagan administration the average number of total violations issued was 106,438, representing a 24 percent decrease from the Carter administration years.

Perhaps more interesting than the total number of violations is the breakdown of violations by various categories. One of the criticisms of OSHA under the Reagan administration until its final years was that there had been a weakening of penalties against businesses that were found to be in violation of OSHA regulations. This is discussed in more detail later. There is some evidence of the validity of this claim in Table 2-5. Interestingly, though, the data indicate that this trend began considerably before the Reagan administration took office. In fact, it seems to have begun in 1976, the last year of the Nixon/Ford administration.

The important statistics to consider in this regard are the numbers and percentages of serious, willful, repeat, and other violations with penalties listed in the last two columns of Table 2-5. Together, these represent all OSHA violations considered to be of great enough concern to merit a penalty. While the number of these penalties increased during the 1972-75 time period, the percentage of total violations with penalties actually declined from 38.3 percent in 1973 to 23.9 percent in 1977. During the last three years of the Carter administration, both the number and the percentage of these violations

TABLE 2-5
OSHA VIOLATIONS ISSUED

Year	Total Violations #	Serious Violations #	Serious Violations %[1]	Willful Violations #	Willful Violations %[1]	Repeat Violations #	Repeat Violations %[1]	Other Violations #	Other Violations %[1]	Other Violations With Penalties #	Other Violations With Penalties %[1]	Total Serious Willful, Repeat And Other Violations With Penalties #	Total Serious Willful, Repeat And Other Violations With Penalties %[1]
1972[2]	55,072	729	1.3	5	.009	24	.04	54,314	98.6	19,990	36.0	20,748	37.7
1973	236,522	2,949	1.2	96	.04	328	.14	233,149	98.6	87,190	36.8	90,563	38.3
1974	313,273	3,364	1.1	127	.04	1,704	.54	308,078	98.3	98,398	31.4	103,593	33.1
1975	369,950	5,847	1.5	206	.055	3,429	.93	360,468	97.4	111,960	30.3	121,442	32.8
1976	315,588	9,822	3.1	256	.081	5,047	1.59	300,463	95.2	83,046	26.3	98,171	31.1
1977	169,207	26,778	15.8	317	.187	4,695	2.77	137,417	81.2	8,724	5.1	40,514	23.9
1978	132,182	36,238	27.4	947	.716	4,087	3.09	90,910	68.7	3,194	2.4	44,466	33.6
1979	132,646	40,847	30.8	1,143	.861	4,003	3.01	86,653	65.3	2,441	1.8	48,434	36.5
1980	128,481	42,878	33.3	1,009	.785	3,348	2.6	81,246	63.2	1,736	1.3	48,971	38.1
1981	107,056	29,001	27.0	269	.251	1,710	1.59	76,076	71.0	957	.89	31,937	29.8
1982	100,708	22,440	22.2	100	.092	1,212	1.20	76,956	76.4	926	.91	24,678	24.5
1983	111,549	27,704	24.8	164	.147	1,685	1.51	81,996	73.5	1,762	1.52	31,315	28.1

Source: U.S. Occupational Safety and Health Administration

[1] Percent of total violations.

[2] For 1972, data are for July to December only.

with penalties increased. In the last year of the Carter administration, the percentage of total violations with penalties, 38.1 percent, almost matched the historical high of 38.3 percent set in 1973.

Overall, the average yearly totals of the serious, willful, repeat, and other violations with penalties declined from 103,442 during the Nixon/Ford years to 45,596 in the Carter years to 29,310 during the Reagan years, representing decreases of 56 percent and 36 percent, respectively. The proportion of these violations (i.e., serious, willful, repeat, and other violations with penalties) to total violations also declined during this time period. This proportion was 33.8 percent during the Nixon/Ford years, 33.0 percent during the Carter years, and 27.5 percent during the Reagan years.

It is easy to see a pattern in these changes. The first year of decline for five of the dimensions considered (total inspections, percentage of initial inspections with citations, percentage of initial inspections with penalties, total violations, and total serious, willful, repeat, and other violations with penalties) was the election year of 1976. This seems highly unlikely to have occurred by chance.

During this election campaign, candidate Jimmy Carter emphasized the theme that the federal government had grown out of control. Thus, it was necessary for outsiders to come to Washington to reassert popular control over the apparatuses of government. Popular discontent with government was quite high at the time, with the Watergate controversy a recent memory for the public. Criticism of excessive and burdensome regulations struck a responsive chord among Republicans and Democrats alike. Jokes about "nonsense regulations" at OSHA reflected popular feelings at the time. Critics ridiculed OSHA for having regulations on such matters as toilet-seat dimensions and the proper height of doorknobs. Even those sympathetic to the federal regulatory system participated in poking fun at OSHA, no doubt because it was so easy to do so. The authors of a leading social issues in management text simply quoted OSHA regulations appearing in the *Code of Federal Regulations* of July 1, 1975 to demonstrate their silliness.

Section 1910.35(b): Exit access is that portion of a means of egress which leads to the entrance to an exit.

Section 1910.25 (d) (vii) [out of 21 pages of fine print devoted to ladders]: When ascending or descending, the user should face the ladder; (d) (2) (xx): The bracing on the back of step ladders is designed solely for increasing stability and not for climbing.

Section 1910.244 (a) (2) (vii): Jacks which are out of order shall be tagged accordingly, and shall not be used until repairs are made. (quoted in Steiner and Steiner, 1980, p. 165)

There now seems to be a general agreement among the concerned parties--including labor representatives, OSHA officials, business people, and congressional oversight committees--that there were regulatory excesses during OSHA's early years.

During the 1980 presidential campaign, there was continued political rhetoric and public support regarding the need to "get government off the backs of the people." This antiregulatory movement culminated in the election of Ronald Reagan as president. Critics of government regulation frequently singled out OSHA for criticism. The costs of both issuing and complying with these and other regulations were frequently cited as creating inefficiency and waste in the U.S. economy (Arthur Andersen and Company, 1979; *Business Week*, 1980; Weidenbaum, 1981).

Given the political popularity of deregulation at that time, the increase in numbers of inspections during 1980 may be somewhat surprising. However, this may have reflected a recognition by the Carter administration that candidate Reagan had already preempted the deregulation/big government issues. In light of this, there may have been an attempt to curry favor with labor through closer scrutiny of the workplace.

The decline in the number and seriousness of violations and penalties may not be due solely to political considerations; there are other possible explanations. It may be that the workplaces actually did become safer. As noted, there has been a decline over time in injury rates. Also, it may be that as managers have become more aware of OSHA, its regulations, and the consequences for being out of compliance with them, fewer violations exist and, therefore, fewer are found. Those that are found are corrected. This is a popular explanation with OSHA administrators, because it suggests that the agency has been effective. Industry sources agree that there have been improvements in safety and health conditions. Any political motivation behind changes in violation and penalty statistics, they feel, is a welcome change from the harassment they believe was experienced in the past. Labor officials ridicule the view that these changes in the violation and penalty statistics are due simply to changes in working conditions although they concede that there have been improvements. They place much greater emphasis on political influence in explaining these changes. Moreover, they are highly critical of the direction of that influence under former president Reagan.

It has been claimed by OSHA administrators that the agency's increased emphasis on education and training under the Reagan administration has resulted in greater compliance with regulations and safer workplaces. Although education and training should have *some* effect on workplace safety, it is hard to believe that these are the principal causes of the changes in violation and penalty statistics. There are several reasons for this skepticism. First, research on the effectiveness of OSHA has not provided convincing evidence that workplaces have, in fact, become safer as a result of OSHA. Second, the great differences in the number and severity of citations and penalties during the first years of new administrations are more likely to come from policy changes regarding issuing citations and penalties rather than from a new OSHA administration's effect on workplace safety. Decreases in the number and severity of violations later on in an administration could more plausibly be attributed to the improvements in workplace conditions under the new OSHA leadership. Also, anecdotal evidence (Simon, 1983) suggests that administrative pressure was actually applied to field inspectors to urge them to reduce the number and severity of violations.

Further evidence to support the position of the critics of safety and health regulation under Reagan was provided by major penalties issued toward the end of his administration. These were fines in the hundreds of thousands of dollars issued to several firms, including Ford, Chrysler, and General Motors, for underrecording work injuries. Critics cite these penalties as evidence that the claimed improvements in worker safety are spurious. Not surprisingly, supporters of the Reagan administration's policies cite these same penalties as evidence that cheaters do get caught and, once caught, are heavily penalized. Given the controversy over policy changes that have taken place during OSHA's history, it is instructive to consider the political controversies surrounding OSHA under the Reagan administration in greater depth.

OSHA UNDER THE REAGAN ADMINISTRATION

Ronald Reagan took office in January 1981 with a mandate for change. His administration did, in fact, bring about dramatic changes in the orientation of government regulatory policies in general and those of OSHA in particular over the next eight years. The changes at OSHA were great in spite of the fact that the Carter administration had previously begun a process of "regulatory reform," eliminating many of the so-called "nonsense regulations."

President Reagan appointed Thorne G. Auchter as the chief administrator of OSHA. He shared Reagan's disdain for how OSHA had been run under previous administrations, and he shared Reagan's enthusiasm for the deregulation of industry in general. Under Auchter's direction, OSHA attempted to eliminate many of the adversarial aspects of its regulatory activities and replace them with cooperative ones. This was to be accomplished through a shift of emphasis in government-industry relations away from punitive enforcement and litigation. These were to be replaced with emphasis on education and reconciliation of differences. Consistent with this orientation and consistent with Reagan's efforts to scale back nondefense government spending, substantial cutbacks were made in OSHA funding. In the 1982 fiscal year budget, the first one developed under the Reagan administration, funding fell to $195 million from $209 million for the fiscal year 1981, in unadjusted dollars. Funded positions were reduced 19 percent, from 2,922 to 2,354 in this same year.

The reorientation of OSHA and the cutbacks were criticized vociferously by organized labor. It was argued that these represented an abrogation of OSHA's duty to protect the workers. The budgetary cutbacks and the appointment of Auchter have been cited as evidence of an attempt to decimate the agency. Auchter's own construction company had been previously cited by OSHA for safety and health violations. His designation to head OSHA was characterized by critics as "the fox guarding the chicken coop." Critics also contended that the new cooperative relationships involved only government cooperation with business and that labor representatives were systematically excluded from participation. Auchter resigned as the head of OSHA in mid-1984, with high praise from industry for what he had accomplished. Although his policies had been unpopular with labor, he had managed to win a certain degree of respect from that sector over time.

Auchter's successor, Robert A. Rowland, followed the same policies, and labor criticism continued. However, due to his management style and certain alleged conflicts of interest, the criticism of Rowland was sharper and took on a much more personal tone. There were also newspaper reports that purges reminiscent of the McCarthy era were being conducted at OSHA. Top level lieutenants of Rowland were quoted as urging subordinates to get rid of the "communists" at the agency. Rowland resigned under pressure in 1985 and was replaced by an acting administrator, Patrick Tyson. John Pendergrass who was appointed chief administrator of OSHA in 1986 is praised in many quarters for making the agency tougher on employers who violate the rules. Even more credit for this tougher enforcement is given to William Brock, who became secretary of labor in 1985 when Raymond Donovan was forced to resign due to legal problems. The major fines for underrecording injuries were imposed after both Pendergrass and Brock took office.

In the remainder of this section, several OSHA programs and policies exemplifying the cooperative orientation of OSHA under Reagan are detailed. They include the inspection targeting program, enforcement activities, and several voluntary protection programs. The various criticisms these approaches have generated are considered, and some assessments of the cooperative/conflictual aspects of these programs and policies are made.

Inspection Targeting

This program calls for OSHA inspection officers to concentrate their safety inspection activities on those workplaces deemed to be the most hazardous. A program for targeting health inspections at workplaces based on OSHA citation statistics was also instituted.

There are basically two steps for prioritizing workplaces for safety inspections: an industry-level step and a workplace-level step. The first step was initiated by the agency when Eula Bingham was the director during the Carter administration. It involves concentrating inspections on workplaces in high-hazard industrial sectors. These were defined as those manufacturing industries with a lost-time injury rate greater than the average for the entire manufacturing sector. This rate, provided by the U.S. Bureau of Labor Statistics (BLS), was 4.2 injuries per 100 workers in 1983.

The second step, instituted during the Reagan administration, involves concentrating within the targeted industries on those workplaces that have a higher injury rate than the national average for all manufacturing. In this step, the focus is on the injury rate of the workplace itself, rather than on that of its industry. Thus, unless there was some special reason for an inspection, a firm would be exempt from inspections either if it was in an industry with an injury rate below the average for all manufacturing or if its own injury rate was below the manufacturing sector average rate.

This targeting was operationalized as follows. An inspector would visit a workplace in a high-hazard industry. The inspector would then check the injury log and conduct an actual shop-floor inspection only if the injury rate at that particular workplace exceeded the national average for all manufacturing. The inspector could also conduct an inspection if a formal employee safety complaint was received or if there was some other evidence of a particularly hazardous condition.

The notion of setting criteria for inspections and concentrating on those workplaces that are most hazardous makes a great deal of sense and is widely supported. Although many critics feel that more resources should be devoted to inspections, they recognize that with approximately 5 million workplaces in the United States, some form of targeting is necessary. In recent years, OSHA has conducted between 60,000 and 70,000 inspections per year. Thus, only about 1 in every 70 workplaces is inspected in a given year.

Despite the general support for the targeting concept, the way in which it was carried out under the Reagan administration came under intense criticism, especially from organized labor. Interviews with AFL-CIO and UAW health and safety officials uncovered a number of specific complaints about the program. These complaints echoed those in published reports of labors' views (Simon, 1983). First, concern was raised that the targeting procedure virtually exempted from inspection a very large percentage of the nation's workplaces. It was felt that much of the incentive for maintaining a safe workplace would be eliminated if the firm was almost certain that it would not be inspected. Labor officials would have preferred a targeting approach that presented the employer with a greater degree of uncertainty concerning whether or not the worksite would be inspected. Something akin to the Internal Revenue Service's auditing procedure would have been more to their liking. Under it, targeting would exist, but there would still be some randomness in choosing workplaces to be inspected to "keep everyone honest."

Second, concern was expressed that some hazardous firms are exempted from inspections by the first targeting step. Workplaces with a higher injury rate than the national average for manufacturers were exempted from inspections by the first targeting step if they were in an industry with an injury rate below the national average.

Third, several criticisms of OSHA's use of injury statistics for targeting purposes were raised. For example, the use of only the most recent two or three years of injury statistics for targeting purposes was criticized. It was argued that an inherently unsafe firm could have low injury rates for two or three years without having resolved its safety problems. It could simply be lucky, or its workers could be more cautious than normal for a given period of time. An inspection or the threat of an inspection could presumably motivate such a firm to solve these problems. Moreover, it was felt by some that OSHA's heavy reliance on injury statistics could encourage cheating on injury rate recording. Employers could, for example, simply not record injuries; they could reassign injured workers to very simple jobs and (illegally) not record the injury; or they could attempt to influence the judgment of the physician who determines the type of treatment provided and who decides whether or not the employee can work. The avoidance of inspections was apparently one of the motivations of the firms that were fined by OSHA for underrecording injuries.

The use of injury statistics for inspection targeting was criticized on several other grounds. It has been argued that some dangerous condition in a plant that has not yet resulted in a high injury rate could be uncovered in a routine safety inspection. Additionally, reliance on injury rates could exempt workplaces from inspections if they have a relatively high percentage of workers in safe white-collar jobs, even if there is a high injury rate among blue-collar workers. This is because only the overall injury rate for the whole establishment is typically considered when determining whether or not it should be inspected.

A final criticism of the inspection targeting program pertains to the amount of advance warning time employers get before an inspection takes place. Since the OSHA inspectors examine the firm's injury log first, there would be time for the employer to correct unsafe conditions before a work-area inspection was initiated. Previously, OSHA inspectors would proceed more quickly to the work area. Moreover, under Reagan-appointed OSHA administrators, OSHA inspectors are much less likely to be allowed to obtain a search warrant prior to being denied entry into a plant. Thus, an employer could obtain even more time to correct unsafe conditions by denying entry into the plant and forcing the inspector to obtain a search warrant.

In an apparent concession to labor, an important change in the inspection targeting program was instituted in early 1986 (Trost, 1986).

OSHA announced that, in the future, approximately 10 percent of its inspections would be spot checks on firms in low-hazard industries and firms with injury rates below the national average--groups that had been previously exempted from inspections. This change was instituted under Secretary of Labor William Brock and OSHA Chief Administrator John Pendergrass. It may be that they were more sympathetic to labor's position on safety and health issues than their predecessors. The large increase in occupational injury and illness rates in 1984 may have also been a motivating factor. This policy change was welcomed by labor representatives, although they would have preferred a higher percentage of such spot checks. In contrast, this new policy was criticized by industry. The *Wall Street Journal* quoted Mark de Bernardo, the manager of labor at the U.S. Chamber of Commerce, describing this change as "a retreat from the positive concept of rewarding the good actor and a movement in the wrong direction" (Trost, 1986, p. 56).

Despite this change, it is clear that under the Reagan administration, OSHA had a different view of the role of the agency and the purpose of inspections than did organized labor. OSHA's inspection policies were geared to bring about a speedy elimination of workplace hazards with a minimum of confrontation and conflict between workplace managers and OSHA inspectors. Labor would have preferred to see the inspections serve as more of a deterrent against hazardous conditions in workplaces by penalizing those firms found to have such conditions. These differences between OSHA and labor were bridged somewhat by the changes in inspection policies. However, labor-management differences over the fundamental role of OSHA have continued.

Enforcement and Citation Policies

Dissent over the proper role of OSHA can be seen vividly in debates over OSHA enforcement and citation activities. These policies/activities are described first and then the controversies are considered.

When a workplace is found to violate an OSHA regulation, a citation is issued. The firm is ordered to comply with the standard within a specified time period; and it may be fined up to $1,000 for each serious or repeat violation. In addition, fines of up to $1,000 per day can be levied for failure to correct the problem within the specified time period. After a citation is issued, the employer may appeal the citation to the regional supervisor of inspectors. If dissatisfied with this appeal, the employer may file a suit to contest the citation in court.

OSHA fines had been a source of considerable resentment among many employers who felt inspectors were "out to get" them. This resentment surfaced in the anti-OSHA backlash in the 1976 and 1980 elections. It also was evidenced by businesses regularly contesting citations--contested claims occurred in one quarter of all citation cases in 1980 (Auchter, November 9, 1983)--and by frequent litigation.

Under Auchter, OSHA took a number of steps to reduce the level of acrimony in its relations with businesses, in particular, regarding its enforcement activities. Auchter explained this approach as follows:

> In an effort to promote the kind of cooperation that can lead to a reduction in job-related injuries and illnesses one of our top priorities has been to eliminate the adversary atmosphere that has all too often characterized the OSHA program. (Auchter, 1983, p. 2)

To this end, OSHA has placed greater emphasis on education and consultation activities and less emphasis on citations and fines for bringing about safer and healthier work environments. Employers undergoing inspections are requested to complete a survey form that goes so far as to ask whether the inspection was conducted in a courteous, nonadversarial manner.

OSHA inspectors under Reagan appeared willing to assume that violations of OSHA regulations were the result of good-faith mistakes unless there was strong evidence to the contrary. This would explain the dramatic decrease in the number of willful violations after the Reagan administration took office. These declined from 1,009 in 1980 to 269 in 1981, 100 in 1982, and 164 in 1983 (see Table 2-5). A component of this new orientation was an effort to reduce the number of contested cases and the amount of litigation. After receiving a citation, employers were invited to request an informal reconciliation conference with the area director. At these conferences, an effort was made to resolve any employer grievances and to reach a negotiated settlement for eliminating the hazard. Often, the negotiated settlement called for a reduction in the severity of the citation or the amount of the fine.

Because employers did not need to correct a cited condition while it was being contested, OSHA officials felt that negotiated settlements achieved safe working conditions more quickly. Moreover, they contended that inspectors did not have as much of their time tied up in court. As evidence of the effectiveness of this approach, Auchter cited the reduction in contested citations as a percentage of total inspections from 25 percent in 1980 to between just 3 percent and 4 percent in 1983 (Auchter, November 9, 1983).

Another change in the enforcement policy was a reduction in the number of follow-up inspections conducted to determine if cited conditions had been corrected. OSHA began to rely more heavily on letters from employers to determine whether the situation had been corrected. These letters were supposed to be posted in the workplace. Workers who knew of the citation could report the company to OSHA if the letter was not posted and/or if the reported correction had not been undertaken.

These changes in OSHA enforcement policies generated considerable criticism, particularly from labor. The criticisms of enforcement policies, like those directed at targeting policies, reflected fundamental philosophical differences concerning the purpose of enforcement activities. In short, OSHA began to follow enforcement policies designed to correct hazardous workplace conditions as soon as possible. Labor representatives, however, emphasized the deterrence effect of citations and fines. They felt that it was necessary to intimidate employers into providing safe working conditions with the threat of citations and fines. This is why they were especially concerned that some employers knew their workplaces were exempted from inspections through the targeting program. One of the major concerns of labor regarding enforcement activities was the decrease in the number and severity of citations and fines at OSHA under Reagan (at least until near the end of his administration). The enforcement effort was viewed as being designed more to maintain harmonious relations between the business community and OSHA rather than to ensure safe working conditions. This was regarded by labor as yet further evidence of a probusiness/antilabor orientation of the Reagan administration.

Part of the enforcement program that labor particularly opposed was the practice of holding informal conferences between management and OSHA area coordinators to resolve disputes and thereby reduce the number of contested citations. Labor representatives contended that because area directors were evaluated by OSHA, in part, on their ability to minimize the number of contested claims, there was a strong incentive for them to reduce the severity of the citation and fine during these conferences. This obviously conflicted with labor's view that fines help to deter safety violations. Moreover, labor representatives complained that they were being systematically excluded from a matter that vitally concerned them and with which OSHA legislation specifies that they should be involved. OSHA officials acknowledged that labor representatives were often not invited to these informal conferences; but this was not to exclude labor from the dispute resolution process. Instead, they contended that it was to avoid confrontational meetings where compromise would be unlikely. They held separate meetings with labor representatives in such circumstances.

Other features of OSHA's new orientation to enforce activities were criticized for similar reasons. Thus, labor representatives objected to the decreased number of follow-up inspections because they didn't trust employers. They felt it was necessary to have an inspector certify that the changes called for were actually made. Labor also felt that the practice of having safety inspectors evaluated by employers whose worksites had been inspected places cooperation with business above worker safety.

Voluntary Compliance Programs

One final OSHA policy initiative worth considering for its bearing on cooperation and confrontation in safety and health pertains to a group of voluntary compliance programs. Included in this group are programs called "Star," "Praise," and "Try." These programs were initiated to encourage a greater degree of self-regulation by industry in safety and health. Worksites with better than average health/safety records and an in-house safety and health program were exempted from routine OSHA inspections for a specified period of time.

The Star Program is the most relevant to this research because it involves labor-management cooperation. It is also interesting because participation in the Star Program was viewed as the ultimate goal for firms participating in the other two programs. To be eligible for the Star Program, a worksite had to meet three criteria: (1) have an injury rate at or below the average for its industry, (2) have a good record in OSHA inspections, and (3) have a formal safety and/or health program that provides for employee involvement. Worksites that participated in the Star Program were exempted from OSHA inspections for an indefinite time period. They were, however, required to submit their injury statistics yearly for review and to undergo an OSHA evaluation of their safety/health program every three years.

Although the Voluntary Protection Programs were initiated in July 1982, only 55 worksites were participating as of the end of 1987. This total included 50 worksites in the Star Program and 5 in the Try Program. The Praise Program was eliminated in December 1987. The low level of participation in the programs was attributed to distrust lingering from OSHA's earlier, more adversarial days. It was also attributed to a feeling among some employers qualifying for participation that the programs were really targeted for improving the performance of worksites with below-average health/safety records. Nevertheless, participants in the Star Program did have exemplary safety records. OSHA reported that worksites in the Star Program had roughly 80 percent fewer lost-work injuries than the averages in their industries (President, 1988).

Labor representatives were critical of the Voluntary Protection Programs. This criticism was, however, attenuated by the fact that so few firms participated in them. Labor criticism focused primarily on the exemption from OSHA inspections of participating worksites. There was no specific opposition to the principle of labor-management cooperation on safety and health advanced by these programs. There was, however, skepticism that these programs would actually promote this cooperation. Labor pointed to the low level of participation in these programs as evidence of their failure. They also argued that, with the other exemptions from OSHA inspections detailed above, firms had relatively little incentive to participate.

The admittedly disappointing results of the Voluntary Protection Programs are interesting in the context of this research. The aim of these programs to promote cooperation on safety and health is similar to the aims of the legislated health and safety structures in many European countries. The fact that neither industry nor labor embraced these OSHA programs with much enthusiasm certainly casts doubt on the ability of government to promote cooperation. Nevertheless, there are several reasons to believe that all cooperative safety and health initiatives need not meet with failure. Elimination of the problems cited above could go a long way toward making such programs viable.

Additional understanding of the low level of participation in these programs can be achieved by comparing the incentives for labor-management cooperation on safety and health in other countries with the incentives in the United States. In Germany and Sweden, joint labor-management safety and health committees have been required by law for many years. It is reasonable to assume that, over time, one can learn to tolerate and even embrace that which one is required to do. Japan, however, is a very different case. The quasi-governmental Japan Industrial Safety and Health Association only recommends joint labor-management safety and health committees. However, in keeping with the Japanese tradition of harmonious relations among labor, management, and government, these recommendations are almost uniformly followed by major corporations. In contrast to employers in these other countries, there is very little incentive or inclination by employers in the United States to participate in government-sponsored cooperative efforts.

Despite OSHA's disappointing results so far, cooperation among labor, management, and government on health and safety matters has been achieved within the context of the American system of labor relations with beneficial results. Interestingly, much of the impetus for cooperative safety and health agreements seems to have been federal legislation. Various sources (Bacow, 1980; Kochan, Dyer, and Lipsky, 1977; Smith, 1982) suggest that OSHA provided employers with the motivation and workers with the negotiating leverage to work out negotiated and/or cooperative approaches to safety and health in recent years. Even earlier legislation, notably the National Labor Relations Act of 1935 (the Wagner Act) and its amendments of 1948 (the Taft-Hartley Act) and 1959 (the Landrum-Griffin Act), provided the legal framework for negotiated safety and health agreements.

Although there has been a long tradition of labor-management negotiations and contractual agreements over working conditions, including safety and health conditions, following the passage of the OSH Act there has been greater emphasis on safety and health committees as a vehicle for cooperation on safety and health issues. A U.S. Department of Labor, Bureau of Labor Statistics study (1976) of 1,724 collective bargaining agreements revealed that 45 percent (407 of 908) of the agreements in manufacturing industries and 21 percent (169 of 816) of agreements in other industries stipulated provisions for some form of labor-management health and safety committee. These committees vary a great deal in terms of their responsibilities and authority, but they each provide a forum for potential cooperation on safety and health matters.

Kochan, Dyer, and Lipsky (1977) studied labor-management safety and health committees in plants organized by the International Association of Machinists and Aerospace Workers. These committees were found to vary a great deal in terms of their level of interaction and their output, as measured by the number of suggestions and recommendations. Nevertheless, it was concluded that cooperation on safety and health matters was both achievable and beneficial. Specifically, they found that there was a greater level of interaction and a greater degree of continuity in those committees where

> OSHA pressure is perceived to be strong, the local union itself is perceived to be strong, rank-and-file involvement in safety and health issues is substantial, and management approaches safety issues in a problem-solving manner. (p. 80)

Interestingly, the researchers also found that there is less labor involvement in safety and health matters when OSHA is viewed as adequately ensuring safe working conditions. This is consistent with Bacow's (1980) finding that safety and health issues, not usually important bargaining issues to begin with, are accorded even less importance in negotiations when OSHA is viewed as providing reasonably safe working conditions.

Based upon the foregoing analysis of occupational safety and health activities in the United States, we can now plot on Figure 1-1 the nature of the behaviors of labor, management, and government for coping with occupational safety and health conflicts. The typical approach taken by management in relations with both government and labor is at a point characterized by high levels of assertiveness and moderately low levels of cooperativeness. This point is in the competitive region of Figure 1-1. (This region is also labeled "domination" but that label would only be accurate where labor's or government's assertiveness was low.) Competition is a less effective method for handling conflicts such as those associated with safety and health than, for example, collaboration, which entails higher levels of cooperation. Both U.S. labor and government typically engage in reciprocal competitive conflict-coping behaviors toward management. Moreover, relations here between labor and government could also be characterized as competitive in most cases.

This chapter has set the stage for consideration of labor and management efforts to deal with occupational safety and health on a more cooperative basis in the U.S. auto industry. These efforts are considered in the next chapter. Following that, we examine the national contexts in which occupational safety and health systems operate for several other countries. Along with general background information that will illuminate subsequent international comparisons, that chapter focuses on cooperative and conflictual aspects of national orientations to handling occupational safety and health. Comparisons of national injury experiences in Chapter 5 allow us to make some qualified assessments of the relative effectiveness of different national approaches. The national-level analysis, along with the industry-level analysis contained in the following chapter, will provide the context for the comparative analysis of safety and health activities and experiences of several multinational automotive companies both in their domestic and international operations. This will permit us to make some judgments regarding the extent to which corporate safety and health activities and their success or failure are dictated by national contexts in which the firms operate (i.e., the environmental determinism view) or are determinable by managerial discretion (i.e., the strategic-choice view).

3

WORKER SAFETY AND HEALTH IN THE U.S. AUTO INDUSTRY

The auto industry is an especially important one in which to consider the development of occupational safety and health issues in the United States for several reasons. First, by virtue of its size alone, the automotive industry plays an important role in labor-management relations in the U.S. economy. The U.S. Department of Labor, Bureau of Labor Statistics (1985b) reported that in 1983, 758,000 individuals worked in the motor-vehicle and equipment-manufacturing sector of the U.S. economy, accounting for 1 percent of the total private-sector work force of 74.7 million and 4.1 percent of the total of 18.5 million workers engaged in manufacturing. When one considers employment in supplier firms and in related industries, such as steel, rubber, and petroleum, a strong case can be made that the automotive industry is the dominant industry in the United States. This is so despite the sharp contraction of the industry that started at the end of the 1970s.

Second, developments in the area of occupational safety and health in this industry have reflected and, to a certain extent, foreshadowed trends in the wider economy. The tendency of other U.S. industries to follow precedents set in the auto industry is readily apparent to those who have observed developments in the areas of wage settlements and employee participation in decision making. The employee wage concessions negotiated in auto industry contracts during the depths of the last recession were followed by similar agreements in other industries. In the auto industry, employee participation in decision making in the realm of product quality, productivity improvement, and quality of work life have been widely publicized by the automotive firms themselves and by the news media. This publicity, no doubt, has influenced other industries to adopt similar practices. Not so widely reported has been the participation by labor in safety and health matters. However, the potential exists for automotive industry arrangements in these matters to serve as a model for other industries as well.

Third, focusing on the auto industry permits interesting comparisons among the structures and practices for handling occupational safety and health in the different countries in which these multinational firms operate. These comparisons are especially interesting when countries such as Germany, Sweden, and Japan, with traditions of labor participation in management, are included. Because workers in the U.S. auto industry are represented by a strong union, they have been able to bargain for certain safety and health provisions in contracts beyond those guaranteed by law. Unlike workers in other industries in the United States, auto workers have been able to negotiate successfully for the rights to participate in safety and health. These rights are similar in certain respects to those mandated by law for workers in many European auto firms and those developed as an extension of participatory management techniques in Japanese auto firms.

HISTORICAL BACKGROUND

Some industries such as steel making and coal mining were organized by labor earlier than the automotive industry and have longer traditions of promoting safety and health concerns of their members. However, in more recent times, the UAW (officially titled the International Union, United Automobile, Aerospace and Agricultural Implement Workers of America) has been at or near the forefront of the labor movement in promoting safety and health concerns. A UAW publication (1979) on safety and health contends that the union has been a very strong advocate of safety and health in its plants since it was organized in the 1930s and 1940s. It cites vigorous efforts beginning at that time at the plant level to get hazards eliminated. It also states that:

> In the 1950's the UAW hired some of the first health and safety experts into the labor movement to help rank-and-file members to recognize and eliminate job hazards. In the 1960's progress continued on a local level. (United Auto Workers, 1979, p. 2)

Since that time, the UAW and the auto industry have taken important additional steps to promote occupational safety and health.

SAFETY AND HEALTH COOPERATION AGREEMENTS

In 1973, the UAW and the major automotive firms negotiated landmark agreements regarding labor's cooperation with management on safety and health. Subsequent contracts built upon and strengthened the safety and health provisions of these early contracts. Prior to 1973, there had been a limited amount of largely informal labor participation in safety and health. For example, some individual management safety specialists relied on line workers for detecting hazardous conditions and for recommending and/or implementing solutions, although others did not. The formal agreements standardized and significantly extended worker participation in safety and health matters.

The safety and health agreements in 1973 and beyond established the position of plant union safety and health representative (sometimes referred to as the safety representative) and spelled out his/her authority and responsibilities. Significantly, these contracts stipulated that the union safety and health representative was to be appointed by the UAW but paid by the company. Appointment rather than election was intended to shield the representative from political pressure from coworkers. Management negotiators successfully argued that if union safety and health representatives had to stand for reelection, they would be less helpful in the enforcement of health and safety rules viewed as inconvenient by workers.

The agreements stipulated that the union safety and health representative, together with a management safety and health officer(s), would form the plant safety and health committee. They were to work together on a wide range of safety and health matters, including inspections, training, record keeping, and handling of grievances. Procedures were specified for handling safety and health disputes outside of the normally cumbersome grievance procedures. These agreements did, however, continue to permit strikes during the course of a contract over safety and health grievances that could not be satisfactorily resolved. They also provided for union access to company safety and health records and to scientific instruments for monitoring conditions relevant to safety and health in the work environment. Additionally, certain guidelines pertaining to the number of safety and health representatives and their full-time or part-time status were specified. These depended on the number of employees and the physical layout of the plant (e g , whether or not different parts of the plant were geographically separated such that it would be difficult for one person to be responsible for the whole plant). There are certain differences in the provisions of the contracts with the various automotive-industry employers, but one example is provided for illustrative purposes. At this company, the contract specifies that one full-time union safety and health representative is to be appointed in plants that have between 600 and 10,000 employees and that do not have any special physical layout problems.

These agreements also set up joint labor-management safety and health committees at the corporate level. These committees were intended to serve as forums to resolve disputes before they led to OSHA intervention, litigation, strikes, or other confrontational dispute resolution approaches. The committee could also participate in negotiations on safety and health provisions of future contracts. The functioning of these committees in Company X and Company Y is discussed in Chapters 6 and 7.

Management and labor representatives who have participated in these corporate safety and health committees have been very pleased with their operations. According to them, these committees have promoted cooperation on safety and health matters between labor and management as intended. There is general agreement that the operations of these committees have improved over time as the members have grown accustomed to working together. Improvements in operations were also attributed to some changes in committee composition and to the development of a greater spirit of labor-management cooperation throughout the industry since the time the first corporate safety and health committees were established.

One can visualize the changes over time regarding cooperation and conflict on safety and health in the auto industry by referring to Figure 1-1 in Chapter 1. In a typical auto company or plant covered by these agreements, management's conflict-coping behavior toward labor (and labor's toward management) has moved from a position of near competitiveness (high assertiveness, low cooperativeness) to a position closer to collaboration (high assertiveness, moderate cooperativeness). The reasons behind these changes are explored below.

Labor and management sources differ considerably in their explanations of the motivations behind these formal agreements on safety and health. An issue of particular contention is the role the establishment of OSHA played in bringing about these agreements. Labor officials contend that the passage of the OSHA legislation in 1970 was the primary motivation for management's willingness to agree to labor's request to participate in safety and health matters through the establishment of joint committees at corporate and plant levels. According to this view, the OSHA legislation increased the threat of sanctions against management for poor performance on the safety and health dimension. Thus, there was more of an incentive for management to concede to labor participation to improve performance in this area. Moreover, should there be any problems, there would be another party with which to share the blame.

A related explanation was offered by one labor official who contended that management was concerned that OSHA might dictate some mandatory form of labor-management cooperation in the area of safety and health. By negotiating labor participation, management would be able to structure that involvement in a less rigid and, presumably, more cost-effective way than OSHA would mandate. Although OSHA never attempted to do this, it certainly was plausible enough such that management might be concerned about this prospect given the reformist spirit of the times.

The union view on the motivations for the agreements on safety and health reflects the UAW view on the auto companies' motivations for cooperation in general. That is, that the union must be able to pose some credible threat of confrontation or have the potential to impose some cost on firms before they are willing to cooperate. Regarding safety and health, the union position is that its own bargaining credibility is enhanced by the threat of OSHA imposing sanctions on firms with poor safety and health performance. Given this perspective, it is easy to understand criticism of the Reagan administration's OSHA policies. These policies forsake government confrontation with industry in pursuit of more cooperative relations. Labor officials feel that this reduces their own bargaining leverage and lessens the incentive for industry to cooperate with labor.

According to management, there was no OSHA-related incentive to agree to labor participation in safety and health. It was noted that, while the OSH Act encouraged labor-management cooperation, it did not require it, and management thought it highly unlikely that this ever would be required. Also, the law does not absolve management of any responsibility or liability in the safety and health area when there is labor participation. So, according to management, OSHA was simply not a factor in these agreements.

Two alternative explanations of the motivations for these agreements were provided by management. One explanation was that the 1973 agreements were simply concessions to labor. They admitted to being initially skeptical that this arrangement would work, and they were pleasantly surprised when it did.

A second and understandably more popular explanation offered by management was that this agreement represented an early recognition on management's part of the value of cooperation with labor to resolve matters of mutual concern. To understand this position, one must first consider management's view of safety and health negotiations prior to the 1973 agreements. At that time, it was felt that management and labor had separate safety agendas. As one management negotiator described it, labor representatives would come to contract negotiations with a "laundry list" of safety and health demands that management negotiators often opposed. Management negotiators would occasionally propose certain changes in work safety rules that were conceded to but not endorsed by the labor negotiators. Agreements on safety and health negotiated under these conditions were often implemented without much enthusiasm. Under such conditions supervisors frequently were required to act as police officers to enforce new regulations and to penalize those workers who violated them. Workers receiving penalties for unsafe work practices often filed grievances, and they were supported in these grievance procedures by the union.

Given management's view of conditions prior to these cooperative agreements, it is easy to see why management would want union cooperation on safety and health. The agreements promised to make negotiations on safety and health less of a zero-sum exercise. More important, they would provide for more union assistance in the implementation of agreements. This interpretation of events then suggests that these agreements were not concessions but were legitimate cooperative approaches to solving a problem of mutual concern between labor and management.

There may be some element of truth in each of the above explanations. However, it is clear that even if OSHA was not directly responsible for motivating this agreement, it was an indirect factor. The passage of the OSHA legislation reflected the growing concern for occupational safety and health in this country. It greatly increased the role of government in regulating working conditions in factories. It also brought increases in the number and severity of penalties, even for conditions that management felt were trivial violations. Also, with the passage of the OSH Act came the prospect of ever-increasing numbers of rules and regulations pertaining to safety and health. Gaining labor's assistance in achieving compliance with these rules and regulations certainly held considerable appeal. Although the likelihood of laws similar to those in Europe mandating cooperation on safety and health was slim at that time, it was not altogether inconceivable as a future possibility.

AN ASSESSMENT OF RESULTS TO DATE

Whatever the reason(s) for the agreements leading to labor-management cooperation on safety and health issues, there is now a widespread belief by both labor and management that this cooperative approach has been successful. In the early 1980s both sides were extremely enthusiastic about the results of this approach. They cited reductions in the industry injury rates of about 80 percent from 1973-82 as evidence of their joint success.

Since then, however, this enthusiasm has been tempered. There is some concern about modest increases in injury rates since 1982. The overall decline in the injury rates from 1973 to 1986 has diminished to 70 percent due to these later increases. More sobering still is the evidence of deliberate underrecording and misrecording of injuries in the auto industry that surfaced with the OSHA fines in 1986 and 1987. Fines of several hundred thousand dollars each were levied against all the major U.S. auto firms for alleged willful record-keeping violations at one or more plants. Collectively, these involved not recording or inaccurately recording hundreds of injuries, including fractures, lacerations, strains, sprains, and burns. Some of these nonrecorded injuries were said to be serious enough to require surgery.

Since these revelations, UAW officials are more circumspect about the benefits of the safety and health agreements. They suspect that the actual injury rates are considerably higher than the reported rates. One official guessed that they may be three times as high as reported. Still, they feel that progress has been made. This is based on the belief that the level of underrecording has been more or less constant over the course of the agreement. The only exception to this is the perceived added motivation for low recorded injury rates provided by the inspection targeting procedures of OSHA under the Reagan administration. However, since this policy did not take effect until after the major reduction in injury rates had been achieved, it is not regarded as having affected these reductions.

Some discrepancies exist between the above injury incidence statistics and Bureau of Labor Statistics (BLS) injury data reported below. The statistics cited above indicate a somewhat greater improvement in the safety performance in the automotive industry than do the BLS data. The injury incidence declines cited by labor and management are based on data collected by the auto industry in cooperation with the UAW. Despite the record-keeping problems noted above, individuals citing these statistics placed greater faith in them than in the data collected by the government. They noted that the industry data comes from the universe of UAW-organized automotive employers in the United States rather than from a sample of automotive industry employers that the Bureau of Labor Statistics uses. Moreover, a UAW official contended that the union's involvement in the compilation of these statistics would place some constraints on industry's attempts to fudge the numbers. Thus, while there are obviously problems with both sets of statistics, these industry safety and health data may give a better picture of injury trends over time in the automotive industry. However, it is necessary to rely on BLS statistics to compare auto industry injury experience with that of other sectors of the economy. In making these comparisons, we will operate on the assumption that whatever underrecording there is is relatively constant across industries and over time.

Tables 3-1, 3-2, and 3-3 are constructed using injury and illness data published by the U.S. Department of Labor, Bureau of Labor Statistics in *Occupational Injuries and Illnesses in the United States by Industry* (successive years). These indicate that the automotive industry has improved its safety and health performance over time on several safety and health dimensions and that it has done so at a greater rate than either the entire private sector of the economy or the manufacturing sector. Despite the overall declines in injuries in each of these three sectors over the entire 1973-84 time period, there were substantial increases in injury rates for each of these following 1983, the last year of the deep 1981-83 recession.

As Table 3-1 indicates, the automotive industry incidence rate of total recordable injury cases was reduced from 16.1 per 100 full-time workers in 1973 to a low of 8.2 in 1982. After that this rate increased to 9.7 by 1986, with a large increase occurring between 1983 and 1984. Total recordable injury cases are comprised of "lost-workday cases," "nonfatal cases without lost-workdays," and fatalities. These component measures also showed declines during this time period. The lost-workday case rate dropped from 4.5 per 100 full-time workers to 3.4 in 1982, but then jumped back up to 4.2 in 1986. The incidence rate for nonfatal cases without lost workdays dropped from 11.6 to 4.8 per 100 full-time workers in 1982 and then increased to 5.5 per 100 full-time workers in 1986.

Impressive declines in occupational illness rates are evident in Table 3-1. Total recordable illnesses declined from a rate of .9 per 100 full-time workers in 1973 to .5 in 1986. The lost-workday illness rate ended this period at the same level it began it, .2 cases per 100 full-time workers; the rate of nonfatal illness cases without lost workdays declined from .6 to .3 during this time period.

TABLE 3-1

OCCUPATIONAL INJURY AND ILLNESS RATES IN THE U.S.: AUTOMOTIVE INDUSTRY[1]

	Injuries and Illnesses per 100 Full-Time Workers			Injuries per 100 Full-Time Workers			Illnesses per 100 Full-Time Workers		
	Total Recordable Cases	Lost-Workday Cases	Nonfatal Cases Without Lost Workdays	Total Recordable Cases	Lost-Workday Cases	Nonfatal Cases Without Lost Workdays	Total Recordable Cases	Lost-Workday Cases	Nonfatal Cases Without Lost Workdays
1972	20.1	4.4	15.7	19.0	4.1	14.9	1.1	.3	.8
1973	17.0	4.7	12.3	16.1	4.5	11.6	.9	.2	.6
1974	15.7	4.8	10.9	14.3	4.4	9.9	1.4	.4	1.0
1975	13.7	4.6	9.1	12.9	4.3	8.6	.8	.3	.5
1976	12.4	4.5	7.9	11.8	4.3	7.5	.6	.2	.4
1977	11.5	4.9	6.6	11.0	4.6	6.4	.5	.3	.2
1978	11.3	5.1	6.1	10.8	4.9	5.9	.5	.2	.3
1979	11.6	5.5	6.1	11.1	5.3	5.8	.5	.2	.3
1980	9.9	4.3	5.6	9.5	4.2	5.3	.4	.1	.3
1981	9.1	4.0	5.1	8.7	3.8	4.9	.4	.2	.2
1982	8.5	3.6	4.9	8.2	3.4	4.8	.3	.2	.1
1983	8.7	3.7	5.1	8.3	3.5	4.9	.4	.2	.2
1984	10.1	4.5	5.7	9.7	4.3	5.5	.4	.2	.2
1985	9.2	4.1	5.1	8.8	3.9	5.0	.4	.2	.2
1986	10.2	4.4	5.8	9.7	4.2	5.5	.5	.2	.3

Sources: U.S. Department of Labor, Bureau of Labor Statistics. *Handbook of Labor Statistics, 1977.* Washington, D.C.: U.S. Government Printing Office, 1977; U.S. Department of Labor, Bureau of Labor Statistics. *Occupational Injuries and Illnesses in the United States by Industry.* Washington, D.C.: U.S. Government Printing Office, successive years.

[1] SIC code 3710, motor vehicle and equipment manufacturing

Comparing the injury experience of the auto industry over the 1973-84 time period with that of the private sector and the manufacturing sector is instructive. This time period is particularly interesting because it also corresponds to the first 11 years of OSHA's existence. The auto industry began this time period with injury and illness rates much higher than those for the private sector as a whole and somewhat higher than those for the manufacturing sector. Since then injury and illness rates in the auto industry declined much faster than those in the private sector and the manufacturing sector. For the most recent year, although they are still higher than those of the private sector, they are lower than those of the manufacturing sector.

TABLE 3-2
OCCUPATIONAL INJURY AND ILLNESS RATES IN THE UNITED STATES: PRIVATE SECTOR EMPLOYEES

	Injuries and Illnesses per 100 Full-Time Workers			Injuries per 100 Full-Time Workers		
	Total Recordable Cases	Lost-Workday Cases	Nonfatal Cases w/o Lost-Workdays	Total Cases	Lost-Workday Cases	Nonfatal Cases w/o Lost-Workdays
1972	10.9	3.3	7.6	10.5	N.A.	N.A.
1973	11.0	3.4	7.5	10.6	3.3	7.3
1974	10.4	3.5	6.9	10.0	3.4	6.6
1975	9.1	3.3	5.8	8.8	3.2	5.6
1976	9.2	3.5	5.7	8.9	3.4	5.5
1977	9.3	3.8	5.5	9.0	3.7	5.3
1978	9.4	4.1	5.3	9.2	4.0	5.2
1979	9.5	4.3	5.2	9.2	4.2	5.0
1980	8.7	4.0	4.7	8.5	3.9	4.6
1981	8.3	3.8	4.5	8.1	3.7	4.4
1982	7.7	3.5	4.2	7.6	3.4	4.1
1983	7.6	3.4	4.2	7.5	3.4	4.1
1984	8.0	3.7	4.3	7.8	3.6	4.2
1985	7.9	3.6	4.3	7.7	3.6	4.2
1986	7.9	3.6	4.3	7.7	3.6	4.2

N.A. = Not available
Sources: U. S. Department of Labor, Bureau of Labor Statistics. *Handbook of Labor Statistics, 1977.* Washington, D.C.: U.S. Government Printing Office, 1977; U.S. Department of Labor, Bureau of Labor Statistics. *Occupational Injuries and Illnesses in the United States by Industry.* Washington, D.C.: U.S. Government Printing Office, successive years.

These changes can be seen most clearly by reference to the total recordable cases of injuries and illnesses in the first column of Tables 3-1, 3-2, and 3-3. The injury statistics make up the overwhelming majority of the cases in the combined injury and illness statistics on these tables. Illnesses can be computed in Tables 3-2 and 3-3 as the difference between categories of combined injuries and illnesses totals (total recordable cases, lost-workday cases, and nonfatal cases without lost workdays) and the corresponding columns of injury statistics on the right-hand side of the tables.

TABLE 3-3
OCCUPATIONAL INJURY AND ILLNESS RATES IN THE UNITED STATES: MANUFACTURING SECTOR

	Injuries and Illnesses per 100 full-time workers			Injuries per 100 full-time workers		
	Total Recordable Cases	Lost-Workday Cases	Nonfatal Cases w/o Lost Workdays	Total Cases	Lost-Workday Cases	Nonfatal Cases w/o Lost Workdays
1972	N.A.	N.A.	N.A.	14.9	N.A.	N.A.
1973	15.3	4.5	10.8	14.7	N.A.	N.A.
1974	14.6	4.7	9.9	14.0	4.5	9.5
1975	13.0	4.5	8.5	12.5	4.3	8.1
1976	13.2	4.8	8.3	12.6	4.6	8.0
1977	13.1	4.5	8.0	12.6	4.9	7.7
1978	13.2	5.6	9.2	12.8	5.4	7.4
1979	13.3	5.9	9.0	12.8	5.7	7.1
1980	12.2	5.4	6.8	11.8	5.2	6.6
1981	11.5	5.1	6.4	11.1	4.9	6.2
1982	10.2	4.4	5.8	9.9	4.3	5.6
1983	10.0	4.3	5.7	9.7	4.2	5.5
1984	10.6	4.7	5.9	10.2	4.5	5.7
1985	10.4	4.6	5.8	10.0	4.4	5.6
1986	10.6	4.7	5.9	10.2	4.5	5.7

N.A. = Not available
Sources: U.S. Department of Labor, Bureau of Labor Statistics. *Handbook of Labor Statistics, 1977.* Washington, D.C.: U.S. Government Printing Office, 1977; U.S. Department of Labor, Bureau of Labor Statistics. *Occupational Injuries and Illnesses in the United States by Industry.* Washington, D.C.: U.S. Government Printing Office, successive years.

From 1973 to 1986, the incidence of injuries and illnesses in the automotive industry fell from 17.0 total recordable cases per 100 full-time workers to 10.2, representing a 40 percent decline. This was greater than the 28 percent decline (11.0 to 7.9) on this same dimension in the same time period experienced by the private sector, and it was greater than the 31 percent decline (15.3 to 10.6) experienced by the manufacturing sector. For this same time period, the auto industry experienced a slight (6%) decline in the lost-workday case rate (4.7 to 4.4 cases per 100 full-time workers). In comparison, the rate for the private sector as a whole rose 6 percent (3.4 to 3.6), and the manufacturing sector experienced a slight increase of 4 percent on this dimension (4.5 to 4.7) during this time period.

The greatest declines for all three sectors were in the dimension of nonfatal cases without lost workdays. The auto industry reported a decline of 53 percent, dropping from 12.3 such cases per 100 full-time workers to 5.8 during this time period. Again, this was better than the 43 percent decline on this dimension for the private sector as a whole, which declined from 7.5 to 4.3 cases per 100 full-time workers. It was also better than the 45 percent decline in the manufacturing sector that dropped from 10.8 to 5.9 cases per 100 full-time workers during this time period. In sum, these statistics indicate that the auto industry has done a much better job of controlling injuries and illnesses during the time period of the cooperative agreements than was done in the private sector as a whole or in the manufacturing sector.

The fact that the auto industry still has injury and illness incidence rates even slightly higher than those of the private sector is understandable. This can be attributed to the large representation of inherently less dangerous service-sector jobs in the private-sector statistics. The manufacturing sector represents a much more meaningful comparison for the absolute level of performance on injury and illness dimensions, and the auto industry improved its performance relative to this sector in the years since the cooperative agreements first came into existence.

Several points should be made regarding the interpretation of the above statistics. Direct comparisons of injury statistics before and after 1973 (the year OSHA started functioning) are not possible due to changes in injury definitions that took place in that year. Also, there are at least two likely biases in the data. One is the underrecording of injuries that took place in the first few years that OSHA was in existence due to misunderstandings regarding injury-recording requirements. These misunderstandings were reportedly corrected in later years. The second is the underrecording of injuries for which automotive firms were fined in 1986 and 1987. There is no way to know for sure, but it is suspected that such intentional underrecording would be randomly distributed over time and across industries. If this is the case, then this intentional underrecording should not affect the comparisons within the automotive industry over time or between the automotive industry and other industries for the time period prior to the fines. The early unintentional underrecording, which is probably also randomly distributed across industries, is likely to result in an understatement of the decline in injury rates for all industries over time, but it too should not affect comparisons among industries.

The postfine era, however, is clearly a different ball game. Early indications are that *recorded* injury rates in 1987 and beyond are going to be much higher, especially for the automotive industry. Safety and health managers in the auto industry concerned with the possibility of being hit with more fines contend that they are now overrecording injuries. They claim to be recording certain injuries that, in their judgment, they are not required to record but that could be questioned later.

Using a different database and a different method of calculation, the National Safety Council also shows an improvement in the safety performance record of the auto industry over a time period including years before and after the cooperative agreements. Table 3-4 contains National Safety Council data on occupational injuries and fatalities in the automobile industry for the years 1952-76. A note of caution is given for interpreting these data. Because they are collected from voluntary participants in National Safety Council surveys, the respondent sample varies from year to year, making precise charting of the industry injury experience impossible. Also, comparisons with more recent years are not possible because the method of calculating these rates was changed in 1977 to conform with OSHA record-keeping practices. Nevertheless, we are able to identify some interesting trends in injury rates for the time period covered.

The frequency rate is the number of disabling injuries per one million hours worked. This showed an overall downward trend during this time period. The injury frequency rate decreased in all but 6 years in this 24-year time span, dropping from 3.62 injuries per million hours worked in 1952 to 2.30 in 1976. The largest 1-year increase during this time period occurred from 1975 to 1976 when the rate increased from 1.47 to 2.30. It is likely that this is attributable to a 1-year measurement error due to confusion resulting from the planned changeover in injury definition. There were only 97 employer units that responded to the National Safety Council occupational injury survey in 1976, compared with more than 300 respondents for every other year back to 1952. Also, there was no corresponding increase in the injury rate from 1975 to 1976 according to the Bureau of Labor Statistics data cited in Table 3-1, reinforcing the view that this is a statistical aberration.

The severity rate is the total "charges" (in days) due to injuries per million hours worked. These charges include lost workdays due to injuries, and specified numbers of days for fatalities and different types of permanent partial disabilities. The severity rate also showed a downward trend during this time period, dropping from 350 in 1952 to 161 in 1976.

The fatality rate is the number of occupational fatalities per one million hours worked. The fatality rate has not demonstrated any

TABLE 3-4
NATIONAL SAFETY COUNCIL
OCCUPATIONAL INJURY RATES
IN THE AUTOMOBILE INDUSTRY

	Number of Reporting Units	Frequency[1] Rate (All Disabling Injuries)	Severity[2] Rate	Fatality[3] Rate
1952	324	3.62	350	.01
1953	326	3.39	380	.02
1954	318	2.68	310	.02
1955	304	2.76	303	.02
1956	321	2.56	280	.01
1957	341	2.57	326	.02
1958	326	2.44	247	.01
1959	333	2.41	265	.01
1960	344	2.20	261	.02
1961	338	1.76	219	.01
1962	332	1.73	202	.01
1963	341	1.71	223	.01
1964	354	1.86	196	.01
1965	360	1.72	215	.01
1966	363	1.67	235	.02
1967	348	1.64	179	.01
1968	363	1.63	189	.01
1969	369	1.67	256	.02
1970	360	1.48	196	.01
1971	330	1.44	140	.01
1972	354	1.62	229	.02
1973	323	1.60	176	.01
1974	333	1.58	204	.02
1975	314	1.47	179	.01
1976	97	2.30	161	.01

Source: National Safety Council.   *Work Injury and Illness Rates*, Chicago, successive editions.

[1] Number of disabling injuries multiplied by 1 million and divided by the number of hours worked.

[2] Number of days lost and specific charges (in days) multiplied by 1 million and divided by the number of hours worked.

[3] Number of fatalities multiplied by 1 million and divided by the number of hours worked.

discernible trend during this time period, fluctuating between .01 and .02. The fatality rate began and ended the period at .01 fatalities per one million hours worked.

While individual yearly comparisons may not be significant, these data do offer strong evidence that there has been a long-term downward trend in nonfatal injury rates in the automotive industry. Unfortunately, direct comparisons of data collected prior to and after the 1973 cooperative agreements using the National Safety Council data are not very meaningful. This is because there were only three years after the 1973 agreements before the National Safety Council changed their record keeping to conform with OSHA.

One indirect comparison lends support to the view that the agreements have been effective in reducing injuries. In the nine years preceding 1973, there was a 14 percent reduction (1.86 in 1964 to 1.60 in 1973) in the auto-industry injury frequency rate according to National Safety Council data and a 10 percent decrease in the severity rate (196 in 1964 to 176 in 1973). According to auto industry data previously cited, there was an 80 percent decrease in injury rates in the nine years following the agreements.

Given the major contraction in employment in the auto industry that has taken place in recent years, it is reasonable to consider whether this has led to the reported decline in injury rates. A plausible argument could be made that during the contraction the companies laid off their least experienced and, presumably, most accident-prone workers. Thus, in the aftermath of the contraction, there should be a more experienced, safer work force. This, rather than the cooperative arrangements, could then account for the decline in injury rates.

To address this argument, one would like to test statistically the effect of job tenure on injury rates through regression analysis or similarly rigorous statistical techniques. Unfortunately, historical job tenure statistics are not available from industry or union sources. Therefore, several items of indirect evidence are considered.

First, greater reductions in injury rates took place prior to the contraction of the auto industry than after it. The contraction in the auto industry did not begin until 1979; automotive production in the United States reached an all-time high in 1978. According to industry sources, most of the reported 80 percent decline from 1973 to 1982 had occurred prior to 1979. This can also be seen by reference to BLS statistics in Table 3-1. More than two-thirds (69%) of the overall 48 percent decline in injuries from 1973 to 1983 occurred during the first five years of this ten-year period. Thirty-one percent of the decline occurred during the latter five years. Thus, it does not seem reasonable to ascribe the reduction in injury rates to a phenomenon that began in 1979.

Moreover, there is some question about the validity of the conventional wisdom that more experienced workers have fewer accidents. They would have fewer accidents attributable to ignorance, but they might have more accidents attributable to carelessness. This is suggested by a study (UAW, 1987) of worker fatalities from 1973 to 1986 among skilled trade workers in the automotive industry. According to this study, the mean age of these workers accidentally killed during this period was 46 and the mean seniority level was 15 years. This would seem to indicate that inexperience was not a major factor in most of these fatalities. Further research would be necessary to determine if such trends hold for nonfatal accidents. However, given the available information and data, there does not seem to be any evidence to support the view that greater worker seniority caused the reported decline in injury rates.

It is clear that the auto industry has been successful in reducing the rates of injuries and illnesses during the course of the cooperative labor-management agreements on safety and health. It has also been shown that the auto industry has been more successful in reducing injury and illness rates during this time period than have the private sector or the manufacturing sector. While this statistical evidence may not *prove*, in a scientific sense, that these agreements have been effective, it certainly lends strong support to this view. The statistical evidence of the effectiveness of the cooperative agreements on safety and health in the auto industry is corroborated by testimonials from auto-industry officials who have participated in these cooperative ventures. They firmly believe that these ventures have improved safety and health operations in the industry. Safety and health experts from both union and management spoke very favorably of an atmosphere of cooperation at the plant level and at the corporate level that allows the parties to resolve matters of mutual concern. They indicated that there has been a dramatic improvement in labor-management relations regarding safety and health since the cooperation agreements were reached. The OSHA fines have, to an extent, undermined the trust upon which this cooperation is based. Nevertheless, every indication points to the continuation of cooperative efforts even if the parties are suspicious of each other.

These testimonials confirm and update earlier findings by Bacow (1980) at General Motors. He found general labor and management satisfaction with the GM-UAW agreement. Management was satisfied because of reductions in injury rates and in the filing of groundless or trivial safety and health grievances. In addition, management was satisfied with an improvement in worker compliance with safety and health regulations. The union was viewed as being more reasonable to deal with than OSHA. Labor satisfaction stemmed from the reduction in injury rates, the increased union role in safety and health matters, and the increased company resources devoted to safety and health, including the funding of safety and health representative jobs filled by union members.

CURRENT CONCERNS

Despite the accomplishments to date in the auto industry, it is not surprising or even necessarily undesirable that there remain a number of safety and health issues that are sources of conflict in labor-management relations. It is highly unlikely that labor and management safety and health experts and negotiators will ever see eye-to-eye on all safety and health issues. The main reason for this is the fact, generally conceded by safety and health experts (although usually only grudgingly so), that safety pays, but only to a point. At some point, increased precautions and expenditures can have a negative impact on corporate profits. Thus, there are disagreements over various safety and health initiatives that are not viewed as being mutually desirable by labor and management.

Controversies over what to do about two safety and health issues--noise control and ventilation--further illustrate inherent labor-management differences. In both of these cases, there are different means available to protect workers. Personal protection devices (ear plugs, face masks, etc.) are effective, but they are generally disliked and rejected by workers on the grounds that they are uncomfortable. Labor, instead, favors engineering controls for these problems, but management complains that they are too costly. In cases like these, management would like to use cost-benefit analysis to determine the most cost-effective way to deal with a problem. This has been resisted by workers for two reasons. First, it suggests the ability to place a dollar value on human life. Second, they have argued that workers have a basic right to a relatively safe work environment that should not be subject to cost-benefit analysis. The Supreme Court used this second argument as the basis for its decision banning the use of cost-benefit analysis in setting cotton dust standards in workplaces (*American Textile Manufacturers Institute v. Donovan,* 1981). Still, OSHA has continued to use cost-benefit analysis in other rule-making activities (Earley, 1985).

Reflecting trends in the wider economy, and indeed in other countries as well, there has been increased concern and controversy over cumulative trauma disorders in the auto industry during the 1980s. Perhaps most notable among these disorders is carpal tunnel syndrome, which involves damage to the tendons and soreness of the wrists. It often affects workers who engage in repeated gripping and twisting of tools and work materials, which are common activities in assembly-line work. It also affects office workers, including managers, who spend large amounts of time working at computer keyboards and video display terminals. One controversy regarding this condition concerns whether or not individual cases of carpal tunnel syndrome are incapacitating and therefore whether or not the employee should be eligible for workers' compensation. Workers often seek disability pay for such a condition in the face of management opposition. Another point of contention concerns whether assembly-line jobs that are likely to produce such a condition should be automated. There is no interest among labor in seeing workers replaced by machines, but there is an interest in seeing certain of the more difficult parts of some jobs performed by machines. From management's perspective, automating certain tasks on the assembly line is likely to be a financially attractive option only if some jobs can be eliminated. Still, it is ironic that automation has in many ways contributed to the problem of carpal tunnel syndrome through the proliferation of computers in the workplace and the high incidence of this malady among keyboard operators.

Another area of controversy that had been brewing for a number of years was the so-called "right-to-know" issue. Workers in many industries had been pressing for information on chemicals and substances present in their work environments so that they could take appropriate action if some substances were considered hazardous. Employers opposed providing this information, among other reasons, on the grounds that doing so might compromise trade secrets. This matter was settled by OSHA, with the promulgation of the Hazard Communication Rule, also known as the Right-to-Know Rule, that took effect in 1986. The standard that was enacted did not contain all the provisions that labor had sought, but labor officials were pleased with the added protection provided for workers by this rule. For management safety and health specialists, the rule required the establishment of comprehensive training programs to communicate information about hazards in the work environment.

A safety and health dispute that resulted in a short strike at a Ford auto plant in Lorain, Ohio (Perl, 1985b) may be symptomatic of other underlying conflicts. The stated reasons for the strike were worker concerns about adverse safety and health effects due to the speedup and increase of work. To meet foreign competition, the plant management had been cutting labor costs by eliminating some jobs and assigning more tasks to the remaining workers to perform in the same amount of time. Union officials claimed that 2,000 jobs were eliminated from 1980 to 1985 from an original work force of 7,200 but that production levels remained the same. Workers contended that the increased work for individuals led to greater stress and a higher incidence of work-related injuries and illnesses. Management felt that these changes were essential for the plant to remain competitive and questioned the legitimacy of the stated safety and health concerns.

Circumstantial evidence in this case suggests that the safety and health issue was used as a proxy to pursue other concerns. The union had an explicit right to strike over safety and health issues but did not have any right to strike over work-pace disputes. Also, corporate safety and health people were not involved in the resolution of this strike, which would be unusual if safety and health matters were the real sticking points. Eventually, when other concerns of workers were satisfied, the safety and health complaints were dropped.

Finally, and most ominously, the aforementioned OSHA penalties on automotive firms for underrecording injuries have exacerbated old conflicts and renewed old suspicions between labor and management. Only in time will we see the full effect those incidents have had on labor-management cooperation regarding safety and health.

Whereas the above describes some issues of labor-management conflict regarding safety and health, there are other types of safety and health conflicts within the industry that also present problems. There are, for example, individual managers/supervisors and production workers who do not place a high priority on safety and health. Such individuals engage in unsafe practices themselves or, in the case of supervisors, permit or encourage others to do so. This individual lack of concern for safety and health runs counter to the labor-management agreements and reduces their effectiveness. These agreements do, however, provide a vehicle for confronting such individuals. The agreements also provide a forum for the parties involved to address the other conflicts mentioned above. These confrontations and the conflict-resolution process often involve a considerable amount of acrimony, but they allow the parties to reconcile their differences to the degree that it is possible to do so.

Recent Developments

The UAW agreements with the auto firms in 1982 and 1984 brought additional changes in the safety and health arena. (One exception to this was Chrysler, where safety and health provisions of contracts had been frozen since the firm's near bankruptcy in 1979.) The 1982 and 1984 agreements provided for increased safety and health training for union representatives, supervisors, and workers. These agreements also provided for union safety and health representatives to have additional access to work-environment monitoring equipment and company safety and health records. Research programs were also established involving company funding of scientific research to be carried out by independent scientists on safety and health topics jointly selected by labor and management. Like other areas of labor-management negotiations, these agreements were reached only after hard bargaining among the participants.

As alluded to above, the focus of concern over the years regarding safety and health issues in the automotive industry has shifted in directions that reflect societal trends. With the apparent decline in the injury and fatality rates in the auto industry and the nation as a whole in recent years, there has also been somewhat of a shift in the focus of safety and health concerns. Greater attention has been paid to occupational illnesses, such as carpal tunnel syndrome and other less obvious safety and health concerns, as many of the more immediately dangerous working conditions have been corrected. Nevertheless, concern over injuries continues, especially in the aftermath of the underrecording revelations. This concern focuses both on the overall number of injuries and specific types of injuries such as those occurring when workers try to fix malfunctioning machinery.

The occupational illnesses that are now receiving more attention may be less obvious than traditional safety concerns, but they are no less serious. Exposure to various potentially harmful substances is a case in point. Diseases resulting from exposure to certain substances can be just as deadly as work accidents.

The change in emphasis of safety and health concerns is not just the result of success in reducing injuries. It is also the result of improvements in technology and changes in work processes and work pace. Certain hazards of work have been eliminated, some previously existing hazards have been recognized just recently, and some new hazards have developed.

UAW safety and health officials acknowledge that there has been a reduction in the number of hazards existing in the jobs performed by their members, however, they believe that there are a number of remaining hazards faced by UAW members. Exposure to silica dust in foundries that auto companies operate is viewed as the most serious hazard. Other serious hazards include exposure to lead in battery operations and painting, exposure to manganese, copper, zinc, and vanadium in welding, and exposure to cadmium and beryllium in brazing and soldering operations. Exposure to other chemicals and to noise are also noted as serious health concerns of the union. Ergonomics, safe work design, and "lockout/tagout" procedures (i.e., steps that can be taken when repairing a malfunctioning piece of equipment to ensure that it is not unknowingly activated by someone else) are also union priorities.

Increased automation has eliminated some hazards while creating others. For example, parts and components are now moved by conveyor systems rather than manually. This reduces the risk of strains and sprains associated with lifting and pulling. In many plants, automatic (or robotic) painters are now being used. These reduce the risk of illness due to inhaling paint fumes containing lead, and they eliminate the risk of a human painter being crushed underneath a vehicle while painting it. They also eliminate strains resulting from painters twisting their bodies to paint hard-to-reach parts of the vehicles. Robotic welders are also in wide use in the industry, performing difficult and hazardous tasks. Despite safety and health advantages of robots, there is now the new risk of injury by the robot itself; there already have been a number of reports of such injuries. The auto industry, which is one of the heaviest users of robots in the United States, has had two reported robot-related fatalities as of early 1987 (UAW, 1987). In Japan, where the use of robots is even greater than in the U.S., there had been ten industrial fatalities involving robots reported by early 1987 (*Roanoke Times and World News*, 1987). Moreover, as evidenced by the example of carpal tunnel syndrome affecting video display terminal (VDT) operators, the hazards of advanced technology are not restricted to the factory floor. In addition, concerns about eye strain, back problems, and radiation leakage have also been expressed by workers who work long hours at VDTs.

One unexpected and ironic outcome of changes in the organization of production has been the increase of sports injuries. These have occurred in plants where fixed production quotas are set and workers can engage in sports or other recreational/leisure pursuits if they achieve their scheduled production before quitting time. One auto firm reported six hand fractures of individuals who injured themselves trying to slam dunk basketballs during working hours after they had achieved their scheduled production. Because these injuries occurred on company premises during working hours, they were classified as work injuries.

Whereas some of the new safety and health concerns could not have been imagined 50 years ago, other hazards remain from earlier days of the industry. These include the risk of workers getting limbs caught in stamping presses, the risk of being run over by material-handling vehicles, the hazards of working around molten metal in foundry operations, and the hazards incurred by skilled craftsmen working in nonroutine situations to repair machinery.

UAW AND AUTO INDUSTRY VIEWS ON OSHA

There is probably no issue on which labor and management views diverge so much as on the perceived value of OSHA. These disagreements apply not only to OSHA's operations under the Reagan administration but also to its earlier activities. Reflecting the views of organized labor in general, members of the UAW believe that OSHA had performed an important function earlier in its history when it was, in their view, an effective, although at times disorganized, watchdog of business. Along the same line of thought, UAW officials feel that under the Reagan administration, the agency's effectiveness was greatly reduced. This is attributed to a probusiness orientation of the Reagan administration in general and of the OSHA political appointees in particular.

As one might expect, auto-industry officials are much more favorably disposed to the current operation of OSHA although they expressed some concerns about it. Management representatives believe that the orientation of OSHA under Reagan was only a correction of an antibusiness orientation of the agency during earlier years. They were, however, surprised and shocked by the size of the OSHA fines imposed upon them. These different UAW and auto industry views of OSHA are elaborated upon in this section.

Before considering their differences, it is interesting to note that there are some points of agreement between labor and management regarding OSHA. UAW officials concede that there were some problems with OSHA in the beginning of its operations, although they view these as being less serious than do management critics of OSHA.

There was general agreement that early OSHA officials were undertrained. This may have contributed to the resentment against OSHA that quickly developed. Most UAW safety and health officials would probably agree that OSHA at least failed to adapt to a changing political climate in the latter part of the 1970s. The agency ended up being redirected by political appointees to reflect the new philosophy of deregulation of the Reagan administration. Whether or not OSHA was, in part, responsible for the changing political climate, because of overplaying its hand in its early days, is the subject of differing speculation among union members.

Another point of agreement between labor and management is the lack of interest in the OSHA-sponsored labor-management cooperation programs (Praise, Star, and Try). This disinterest is noteworthy, because the cooperative agreements in the auto industry have features that OSHA is apparently trying to encourage by means of these programs. The reasons labor and management are not interested in these programs are very different. They are also illustrative of their views of OSHA in general.

Management representatives from the auto industry subscribed to the now popular view that OSHA, at least initially, was "a royal pain in the neck." They felt that their companies' safety and health programs were very good prior to the enactment of OSHA and that this agency did very little to improve safety and health in their operations. If federal regulation in this area were necessary, management felt that the regulators should concentrate on the smaller more hazardous firms rather than on large auto firms that had good safety and health programs in operation. This was not done, in their view, because the auto companies and other large employers made such inviting targets. By visiting a plant with 10,000 employees, OSHA inspectors could visit the worksite of the same number of workers as if they had visited 100 establishments with 100 employees each. For inspectors and supervisors, who are evaluated in part on the number of workers covered in inspections conducted, the choice is obvious.

It was also felt that at a higher level in OSHA, administrators found it politically advantageous to target the auto companies. OSHA, like any other bureaucracy, operated in the political arena where it was important to build a constituency to ensure continued funding. One way to do this was to find safety and health violations and to penalize the firms responsible. This would demonstrate that the agency's existence was necessary. They felt that this mode of operation was especially problematic at the start-up of the agency and that it became even worse under Eula Bingham's administration of OSHA during the Carter presidency.

Another view of the targeting of the auto industry for inspections in OSHA's early days was provided by one management safety specialist. He characterized the inspections of auto plants as "good training" for the relatively new OSHA inspectors. This assessment was good-natured, cynical, and self-congratulatory, all at the same time. According to this view, the OSHA inspectors had an opportunity to see how a relatively safe manufacturing plant operated; moreover, because the inspector would feel compelled to cite the plant for some safety or health violation, finding a citable violation would be more of a challenge at an auto plant.

Management's views on penalties imposed by OSHA were interesting. One safety manager noted that from 1972 to 1985 his entire corporation had received fines from OSHA of just $262,000, which he described as "peanuts." Emphasizing the insignificance of these fines, he quoted a plant manager who once remarked that if OSHA gave him a $900 fine he would "fall asleep." The manager did note that willful violations, which carry up to a $10,000 per day fine for every day that a condition is not corrected, do catch the attention of even the largest corporations. Nevertheless, even if the size of a given penalty is relatively small, managers have had to be concerned about precedents set by any penalty that they feel is unwarranted. Because the companies are so large, discovering that a standard work practice or condition that exists throughout the firm is in violation of OSHA regulations could have enormous ramifications. The fines for underrecording injuries were between $4,000 and $5,000 for each record-keeping violation, yet they amounted to hundreds of thousands of dollars per plant for the firms involved. If evidence of similar violations was found at other plants, the fines could be enormous. Recognizing the potential for penalties to multiply like this, firms have been very active in contesting citations and penalties through OSHA provisions to appeal citations and penalties at regional offices and through legal proceedings. The firms are not at all hesitant to resort to these adversarial conflict resolution procedures with OSHA when a penalty or citation is considered unfair.

Other OSHA-related costs cited by management safety specialists indicate that OSHA is not an agency whose cost impact can be ignored. These include the cost of managers' time required for record keeping and various other compliance-related activities, for accompanying OSHA inspectors around the plant, and for appealing contested citations even to the point of testifying in court. Other legal expenses can be even greater.

Although the above suggests that management felt that OSHA was largely unnecessary, several managers went even further to argue that OSHA was actually counterproductive during its early years. When OSHA was instituted, managers were overwhelmed with the new rules and regulations with which they were obliged to comply or be penalized. They felt that they were spending so much time trying to ensure compliance with the technical details of OSHA regulations that they did not have enough time to be concerned with actual hazards. One safety manager noted that his firm had experienced a significant increase in the number of fatalities during OSHA's first year of operations.

The one benefit of OSHA that safety managers did concede was the elevation of the status of safety and health issues and the individuals responsible for safety and health in their companies. The threat of penalties and sanctions that OSHA could impose caused other managers to take safety and health more seriously. This enabled them to further the cause of safety and health more than before OSHA's inception.

As one might imagine, the auto-industry safety and health managers are generally pleased with the changes that took place under the Reagan administration. But contrary to the aims of these changes, these managers have never come to view OSHA as a partner in promoting safety. In their view, reduced "harassment" by OSHA was desirable. The initial reaction to the change was that the agency was now largely irrelevant rather than helpful or harmful. Safety and health managers were pleased with the more conciliatory approach of regional OSHA administrators who considered their complaints about citations and usually reduced the severity of penalties. In their view, this did not lessen their concern or discourage good performance in the area of safety and health, because their own corporate and union structures for dealing with safety and health could do the job perfectly well without government interference. In recent years, if nothing else, the major fines imposed by OSHA have earned the agency more respect.

Management concerns about safety and health regulations now focus more on certain states that administer safety and health regulations themselves. Michigan is one of those states. Because much of the auto industry is located there, the Michigan OSHA (MIOSHA) plays a very big role in the regulation of safety and health in the auto industry. Comments about MIOSHA suggest that it is regarded by industry with at least as much disdain and contempt as was OSHA under Eula Bingham. Managers feel that because of the large representation of union workers in the electorate, Michigan is a "labor state." According to this view, MIOSHA simply reflects the politicians' desires to court labor by pursuing policies that promote the interests of labor and hurt the interests of industry.

Management and the UAW views on the Star, Praise, and Try programs are consistent with overall views toward OSHA. Managers believe that these programs are irrelevant for them, because they can handle safety and health issues adequately without any OSHA assistance. It is interesting to note, however, that there was a certain degree of misunderstanding of these programs. One corporate safety official said that his reason for not wanting to participate in these was that he felt no need to have OSHA people come in to help. However, these programs specifically exempt companies from inspections by OSHA officials when there is labor-management cooperation on safety. His firm would have been eligible for this exemption, although labor would almost certainly have protested participation by this firm. Still, he and the rest of the safety and health personnel in this company obviously did not believe there was enough incentive to participate.

Labor's views regarding OSHA under the Reagan administration are quite uniform and predictable. The consensus view among UAW members is that OSHA, at least prior to the fines, was ineffective in protecting the safety and health of workers. They feel that their own workers are generally well protected, but only because they have a strong union. Workers in other industries who are not so well represented are at risk. Also, according to their view of OSHA, they need to work harder to promote the safety interests of workers, because cooperation is more difficult when there is a reduced threat of sanctions by OSHA. Thus, UAW officials pursue stronger safety and health provisions in their negotiations with the auto companies.

The above helps explain labor's lack of interest in the Star, Praise, and Try programs. Labor officials feel that they have nothing to gain from participation in these programs but something to lose, namely, the already diminished threat of OSHA inspections. According to their view, the sole benefit that labor might obtain from involvement in these programs is the right to participate in decision making regarding safety and health--a right they have already won in negotiations. In exchange for this, labor must effectively give up the already lessened threat of OSHA inspections.

The fines produced mixed emotions among labor leaders. There was a certain "I told you so" reaction. These fines confirmed suspicions about management and the need for OSHA to pose a threat, which they felt was lacking in the past, to keep the companies honest. There was certainly also a sense of gratification that the cheating had been caught and at the prospect that OSHA would pose a greater threat in the future. Finally, there was a sense of embarrassment. This was due to the involvement with management of one UAW local in an injury underrecording scam. In this scam, when a worker became injured, he/she was "laid off" and then rehired when well again. The injury was not recorded and during the "lay-off period" the worker received government unemployment compensation and certain benefits from the employer.

One UAW safety and health expert had an interesting view on management's objections to OSHA and its reasons for not wanting to participate in OSHA-sponsored programs. He cited a desire by factory managers to maintain complete control over their operations. He characterized this as a "my plant is my castle" ideology. The existence of such an ideology would also help explain the rancor evident in the disputes between line managers and safety and health managers within plants. And it explains why corporate safety and health officials reported that their visits to plants are often resented by plant managers and other line personnel. Viewed in this light, many safety and health controversies can be considered disputes over *control* rather than over safety and health per se.

SAFETY AND HEALTH AS A MODEL FOR COOPERATION

The 1973 agreements on labor-management cooperation with respect to and health were part of broader agreements on cooperation to improve the quality of work life. These broader agreements were intended not only to increase workers' job satisfaction but also to improve productivity and quality and to control absenteeism. It is particularly noteworthy that cooperative arrangements and program results were achieved much more rapidly on safety and health than on these other issues. Kochan, Katz, and McKersie (1986) note that it was not until the end of the 1970s that most firms in the auto industry made a serious effort to pursue quality-of-work-life programs. These were emphasized mainly in response to the severe competitive pressures and the economic difficulties that had hit the auto industry as a result of the 1979 oil crisis. By this time the safety and health programs were in full gear and were available as models for these other programs. Managers and labor leaders who saw a framework for enhancing cooperation between labor and management adopted certain successful features of the safety and health programs in these subsequent cooperative ventures.

It is interesting to speculate about why the area of safety and health initially proved to be a more fertile ground for cooperation between labor and management. As noted previously, there is a large intersection of interests among labor and management regarding safety and health, because the costs of injuries and illnesses accrue to both employees and employers. Still, there are many incentives for cooperation on these other issues as well.

One explanation is that safety and health is essentially a "motherhood and sin" type of issue. It is easy to support these aims rhetorically; it is hard to argue against them without appearing to be a cruel or stupid person. Typically, the only credible management argument opposing some specific safety or health provision is that the same result could be obtained more cheaply with another approach. For example, management might argue for the use of ear plugs and masks rather than engineering controls to reduce exposure to noise and inhalation of hazardous substances. Workers often present the opposing argument that the personal protective devices are too inconvenient and uncomfortable and that engineering controls should be provided to achieve the same ends. This is a disagreement over means to an end, not over the goal itself. Occasionally, management might argue that reducing injuries or illnesses is not worth the cost, or workers might claim that it's not worth the inconvenience, but these arguments about the value of safety and health as a goal typically are not stands that can be publicly defended or around which others will rally in support.

Thus, it may be that rhetorically and emotionally it is easier to get various factions to agree on the need to cooperate on safety than on other issues, even if the commonality of interests is just as great for these other issues. Moreover, some workers, no doubt, have felt that productivity and quality improvement programs were simply measures to get them to work harder. Likewise, absenteeism-control programs are viewed suspiciously by some workers as attempts to get them to work when they are not able to do so. Some managers surely felt that allowing workers to participate in decisions regarding these matters was simply abandoning an area of management prerogative. It is interesting to note that this argument was also made regarding safety and health by one plant safety manager whose firm was not involved in labor-management cooperation, but it was not very convincing given workers' strong stake in decisions regarding safety and health. Overall, then, there seem to be more convincing arguments available to both labor and management for objecting to cooperation in areas other than safety and health.

In addition to convincing the opposing faction in negotiations of the need to cooperate on safety and health, negotiators who came to tentative agreements on cooperation would have a relatively easy time persuading their constituents to support the agreement. Management safety and health experts, who might naturally be more inclined toward this sort of thing to begin with, would be able to persuade their management colleagues to support this notion on economic grounds. Union negotiators would be able to "sell" this idea to their labor constituents on the promise of obtaining a less hazardous work environment and gaining greater influence over working conditions.

VIEWS ON EUROPEAN SAFETY AND HEALTH SYSTEMS

Neither labor nor management representatives in the auto industry indicate any desire to see a European-style codetermination system for promoting safety and health. Management's position is certainly understandable, because it could retain more autonomy by negotiating a system for worker participation in the safety and health arena than by having it dictated by the government. In this way, management could retain the flexibility to try to structure the system in a way that fits the special circumstances of its industry and firm.

Labor officials conceded that because they did not have the political clout of the European labor unions, it was unlikely that codetermination on safety and health would be legislated. Moreover, they expressed no desire to see such legislation passed. In considering codetermination in general, many labor officials over the years have felt more comfortable in the role of a friendly adversary and have feared being co-opted by too close a relationship with management (Furlong, 1977; Thimm, 1980). Regarding safety and health in particular, a view was expressed that cooperation is likely to be more effective when undertaken voluntarily than when imposed. In this context, it is instructive to consider how cooperation is viewed by one of the UAW's chief safety and health officials:

> My functional definition is that cooperative relations are stable, polite, honest, rational, competent and structured interactions without resort to the courts, strikes, or political confrontation. "Problem solving" is a popular term for this; it implies that the parties recognize each other's problems and have an interest in resolving them. Parties with quite divergent, and even fundamentally adversary interests can have cooperative relationships in certain areas. No continuing relationship is either completely cooperative or completely confrontational. (Mirer, 1983, p. A-13)

This problem-solving relationship involving both cooperative and adversarial elements is a good characterization of labor-management relationships in the safety and health field in the U.S. auto industry today.

UAW officials noted that while they felt comfortable with the safety and health system within their industry, workers in other industries where labor unions are weak or nonexistent are not as well protected. These workers are unable to negotiate the sort of safety and health protection that the UAW has been able to obtain. In these cases, they preferred stronger OSHA enforcement of existing laws to legislated rights of participation by labor as the most desirable way to protect these workers.

SUMMARY

The degree of labor-management cooperation on occupational safety and health that has developed in the U.S. auto industry in recent years is indeed significant. Although the problem of injury underrecording clouds the matter, the safety and health performance of the auto industry seems to have improved substantially under these cooperative agreements. An issue that was once seen as predominantly adversarial has developed into a model for cooperation in other areas. Nevertheless, both labor and management maintain their assertiveness along with their cooperative orientation in handling safety and health conflicts.

There are certainly a great many safety and health issues on which the interests of management and workers are the same, but there remain others on which they presently diverge and probably always will. Potential health and safety hazards of accelerated work pace is an example. Divergent interests also include the use of personal protective devices as opposed to more expensive engineering controls to eliminate hazards such as exposure to noise and dust. Regardless of their effectiveness compared with engineering controls, they may be uncomfortable, and, like seat belts, not worn by some, although the evidence of their life-protecting value is overwhelming. Management will, in almost every case, be concerned with the impact of safety and health measures on profits, whereas this impact may be of little importance to workers concerned with their own safety and health or even their own convenience. Also, managers who are rewarded for short-run performance are not likely to recognize or be concerned with long-run cost savings of certain safety and health measures.

Responsibility and concern for safety and health has, for the most part, been assumed by safety and health professionals in the firms. Efforts to make line managers more responsible for these functions are being undertaken within the industry but with mixed results so far. Also, workers are becoming more aware of the financial implications of safety and health. Workers have, in recent years, become more concerned with the possibility of job loss or smaller wage increases due to poor financial performance by the firm. This concern improves the prospects for cooperation between labor and and management on a wide range of issues, including safety and health.

The agreement to freeze safety and health provisions at Chrysler while it was undergoing restructuring after its near bankruptcy in 1979 is telling. Contrary to the "safety pays" jargon, this confirms the view that beyond a certain point, safety and health expenditures are considered to represent a net cost to the firm. Both workers and managers were willing to forego added protection that could be provided through safety and health initiatives when the Chrysler Corporation was on the verge of bankruptcy. This is yet another example that, except for the most immediately dangerous conditions, occupational safety and health can be characterized as a higher-level need according to Maslow's terminology.

4

OCCUPATIONAL SAFETY AND HEALTH IN FIVE COUNTRIES

Having considered occupational safety and health issues at the national level and within the automotive industry in the United States, we are now ready to shift our attention overseas, where we will consider many of the same issues in other national contexts. This international perspective will shed light on the degree to which the experiences and methods of handling safety and health issues that we have seen in the United States are characteristic of the issues themselves (i.e., the same patterns are seen in all countries) or are dependent on the national contexts (patterns vary). This will set the stage for the international comparisons of occupational safety and health activities at the corporate and plant levels contained in later chapters. It will also make the comparisons of national work injury experiences in the next chapter more meaningful.

Occupational safety and health systems in West Germany, Sweden, the United Kingdom, Japan, and Kenya are considered in this chapter.[1] These countries represent considerable diversity with respect to social, economic, and political conditions and with respect to the institutional structures used to promote occupational safety and health. This diversity provides contrast for comparing occupational safety and health issues among these countries and between each of them and the United States.

Each of the countries considered makes a distinct contribution to our understanding of the regulation and management of occupational safety and health. The United Kingdom is often cited as the classic example of a national industrial failure. It is frequently included in discussions of national economic, industrial, and labor-relations policies to provide examples of policies to avoid. West Germany, Japan, and Sweden are widely recognized for economic success and for their cooperative labor-management-government relations on a broad range of work-related issues. These three countries, particularly Japan, are frequently examined in attempts to discern the reasons for their success. Both West Germany and Japan had spectacular economic recoveries from the devastation of World War II. Sweden has a very high standard of living, along with strongly labor-oriented policies at both the national and corporate levels. Kenya is a developing country that is impoverished compared with the other countries of this study, and it is rarely considered in discussions of national economic and industrial policies, yet it provides some perspective to the analysis of worker safety and health. By examining occupational safety and health at the national level in these countries, we are able to gain insight into the influence of various social, economic, and political conditions on occupational safety and health systems.

This chapter is organized in the following way. Country profiles are provided first, which discuss important aspects of the national contexts in which the occupational safety and health systems operate. These offer a basis for understanding differences in the structures, operations, and results of national safety and health systems. Following this is a review of major legislation and institutional structures pertaining to occupational safety and health in each of these countries. Early safety and health legislation is discussed first, and then more recent laws are considered. Other structural aspects of national occupational safety and health systems are deliberated at this point. The final section is a discussion of the cooperative/conflictual aspects of occupational safety and health relationships in each of these countries. The next chapter looks at the occupational injury and fatality experiences in these countries compared with those of the United States.

NATIONAL CONTEXTS

It is clear that to understand the operation of occupational safety and health systems, one must understand the national contexts in which these systems function. The broad frameworks of these systems and their day-to-day implementations are the results of legislation and regulations that are developed in the political, governmental, and judicial arenas and that are influenced by various economic, social, political, and other considerations.

In the country profiles provided, general economic, social, governmental, and political factors are outlined and put in historical perspective. So too are important aspects of labor law, the role of labor in society, and labor-management relations. Much of the relevant economic and industrial relations data for these countries are contained in Tables 4-1 and 4-2. Table 4-1 has per capita gross national product (GNP) and per capita GNP growth data, along with recent unemployment statistics for each of these countries. Table 4-2 contains data on the percentage of the work force that is unionized, and it repeats industrial dispute rate data from Table 1-1. It also contains an assessment of the relative degree of labor and industrial political influence. In addition to the national unionization rate for labor, this assessment is based on the extent to which individual unions and employers are unified by confederations or other bodies that can represent their interests on matters of political importance. Important employee and employer confederations (or peak organizations) also are cited on Table 4-2. The relationships of these various nation-specific factors to the structure and operation of national and corporate safety and health systems are considered in this and subsequent chapters.

United Kingdom

The economic and industrial problems of the United Kingdom[2] are well known. As indicated in Table 4-1, the United Kingdom had the lowest per capita GNP of the industrialized countries considered here, U.S. $8,460 in 1985. This was only 51 percent of the U.S. per capita GNP in the same year. The real income in the United Kingdom rose only a modest 1.6 percent annually during the 1965-85 period, and the unemployment rate stood at 11.9 percent in 1985. The relatively poor economic conditions are noteworthy, because the United Kingdom was the dominant industrial country in the world in the nineteenth century and the early years of the twentieth century. The decline of the country from its dominant position as a world power has been exhaustively analyzed for what it can tell one about the root causes of industrial decline. Pundits who feel the United States is following the United Kingdom's path of decline occasionally suggest that Americans are suffering from the "British disease."

TABLE 4-1
KEY ECONOMIC STATISTICS

GNP per Capita

	U.S. Dollars[1] (1985)	Annual Real Growth Rate[1] (1965-1985)	Unemployment Rate[2] (1985)
United States	$16,690	1.7%	7.1%
United Kingdom	8,460	1.6	11.9
West Germany	10,940	2.7	9.3
Sweden	11,890	1.8	2.8
Japan	11,300	4.7	2.6
Kenya	290	1.9	13.0[3]

[1] Source: The World Bank. *World Development Report, 1987*. New York: Oxford University Press, 1987.
[2] Sources: International Labour Office. *1986 Yearbook of Labour Statistics*. Geneva, Switzerland, 1986; and Economist Intelligence Unit. *Country Profile Kenya*. London: 1987.
[3] Kenya's unemployment statistics are for 1986 and they do not include unemployed or underemployed workers in the large informal sector of the economy.

Frequently diagnosed as a symptom of the "British disease" is industrial strife involving adversarial relationships between labor and management. As can be seen in Table 4-2, the United Kingdom had by far the highest rate of industrial disputes of the countries considered, with an average of 494 days lost per 1,000 workers for the years considered. Only the United States, with an average of 216 days lost, had an industrial dispute rate of more than one-fifth of that of the United Kingdom. The fragmented structure of labor's participation in collective bargaining is seen as a contributing factor to the high rate of industrial disputes in the United Kingdom (U.S. Department of Labor, Bureau of International Labor Affairs, 1980b). Typically contracts must be negotiated with separate unions within companies and plants.

The United Kingdom is a constitutional monarchy with a parliamentary form of government. This type of government provides for much more concentration of power in the central government than is the case with the federal-republic form of the United States.[3] The prime minister is selected by the majority party in Parliament. Thus, there is never a situation, as often occurs in the United States, in which the executive and legislative branches are controlled by different parties that sometimes send conflicting signals to the various agencies and departments of government. Cabinet-level officials are appointed by the prime minister and are typically members of Parliament themselves. Because of this, these cabinet ministers can be held directly accountable for their actions by voters.

Labor unions have significant political influence in the United Kingdom, despite their fragmented structure. The overall rate of unionization, at 54 percent, is second only to Sweden among the countries considered (see Table 4-2). The unions have, for the most part, supported the influential Labour party, which has taken turns in office with the Conservatives since World War II. In addition to the cohesion provided by the Labour party, labor's political unity is promoted by union membership in confederations. The Trade Union Congress is the peak labor confederation and serves as the national spokesperson for labor.

There is also a high degree of industrial political influence. The Confederation of British Industry serves as the business counterpart of the Trade Union Congress. Along with the Conservative party, which is aligned with business interests, the confederation is a unifying factor in promoting business' political influence.

Since 1979 the Conservative government of Margaret Thatcher has been in power; Labour last held power from 1974 to 1979. The Conservative government has been true to its name and has, in fact, followed conservative policies. These have, in many respects, mirrored the policies of the Reagan administration. The Thatcher government embarked on policies of deregulation of industry, privatization of government-owned firms, and cuts in government social welfare spending. Efforts to revive the failing economy led to

TABLE 4-2
INDUSTRIAL RELATIONS FACTORS

	Unionization (Percentage)[1]	Working Days Lost Due to Industrial Disputes per 1,000 Workers (1972-1984 Average)[2]	Union Political Influence (and Peak Organization(s))	Industry Political Influence (and Peak Organization(s))
United States	25%	215.96	Moderate; (AFL-CIO)	High; (Chamber of Commerce)
United Kingdom	54	494.10	High; (Trade Union Congress)	High; (Confederation of British Industry)
West Germany	43	39.48	High; (German Federation of Trade Unions; German Federation of Civil Servants; German Salaried Employees; German Christian Trade Union Confederation)	High; (BDI-Federation of German Industry; DBA Confederation of German Employers)
Sweden	85	98.29	High; (LO-Swedish Confederation of Trade Unions; TCO-Central Committee of Salaried Employees; SACO/SR-Swedish Confederation of Professional Organizations)	Moderate; (SAF-Swedish Employers' Confederation)
Japan	30	50.86	Moderate; (Sohyo; Domei; Shinsanbetsu; Churitsuroren; Zenmin Rokyo)	High (Keidanren; Nikkeiren; Keizai Doyukai; Nissho)
Kenya	43	41.67[3]	Moderate; (COTU-Central Organization of Trade Unions)	Moderate; (FKE-Federation of Kenyan Employers)

[1] Source: Walsh, K. and A. King. *Handbook of International Manpower Market Comparisons.* New York University Press, 1986.
[2] Source: International Labour Office. *1982 Year Book of Labour Statistics.* Geneva; 1983; International Labour Office. *1985 Year Book of Labour Statistics.* Geneva; 1986.
[3] Data for years 1979 and 1980 are missing.

the adoption of a "get tough" policy with organized labor. This policy appears to have sharpened the conflicts among labor, management, and government, the intensity of which peaked with the 1984-85 strike of the mine workers' union.

The history of labor legislation in the United Kingdom is both long and convoluted. One of the earliest labor laws was the Ordinance of Labourers of 1349. The Black Death plague had reduced the working population dramatically and those surviving demanded higher wages for their services. To prevent such wage increases the government fixed wages and prices to their level before the onset of the plague. Though the wage/price controls were not always enforced and sometimes enforced inadequately, the system of wage and price controls was not repealed until 1813. From 1360 onward, increasingly punitive laws were passed to prohibit workers from organizing for the purpose of trying to increase wages. In spite of these laws, workers combined together in ever greater numbers to promote their common interests, which were undermined by the awkward wage/price control system.

Due to labor's persistence, the Combination Laws Repeal Act of 1824 and subsequent amendments repealed earlier combination acts and decriminalized union combinations. Still, employers were able to use common-law prohibitions against restraint of trade to challenge many union activities. Subsequent legislation alternately made it easier and then more difficult to prosecute union activities (Economist Intelligence Unit, 1987d).

During the twentieth century the interests of labor have been advanced most during years of ascendancy of the Labour party. However, laws promoting union activities passed under Labour governments frequently have been repealed or modified under subsequent Conservative governments. Most recently, the Tory Employment Acts of 1980 and 1982, and the Trade Union Act of 1984, restricted closed shops and picketing and removed certain union immunities from prosecution.

Labor's efforts to advance its interest through oftentimes bitter negotiations with management have followed a similar pattern of success and failure over the years. However, the incremental advances and setbacks in the collective bargaining arena have been relatively minor (Dore, 1973).

In spite of the legacies of adversarial relations in political and collective bargaining domains, there has developed a national-level system of cooperation among labor, management, and government with respect to regulation. This tripartite approach to handling problems is quite common in the United Kingdom. For example, Vogel (1983) describes the regulatory process in the United Kingdom regarding environmental issues as very flexible and encouraging of participation by affected parties. This approach no doubt stems from the tradition of heavy government involvement in national economic planning. The extremely high regard in which the professional British civil service is held certainly also contributes to the success with this approach.

West Germany

The Federal Republic of Germany, along with Japan, staged a remarkable economic recovery following World War II. The *Wirtschaftwunder,* or economic miracle, propelled Germany to the forefront of international economic prosperity. As indicated in Table 4-1, the per capita GNP in Germany stood at U.S. $10,940 in 1985, ranking it just behind the United States and Sweden among the countries considered in this study. The 1965-85 average annual real growth of 2.7 percent is the second highest of the countries considered here. Moreover, the 1985 per capita GNP figure does not reflect the substantial appreciation of the Deutschemark relative to the dollar since then. The unemployment rate stood at 9.3 percent in 1985.

As its official name suggests, West Germany is a federal republic; this structure functions in the context of a democratic parliamentary regime. As with the United States, powers are divided and shared between the federal and state *(Länder)* governments. At the federal level power is concentrated in the chancellor and his ruling party; however, the *Länder* have the responsibility for administering and enforcing federal legislation, including that related to occupational safety and health. As is the case with the other countries that possess the parliamentary form of government, cabinet members of the government are typically members of the legislature who belong to the ruling party.

Much of the credit for the economic recovery following the war has been given to the cooperative relationships between labor and management. Germany had the lowest rate of industrial disputes in Table 4-2, with only 39 days lost due to industrial disputes per 1,000 workers. This is less than one-fifth of that of the United States and less than one-twelfth of that of the United Kingdom. The cornerstone for this cooperation has been the system of codetermination *(Mitbestimmung)* in Germany. This calls for worker participation in decision making at both the shop-floor level and the board-of-directors level.

Although it has been suggested by some that this system was imposed upon Germany by the Allies in the aftermath of World War II, this is only partly true. Germany had a tradition of labor participation in decision making dating back to the 1830s and a system of codetermination similar to the current structure was established by the Works Council Act of 1920. This was later abolished by the Nazis, who also suppressed all meaningful union activity. During the war, this was accompanied by severe oppression of workers and drastic deterioration of working conditions, particularly as the war progressed (Furlong, 1977). Following the war, the Allies did use their influence to reinstitute codetermination. This was done with the hope of ensuring the rights of labor and preventing the reestablishment of the dominant economic and political influence of the cartels that had supported Hitler's war efforts. It was also hoped that it would promote labor-management cooperation, because industrial disputes had contributed to the downfall of the Weimar Republic and the accession to power of the Nazis (Berghahn and Karsten, 1987).

Labor has a very influential position in German society, with the overall rate of unionization in Germany at 43 percent (Walsh and King, 1986). Unions are very active politically, having close ties with the Social Democratic Party. This is the more liberal of the two major political parties that have alternately controlled the government since World War II. The Christian Democrats under Helmut Kohl have, however, been in power since the end of the Social Democratic administration of Helmut Schmidt in 1982.

The unions in Germany are few but very large. They negotiate with large employers' associations on wages, hours, and working conditions. The auto workers, for example, belong to the I. G. Metall Union, which has a total of 2.7 million workers. This union also includes shipbuilders, iron and steel workers, and other metal workers. I. G. Metall, along with 16 other major trade unions, belong to a confederation of unions, the German Federation of Trade Unions (DGB). This confederation accounts for over 7.7 million workers in Germany, a sizable number in a country of just over 60 million people. As indicated in Table 4-2, there are also several smaller confederations. The unification of union members in a few large unions and confederations contributes to the relatively high labor political influence. This influence is further reinforced by labor's alliance with the Social Democrats.

Employers' interests in Germany are represented by two principal confederations that promote a high degree of industrial solidarity and political influence. The BDI (Federation of German Industry) is chiefly involved with collective bargaining and economic matters. The DBA (Confederation of German Employers) is principally concerned with influencing government policies on labor and social issues. These groups are informally aligned with the Christian Democratic Party and its allied parties.

The overall framework for industrial relations is provided by the Basic Law or constitution of Germany that was enacted under Allied direction in 1946. It stipulates basic aspects of the functioning of the economy. Specifically, it guarantees the rights of workers and employers to join together among themselves to promote their interests and to negotiate with the other party. Specific rights of workers have been spelled out in codetermination legislation beginning with the Allied Control Law No. 22 and continuing with laws established by the Germans themselves in the 1950s, 1960s, and 1970s. The most recent major revisions of codetermination legislation, the Works Constitution Act of 1972 and the Codetermination Act of 1976, have, in theory (although not as much in practice), given workers nearly equal authority to management in the control of major corporations. As we will see, these codetermination rights have had an important bearing on workers' rights with respect to occupational safety and health. Like codetermination in general, there are discrepancies between the theoretical and actual influence of labor in regard to occupational safety and health.

Germany is noted for the cooperative relations between labor and management, and this is borne out by the statistics on industrial disputes. Germans, however, have been concerned that the cooperative labor-management relations that have been prevalent in the past might be unraveling. During the 1980s there has been a notable slowdown in the rate of economic growth and in the creation of jobs in Germany. As a result, labor has sought a shorter work week to spread the existing work among a larger number of workers. This labor demand resulted in contentious labor-management relations, particularly in the metal-working industry. A bitter strike over this issue by I. G. Metal in 1984 was settled after 7.5 weeks when an agreement was finally reached on a 37.5-hour work week. The length of the work week has continued to be a point of contention in labor-management relations since then despite the fact that German industrial workers are reported to work fewer hours than industrial workers in any developed country (U.S. Department of Labor, Bureau of International Labor Affairs, 1986).

Sweden

Sweden is often included in discussions of international economic and labor issues due to the success that it has experienced with its distinctive economic and labor policies. As indicated in Table 4-1, the per capita GNP in Sweden is U.S. $11,890, ranking it just behind the United States among the countries considered. Other estimates using different exchange rates have actually placed the Swedish per capita GNP higher than that of the United States (U.S. Department of Labor, Bureau of International Labor Affairs, 1987a). In addition, the per capita GNP growth of 1.8 percent exceeded that of the United States in the 1965-85 time period. Moreover, Sweden has an extremely low unemployment level that stood at 2.8 percent in 1985. Because of such economic success, its mixed market economic structure has frequently been suggested as an alternative to both capitalism and communism.

Apart from its economic success, Sweden has attracted much attention by business and management scholars due to its industrial-relations system that is reputed to promote cooperative labor-management relations. Harmonious relations between labor and management are evidenced by the relatively low rate of industrial disputes of 98 days lost per 1,000 workers for the 1972-84 time period.

An aspect of industrial relations in Sweden that makes this country interesting to consider is the prolabor policies at the national and corporate levels. Throughout this century, Sweden has been very progressive in promoting the rights of labor in the workplace and in improving the quality of work life. In the other industrialized countries considered here (including the United States), labor critics frequently compare their own rights unfavorably with those of labor in Sweden. In particular, Sweden probably has been the most aggressive nation in promoting worker safety and health rights.

Sweden's government is a parliamentary democracy. As noted previously, this form of government allows a large degree of concentration of power. However, Swedish agencies, including the National Board of Occupational Safety and Health, have considerable autonomy from the governmental ministries that are headed by majority-party Parliament members and that technically have jurisdiction over them (Kelman, 1981).

Sweden is a country that epitomizes the notion of a social welfare state. Its elected governments have, for the most part, pursued quite liberal political policies throughout this century. They have promoted extensive government involvement in the market, albeit still maintaining a strong private sector, and high levels of government social welfare spending. The Social Democratic Party, which we in the United States sometimes refer to as the Socialist Party, held power from the early 1930s to the mid 1970s. Much of the credit or blame for the shape of economic and government policies up to that point in time thus could be attributed to it. Since 1976 a number of short-lived governments have been formed, including conservative-led coalition governments that instituted numerous policy changes. Nevertheless, the overall framework of economic and industrial-relations policies has remained more or less intact. Moreover, at the time of this writing, the Social Democrats were back in power.

Accompanying the traditional liberal orientation of national politics, and, to a considerable extent, causing it, has been the strong labor influence. The overall rate of unionization in Sweden, at 85 percent, is the highest of all the countries considered (Walsh and King, 1986). Blue-collar labor unions are joined in a union confederation known as the "LO" *(Landsorganisationen)*, which has strong ties to the Social Democratic Party. Symptomatic of the strong labor-union orientation in Sweden, white-collar workers are also unionized and their unionization rate is only slightly lower than that of blue-collar workers. The organization of white-collar unions, the TCO or *Tjänstemännens* Central Organization (the Swedish Federation of Salaried Employees in Industry and Service) is relatively conservative in political orientation compared with the LO. A professionals' union, the Swedish Confederation of Professional Organizations (SACO/SR), which represents academicians and upper-level civil servants, is more liberal in orientation. It should be noted, though, that such terms as "liberal" and "conservative" must be considered in the Swedish political context, where the ideological spectrum can be viewed as shifted to the left compared with that of the United States. Liberal policy initiatives such as national health insurance and national economic planning, which have stirred debate in the United States in recent years, enjoy a broad consensus of support across the entire political spectrum in Sweden.

The extraordinarily high rate of unionization guarantees a high level of political influence by labor. However, there is a certain degree of splintering of labor's interests due to this high unionization rate and the diverse ideological orientations of the confederations that represent labor. For example, a 1986 strike by public-sector workers who were attempting to achieve wage and salary parity with the better-paid private-sector workers created considerable dissension within labor's ranks. Private-sector unions severely criticized this strike action (Economist Intelligence Unit, 1987c).

Employers' political influence is more focused than that of labor. They are joined in one confederation, the Swedish Employers Confederation (SAF). Overall, the political influence of employers is judged as moderately high.

One other factor that explains the concern with worker safety and health and other quality-of-work-life and general social welfare issues in Sweden is the high standard of living. It has been argued that worker safety and health can be viewed as a higher-level need in terms of Maslow's hierarchy of needs. Because many of the lower-level needs are satisfied in Sweden, more attention can be focused on such higher-level needs.

In the other countries considered here, landmark pieces of legislation have dictated the broad framework of labor-management relations. This traditionally has not been the case in Sweden, where these relations, at least until recently, were largely determined within the context of collective bargaining agreements (U.S. Department of Labor, Bureau of International Labor Affairs, 1979b). Reflecting a general distrust of government, work laws have been typically nonspecific in nature, with details worked out in national and local collective bargaining agreements. In 1928 the Swedish government passed the Act on Collective Agreements and the Act on the Labour Court to establish judicial authority and procedures for adjudicating disputes about labor-management agreements. In an effort to preempt further legislation, the "Basic Agreement" or *Huvudavtal* was reached in 1938. This was intended to provide a framework for labor and management to negotiate and yet to protect the interests of third parties and the general public in industrial disputes. Labor, in particular, desired to avoid government regulations of work and negotiating guidelines due to a general distrust of government. The cooperative character of this agreement between labor and management is so dominant that it is customary to refer to "the spirit of Saltsjobaden," the place in which the agreement was negotiated and signed (Schmidt, 1977). In the past decade or so, however, there has been a tendency to rely more on government regulation of work than in the past.

Swedish workers have gained certain codetermination rights similar to those in Germany both through legislation and collective bargaining agreements in the past few years. Workers have gained codetermination rights in traditional areas of managerial prerogatives such as hiring, firing, and directing workers, and determining the nature and type of production. Most significant in establishing these latter rights was the passage of the Codetermination Act of 1977. Prior to this time, there existed agreements that called for management to consult with labor on important decisions in these areas, but this arrangement was deemed inadequate. As is customary in Sweden, these legislated codetermination rights were to be spelled out in greater detail through national collective bargaining agreements. Thus, along with worker representation on company boards of directors, these agreements were to be the vehicles for implementing these rights. However, critics of the codetermination system in Sweden contended that the general laws setting forth these rights were not adequately supplemented in the private sector by detailed negotiated agreements that would permit the system to operate as intended (Abrahamson and Broström, 1980; Enström and Levinson, 1982). An agreement that worked out the details of codetermination was negotiated in the large public sector in 1979, and in 1982 an agreement in the private sector was reached. Overall, Swedish workers have tended to trail German workers in achieving and exercising codetermination rights. Such is not the case, however, with respect to codetermination in the field of occupational safety and health.

One recent legislative initiative that generated considerable controversy was the establishment of "wage earner investment funds." These funds use company profits to buy company stock or make other investments in the name of the workers. The legislation proposing to establish these funds faced strong opposition from management and from the owners of capital. It was argued that this initiative would tilt the balance of power in society toward labor by allowing workers or the regional funds representing them to become majority stockholders in many businesses. After vigorous debate, the legislation that was passed was more moderate than that originally proposed and, to date, the impact of these funds has not been as dramatic as predicted or feared.

The passage of the wage earner investment fund initiative notwithstanding, there was somewhat of a conservative backlash in recent years marked, most notably, by the 1976 defeat of the Social Democrats. This backlash forced subsequent Swedish governments, including those formed by the Social Democrats, to modify some of their economic and industrial policies. Sweden, which is highly dependent on international trade, was particularly hard hit by the energy crisis and the emergence of low cost international competitors to two important Swedish industries, steel making and shipbuilding (Weaver, 1987). Sweden's economy grew at a historically low .8 percent real annual rate during the 1973-83 time period. Faced with a 1983 budget deficit that exceeded 12 percent of the GNP (more than twice as large as the U.S. budget deficit in relative terms), the Social Democratic government in Sweden began serious budget cutting. It also cut subsidies to public and private firms and started to sell off state-run firms to private investors with the belief that private entrepreneurs could run them more profitably than the government (Moore, 1984). Since that time, Sweden's economy has improved substantially due to the recovery of the world economy and improved competitiveness, attributed largely to the devaluation of Sweden's currency (Rivlin, 1987). The budget deficit has become much more manageable, and further nationalization of failing firms has taken place.

Japan

Given the current fascination with Japan in the United States, any international study of management practices, government policies, or industrial relations would not be complete without consideration of Japan. This interest in Japan is well founded due to the tremendous economic success that the Japanese have achieved in recent years. As can be seen in Table 4-1, Japan's per capita GNP stood at U.S. $11,300 in 1985. As with Germany, this figure understates the economic prosperity in Japan due to the sharp appreciation of the yen versus the dollar since that time. Also of note is that Japan's economy had an extremely high 4.7 percent growth of per capita GNP from 1965 to 1985. The unemployment rate, which is extremely low by U.S. standards, was 2.6 percent in 1985, but it reached a postwar high of just over 3 percent in 1987, largely due to the appreciation of the yen. The concern in Japan over this unemployment increase might seem unwarranted in the United States, however, differences between United States and Japanese statistical techniques may cause Japanese unemployment statistics to appear artificially low (Taira, 1983).

The government of Japan was significantly altered by the constitution adopted in the aftermath of the defeat of World War II. Japan is a constitutional monarchy operating under a parliamentary democracy. Since World War II, the emperor has served only as a figurehead, albeit a revered one. Although there is a federal structure to the government, most of the power is concentrated in the central government. As with other parliamentary democracies, cabinet ministers are selected from the ruling party.

There has been great political stability in Japan since World War II. Except for a brief government by the Socialist Party shortly after the war, the Liberal Democratic Party (LDP) has held power without interruption since then. Still, there are a number of factions within the LDP that have been in control at various times.

It should be understood that, although much attention has been focused on Japan's postwar recovery, its remarkable economic progress predates World War II. Japan remained isolated from the rest of the world throughout most of its history, in part due to its geographical separation as an island nation and, in part, by design. As a result, it lagged behind the United States and Western European countries in the industrialization process. Consequently, Japan also trailed the other industrialized countries of this study in the regulation of industrial-working conditions. Until the second half of the nineteenth century, Japan was still a feudal society. Industrialization only began following Japan's forced opening to the West by U.S. Admiral Perry (1854) and the subsequent Meiji Revolution (1868). The Meiji government expanded contacts with more advanced nations to acquire basic scientific knowledge to bolster both national defense and the economy.

The Ministry of Industry, *Kobusho,* was formally established in 1870 to serve as the governmental vehicle in industrial development (Tsurumi, 1978). One of its primary strategies was to absorb foreign technologies. Two factory systems subsequently evolved. Factories established by the government served as models of technology and organization (Patrick, 1976). Aspects of the work environment tended to be Western in orientation.

By contrast, workers at private factories faced longer hours, lower wages, and minimal-standard working conditions (Tsurumi, 1978; Patrick, 1976). These were improved somewhat with the passage of the Factory Law of 1911. Along with safety and health aspects discussed below, this imposed limitations on working hours and night work (Japan Institute of Labour, 1982).

In the years that followed, conditions improved as employers attempted to preempt the rise of unionization by bettering employee benefits (Fujita, 1984). However, with the onset of the Great Depression, unions and their influences declined. World War II marked an even greater decline in workers' rights and in working conditions. Union activity was forbidden during World War II. To meet production schedules, employers resorted to harsh discipline of workers. Toward the end of the war, as the military regime became more desperate and as Japanese factories became targets of U.S. bombing, working conditions were extremely poor and hazardous.

Cessation of hostilities put an end to the extremes in working conditions. Moreover, philosophies concerning working conditions shifted dramatically during the occupation of Japan by U.S. forces following World War II. Three major pieces of legislation affecting labor and working conditions were enacted. The Labor Standards Act, passed in 1947, addressed work-place issues such as hours of work, safety regulations, industrial-injury compensation, and prohibition of specific worker categories from night work. This act, along with the

Trade Union Act of 1945 (amended in 1949) and the Labor Relations Adjustment Act (1946), formed the framework for modern Japan's labor and management relations. Unions were at this time officially recognized. Systems for permanent disability pensions and long-term sickness payments were established during the 1960s.

The years following World War II marked a tremendous economic growth period in Japan and the accompanying improvements in the standards of living of the workers. Much credit for this has been attributed to the cooperative relations among labor, management, and government. Government provided the conditions for economic growth to occur and played a major role in targeting certain industries for growth. However, improvements in wages, hours, and conditions of work occurred through negotiated rather than legislated changes.

The Japanese corporation has long been pictured in the Western press and business publications as a paternalistic organization, harmoniously cooperating with labor. This is an accurate portrayal but only for master employers. These are companies such as Toyota, Nissan, Toshiba, Sony, and Canon that are familiar names in the West. In such companies one will find good wages, lifetime employment, pleasant working conditions, and worker participation in decision making, all of which have been cited as contributing to the success of Japanese industry. These employers also look after a wider range of workers' needs than do Western companies. For example, company-owned housing and hospitals are common in large corporations. The company also typically provides financial and material assistance at major points in an employee's life, such as beginning employment, buying a house, getting married, and so on.

In return for providing for workers' needs, the company expects a high degree of loyalty from the workers and cooperation from the unions. Unique among the nations considered here, the unions in Japan are organized on a company basis rather than on a national or industrial basis. The cooperativeness of these unions has been credited with contributing to the economic welfare of Japan and the workers they represent. They are credited with being more realistic in their demands during negotiations and in taking efforts to understand the company's needs and financial constraints. This is reflected in the statistics on industrial disputes. Japan ranks behind Germany and Kenya with the third lowest rate of industrial disputes with 51 days lost per 1,000 workers.

In general, unions do not play as great a role in Japanese society as they do in the European countries of this study; there is only a moderate degree of union political influence. The overall rate of unionization in Japan is 30 percent. Unions are organized into five different confederations--Sohyo, Domei, Shinsanbetsu, Churitsuroren, and Zenmin Rokyo--which are differentiated both by industrial sector and ideological orientation of the member unions. The diversity of ideological orientation and the tendency of many private unions to support the political initiatives of employers fragment and dilute union political influence.

Employers have a high degree of political influence in Japan. This is the case although there are four different confederations that represent their interests (Keidanren, Nikkeiren, Keizai Doyukai, and Nissho). Employers and certain private-sector unions are affiliated with various wings of the Liberal Democratic Party and they assert their political influence through them.

In contrast to private-sector unions the political activities of public-employee unions are much more distinctive. Moreover, these unions engage in activities that are very much at variance with the stereotypic Western view of compliant Japanese unions. The controversy surrounding the privatization of the Japan National Railway system, though perhaps an extreme case, demonstrates this. Due to this privatization that took place in 1987, thousands of workers were laid off. Although the government coordinated efforts to place these redundant workers with other employers, the workers and the union fiercely resisted privatization. There were murders of union officials believed to be not strong enough in their opposition to privatization and close to 100 suicides in 1985 and 1986 among soon-to-be displaced workers. As the union confederation representing most public-employee unions, Sohyo is a strong critic of the ruling Liberal Democratic Party, which has been in power since World War II, and it actively supports the Socialist Party, which is a distant second in political strength.

The degree of industrial and union involvement in party politics is an interesting feature of the political landscape in Japan. It is not uncommon for a corporation or union to support and elect one of its members to political office in collaboration with one of the parties.

Much of what has been written about the Japanese economy and about labor-management relations in Japan has focused on career workers in the well-known and highly successful master-employer companies. However, these master employers employ only about 30 percent of the work force. There exist other sectors of the economy in which such conditions do not prevail. These include employers who are subcontractors to the master employers. These employers are mostly small and medium-sized businesses. These companies are under extreme pressure from master employers to control costs and they are also forced in various ways to bear the brunt of fluctuations in demand so that master employers can maintain lifetime employment policies. Thus, they are not able to provide the favorable employment and working conditions offered by the master employers. Also such benefits do not apply to temporary workers nor to most female workers even in master-employer firms.

The Japanese economy is currently entering a critical era. Due to the rise in the value of the yen, unemployment has become a national concern. It is also clear that the days of dramatic growth are over. Economic growth is predicted to average around 2 percent to 4 percent in the foreseeable future. This is far lower than the double-digit growth rates of the 1960s and lower also than the more moderate growth of the 1970s. Moreover, there is concern in Japan about the "hollowing" of the economy as manufacturing operations are moved overseas in search of cheaper labor. Whether the predominantly cooperative relations among labor, management, and government can continue in an era of lower growth is an important question.

Kenya

The other countries considered in this study are ones that have achieved a high level of economic development. These countries have sophisticated systems for regulating industries and providing various social welfare benefits to their populations. An interesting contrast is provided by considering a developing country such as Kenya.

The influences on work of such factors in Kenya as the pre-industrial/agrarian economy, the educational level and standard of living of the work force, legislative and regulatory traditions, the country's colonial heritage, and the lack of a national welfare system are striking. These influences are so great that differences in the work environment among the United States, Japan, and European countries seem almost trivial by comparison.

Although Kenya is one of the more economically and socially advanced countries in Africa, it is impoverished in comparison with the industrialized nations of this study. Its 1985 per capita GNP of U.S. $290 is less than 2 percent of that of the United States. Also, with a 1965-85 annual per capita GNP growth rate of 1.9 percent, Kenya is not making appreciable progress in catching up to the industrialized countries. Kenya's literacy rate of 47 percent is about average for Africa (Rake, 1983), but much lower than the nearly universal literacy in the developed countries.

Precise statistics on unemployment are not available, and estimates vary widely. One source placed national unemployment at 13 percent (Economist Intelligence Unit, 1987b). Estimates of the urban unemployment rate have been placed at between 25 percent and 40 percent during this decade. Based upon these estimates it is clear that unemployment, especially in urban areas, far exceeds that of the industrialized countries in this study. Moreover, unemployment is almost certain to worsen given the extraordinarily high population growth rate of 4.4 percent per year, which is cited by some sources as the most rapid of any country in the world. This population growth rate negates the employment benefits of the relatively high overall rate of economic growth in Kenya. The GDP (gross domestic product) increased at an annual rate of 3.1 percent from 1980 to 1985.

In considering the above statistics one should note that only about one million workers out of a total labor force of approximately seven million are in the wage economy. Reflecting the agrarian nature of the economy, a large percentage of Kenya's population is composed of subsistent farmers and cattle herders who are not considered in the urban unemployment statistics. In addition to the farmers and herders, a large percentage of the population is involved in the "informal economy." Members of the informal economy include the self-employed and individuals who work for family members without receiving any wages. They are typically engaged in such activities as making or selling souvenirs (tourism is the country's third leading industry) or in fabricating salable products out of scrap (e.g., cooking utensils out of old metal drums or rubber sandals out of bald tires). Many of these self-employed individuals also would not be counted as unemployed although they may work only part time and earn a barely subsistent income.

The labor movement in the formal sector of the economy is quite strong and politically significant. Approximately 43 percent of wage earners are unionized, although this is only about 6 percent of the work force. Still, most of these unionized workers are concentrated in the principal cities where they are strategically positioned to influence the government. The unions' political influence is moderately high. All but two major unions belong to the Central Organization of Trade Unions (COTU). These two exceptions are the unions of teachers and civil servants, which for political reasons were forced to withdraw from COTU by the government.

The Federation of Kenya Employers (FKE) is COTU's industrial counterpart. It negotiates with COTU and the government over various matters related to work. Although most employers belong to the FKE, industry's political influence is moderated by the formal sector's minor role (relative to the industrialized countries) in the economy and the diversity among the employers. In addition to the tribal differences among ethnic Kenyan employers, many companies are owned by foreign individuals, by multinational corporations, or by nonethnic Kenyans (e.g., British and Indian immigrants and their descendants).

Another important factor to consider in comparing work-related issues in Kenya with those of the United States and European countries is Kenya's colonial heritage; it won its independence from British colonial rule only in 1963. This colonial heritage is evident in a number of ways. Many British rules, regulations, and traditions for handling various issues, including work-related ones, remain in effect. Laws pertaining to employment of women and children and to wages, hours, and conditions of work were enacted while Kenya was under British colonial rule. Also, British companies and individuals holding dual British/Kenyan citizenship continue to play prominent roles in the economy.

The government of Kenya is a republic with a democratic parliamentary regime. The president is directly elected, and his vice-president and the members of his cabinet are appointed from party members in the legislature. Over the years there has been an increasing centralization of power in the presidency. One significant difference between Kenya and the other parliamentary democracies considered is that there is only one legal political party, the Kenyan African National Union (KANU). KANU has ruled since independence in 1963, first with Jomo Kenyatta serving as president until his death in 1978. He was followed by Daniel Arap Moi, who has served since then, winning two uncontested party nominations and elections. There is, however, considerable within-party political competition based to a large extent on tribal ties. This is reflected in the extensive turnover in the legislature in the periodic elections. Moreover, there has been at least one coup attempt in recent years, reflecting a degree of political instability.

The relatively high degree of government involvement in the marketplace is another important factor relevant to the study of work issues. Although the government supports the philosophy of "African socialism," it should be noted that, relative to other African countries, there is a considerable amount of private enterprise in Kenya and the role of government in the marketplace is more limited. However, when compared with the industrialized countries in this study, the role of the government in Kenya's economy is extensive. The government's role as an employer is illustrative of this. In 1978 the government employed over one-third of the 911,500 wage employees in the economy, many in various state-owned businesses (U.S. Department of Labor, Bureau of International Labor Affairs, 1980a).

The Industrial Relations Charter of 1962 and subsequent amendments established a tripartite system of relations among labor, management, and government that reflects Kenya's historical ties with the United Kingdom. This provides a framework for resolving labor-management disputes, without having to resort to strikes or lockouts. Settling these disputes amicably is imperative given the potentially grave political repercussions of work stoppages. When industrial disputes arise, the government becomes involved in settling the dispute through a number of possible avenues, including the appointment of arbitrators and adjudication of disputes. The Industrial Court, established in 1964, is the final arbiter of industrial disputes and a central mission of the court is to resolve disputes without any stoppage of work. Strikes and lockouts are, at least in theory, illegal. Nevertheless, as Table 4-2 indicates, there were still some strikes occurring as recently as 1984. These were typically unofficial "wildcat" strikes that occurred infrequently and for a short duration. Since the early 1960s, the number and duration of strikes have decreased (U.S. Department of Labor, Bureau of International Labor Affairs, 1980a; Cockar, 1981). Table 4-2 shows that the average number of working days lost due to strikes per 1,000 workers was 42 for Kenya during the years for which data are available. This rate is lower than the averages for all the industrialized countries considered except Germany.

Although the tripartite model is designed to encourage cooperation among labor, management, and government, it is clear that the Kenyan government is the dominant actor in this triumvirate. The government certifies unions and supervises union elections in addition to requiring that actual and even potential labor-management disputes be reported. The government maintains a comprehensive set of regulations of business activities; it issues wage guidelines for negotiations and must approve all new contract agreements. As noted above, it also has a very active and direct involvement in the economy as an employer in various state-run enterprises. Nevertheless, on a continent where many governments have outlawed labor unions and have nationalized much of private industry, the degree of business and labor autonomy and participation in decision making is significant.

The governmental control of labor unions can best be understood in a historical context. During much of the period of British colonial rule, union activities were officially discouraged, because organized labor was considered to be a significant source of political power. Even traditional union activities related to seeking improvements in wages and working conditions took on a political meaning, as employers were mostly British and from the same ruling elite as the colonial administrators. The British concern over the political role of the unions proved to be well founded because they played a key part in the struggle for independence (Iwuji, 1979).

For a period of time following the achievement of independence, the unions struggled for power with the ruling political party, KANU. The government eventually asserted its dominance and imposed numerous restrictions on union activities to prevent the unions from achieving the political power they previously had held. Political parties other than the KANU party are illegal in Kenya, and all government employees must belong to this party. Another factor contributing to the weakness of labor unions is their financial position. The unions are funded by dues paid by members. However, given the low wages of the workers and the high unemployment rates, unions are not able to raise sufficient funds to support many activities.

Unions are not at so great a disadvantage with respect to management as they are relative to government in this tripartite system. As already described, various labor rights are mandated by law; others have been achieved through collective bargaining. Still, jobs are scarce while the pool of unemployed workers is large and growing, thus giving management leverage over labor.

Management, although not required to do so, has permitted worker participation in decision making at some plants. Labor obviously is not in a position to seek such rights through legislation or negotiation as has been done in the European countries. Typically, workers are satisfied simply to have a job in the wage economy; participation in decision making is not of priority concern.

The extent of government involvement in the Kenyan economy is comparable to and perhaps even greater than that in Sweden. However, due to the enormous differences in the economic circumstances of these two countries, the nature of this involvement is quite different. In Sweden, due to the high degree of economic development, government involvement in the economy is designed to ensure that everyone is able to maintain a relatively high standard of living and a high quality of life. In terms of Maslow's needs hierarchy, the government attempts to ensure that higher-level needs that might not be fulfilled by the private market are guaranteed by the state.

In Kenya, the focus of government involvement is on fulfilling lower-level needs. Thus, the government imposes price controls on basic foodstuffs and plays the leading role in setting the minimum wage. The minimum wage is a much more important factor in this country than in the United States, because it is the effective wage for most wage earners. The government also participates in the marketplace through quasi-government institutions known as parastatals that are chartered to fulfill various economic functions (e.g., selling seed and fertilizer, providing credit to farmers, marketing produce, and running key industries such as air and rail transportation).

Because unemployment is such a great problem, the Kenyan government also places various controls on multinational corporations to guarantee the employment of Kenyan nationals. This is done directly by requiring multinationals to hire a large percentage of their workers and managers locally. In addition, employment in other local businesses is stimulated by requiring these multinationals to purchase components from local subcontractors. Moreover, the government often requires that multinationals sell majority ownership in their local enterprises to the government as a condition for beginning operations.

EARLY SAFETY AND HEALTH LEGISLATION

Table 4-3 provides a listing of the major safety and health laws in the United Kingdom, West Germany, Sweden, Japan, and Kenya. Included are the early safety and health laws considered in this section and the more recent legislation considered in the next section.

Owing in large part to its lead in industrialization during the early 1800s, the United Kingdom was the first country to enact laws regulating safety and health standards in the workplace. These first pieces of legislation were passed in the early 1800s, several decades before other countries followed suit. Their principal focus went beyond occupational safety and health. For example, the Health and Morals of Apprentices Act of 1802 dealt primarily with sanitation and the hours and time of work. It also required that provisions be made for employees to obtain Christian education on Sundays.

General dissatisfaction with the results of the legislation eventually led to the establishment of a factory inspectorate system under the Factory Act of 1833 that has survived to the present. Although only four inspectors were initially appointed, this was later increased. Reports by these initial inspectors on working conditions prompted even more concern and government activism in the

TABLE 4-3
OCCUPATIONAL SAFETY AND HEALTH LEGISLATION IN
FIVE COUNTRIES

Country	Date	Law	Purpose
West Germany	1884	Industrial Injuries Insurance Law	To establish *Berufsgennossenschaften* responsible for workers' compensation
	1950s, 1972, 1976	Codetermination laws	To establish and strengthen workers' codetermination rights with respect To Occupational safety and health
	1974	Work Safety Act (*Arbeitsicherheitsgesetz*)	To provide a general framework for safety and health laws
United Kingdom	1802	Health and Morals of Apprentices Act	To improve sanitary conditions at work and to regulate hours and time of work
	1833	Factory Act	To provide factory inspectors
	1844	Factory Act	To improve occupational safety and health
	1923	Workers' Compensation Act	To provide for reporting and compensating of work accidents
	1900s	Factories Act, Regulation of Railways and Railway Employment (Prevention of Accidents) Act, Explosives Act, Offices, Shops and Railway Premises Act, Mineral Workings (Offshore Installations) Act, etc.	To regulate safety and health conditions in specific industries
	1974	Health and Safety at Work Act	To establish the Health and Safety Commission and the Health and Safety Executive; to provide an overarching integration for safety and health laws and their enforcement

TABLE 4-3 (continued)

Sweden	1889	Occupational Hazards Act	To improve safety and health conditions at work
	1890	Name uncertain	To establish the Factory Inspectorate
	1905	Name uncertain	To provide workers' compensation
	1912	Workers' Protection Act	To combine and strengthen earlier laws; to establish worker safety representative position
	1949	Worker Protection Act, Worker Protection Ordinance	To establish the National Board of Occupational Safety and Health (NBOSH) and to improve safety and health conditions
	1974	Worker Protection Act	To strengthen earlier laws and to increase authority of safety delegates and safety committees
	1978	Work Environment Act	To strengthen and broaden coverage of earlier laws
Japan	1911	Factory Law	To establish factory inspection and workers' compensation systems; to place limitations on hazardous work
	1947	Labor Standards Law	To establish post-war standards on working conditions (including safety standards); to establish a workers' compensation system and a labor standards inspection system
	1972	Industrial Safety and Health Law	To promote safety, health, and comfort on the job thru specific industrial countermeasures and government assistance
Kenya	1962+	Industrial Relations Charter and amendments	To set broad framework for cooperation and resolution of disputes regarding safety and health and other issues
	1963+	Various safety and health laws adapted from the U.K. and other industrialized countries	To set specific safety and health standards

regulation of workplaces. The Factory Act of 1844 was the first law that dealt exclusively with occupational safety and health. Over the years the acts, along with numerous regulations and orders promulgated under their authority, were variously modified in efforts to promote occupational safety and health. One significant new law was the 1923 Worker's Compensation Act, which provided for the reporting and compensating of work injuries (Ambrose, 1979; Martineau, 1864).

During the nineteenth century, Germany trailed somewhat behind the United Kingdom both in industrialization and the regulation of worker safety and health. The first German general safety and health initiatives were undertaken during the 1830s. These came about primarily due to the poor physical conditions of military recruits. Prior to this time, there had only been industry-specific regulations in mining and craft industries (Hauptverband der gewerblichen Berufsgenossenschaften, n.d.).

The Reich Act of 1871 allowed workers to sue employers for negligence on the part of the employer, or of an agent of the employer, which resulted in an injury. This arrangement, however, proved unsatisfactory due to the difficulties in proving fault and in securing compensation for the victims. The inadequacies of this arrangement led to the establishment of a system of workers' compensation. This was established under the Industrial Injuries Insurance Law of 1884 enacted by Chancellor Otto Bismark. The law also established industrial insurance institutes, known as *Berufsgenossenschaften* (trade cooperative associations or TCAs). TCA membership was mandatory for private employers, and these organizations provided compensation to injured workers, regardless of whose fault the injury was.

In Germany, the codetermination laws of the 1950s, while not specifically designed as worker safety and health legislation, had important bearing on these matters. Workers were given rights to participate in organizational decision making at the shop-floor level and at the board-of-directors' level. Included in the issues over which labor participation rights extended were worker safety and health.

Although Sweden has been at the forefront of the regulation of industrial safety and health in recent years, its initial regulations in this area came about later than those in the United Kingdom and West Germany. Sweden's first law regulating general safety and health conditions at work was passed in 1889. The Factory Inspectorate *(Yrkesinspektionen* or YI), which has responsibilities for overseeing working conditions, including those related to safety and health, was established shortly thereafter in 1890. Legislation providing a framework for workers' compensation was passed in 1905, and a mandatory workers' compensation system was established in 1916. Safety and health legislation that passed in 1912 called for the establishment of the worker representative position that evolved into the safety delegate. Significant modifications of industrial safety and health laws in Sweden occurred in 1949 with the passage of the

Worker Protection Act and the Worker Protection Ordinance. Among other things, the Worker Protection Act created the National Board of Occupational Safety and Health (NBOSH, sometimes also designated as ASV), the Swedish counterpart of OSHA.

Owing to its lag in industrialization, Japan had a late start at coping with the problems of industrialization. Various industrial safety and health problems developed in Japan following the Meiji Restoration, as the country rushed to catch up with the West. The Factory Law of 1911 was the first general health and safety law. This provided a factory inspector system and covered injury compensation, restrictions on employment in harmful and hazardous jobs of protected worker categories (notably females and youths under 14 years of age), and limitations on working hours and night work.

Despite these provisions, working conditions in Japan remained poorer than those in the more advanced industrialized countries. Moreover, these conditions deteriorated significantly in the years leading up to and during World War II. By the end of the war, the working conditions were, by all accounts, terrible. Following the war, U.S. occupation forces in conjunction with the Japanese rewrote major elements of labor law in Japan. As with Germany, the primary intention of this was to weaken the power of the economic conglomerates (called *zaibatsu* in Japan) that had supported the militarization and the war effort. The Labor Standards Act, passed in 1947, addressed workplace issues such as hours of work, safety regulations, industrial-injury compensation, and prohibition of specific worker categories (women and youth) from night work. This act, along with the Trade Union Act (1945, amended in 1949) and the Labor Relations Adjustment Act (1946), formed a framework for modern Japanese labor relations. In addition, the Japanese constitution adopted after the war contains guarantees of the rights of workers to organize, to engage in collective bargaining, and to strike (Japan Institute of Labour, 1983). A comprehensive national work injury insurance program was established with the passage of the 1947 Labor Standards Act. Prior to this time a system existed as early as 1875 for providing "assistance" during periods of work incapacity for certain privileged classes of workers (Bennett and Levine, 1976). Systems for permanent disability pensions and long-term sickness payments were established during the 1960s.

Kenya only received its independence from the United Kingdom in 1963. Prior to that time, various laws regulating the work environment were enacted by the colonial government. Laws pertaining to the employment of women and children and to wages, hours, and working conditions were enacted under British rule and based on British legislation. The basic thrust of labor laws was to develop a tripartite system involving cooperation among labor, management, and government to promote economic development.

The Industrial Relations Charter of 1962 and subsequent amendments specify many of the details of this tripartite system.

These established a system for resolving industrial disputes, including those related to safety and health issues without having to resort to strikes or lockouts. The Industrial Court is the final arbiter of such disputes. Many of the detailed safety and health laws are based on earlier British legislation.

It is clear that the earliest efforts to regulate occupational safety and health took place where the industrialization process was furthest along and where the safety and health problems associated with industrialization were first encountered. It is also clear that the physical welfare of workers was only part of the reason (in some cases, a minor part) for the enactment of these laws. As we will see in the next section, a relationship between stage of industrialization and the enactment of safety and health legislation has persisted over the years. The improvement of safety and health conditions has, however, become more of a central focus of modern legislation.

INSTITUTIONAL STRUCTURES AND RECENT LEGISLATION

Throughout the industrialized world much of the legislation pertaining to occupational safety and health had accumulated incrementally during this century until the early 1970s. Then, almost simultaneously in numerous countries, vigorous movements to strengthen and coordinate national worker safety and health legislation emerged. The motivations for these efforts differed between countries, but they reinforced each other. In this section we consider this recent legislation along with other structural aspects of national occupational safety and health systems that dictate activities in this domain.

United Kingdom

The United Kingdom provides a good example both of the long-term accumulation of safety and health laws and the more recent efforts to coordinate and consolidate them. Numerous acts covering various worker populations and industries were passed in the latter half of the nineteenth century and in the twentieth century. The accumulation over the years of a large and confusing assortment of safety and health laws and regulations, along with new regulatory needs dictated by changes in the workplace, ultimately led to the passage of the Health and Safety at Work Act (HSW Act) in 1974 (Ambrose, 1979). This provided an overlaying integration and organization for earlier legislation.

The HSW Act applies to England, Scotland, and Wales; it does not apply to Northern Ireland, which has its own occupational safety and health legislation (Health and Safety Executive, 1980). This bill imposed new regulations, revised old ones, and provided a mechanism for policy making and enforcement pertaining to occupational safety and health. Specific objectives of the bill pertained to protecting both workers and nonworkers alike from industrial work hazards; controlling explosive, flammable, and otherwise dangerous substances; and controlling air pollution from worksites. The HSW Act describes in general terms how these objectives are to be achieved. A primary vehicle for this was the establishment of two new agencies: the Health and Safety Commission, responsible for policy matters, and the Health and Safety Executive, responsible for administrative and enforcement activities. As with the establishment of OSHA in the United States, central coordination of all national occupational safety and health activities became possible through these two new agencies.

Senior-level officials of the Health and Safety Commission and the Health and Safety Executive are appointed by the secretary of state for employment, who is a member of the ruling party. Just below these senior-level political appointees are members of the respected British civil service, who provide stability and continuity to occupational safety and health regulation.

The HSW Act places general duties on all people at work, although ultimate responsibility remains with management. These duties are stated in very broad terms to cover a wide spectrum of activities and situations. Some of the specified duties are absolute, but many are conditional and specified with phrases such as "so far as is reasonably practicable," "so far as is practicable," and "best practicable means." Unlike in the United States, the use of cost-benefit analysis by employers is condoned for deciding what measures to take regarding hazards. The employer should take account of the risks of a hazard and the monetary and other costs (e.g., time) involved in the various ways of dealing with it.

The HSW Act overlays the earlier acts dealing with worker health and safety, such that most previous regulations still apply. Also, the enforcement activities of the existing inspectorates were integrated into the Health and Safety Executive, although enforcement procedures were modified. The HSW Act applies to all types of workplaces, whether it is the regulations of earlier acts or HSW Act regulations that are being enforced. The aim is to eventually replace earlier regulations with revised rules to be promulgated under the jurisdiction of the HSW Act.

Worker safety representatives and labor-management safety committees are specifically called for by the HSW Act. These are similar in many respects to like structures formally established earlier in Sweden and Germany. Safety representatives and committees were called for because it was viewed as impossible to create detailed regulations covering all the types of worker safety and health problems that could arise. They are envisioned as agents responsible for providing and utilizing a framework through which management and employees can develop effective working arrangements for their individual situations. Safety representatives and safety committees also provide vehicles for worker input into decision making, and they are closest to and most affected by conditions on the shop floor.

The size of safety committees varies from establishment to establishment, but the number of management representatives is not to exceed the number of employee representatives. These committees are involved with all relevant aspects of workers' safety, health, and welfare, including the following:

Statistical studies of injuries and diseases

Examinations of reports provided by inspectors or safety representatives

Assistance in the development of safety rules or systems in the workplace

Evaluation of the safety and health network in the workplace

Just as the British occupational safety and health system is flexible at the factory level, where labor and management are involved in implementation, so too is it flexible at the national level in rule-making and rule-enforcing activities. It is designed to elicit input and ideas from labor and management regarding proposed rules and regulations. The rules themselves are flexible so that labor and management participation is elicited in their interpretation and enforcement. This flexibility is described by Brickman, Jasanoff, and Ilgen (1985) in a study of the control of chemicals in the workplace as follows:

> The British carry flexibility to the extreme, developing policy, wherever possible, through close informal contacts among government officials and private groups. Flexibility characterizes policy outcomes as well, with guidelines, recommendations, and informal persuasion substituting as far as possible for statutory orders and prosecutions. (p. 53)

In summary, the occupational safety and health system that has been dictated by the HSW Act differs from the earlier system in that it requires a "tripartite" institutional structure containing equal representation from government, labor, and management. Implicit in this system is a less intrusive regulatory role for government due to greater reliance on self-regulation of the workplace.

West Germany

In Germany significant changes in general codetermination rights were dictated by the passage of the Works Constitution Act of 1972 and the Codetermination Act of 1976. These laws also strengthened codetermination rights with respect to occupational safety and health. Moreover, the laws governing the safety and health system in Germany were significantly modified in 1974, shortly after the passage of the OSH Act in the United States, with the enactment of the Work Safety Act (ASiG or *Arbeitssicherheitsgestz*). This provided a general framework for safety and health laws and regulations in Germany. As Mertens describes it: "The Occupational Safety Act is a skeleton law. It lays down the employer's basic responsibilities, the plant physicians' and safety officers' duties and rules for cooperation and the organization of occupational safety and health in the plant" (Mertens, 1979, p.10).

Responsibilities for worker safety and health are delegated throughout various branches and levels of government in Germany and to nongovernmental organizations. General worker safety and health legislation such as the ASiG is considered by the German national assembly, the Bundestag. The Ministry of Labor and Social Affairs promulgates regulations that have general applicability and coordinates the activities of the various players in the safety and health arena. Technical support for its activities is provided by the Federal Institute for Occupational Safety and Accident Research.

The independent TCAs, organized along industrial lines, fulfill a variety of functions in the German safety and health system. In addition to providing industrial insurance, they have regulatory enforcement and training responsibilities and they provide medical treatment and rehabilitation therapy in their hospitals. The TCAs issue industry-specific work safety and health regulations and monitor compliance through inspections. TCA-promulgated regulations provide much of the content to fill in the broad outline of safety and health law stipulated by ASiG. (Even more specific regulations and directives are given by two organizations, German Industrial Standard and the Association of German Electrotechnicians.) The Ministry of Labor and Social Affairs must, however, approve such regulations.

The principle of worker participation in occupational safety and health extends to the TCAs. Employees and management representatives each make up 50 percent of the members of an oversight assembly or board for each TCA (McCall, 1977). In addition to carrying out research dictated by the Ministry of Labor and Social Affairs, a TCA board researches topics of interest to labor and management and it conducts safety tests on equipment and machinery for companies that elect to use this service on a voluntary basis. It also provides free training for company safety engineers and safety committee members.

Safety and health inspections are carried out not only by the TCAs in their respective industries but also by the individual states or *Länder* in Germany on a geographical basis. These *Länder* vary significantly in the amount of resources they commit to safety and health (Brickman et al., 1985). Germany and the United States, which both have the federal-government structure, are the only countries considered here (save Northern Ireland in the United Kingdom) in which states or other regional/local political jurisdictions play such a significant role. Moreover, due to the central role of the TCAs, safety and health regulatory responsibilities are even further spread out than in the United States. While the extent of overlapping of responsibilities would seem to be a prescription for failure were it to be tried in the United States, the operation of this system is quite smooth and devoid of the sharp political controversy that surrounds occupational safety and health regulations in the United States.

Safety and health provisions beyond the legal requirements are occasionally negotiated between labor and management within individual industries. Certain safety and health provisions were under consideration in the 1984 round of labor negotiations in the automotive industry. These safety and health provisions were, however, not pursued as aggressively by labor in these negotiations as other matters.

The general organization and scope of a plant's safety and health operations are dictated by law. Plants with employment above a certain level, which varies depending on the degree of hazard of the industry, must appoint a safety officer in consultation with the works council. The safety officer advises management on safety and health matters; however, as in other countries, management retains ultimate responsibility for these concerns. Also required by law is the provision of plant physician services and services by other safety/health professionals. The numbers of hours of work that must be provided by a safety officer, plant physician, and other safety/health professionals for a plant are functions of such factors as the number of employees, the injury risk of the industry in question, and the type of jobs performed. The TCAs dictate the details of these calculations. For small plants, these services are likely to be provided by employees who work in these jobs part time or by contracted outside safety/health service providers. A plant in the metal industry (in which the automotive industry is classified) would be required to have a full-time safety officer for every 780 employees and a full-time plant physician for every 3,280 employees.

Workers participate at both the shop-floor level as safety stewards and at the plant level as safety committee members. Appointed by management, the safety stewards are responsible for looking for safety and health hazards on the shop floor, receiving complaints from other workers about such hazards, and communicating these to foremen, supervisors, and ultimately to the safety officer if the matter is not resolved satisfactorily at an earlier stage. For plants above a certain minimum-size criterion, a joint labor-management safety committee is also required by law to meet quarterly to discuss various safety and health matters. This committee typically is comprised of the plant manager or a safety representative of the plant manager, the safety officer(s), the plant physician(s), along with safety stewards and works-council members nominated by the works council. The exact numbers may vary, but management and management representatives maintain a majority on this committee.

As in the United States, there is a strong engineering orientation to the promotion of occupational safety and health in Germany. This is a tendency to try to engineer safety into machinery and the rest of the work environment rather than relying on workers to avoid accidents by being careful.

Sweden

Along with the other industrialized countries, Sweden passed major occupational safety and health legislation in the 1970s. Prior to this time, the NBOSH maintained a low profile in Sweden despite complaints about occupational safety and health conditions by the politically powerful unions. Increased funding and public attention to NBOSH emerged slowly at first but accelerated in the late 1960s (Kelman, 1981). Major legislation was passed then in the form of the Worker Protection Act of 1974 and the Work Environment Act of 1978. The former legislation strengthened the authority of safety delegates and safety committees. The latter legislation extended the coverage of existing safety and health legislation to include even military conscripts, prison inmates who are engaged in work, and schoolchildren. Also important was the action of the Social Democratic government in 1974 when it froze 20 percent of corporate profits for use in upgrading safety and health conditions in the workplace, with specific projects subject to approval by the unions.

The occupational safety and health regulatory system in Sweden has considerable stability and insulation from party politics owing to the relative independence of regulatory agencies in Sweden. For example, Kelman (1981) notes that the NBOSH had only three director generals in its first 27 years of operation, compared with three OSHA directors in its first 6 years of existence. This stability is not solely due to the dominance of the Social Democratic Party, because one NBOSH director general even survived the fall of the Social Democratic government in 1976.

There are also important structural differences between NBOSH and OSHA. NBOSH policies and activities are governed by a board of directors that includes representatives of organized labor, employer organizations, and the Swedish Parliament. This structure facilitates labor-management-government cooperation on safety and health at the national level. OSHA has no such structure or even anything remotely similar. Another structural difference is that the Swedish equivalent of NIOSH (National Institute of Occupational Safety and Health), which conducts research on occupational hazards, reports directly to NBOSH. In the United States, NIOSH is independent and essentially co-equal with OSHA (Lichty, 1982). The Swedish structure thus entails greater centralization of the occupational safety and health regulatory and research functions although oversight authority for them is shared by the government with labor and management.

Although legislation has been important in modifying worker health and safety structures, negotiated national labor-management agreements between the Swedish Confederation of Labor (Landsorganisationen--LO) and the Swedish Employers Confederation (Svenska Arbetsgivareföreningen--SAF) have been even more important. Many of these agreements have served as models for subsequent legislation. The legislation typically codified, but in some cases modified, existing arrangements. For example, the 1949 Worker Protection Act and the Worker Safety Ordinance were largely based on a 1942 SAF-LO agreement regarding labor-management cooperation on health and safety. This agreement was then modified in 1951 in accordance with the legislation. Also, a 1967 SAF-LO agreement on company health services served as the basis for legislation passed in 1971 by the Swedish Parliament. Other significant work-environment agreements were reached in 1976, 1978, and 1983. Such national agreements are a distinctive feature of Sweden's occupational safety and health system, unparalleled in any of the other countries of this study. The closest counterpart to it is the landmark 1973 UAW-auto industry agreement in the United States to improve safety and health conditions, but this involved only one industry.

Numerous features of the structure of company safety and health programs in Sweden are dictated by the above-cited laws and agreements. Each workplace with five or more workers is required to select safety delegates to serve as representatives of workers in matters of health and safety. Regional representatives are required for worksites with fewer than five employees. Also, companies with 2,000 or more employees are required to provide comprehensive health and safety services, employing, among others, a full-time medical doctor and safety engineer on the premises. It is recommended that these comprehensive services should be provided when there are as few as 1,500 employees where particularly hazardous work conditions exist. Companies with fewer employees are encouraged to set up joint health and safety services organized sometimes on regional bases and sometimes on industrial bases. Approximately 65 percent of all employees were covered by health and safety services as of 1987.

Another requirement is that companies with 50 or more employees must establish labor-management safety committees that are required to meet at least four times a year to deliberate on safety and health matters. Responsibilities of the safety committees are broader than those of the other countries considered and include the following:

Setting safety goals

Dividing the workplace into safety areas

Planning safety training

Determining the number of safety delegates

Altering work methods, processes, and equipment to improve safety

Reviewing health and safety statistics

Overseeing inspections, studies, and investigations, including accident investigations

Ensuring that safety regulations are obeyed

Administering a budget for safety activities (the size of the budget is, however, established by the firm)

Overseeing the operation of the company health services, including approving the appointment of company doctors and safety engineers (SAF, LO, PTK, 1979)

Significantly, workers comprise a majority on these committees, the only country in this study where this is the case.

Worker safety delegates or stewards provide an important component of a company's safety and health system. Both individually and collectively, the safety stewards have considerable authority. They have the legal right to obtain any information pertinent to safety and health. This includes information regarding the chemical composition of substances used in the work environment, an information right extended much more recently to workers in the United States through the Hazard Communication (Right-to-Know) Rule. Even more significantly, a safety steward has the authority to suspend work activities until a government inspector arrives if he/she considers the work environment to be too dangerous. This is a right unmatched in any of the other countries considered in this study.

A safety steward is typically a full-time worker who performs this role part time. In larger companies there is, however, usually one full-time safety steward. The part-time safety stewards decide how much time and effort to spend on safety and health matters. Safety stewards are also protected by law from any company retribution for unpopular safety/health decisions.

Plant physicians typically spend about half their time caring for people suffering from job-related disabilities and the other half on preventative medicine, such as monitoring the health of workers or researching potential hazards. One U.S. labor leader (Empsak in Einhorn and Logue, 1982) noted that safety and health personnel in

Sweden were able to research topics that would be considered taboo by U.S. companies. One example is the carcinogenicity of work-environment substances that are not currently considered hazardous by the government. This was attributed to the greater influence of labor over safety and health services in Swedish companies. The ability to affect research agendas gives labor greater influence on the designation of industrial diseases in Sweden than in other countries.

In general, Swedish safety and health legislation, coupled with the negotiated labor-management agreements, have given labor a very powerful role to play in the occupational safety and health arena. Moreover, Sweden is regarded by many experts in the field as the country most progressive in protecting the safety and health of workers.

Japan

Although Japan lagged behind other countries in the initial regulation of workplace safety and health, this no longer is the case. Important new safety and health legislation was enacted in Japan in 1972, about the same time as other industrialized countries were passing similar legislation. The Industrial Safety and Health Law of 1972 addressed several problems that had cropped up over the years since the Labor Standards Law was enacted under the direction of the occupation forces in 1947. Since the Labor Standards Law had dealt with a great many work issues, only one chapter was devoted to occupational safety and health, and it was felt that more specific regulations were necessary. The overall purpose of the Industrial Safety and Health Law was to promote not only safety and health but also comfortable working conditions on the job. Improvements in the work environment were the legal responsibility of the employer. Government's role was to guide and supervise employers and to research new technologies.

The law stipulates safety and health provisions in the following areas:

1. Organization (within companies and plants) for safety and health management

2. Measures to prevent accidents and illnesses to be taken by the employer and/or by the principal employer (where a contractor-subcontractor relationship exists)

3. Regulations concerning the use of machines and harmful substances

4. Regulations pertaining to the training and placement of workers

5. Measures to promote health of workers (including such things as medical exams and work environment measurements)

6. Licensure of workers in certain skilled occupations

7. The establishment of a comprehensive safety and health improvement program when such a program is deemed necessary by the Labor Ministry

8. Periodic inspections of worksites and advance review of plans of new work facilities

9. Penalties for noncompliance (Japan Institute of Labour, 1982).

The last provision is significant because Japanese business regulations often do not carry with them penalty provisions for noncompliance. Still, prosecution of firms for safety and health violations is rare in Japan. In addition to employer responsibilities, the law specifies responsibilities for the government, for company safety and health officials, for safety and health committees, for the union (where one exists), and for individual employees.

Rule making, and inspecting and enforcing responsibilities for occupational safety and health are housed within the Labor Ministry in the Labor Standards Bureau. Owing to the stability of national governments, the Labor Standards Bureau has not been as affected by national political changes as has OSHA. Moreover, beneath the Labor Minister, who is a member of the Japanese legislature, is the highly respected civil service, which lends even more stability to the ministry and the Labor Standards Bureau.

The Industrial Safety and Health Law recommends (but does not require) an organizational structure for companies to follow to promote safety and health. Major employers typically follow these structural recommendations although the practices of smaller subcontractors are not so uniform. In the factories of major employers the plant manager serves as the general safety and health supervisor. Production-line personnel are, in effect, the line organization responsible for management of safety and health. A separate division exists for safety and health personnel, including an industrial physician. To a far greater extent than in the United States and other countries considered, the line managers really do assume the safety and health responsibilities assigned to them. The safety and health staff act primarily as technical advisors.

Workers' input regarding safety and health is provided in large part through a company or plant safety and health committee, the membership of which is jointly determined by labor and management, with about half of the seats designated for workers. The committee investigates the causes of injuries and illnesses, proposes countermeasures to eliminate them, considers workers' complaints, and deliberates on other safety and health matters. In some larger firms, instead of a committee, a joint-consultation scheme is used. This approach, based on union-management contract, predates the Industrial Safety and Health Law.

Unions often have their own safety and health experts and parallel systems to promote safety and health. Shop stewards typically have safety and health responsibilities along with their other union duties. Workers are also involved in safety and health activities as instructors. Labor unions nominate individuals to attend training courses sponsored by the government and organizations such as the Japan Industrial Safety and Health Association to prepare them to serve as safety and health instructors at their plant.

Yet another aspect of worker involvement in safety and health is through "toolbox meetings" at the plant-floor level. These are short meetings that occur within work groups to discuss safety and health issues before the start of work. Sometimes similar meetings are held after work to discuss safe commuting.

Japanese companies, far more than companies of the other nations considered, emphasize the relationships among safety, productivity, and product quality. This can be seen in the emphasis on slogans such as "there can be no production without safety" and in the pursuit of zero-accident campaigns that are derived from and associated with the zero-defect movement. This results in considerable efforts by major employers to promote safety and health beyond those that are required by law.

Other government-encouraged safety and health procedures that have been instituted by various companies involving employee participation include training to foresee danger, safety check through finger pointing and calling, suggestion systems for industrial safety and health, rotating employees in charge of safety, and a morning safety meeting. Also, safety and health issues are often discussed among quality circles. The basic idea underlying these techniques is involvement of employees verbally and physically in safety and health activities to increase awareness. The degree of involvement of the typical line worker (i.e., one who has no special safety and health responsibilities) in Japan far exceeds that of workers in any of the other countries considered. These activities taken together reflect a dominant behavioral orientation in the safety and health system in Japan.

In addition to its regulatory activities, the government promotes voluntary safety and health activities in various ways. The Ministry of Labor is involved in training, financing, consulting, and researching activities to promote safety and health. Of particular note in the area of training are a government-funded University of Occupational and Environmental Health established in 1978 and government-sponsored Occupational Safety and Health Education centers. In the area of financing, government provides funds to assist small businesses and medium-sized businesses with various safety and health expenditures through low-interest loans and direct subsidies. Labor Standards

Bureau inspectors provide technical advice to employers to help them improve safety and health conditions and to help ensure compliance with regulations. Research activities are carried out in several government-sponsored research organizations, including the Research Institute of Industrial Safety, the National Institute of Industrial Health, the Japan Bioassay Laboratory, the Industrial Health Test Center, and the Safety and Health Appliance Authorization Center.

Kenya

The occupational safety and health system in Kenya has a less clearly defined structure that those of the industrialized countries. The responsibility for enacting and enforcing occupational safety and health regulations is housed within the Ministry of Labour. This ministry also administers a workers' compensation program that provides modest support for work-related disabilities. Further details of the structure of occupational safety and health activities within the Ministry of Labour were not available.

Unlike the industrialized countries, Kenya has not adopted any overarching safety and health law in recent years. However, various laws and regulations addressing individual hazards in the work environment have been passed during this time period. Formal safety and health standards in Kenya are surprisingly similar to those in the developed countries. They are, in fact, modeled after them. Typically though, the enactment of new safety and health regulations trail those of developed countries by several years. An example of this is the enactment of noise standards. These have only recently been considered in Kenya, whereas noise-level standards have existed in the other countries of this study for a number of years.

Still, there is a greater disparity in actual safety and health conditions between Kenya and the industrialized countries than there appears in the existing legislation. These differences will become apparent later in this book when we discuss safety and health conditions in Company X's Kenyan plant. Accounting for some portion of this disparity is the fact that certain Kenyan safety and health laws are not actually enforced. A case in point is a requirement of every employer that work facilities be inspected yearly by inspectors from the Ministry of Labour. There are not nearly enough government inspectors to carry out such a schedule. Large employers in the capital city of Nairobi, where one would expect the inspectors to focus their greatest attention, go for years between inspections. The existence of such unenforced safety regulations testifies to the importance placed on occupational safety and health issues, if only from a political or public-relations perspective, even in developing countries.

In considering worker safety and health in industrial settings in Kenya, one needs to place this issue in some perspective.

Government occupational safety and health regulations apply only to the formal work sector; self-employed workers are not covered. Workers in the informal sector work under conditions that westerners would consider grossly unsafe. For example, this researcher visited an area known as "woodcarvers' alley." There, perhaps 100 or more self-employed individuals carve various wooden souvenir items. The carvers have no safety equipment or protective clothing. They often use their feet to hold tiny pieces of wood while they chisel them with inappropriately large tools. The area is extremely dirty and smoky; wood chips and scraps remain where they fall unless they are picked up by someone for use as fuel. Heavy smoke from food vendors' grills fills the air and there are no sanitary facilities in evidence. If such a worker sustained a permanent disability there would be no workers' compensation or free medical care. The individual would have to learn to work with the disability in this or some new line of work. Otherwise, the individual would probably have to beg or rely on the support of family or friends.

SAFETY AND HEALTH SYSTEMS: COOPERATION AND CONFLICT

There are many points at which the interests of labor, management and government relative to occupational safety and health converge in each of these countries. These convergent interests suggest the validity of the old slogan "safety pays" in many situations, and this leads to cooperation among the parties. However, there are many points at which the interests of these parties are divergent, indicating that a more accurate slogan would be "safety pays, but only up to a point." These disharmonies of interest inevitably lead to conflicts, and these are dealt with in both cooperative and assertive ways.

The harmonies and disharmonies of interest, the conflicts and the cooperative and assertive approaches for dealing with them are products of the national contexts in which they develop. Thus, we can understand them better by reference to these contexts.

United Kingdom

The regulatory system for promoting occupational safety and health in Britain is explicitly designed to promote cooperation among labor, management and government. As noted above, cooperation is promoted at both the rule-making and rule-enforcing stages of the regulatory process by structuring a flexible system that requires participation by labor and management to work out details.

On the whole, this flexible approach to regulation works very well in the United Kingdom. Contrary to the stereotypic view in the United States of relations among labor, management and government in the United Kingdom, this cooperative tripartite approach to handling problems is common in the British regulatory process, if not in other aspects of British relations. Favorable reviews have also been given by scholars from abroad who have studied this approach to regulation in general or the regulation of safety and health in particular (Brickman et al., 1985; Vogel, 1983). These cooperatively designed regulations obviously make more sense than they might otherwise, because they take into account the views of affected parties and can be adapted to meet particular circumstances. Also, the behind-the-scenes negotiations on regulations defuse much of the political acrimony surrounding new regulations. This compares favorably with the United States, where the safety and health regulatory process is often heavily politicized and regulations frequently remain controversial long after they are enacted.

Further evidence of the nonconfrontational orientation of safety and health regulatory activities is provided by considering the inspection and enforcement activities of the Health and Safety Executive and by contrasting these activities with those of OSHA. In 1983, the Health and Safety Executive conducted 248,000 inspections and issued 8,700 "improvement, prohibition and crown notices, and infraction letters," or 1 for every 29 inspections. In contrast, 111,549 total violations were found by OSHA in 1983 (Table 2-5) in 69,045 inspections, or almost 2 for every inspection. Moreover, the 8,700 letters and notices issued by the Health and Safety Executive led to 1,377 prosecutions (1 for every 180 inspections). This compares with 31,315 penalties issued in the United States (1 for every 2 inspections). Although British prosecutions may be more serious than U.S. penalties, these statistics still indicate that there is a more frequent utilization of sanctions for noncompliance with safety and health regulations in the United States compared with the United Kingdom.

Despite the generally favorable view of safety and health regulation in the United Kingdom, there are certain problems or perceived problems of this system that reflect conflict or, at least, an absence of cooperation in safety and health relationships. One perceived problem is that the system is not participative enough. Both labor and management complain that their views are not adequately taken into account, particularly in the rule-making stage. Managers, in particular, also feel that the required cost-benefit studies of proposed regulations are not given adequate weight in the decisions that are made.

Another criticism of the consultative process is that it is only open to *officially* sanctioned groups. Thus, nonunionized workers are likely to have less of a voice in the rule-making process than unionized workers. Brickman et al. (1985) have noted that some parties have been so dissatisfied with the process that they have gone public with their complaints. This brings about a greater politicization of the issues.

Yet another problem deals specifically with the downside of the flexibility feature. That is, that the flexibility leads to unpredictability. This is because different inspectors are likely to interpret the regulations differently, making it very difficult for management to know exactly how to respond to a regulation without specific guidance from the Health and Safety Executive/Commission. And this guidance is not always readily available due to the large number of business establishments compared with the number of inspectors. Similar interpretation difficulties confront labor officials concerned with safety and health.

Labor-management relations regarding safety and health have become somewhat more cooperative in recent years, however, elements of adversarial relations that conform to the British stereotype remain strong. This is particularly evident in workers' resistance to wearing proper safety equipment and management's disciplining of such workers. The filing of safety and health grievances that sometimes lead to work stoppages is also common. There is a feeling among management that a substantial number of these grievances, regarding technical violations of health and safety standards rather than truly hazardous conditions, are frivolous. Thus, they believe that workers who file such grievances are doing so just to harass management or to get a break from work. Workers, for their part, feel that managers are not adequately concerned with safety and health conditions. Line-staff conflicts among managers over safety and health are also common as we will see in the discussion of Company Y.

In summary, the occupational safety and health system that has been dictated by the HSW Act differs from the earlier system in that it requires a "tripartite" institutional structure containing equal representation from government, labor, and management. There is also a reduced regulatory role for government due to greater reliance on self-regulation of the workplace. This self-regulation is driven not by altruism but by the threat of government sanctions and the assertiveness of unions. Though somewhat at odds with the traditional U.S. view of labor-management-government relations in the United Kingdom, this system is well accepted and viewed on the whole as effective by those directly involved in it and by scholars who have studied it.

The cooperative and assertive behaviors of managements' safety and health relationships can be visualized by reference to Figures 4-1 and 4-2, which use Ruble and Thomas's (1976) two-dimensional model of conflict-coping behavior. Management's behavior toward government is high on assertiveness and moderately high on cooperativeness. This can be plotted in the "collaborative" region of Figure 4-1. Government also engages in collaborative behavior toward management. Management and labor also both engage in highly assertive behavior toward each other. Cooperativeness, however, is only moderate. Still, these relations border on collaboration, which is characterized in the literature as an effective mode of handling conflict (Thomas, 1976). The effectiveness of the British approach to handling occupational safety and health in the

FIGURE 4-1
MANAGEMENT'S CONFLICT-COPING BEHAVIORS TOWARD GOVERNMENT

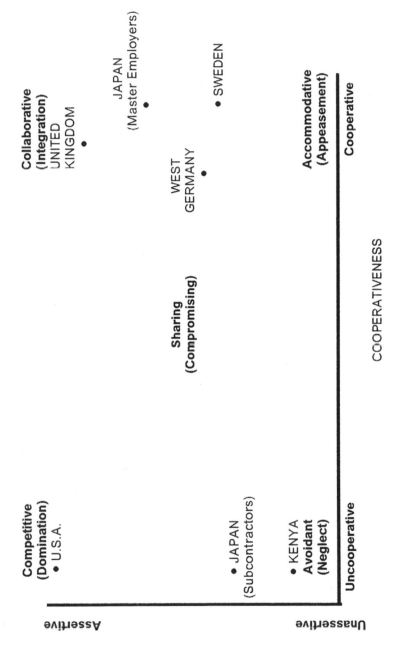

FIGURE 4-2
MANAGEMENT'S CONFLICT-COPING BEHAVIORS TOWARD LABOR

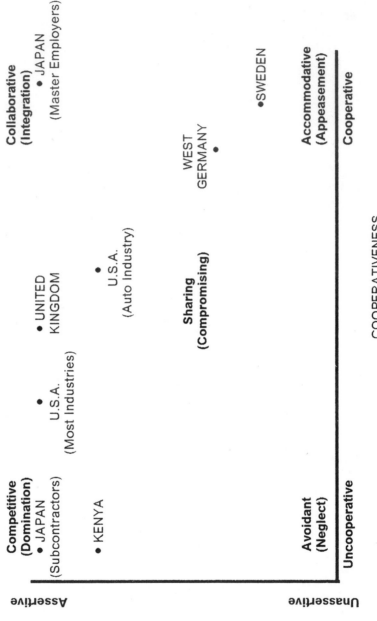

United Kingdom is evidenced in national injury statistics considered in Chapter 5.

West Germany

As is evident from earlier descriptions, the German worker safety and health system relies on cooperative relations among the various participants of the system. In some cases, cooperation has been mandated by law; in other cases, it has developed in response to the need to coordinate the activities of the several parties involved. As noted, worker involvement in safety and health activities is required at the shop-floor level and the board-of-directors level through *Mitbestimmung* legislation. The multifaceted involvement of the quasi-public TCAs is also legally mandated. The individual states, or *Länder* in Germany also have legally mandated safety and health responsibilities intersecting those of the TCAs. This situation does not create any serious conflicts, but it does bring about certain regional disparities in the enforcement of safety and health regulations.

Cooperation is clearly evident between the TCAs and the companies, and between labor and management. Because the TCAs function as the insurance carriers, promulgators, and enforcers of safety/health standards, they have a very strong economic incentive to ensure that their activities have the ultimate effect of minimizing injuries and illnesses in the plants they cover. This leads representatives of TCAs occasionally to seek advice from the safety managers of the plants they cover regarding how best to deal with various hazards. This is particularly common with automotive plants because they are very large employers and have the expertise available to develop state-of-the-art solutions to problems encountered by them and smaller firms alike.

Cooperation among firms on safety and health issues is quite striking. It is not uncommon for plant safety officers to meet with their counterparts at other German automotive plants (and at plants in other countries as well) to exchange information on worker safety and health. Industry-government cooperation on safety and health matters is also quite common. Support of corporate safety and health efforts is provided by various government agencies or agencies receiving government support.

Available evidence supports the view that safety and health relationships are primarily cooperative in nature. The organizational structures for labor-management cooperation usually facilitate amicable compromises on safety and health matters. The overwhelming majority of individuals involved with the safety and health system feel that this cooperative approach is both desirable and effective. Moreover, they believe that this approach should and would be continued even if it were not required. Criticisms of the system are, for the most part, aired by individuals who want to modify and improve it within the present general framework rather than dismantle and replace this system with something else.

Despite the overwhelmingly cooperative orientation of the health and safety system in West Germany, there is ample evidence of conflict on several levels. The close relationships between the TCAs and the covered firms may create certain problems. There is certainly the possibility for conflicts of interest to arise because the TCAs set standards, advise the firms on the meeting of these standards, inspect the firms for compliance with the standards and provide insurance coverage for injuries.

Evidence exists that both the spirit and the letter of the law regarding occupational safety and health legislation are often violated. Various problems arise due to deviations between the intent or prescriptions of the law and actual practice. An example of this is the lack of functioning safety committees in workplaces. One researcher found that safety committees did not exist in 30 percent of the workplaces surveyed (Rosenbrock, 1983). Many existing committees were found to be not operating according to specified guidelines and not serving their intended purpose of improving labor-management cooperation on safety and health issues. Blame for these conditions has been placed not only on management for not encouraging employee involvement in safety and health but also on labor for not taking advantage of opportunities for involvement. Managers feel that labor's uncooperativeness stems from the low priority workers themselves place on safety and health and that they communicate to their elected representatives. Labor's position is that they do not have sufficient authority regarding safety and health and therefore should not be held responsible for deficiencies. Their representatives comprise a minority on safety and health committees and, in any event, these committees are only advisory.

Political aspects of the worker representation system also appear to create certain conflicts. Safety officers, who are required to consult with safety representatives in disciplinary matters, complain of a lack of cooperation in disciplining workers not following safety and health work rules. They attribute this uncooperativeness to safety representatives not wanting to be involved in disciplinary matters that might jeopardize their reelection by the workers. Management personnel at two German plants complained that, unlike managers in the United States, they did not feel they could send workers home for such violations. At one of these plants, managers required workers who had violated safety rules to view safety films that graphically depicted gruesome work accidents. Management felt that these films had a certain shock value and motivated workers to comply with safety regulations.

Some critics (Hauss and Rosenbrock, 1982, 1983; Naschold, 1977a, 1977b) contend that an imbalance of power in the favor of management inhibits more cooperation on safety and health from taking place. In such critiques, the German occupational safety and health system is often compared unfavorably with that in Sweden, where greater worker rights are guaranteed. Specifically cited as examples of this imbalance are the weaknesses of labors' rights to refuse dangerous work and to call in inspectors. Labor is also viewed as having a subsidiary role to management and government in the designation of industrial diseases. One alleged result of this imbalance of power is the provisions of technical safety and health services (e.g., safety engineering, medical services) that, it is claimed, place profits over the interests of workers. Another perceived flaw is management's alleged abuse of its power regarding safety and health. For example, Hauss and Rosenbrock (1983) contend that employers dismiss illness-prone or injury-prone workers through a variety of means used to circumvent laws prohibiting this.

Another problem that creates conflicts in safety and health responsibilities is the relatively common practice of companies assigning two or more engineers to part-time safety/health duties rather than employing one full-time safety officer, where one is required by law. Government and labor officials consider this to be a serious problem because other responsibilities of these engineers often take precedence over safety and health responsibilities.

Another conflict between management and government pertains to the rigidity of safety and health regulations. Managers feel that overemphasis on detailed regulations distracts them from seeing the overall picture and improving workplace safety and health. One safety manager familiar with the workplace safety and health system in the United States felt that German regulations were much more rigid and demanding. As an example, he contended that it was permissible in the United States to have warnings or simply to paint a line on the floor to keep workers away from a dangerous machine. (The U.S. guarding requirements are not as lax as he indicated, but the point of the story was interesting, nonetheless.) He argued that in Germany, the laws required the employer to make it almost impossible for workers to injure themselves. This engineering-oriented approach to safety and health is, in fact, quite similar to that in the United States, but it contrasts sharply with the behavioral-oriented approach of Japan.

A final area of inconsistency between the intent and practice of labor-management cooperation on safety and health pertains to occupational injury statistics. Government-published injury statistics are particularly unhelpful; they are broken down into only nine broad industrial categories. Thus, the automotive-industry statistics are combined with statistics for other metal-working industries, such as shipbuilding and iron and steel production, and are reported in this combined metal-working category. Of the countries considered, only Kenya's injury statistics are less informative.

The safety directors of the various German auto companies do, however, exchange their work injury experience data and thus have access to more narrowly defined industry averages. These data have been closely guarded by safety directors in recent years. Previously, the union that represents workers in the auto industry, I. G. Metall, had attempted to use these data to apply pressure on firms with higher-than-average injury rates to improve their safety performance. To avoid such comparisons, safety directors were unwilling to divulge any specific data on injury rates for the automotive industry as a whole. They were also quite hesitant about divulging their own companies' injury statistics. It was, however, learned from other industry sources that the auto-industry injury rate is relatively good compared with other industries and that it is improving.

An alternative explanation of the guarding of injury statistics provided by a corporate safety director was that it was done not to protect management. Rather, he claimed, the intention was to protect the works-council members of firms with higher-than-average injury rates from pressures from their constituencies. Whatever the motivation, this secrecy attests to the sensitivity about work injury experience in Germany.

Despite these criticisms of the safety and health system in Germany, there is no evidence of dissatisfaction with the overall safety and health system and its cooperative orientation. Most critics seek to point out problems that hinder the system from operating as intended. Labor, management, and government representatives contend that insufficient cooperativeness by the other parties is behind the less-than-optimal performance.

Overall, the tone of the debate concerning worker safety and health suggests that there is less conflict and fewer adverse consequences of conflict pertaining to this issue in Germany than in the United States. The nature of the relationships pertaining to occupational safety and health can be summarized by reference to Figures 4-1 and 4-2. Management's relations both with government and labor can be characterized as being moderately high on cooperativeness and moderate on assertiveness. Cooperation is not as great as it could be, but it is clearly greater than in the United States. Assertiveness of these parties in their relationships with each other is lower than that of their counterparts in the United States. There is a general consensus that the safety and health system in Germany is, on balance, quite effective. Industry, government, and labor representatives directly involved with safety and health attest to its effectiveness, although they are quick to point out areas of potential improvement.

Some of the criticisms of the German system have received little or no attention in the United States. For example, concerns have been raised that absenteeism rates in Germany might be *too low* as a result of sick or injured workers going to work, despite their condition, out of fear of job loss. There was concern that these workers could represent a hazard to themselves and other workers. Researchers studying absenteeism in the United States found the notion of absenteeism being too low surprising and, to them, even humorous. To their knowledge, it had not been addressed in the U.S. literature on absenteeism. Another safety and health concern in Germany receiving less attention in the United States is worker mental stress resulting from shift-work and piece-work compensation. Finally, a criticism of the German approach to detecting industrial diseases, that it relies too much on hard science and too little on workers, seems to represent a fundamental difference in the orientation of the debate over occupational safety and health in Germany compared with that in the United States. Critics of the U.S. system would find this an esoteric point far beyond the scope of the debate regarding safety and health in the United States, at least under the Reagan administration. Moreover, recent U.S. labor-management agreements pertaining to occupational safety and health rely increasingly on jointly funded hard-science research as a more objective arbiter to resolve matters of dispute.

Even among critics of the safety and health system in Germany, there is little support for fundamental changes. The lack of pressure for change, at least from labor's perspective, can be attributed partly to slower economic gains in recent years. Labor of late has also been emphasizing other demands in negotiations, such as the reduction of the work week. With the recovery of the economy and union gains on more pressing concerns, safety and health issues could become higher priority items. However, the bitter strike in this 1984 round of negotiations suggests a more pessimistic view. Cooperative relationships between labor and management in general may be unraveling due to the decline in the economic growth rate. As a result, cooperation on safety and health in particular might also decline. Commentators suggest that unions moderated their negotiating demands and cooperated with management during Germany's seemingly miraculous postwar recovery because of their expectations of future benefits resulting from economic growth. Now, as these expectations become more questionable, that moderation and cooperation may be more difficult to maintain.

Sweden

Most observers, including this researcher, have judged the cooperation among business, government, and labor on matters of safety and health to be extremely high in Sweden. This cooperation is greater there than in the United States or any of the other countries considered in this study, except perhaps Japan (in master-employer firms).

There is a general consensus among labor, management, and government on safety and health goals and a willingness to work together in pursuit of these goals. Where one party disagrees regarding the best way to achieve these goals, such disagreements are often sublimated. Interestingly, labor-management cooperation and codetermination regarding safety and health have been widely accepted for a number of years, although codetermination regarding other work issues has been a more contentious topic. A number of factors can be cited to explain the high level of cooperation among labor, industry, and government on safety and health issues in Sweden. Certainly the representation of labor, employers, and the legislature on the board of NBOSH facilitates this cooperation. More fundamentally, workers who are aligned with the ruling Social Democrats clearly have much more political power than does labor in the United States or the other countries in this study. Management may have reached collective bargaining agreements on safety and health with labor to avoid less desirable conditions that might be imposed on them legislatively. Where laws have already been passed, these apparently have been used to strengthen labor's negotiating position at corporate and industry levels.

One American researcher who studied the promulgation and enforcement of health and safety regulations in the United States and Sweden made the following observations:

> Rule-making decisions of the two agencies (OSHA and NBOSH, or ASV) were quite similar and usually favored more protective alternatives over less protective ones.
>
> These decisions were fought persistently by business in the United States but accepted meekly by business in Sweden.
>
> OSHA was bound by a detailed set of procedural requirements while ASV was bound by virtually none.
>
> OSHA adopted a far more punitive approach to compliance than did ASV.
>
> OSHA was far more concerned with controlling field inspectors than was ASV.
>
> Lawyers and courts were highly involved in both rule making and compliance in the United States and virtually uninvolved in Sweden. (Kelman, 1981, pp. 5-6)

The cooperative orientation of government regarding safety and health is further indicated by statistics on inspection and enforcement activities.[4] These data indicate that inspection coverage of worksites is extensive but nonadversarial. NBOSH's 500 inspectors conducted inspections at approximately 60,000 worksites or about two-thirds of the country's 90,000 workplaces in 1986. In contrast, the United States, with employment at approximately 25 times that of Sweden, has only about 1,200 OSHA inspectors (2.4 times that of NBOSH) who visit fewer than 2 percent of U.S. worksites. Even adding state safety and health inspections, it's unlikely that more than 4 percent of the nation's worksites are visited annually. The Swedish inspectors issued written improvement recommendations in approximately 25,000 to 30,000 (about one-half) of their inspections. Violations are not usually charged nor penalties assessed for deviations from safety and health laws found during a first inspection. Only about 400 violations were charged during 1986, in most cases for failure to follow recommendations. This is only a tiny fraction of the safety and health violations issued in the United States, both in absolute terms and in relation to the number of inspections carried out.

The considerable authority of the safety committee, in which worker representatives form a majority, appears to be a significant factor in promoting labor-management cooperation. For example, one of the major worker complaints about the safety and health systems in other countries, that medical and safety services put profit concerns ahead of workers' interests, is not an issue in Sweden. Company safety and health professionals in Sweden are likely to weight workers' safety and health interests more heavily vis-à-vis profit concerns than their counterparts in the other countries considered in this study. This is relevant in considering reported injury statistics for plants operating in Sweden. There is no obvious incentive on the part of the safety and health professionals to limit the number of reported injuries by rejecting bogus injury claims or even not reporting legitimate injury claims as there is in other countries.

Labor-management cooperation on safety and health and on other work issues can also be attributed to the respect the Swedish people generally have for rules and authority. Compared to the U.S. population, Sweden's population has traditionally been quite homogenous along racial, ethnic, and religious lines, eliminating many of the sources of social friction that exist in the United States. In fact, one of the complaints of six U.S. workers who worked in a Swedish automobile plant on an experimental basis was that their Swedish coworkers were too submissive to union and management authority (Schrank, 1979). They felt their own individuality was excessively constrained by stated and unstated norms of behavior. The composition of Sweden's population is changing, however, as is discussed in the next chapter.

Despite the many positive features of the Swedish safety and health system, there are several problem areas as well. Many of these problems, however, might be better characterized in terms of an absence of cooperation rather than a presence of conflict. For example, workers do not take full advantage of general participation opportunities, including those related to safety and health, which are open to them at the plant and company levels. This has been attributed to a union structure that entails a high degree of centralization at the national level (Einhorn and Logue, 1982; Gardell, 1980; Barstow, 1983; Schrank, 1979). The centralization is a by-product of relying on national approaches to resolve labor-management issues rather than on local, company, or industrial approaches. This might take the form of securing national legislation or negotiating an agreement between LO and its employers' association counterpart, SAF. Because so many issues are dealt with at a level far removed from the workers, they may feel that they needn't get personally involved in settling work issues because the union will take care of them. This results in a system of labor-management cooperation that focuses on major safety and health issues with national implications but that overlooks many workplace-specific issues. At the plant level, worker participation in safety and health matters meets the minimum legal requirements, but it does not usually go much beyond that.

To gain an understanding of this apparent lack of enthusiasm for participation requires a short digression. To a visitor, one of the most striking features of the Swedish work environment is the high rate of absenteeism. A 10 percent daily unscheduled absenteeism rate is not at all unusual for blue-collar workers. To put this in perspective, unscheduled absenteeism in the United States is generally less than 2 percent. Several factors can explain this high Swedish absenteeism rate. One reason is the very generous legislated leave policies that are rare in the United States, including maternity/paternity leave (up to 9 months), child-care leave (up to 60 days per year for working couples with children), and educational leave. Another relevant reason in the context of this study is that workers can certify themselves as unfit to work for physical or psychological reasons (work or nonwork related) for up to 7 days at a time while receiving 90 percent of their pay from the federal government. Thus, workers dissatisfied with working conditions have an easier alternative than attempting to alter those conditions--simply not going to work. This may help explain the low level of employee participation in safety and health.

Another problem with the Swedish safety and health system concerns the union safety stewards. In contrast to the United States, where most safety and health representatives are involved with safety and health full time, giving them the opportunity to develop their skills further, most Swedish safety stewards work at this task part time. This results in a conflict between the stewards' regular jobs and their safety steward jobs, at least in terms of time devoted and the ability to develop technical competence.

There have been numerous union complaints in Sweden that the labor inspectorate is lax in its inspection activities and in its enforcement of existing safety laws (Lundberg, 1981). Although some of this laxness may be due to the limited resources of the labor inspectorate, a significant portion of it appears to result from congenial (or perhaps overly congenial) relations between the inspectorate and employers. This has been characterized as cooperation between government and management in exclusion of and at the expense of labor.

Contrasting NBOSH's inspection policy with the more formal and confrontational approach of OSHA, Kelman (1981, p. 203) observes that "Swedish inspections are designed more as informal personal missions to give advice and information, establish friendship ties between inspector and inspected and promote local labor-management cooperation." Using this cooperative approach, inspectors may give advance notice of inspections. They will typically concentrate on encouraging managers to correct conditions that violate safety or health standards rather than on issuing citations.

Critics contend that this approach is not effective (Kronlund, 1979; Lundberg, 1981). They claim that the system is reactive--ignoring conditions until problems develop. Employers have little incentive to correct problems before they are pointed out by friendly inspectors, unless, of course, labor representatives insist upon it. Unsafe and unhealthy conditions, therefore, persist longer than if some greater threat of sanctions existed.

This position portrays inspectors as too cooperative with management. According to this view, excessive inspector-employer cooperation prevents the inspectors from serving as adequate representatives of the employees and thus creates a conflict between the advising and enforcing functions of the inspectors. This criticism would fit the "captured regulator" model frequently posited by critics of the U.S. regulatory system. Consistent with this model is the claim that Swedish regulators too frequently come from the ranks of the regulated. Lundberg (1981) notes that inspectors typically have previous experience as foremen or middle managers rather than as safety engineers or safety stewards.

Another problem with Sweden's approach to safety and health is the permissiveness regarding the usage of protective equipment. Both supervisors and safety stewards usually let the worker decide what protective equipment they will wear. This is the case despite the fact that safety legislation contains provisions for the punishment of workers who violate safety rules. This permissiveness results in a relatively low rate of usage of safety equipment. Immediate convenience and comfort concerns often take precedence over relatively unlikely accidents or long-term health hazards. Such a situation suggests the need for more conflict in the safety and health arena (or, more precisely, for greater assertiveness by safety and health managers and by safety stewards).

Much of the Swedish literature criticizing the health and safety system and worker participation in general takes on a distinctly anticapitalist tone (see Åsard, 1980; Kronlund, 1979; and Lundberg, 1981, for examples). From this perspective, work injuries and diseases are the inevitable results of a basic conflict between labor and capital. This arises as the owners of capital and their representatives in management pursue profit at the expense of workers' interests. According to this view, the only way to redress this problem is to shift more power to the workers. Both codetermination arrangements and the wage-earner investment funds are viewed by certain factions within the labor movement as means of accomplishing this.

Despite such fundamental criticisms, the level of conflict pertaining to occupational safety and health is relatively low in Sweden compared with that in the United States, West Germany, or the United Kingdom. We can summarize the nature of the relationships regarding safety and health in Sweden by referring again to Figures 4-1 and 4-2. Management's conflict-coping behavior toward both government and labor can be described as high on cooperativeness and moderately low on assertiveness. This is characterized as accommodative behavior. This behavior is reciprocated by both of these parties in their behavior toward management. Government's and labor's behavior toward each other may also be described as accommodative.

The overwhelming view by labor, management and government representatives in Sweden is that the safety and health system is quite good overall. Although there is considerable debate about safety and health issues in Sweden, as in Germany, this debate has progressed to a more sophisticated level than in the other countries considered in this book. The literature addresses the safety and health implications of such organizational factors as payment by results/piece-rate payment, employee workload, worker control over work pace, shift work, increasing organization size, routinization of work tasks, and the decrease of social interactions. These concerns receive less attention in the United States, Japan, Germany, and the United Kingdom. There is also greater consideration paid in Sweden to white-collar safety and health issues related to psychosocial factors, such as job stress and monotony (Abrahamsson and Brodström, 1980; Gardell, 1980; Kronlund, 1979; Levi, 1978). Concern with such issues as these can be viewed as evidence of success with other more basic safety and health concerns.

Japan

The occupational safety and health system in Japan is described in most accounts as eliciting near total cooperation among labor, management, and government. In sharp contrast to the situation in the United States, labor and management in Japan have nothing but praise for government's role in occupational safety and health. Each of these three parties is quite satisfied with its working relationships with the other two parties.

The success of government and industrial efforts to work together to promote industrial activity in Japan is legendary. As with other areas of government-industry relations in Japan a great deal of emphasis is placed upon maintaining harmonious relations in matters pertaining to safety and health. Government use of citations and penalties to ensure compliance with safety and health regulations is rare. Much of the emphasis is on government encouragement of voluntary self-regulation by industry.

The Industrial Safety and Health Law of 1972 provides the framework for cooperation. It recommends a safety and health committee structure that facilitates cooperation on these issues between labor and management. The government assists industry in promoting safety and health through training, financing, and consulting activities and government-sponsored research. Industry is relied upon to voluntarily carry out various safety and health measures. Unions often have parallel safety and health programs that complement company programs.

Although the predominant orientation toward safety and health in Japan appears cooperative, below the surface there exist several conflictual aspects of safety and health relations. These conflictual relations pertaining to safety and health reflect broader conflicts in labor-management relations. One such conflict pertains to the reporting of injuries. Japanese culture and industrial relations emphasize group loyalty and a sense of obligation of group members. Being involved in an accident is typically viewed as having let down one's group. This is especially obvious in companies that emphasize the zero-accident campaign. One injury means the entire company fails to meet its goal. Thus, there is a conflict at the group and individual levels regarding injury reporting. Reporting an injury brings attention to the failure of oneself and one's group. Not reporting injuries undermines the recording, reporting, and evaluation systems in place at the plant, corporate, industrial, and national levels.

The extent of the underreporting is difficult to gauge, but some speculation has placed the actual injury rates as high as three times the reported rates. The non-reported injuries are more likely to be minor injuries but there have been reports of workers attempting to conceal broken bones and concussions. Managers may also attempt to conceal injuries that occur to their workers. This can be done by having the worker treated for the injury at the company hospital (a facility that many master employers have). In such a situation, it would be simple to avoid filing a workers' compensation claim.

The economic success of Japan, which in many cases has come at the expense of international competitors, has created international implications for injury reporting. Labor, management, and government officials in other countries have frequently accused the Japanese of exploiting their own workers to gain competitive advantage, forcing them to work long hours in unsafe conditions. These labor practices would, presumably, show up in higher injury statistics as one aspect of this alleged exploitation. Thus, international pressures may create further incentives for the underrecording of injuries to prevent workplace safety and health from becoming more of an issue in trade disputes.

The incredibly high cost of building new facilities in Japan leads to numerous conflicts between labor and management over safety and health hazards in older facilities. Due to the scarcity of land in Japan--it is one twenty-fifth the size of the United States, with much of its land area mountainous, yet it has over one-half the population of the United States--the cost of new building sites is exorbitant. Compared with the United States, there is a much greater tendency for management in Japan to renovate old cramped facilities rather than to build new ones. Thus, typical complaints by Japanese workers about dust, fumes, heat in the summer, and cold in the winter are usually not completely resolved.

Another area of labor-management conflicts pertains to the enforcement of work safety and health rules such as the wearing of protective equipment. Although it occurs less frequently than in other countries, workers in Japan sometimes forget about or disregard long-term or low-probability hazards and seek immediate comfort or convenience by not following these rules. In such a case, managers may remind, reprimand, or in some way penalize the worker. On occasion, Japanese managers mete out a severe form of punishment, particularly for repeat offenders, by capitalizing on the Japanese sense of honor or face and the dread of losing face. One example was cited by a manager who would make the offending worker stop working and stand beside him for the balance of the day. The following day the worker could return to the job but would be required to wear a yellow shirt or some other symbol of shame. Company officials were very sensitive about this example and contended that such a practice is far less common presently than in the past. It was felt that this was an extreme form of punishment, and these officials explained that, in the past, Samurai warriors were given the privilege of being allowed to commit suicide when confronted with such a loss of face rather than having to live with the shame.

Another set of conflicts pertains to the subcontractors. As noted previously, many aspects of the highly touted working conditions in Japan exist only in master-employers firms. Available evidence suggests that safety and health conditions in subcontractors are also inferior to those in the master employers. The Japan Institute of Labor (1982) has reported far higher injury rates in subcontractor firms and in small and medium-sized businesses. It is reasonable to assume that the less favorable financial positions forced on subcontractor firms by master employers result in their cutting corners on safety and health matters. The subcontractor firms may also be assigned more hazardous work by master employers interested in achieving low injury rates.

Partly in response to this situation, the government requests that master employers oversee the safety and health activities of their subcontractors. This oversight typically extends only to the first of many layers of subcontractors. The smaller firms are left to manage their safety and health activities on their own. Neither the master employers nor the Labor Standards Bureau, with its limited number of safety and health experts, provides much assistance. Master employers prefer not even to know anything about the working conditions in these smaller subcontractors for fear that they would be required to help upgrade them. In addition, workers in smaller firms are likely to be more reluctant to complain about hazardous conditions because they lack adequate protection from employer retribution.

While inferior safety and health conditions would be found in the smaller establishments of any of the industrialized countries considered in this book, this disparity appears more obvious in Japan. (The disparity is, however, even greater in Kenya, where regulation of working conditions in smaller establishments is virtually nonexistent.) The contrast in Japan is so great because of the extremely good safety and health conditions in the master-employers' facilities.

The behavior of management (in master-employer firms) can be best characterized as in the collaborating region, that is, high on cooperativeness and high on assertiveness in Figures 4-1 and 4-2. Labor and government also have high levels of cooperative behavior but only moderate levels of assertive behavior toward management. This also describes labor's and government's behaviors toward each other. Overall cooperation among these parties on safety and health matters is extensive, however, there is room for increased assertiveness by both labor and government.

For smaller firms, management would be best characterized as being in a dominant position toward labor and labor in an appeasing position toward management. Government could dominate these employers if it had the resources and the political mandate to do so. The current situation, however, might best be described as one of neglect or avoidance by both government and management toward each other.

Kenya

Kenya relies, to a certain extent, on the cooperation among labor, management, and government to promote safety and health. However, to a far greater extent, labor and government have abdicated responsibility in this area to management. This has happened for a number of reasons. As has already been noted, neither government nor unions have sufficient technical expertise in occupational safety and health. Also, there are simply higher priorities for government attention. Unions are more concerned with using their limited negotiating leverage for more bread-and-butter-oriented issues such as wages, fringe benefits, and the length of the work week.

Still, developing countries like Kenya are sensitized to occupational safety and health issues by the rapid dissemination of information that takes place in the world today. This creates pressure for at least token efforts at addressing workplace safety and health issues. There are numerous vehicles that facilitate this spread of information. Information about occupational safety and health issues is readily available in newspapers, journals, books, and even the electronic media. For example, news about the Union Carbide disaster in Bhopal, India spread almost as rapidly throughout the underdeveloped world as it did throughout the United States. International organizations, like the International Labor Office in which Kenyan officials are particularly active, and the World Health Organization, play a role in the dissemination of information about occupational safety and health. So too do international unions, or international meetings of unions, and multinational corporations, as we will see in the later chapters. And finally, individuals who receive training or experience abroad and then return to their country bring back with them knowledge about state-of-the-art safety and health practices. This dissemination of information and technology obviously has many advantages. In addition, it creates certain expectations that make it imperative that the government at least appear to be as concerned for the welfare of its citizens as are other governments.

In practice, the dismal economic conditions make the duplication of the best available safety and health conditions impossible in Kenya. Concern for occupational safety and health beyond a certain necessary minimum is a luxury that cannot be afforded in this country. Technical and professional expertise and other resources necessary to conduct research on new safety and health issues that are topics of strong current interest in the industrialized countries simply are not available here. Moreover, given the unemployment and poverty in Kenya, allowing enterprises autonomy in the safety and health arena seems like a reasonable compromise. This is readily apparent when one considers the alternatives to employment in industrial settings--usually unemployment or employment in the informal economy in which government safety and health standards do not apply.

Because of other priorities for labor and government, occupational safety and health relations are largely devoid of the various conflicts that are common in labor-management-government interactions in industrialized countries. Referring to Figure 4-1, management's behavior toward government regarding safety and health could be characterized as one of avoidance (neglect), that is, low assertiveness, and low cooperativeness. This also describes government's behavior toward management. Government, however, has the potential to engage in dominant behavior if it ever desired to do so. Management's behavior toward labor regarding safety and health could be plotted as a point with moderately high assertiveness and low cooperativeness. This is in the domination region of Figure 4-2. Labor's behavior toward management can be characterized as appeasing, that is, low assertiveness and high cooperativeness.

There is always the potential for conflict regarding safety and health to develop. Conflict could arise regarding some newly recognized hazard that labor, management, and government might favor handling in different ways. There is also the possibility that technical violations of safety and health standards could be used against an employer for reasons unrelated to safety and health. The threat of penalties could be used to coerce some action on the part of the employer desired by the government.

Further economic development in Kenya could make occupational safety and health a higher-priority issue. This could stem from greater numbers of occupational injuries and illnesses associated with further industrialization, or from greater economic prosperity. However, given the rapid increase in the labor force and the slow increase in the number of jobs, substantial improvement in economic conditions does not seem likely in the near future. Thus, only a disaster or a significant deterioration of occupational safety and health would seem likely to bring about increased attention and commitment of resources to these issues.

SUMMARY

This chapter has described occupational safety and health activities in the United Kingdom, Sweden, West Germany, Japan, and Kenya. In doing so, principal attention was paid to structural aspects of safety and health systems deriving from legislation, regulation, and (in some cases) negotiation. Cooperation and conflict among labor, management, and government pertaining to occupational safety and health have been highlighted. These were seen to be reflections of underlying conditions in these countries. In the next chapter, we will examine occupational safety performance in these countries in terms of occupational injury and fatality experiences, and we will see that these too are largely determined by national contexts.

Even without considering these injury/fatality statistics, it is obvious that there is not any one best way to manage and regulate occupational safety and health. As can be seen in Figures 4-1 and 4-2 there is considerable dispersion in managements' conflict-coping behaviors toward labor and toward government. The particular national contexts dictate what is feasible in terms of assertive/cooperative behaviors relative to occupational safety and health in these countries. Thus, high degrees of political influence by management in countries such as the United States, United Kingdom, West Germany, and Japan make it feasible for management in those countries to be assertive in their relations with government relative to occupational safety and health. Likewise, high levels of political influence by labor in the United Kingdom, West Germany, and Sweden are preconditions of labor assertiveness.

The national contexts also determine what is appropriate behavior in these relationships. Thus, it is obvious that although a dominant behavior by management toward labor might well be appropriate in Kenya, it is not likely to be so in industrialized countries, particularly where the workers are educated and knowledgeable of their rights. By the same token, it is unlikely that Swedish managers' conflict-coping behaviors toward labor and government, characterized by high levels of cooperativeness and relatively low levels of assertiveness, would work in the United States. The assertive behaviors of labor, management, and government are much too ingrained in the U.S. system to expect relationships appropriate in the Swedish context to be effective here.

The political volatility of occupational safety and health is usually assumed to be a negative feature of the system in the United States. It was with this in mind that the occupational safety and health systems of these other countries are considered. It is clear that there are a number of different factors in the various countries that contribute to the less volatile safety and health relationships that exist in these countries compared with the United States. The political stability of national governments in such countries as Japan and Sweden is one such factor. The lengthy traditions in regulating safety and health by established institutions, such as the TCAs in Germany and the inspectorates in the United Kingdom are also factors. So too are the extremely high regards in which the British and Japanese civil services are held and the political insulation of agencies in Sweden. Also, the organization of unions in Japan along company lines contributes to the labor-management harmony there. Finally, the variations of parliamentary government employed by all the nations considered, except the United States, contribute to the within-government political harmony that results in less volatility in occupational safety and health policies at the national level. Obviously, such elements as these are not readily transferable from one national context to another. Moreover, as we will see in subsequent chapters, some degree of conflict (or assertiveness in dealing with conflict) pertaining to occupational safety and health has certain beneficial effects.

In the next chapter, we will consider how the particular national circumstances discussed here affect national work injury experience and the statistics used to measure this experience. Following that, we will consider several case studies of multinational automotive companies that will allow us to see how the national occupational safety and health systems impact upon safety and health experiences at the corporate and plant levels.

NOTES

1. We use the term "occupational safety and health systems" to refer to the whole set of regulatory and managerial practices and labor-management-government relations relative to worker safety and health that are distinctive of individual countries.

2. The United Kingdom is made up of England, Scotland, Wales, and Northern Ireland. Great Britain is comprised of England, Scotland, and Wales only. The national statistical information provided here (which, for the most part, comes from the International Labor Office) is for the United Kingdom. However, as noted below, the discussion

of the occupational safety and health system applies only to Great Britain because Northern Ireland has a separate system. For the sake of simplicity, we will refer to the United Kingdom throughout this book.

3. There is, nevertheless, a certain degree of regional autonomy in the separate entities of England, Scotland, Wales, and Northern Ireland.

4. The source of these statistics is the Occupational Safety and Health Department of the Swedish Embassy in the United States Notably, this is the only embassy of the many contacted in this research (both of the U.S. and of foreign governments) to have such an office. In the other embassies, the labor attaché is the person typically responsible for occupational safety and health concerns although he/she may have little interest or knowledge in the subject.

5

NATIONAL WORK INJURY STATISTICS AND THEIR ECONOMIC/SOCIO-POLITICAL CONSTRUCTION

This study compares the occupational safety and health systems of selected countries. It also compares and contrasts the corporate- and plant-level safety and health activities of several automotive firms operating in these countries. One purpose of these comparisons is to make some assessments regarding whether or not there are any elements of the safety and health systems that can be beneficially transferred from country to country, from firm to firm, or even within firms. Naturally, then, one would like to determine which of the countries, corporations, and plants considered have the most effective safety and health systems, and the most obvious measures of effectiveness are work injury and illness rates.

In an ideal world (ideal at least from a researcher's perspective) such comparisons would be relatively straightforward, and we could recommend that the practices followed by the best performers be considered for adaptation elsewhere. This is, of course, not an ideal world, and these comparisons are extremely complex. Nevertheless, with sufficient care, we can gain some insight into the relative performance of these safety and health systems. We do so by comparing injury rates at the national level in this chapter and at the corporate and plant levels in following chapters. (Work illness rates are not considered due to the even greater comparability problems associated with them.) The national work injury comparisons considered here provide additional statistical background information to make later plant-to-plant and company-to-company comparisons of injury rates even more meaningful.

An important serendipitous result of attempts at comparisons of national work injury statistics is the finding that the injury statistics generated in individual countries are reflections of broad-based legal, social, economic, and political conditions within individual countries. This accounts for the complexity of the comparisons but it also makes this a very interesting exercise. In some ways these comparisons tell us more about the countries themselves than they do about their relative injury experiences.

This chapter is a revision of an earlier article that appeared as Wokutch, R. E. and McLaughlin, J. "The Socio-Political Context of Occupational Injuries." In *Research on Corporate Social Performance and Policy,* edited by L. E. Preston. Greenwich, CN: JAI Press, 1988, pp. 113-137.

COMPLICATING FACTORS

Difficulties in making international comparisons of work injury rates arise from a variety of factors, including: (1) different national and corporate definitions of a work injury; (2) different incentives and disincentives for having an incident counted as a work injury; (3) different methods by which injury statistics are collected that rely on "reported accidents" versus "compensated accidents" and that exclude certain employers on the basis of size or industrial sector; (4) different bases on which injury rates are calculated; (5) different political influences at national levels regarding the compiling and reporting of injury statistics; (6) different national traditions regarding injury reporting; (7) different statuses of industrial relations within countries and companies; (8) different distributions of the industrial composition of national work forces; and (9) different degrees of ethnic homogeneity of the national work forces.

Before considering the injury rate comparisons it is worth looking at the nature and source of the research difficulties more closely for two key reasons. First, to a great extent, they are endemic to any international research in the social sciences. National differences can make international research challenging but it is precisely because of these differences that such research is valuable. Reporting on the difficulties and the measures taken to address them may thus benefit other social scientists interested in international research.

Second, national differences in safety and health systems that lead to these difficulties tell us a great deal about the legal, social, economic, and political forces at work in these countries that are at the root of these differences. The different methods by which the safety and health systems are evaluated in various countries reflect differences in national value systems. So too do differences in national standards for occupational injury definitions, record keeping, and reporting.

Differences in work injury definitions and reporting procedures are not trivial matters. They have major impacts on reported injury statistics, making simple direct comparisons of the published national injury rates meaningless. They also are of such an intrinsic nature, stemming from fundamental national legal, social, economic, and political differences, that elimination of these injury definition differences is highly unlikely. The International Labour Organization has provided certain guidelines for compilation and reporting of work injury statistics through its publication *International Recommendations on Labour Statistics* (International Labour Office, 1976), but significant national differences persist. In most cases, occupational injury compensation is more generous to the worker (and more costly to the employer) than other forms of injury or work absence compensation. Thus, within countries, workers are likely to seek more inclusive work injury definitions and employers are likely to favor more restricted definitions.

Work Injury Definitions

Three primary differences in work injury definitions exist. One is related to the minimum *time* of a worker's incapacity to work before an incident is counted as a work injury. This time period ranges from one day (beyond the day of the injury) in the United States and Sweden, to three full days in Germany and the United Kingdom, to four full days in Japan for one of the several injury-reporting systems there. All things being equal, one would expect to find higher reported injury rates in countries such as the United States and Sweden, which have work incapacity criteria of shorter duration.

A second difference is the *degree* of work incapacity necessary before an incident is considered a work injury. Injuries that result in restricted work activity are counted as work injuries in some countries but not in others. Restricted work activity refers to a situation where a worker is able to report to work but is unable to perform all the duties of his/her job. Restricted work activity incidents are more likely to be considered work injuries where unions are powerful and where they have strict job definitions, such as in the United States. In countries such as Japan, where unions are less powerful and where there are less rigid job descriptions, such incidents are not usually considered work injuries. Again, all things being equal, the inclusion of restricted work activity injuries will increase the number of reported injuries.

Finally, an added difficulty in work injury definitions relates to the *location* in which the injury occurs. In some countries, such as Germany, injuries occurring on the way to and from work are considered work related. These *"Wegeunfälle"* accounted for more than 50 percent of work-related fatalities in Germany in some years. In Sweden, commuting accidents are also included in some reports of work injury statistics (but not in those reported here).

Incentives and Disincentives

National standards establishing the duration and extent of work incapacity necessary for an incident to be considered a work injury are set in the political arena. Thus, various political factors, including the power relations between labor and industry and their national political influence, have a bearing on these standards. The incapacity standards are also likely to be related to the various individual and corporate incentives and disincentives to have an incapacity to work classified as work or nonwork related. These incentives and disincentives also influence injury reporting practices given the different work injury definitions in the various countries. These represent the second source of difficulties in making international comparisons of injury statistics.

Injury Insurance Costs. There are significant differences among countries in the degree of financial incentive for a firm to keep injury rates low. In some countries, costs such as work injury insurance premiums fluctuate significantly as a result of injury experience. In other countries, there is little or no fluctuation. Even within countries there are differences. In Germany, the individual Trade Cooperative Associations that are the insurance carriers set the premiums for their corporate clients. In the United States, state law dictates what type of injury insurance is available: self-insurance, state workers' compensation insurance, and/or private workers' compensation insurance. The correlation between injury rates and payouts or premiums will vary between type of insurance, insurance carriers, and even insured firms of different sizes. The closest correlation is present where there is self-insurance.

Where there is a significant financial incentive to have low reported injury rates, there likely would be greater pressure on employees and managers to report fewer injuries. This pressure can take many forms. Workers can be encouraged to ignore minor injuries. An injured worker can be assigned to a different and very easy job so that the length of work incapacity criterion is not met for the incident to be considered a lost-time injury. This may occur legally in some situations and illegally in others. (Occasionally one hears stories such as a worker confined to a stretcher being assigned to count nails on the factory ceiling. This would, of course, be illegal in the United States.) Plant physicians can be encouraged to scrutinize carefully injury claims to weed out bogus ones. Physicians can also be pressured to consider the injury-recording implications of different medical treatments of an injury. Injury records can be falsified and legitimate injury claims can be denied, particularly when workers do not know their rights. Evidence of these practices was found in the various companies and countries considered in this research.

The differences in employer financial incentives do not occur by chance. They result from different emphases on the two principal purposes of work injury compensation programs: wage continuation and injury reduction. As discussed in the section on workers' compensation in the United States, these are both goals of the system here, but there is considerable question about whether the employer financial incentives are adequately structured to promote injury reduction. Such skepticism was a contributing factor in the passage of the OSH Act. In the other countries considered, different approaches to injury reduction are used more heavily than workers' compensation. Worker participation in safety and health, which is mandatory in Germany and Sweden, is one such alternative approach.

Workers Benefits. The financial incentives for employees to have a condition resulting in incapacity to work considered the result of a work accident (or illness) also vary among countries. They are related in large measure to the availability and comprehensiveness of medical coverage and wage replacement compensation for nonwork-related disabilities. In all the non-U.S. countries considered (save Kenya), some form of national health insurance exists, although coverage for work-related conditions may be more generous in some cases. There are considerable differences among countries in the availability of nonwork disability (wage replacement) payments and in how liberal these benefits are relative to compensation for work-related disabilities. Even *within* the United States there are a great many differences in both medical coverage (usually provided by companies) and wage replacement compensation (dependent on state workers' compensation laws, company policies, and social security guidelines).

The worker's incentive to have a condition considered work related often conflicts with the employer's incentive to have it not considered as such. Where such conflicts arise, the nature of the control system for validating/verifying a condition as work related can have a very important influence on the compensated and reported injury rates. The impact of control systems on reported injury rates is seen most clearly in the comparison of the reported injury rates of the Swedish and U.S. plants of Company Z in Chapter 8.

The distinction between an incapacity to work resulting from a work-related condition versus a nonwork-related condition is typically important in the United States. Medical coverage is generally more generous for work-related disabilities than nonwork-related ones. Also, the wage replacement compensation to workers for absences due to work injuries and illnesses is usually more liberal than for other absences, including those stemming from nonwork-related injuries and illnesses. In some cases, (nonwork-related) sickness and accident benefits of certain companies may be greater than workers' compensation benefits in the short run. However, these sickness and accident benefits typically do not provide coverage comparable to workers' compensation for long-term disabilities. In any event, an employee who anticipates possible long-term effects of an injury or illness is likely to want to have it classified as work related. In contrast, it is usually more costly to a firm if an employee qualifies for workers' compensation.

Swedish compensation systems are designed so that it would not make much difference to the worker or to the firm whether the incapacity to work resulted from a work-related accident or illness or from nonwork-related causes. Only after 90 days of incapacity is the wage replacement compensation for a work-related disability somewhat more favorable to the worker. There are also no significant differences in medical coverage. Moreover, compared to the United States, compensation for both work-related and nonwork-related incapacities are more favorable to Swedish workers.

A similar situation exists in Germany. The national health-insurance system is very comprehensive and generous. Also, although there is a relatively long (3-working-day) incapacity period required before an incident is considered a work injury, the liberal nonwork-related sickness and injury compensation mandated by the federal government makes this situation more palatable to labor. The work-related and nonwork-related disability compensations are roughly comparable except for long-term incapacities. There is a 546-day limit on compensation for nonwork-related disabilities, but benefits for work-related disabilities have no time limit.

As noted earlier, injuries occurring while commuting to and from work are considered work related in Germany and Sweden and therefore are compensated. Commuting injuries are not, however, considered work related in the United States, the United Kingdom, and Kenya. In Japan commuting injuries are covered under workers' compensation but these injuries are not reported in most published statistics. By contrast, commuting injuries account for a large proportion of reported and compensated work-related injuries in both Germany and Sweden. Compensating commuting injuries in the same way as other work-related injuries can be a significant advantage for covered workers in cases of long-term or permanent disabilities.

In Kenya, there is no national system providing medical coverage or wage replacement compensation for nonwork-related disabilities. The only such coverage or compensation in Kenya would be provided voluntarily by employers.

Methods of Data Collection

A third category of difficulties in making international comparisons of injury rates relates to different national methods of data collection. The International Labour Office (1982), which is the single best source for international work injury statistics, shows two broad statistical categories, reflecting two different national record-keeping approaches. "Reported accidents" are based on national compulsory injury reporting systems. "Compensated accidents," as the name implies, are derived from government or industry compensation data.

Reported Accidents. The national injury statistics most widely used in the United States are derived from establishment surveys conducted by the Bureau of Labor Statistics. Injuries compensated through state workers' compensation programs are tabulated on a national basis through the "supplementary data system." These data are not, however, considered to be very trustworthy, given the differences among the 50 state workers' compensation programs. Thus, the federal government's deferral to the states in the matter of workers' compensation in the United States necessitates an alternative record-keeping system. Greater centralization and standardization of workers' compensation in other countries allows for reliance on compensated injury data.

Compensated Accidents. The injury statistics available for Sweden, Germany, and the United Kingdom are derived from workers' compensation programs, as are certain work injury statistics for Japan. This means that whatever incentives there are for employers and employees to have or not to have an incapacity to work classified as a work injury will directly affect the injury statistics. In the United States the effect is indirect. There are different standards and record keeping and reporting requirements for OSHA and for state workers' compensation programs. However, the determination that an incapacity-to-work condition is work related for one system may influence its designation under the other system.

Size and Industrial Sector. Another difficulty in making international comparisons related to national methods of data collection arises from systematic differences in coverage in regard to employer size and industrial sectors included in each data-collection approach. In the United States, for example, nearly all private-sector establishments with 1 or more employees are covered in published injury statistics. One exception to this is agricultural-production establishments (i.e., farms), for which only those with 11 or more employees are covered. Also, published U.S. occupational *fatality* data generally exclude all establishments with 10 or fewer employees. The U.S. fatality data contained in this book, however, include unpublished data on establishments with 1 to 10 employees.

Japanese injury and fatality *rate* statistics come from industrial surveys that cover only establishments with 100 or more employees. Japanese statistics on the *numbers* of "casualties" (i.e., injuries resulting in 4 or more days absence from work) and fatalities come from workers' compensation data and a supplementary fatality reporting system. They cover virtually all private-sector establishments with 1 or more employees, but not the self-employed. Unlike the United States and Japan, Germany includes some self-employed individuals who may voluntarily join the workers' compensation programs from which injury data are derived. Obviously, the greater the number of excluded establishments is, the greater will be the number of uncounted injuries. Injury rates may also be artificially low because of poorer safety conditions in excluded establishments.

The exclusion of smaller establishments from certain Japanese injury statistics is consistent with the characterization of the Japanese economy as comprised of a dual labor market. One segment consists of the workers who enjoy the benefits of lifetime employment, usually from the larger corporations in Japan. The other segment consists of individuals who receive lower wages and bear the brunt of unemployment in economic downturns. This second segment is comprised largely of employees of small firms that subcontract from the large corporations. If the observation is correct that this second segment is not viewed as part of the mainstream of the economy, then it is reasonable to expect that there would not be as much concern about the injury experience in this segment.

In developing countries, the injury statistics are likely to suffer from even greater distortions than those reported by industrialized countries. In Kenya, for example, individual employers are permitted to set their own definitions of a work injury for record-keeping purposes and for reporting to the central government. Statistics on compensated injuries are, therefore, more reliable, especially since workers' compensation is mandatory for employers. However, because a large percentage of the population is self-employed and not covered by workers' compensation, even the compensated injury statistics would need to be viewed with caution. Because self-employed workers often work under conditions that we in the United States would consider grossly unsafe and intolerable, it is likely that work injury rates would be much higher than compensated injury data would suggest. Curiously, unlike the injury statistics published for other countries in the *1986 Year Book of Labour Statistics*, those for Kenya contain no indication of whether they are compensated or reported injuries (International Labour Office, 1986). It may be because the International Labour Organization is unsure which source of data is used or because both sources are used. Still, these statistics represent an improvement because Kenya had not reported any injury statistics to the International Labour Organization for a number of years prior to those published in the 1986 edition of the *Year Book of Labour Statistics*.

Bases for Injury Rate Calculations

The varying bases on which injury rates are computed constitute a fourth set of problems in making international comparisons. The *1986 Year Book of Labour Statistics* (International Labour Office, 1986) reports occupational injuries on four bases: (1) rates per 1,000 man-years of 300 days each; (2) rates per 1,000 wage earners (average numbers); (3) rates per 1,000 persons employed (average numbers); and (4) rates per 1,000,000 man-hours worked. To be meaningful, comparisons must be made on the same basis, but comparable data are not always available. Attempts to convert from one basis to another are complicated by the fact that workers in the countries considered vary widely in the number of hours and days worked.

Political Factors

A fifth factor complicating international comparisons of injury statistics is the political significance of these statistics within countries and among the international community of countries. It is obvious from Chapter 2 that different political factions within the United States attempt to use increases or decreases in reported injury rates to their political advantage. There are also transparent efforts to develop and/or use statistics related to safety and health activities that support certain preconceived ideas of various parties. OSHA's counting of "records inspections" and the criticism it generated are exemplary of this.

The Japanese, who have been accused by their trading partners of overworking and abusing their workers to gain advantage in trade, are very concerned with the international implications of safety and health statistics. Government, industry and, in some cases, even union officials see it as both a patriotic duty and a matter of self-interest to ensure that international visitors receive a favorable impression of the occupational safety and health system in Japan. It is felt that unfavorable reports on occupational safety and health conditions would result in greater pressures on Japan regarding international trade. This provides greater explanation for the exclusion of smaller Japanese firms from injury rate statistics.

The political influences on the compiling and reporting of work injury statistics in the United States and other industrialized countries in this study are, however, relatively minor compared with many other countries. In certain developing countries and countries with single-party political systems, there is a tendency to treat work injury statistics as state secrets. These statistics reflect upon the government in power and the nature of the economic/political system employed, and they affect the international status of the country. If injury statistics are available at all from countries with single-party political systems they must be viewed with great suspicion because there are likely to be no countervailing powers within these countries to ensure validity of the data. Prior to the recent publication of Kenya's injury statistics, all efforts to obtain information on national injury experience were rebuffed or ignored, even when requests came from U.S. diplomatic personnel in Kenya. No doubt, internal Kenyan political considerations and the temerity of government bureaucrats in a single-party state account for the reluctance to divulge this information.

National Traditions

A sixth category of difficulties in comparing national work injury rates relates to differences in cultures and values. Different national and even corporate traditions regarding injury reporting affect the available statistics. Some U.S. and Japanese employees do not report injuries out of a feeling of corporate loyalty, group consciousness, or even out of a sense of fear. In Japan, zero-accident campaigns, coupled with cultural traditions of loyalty and honor, cause underreporting of injuries. Having one work injury makes the zero-accident goal unattainable and is regarded as failing in one's responsibilities to the group. It brings dishonor and shame to the injured worker and his/her work group. Thus, there is a strong temptation not to report injuries. Both Swedish and German national cultures are renowned for engendering respect for authority and laws. This may deter deliberate underreporting of injuries. In general, different national attitudes toward group commitment, toward a goal of a low recorded injury rate in a firm, toward obeying the law, and even toward working with pain will influence the reported injury statistics.

Status of Industrial Relations

The reporting of injuries can be a political exercise influenced by the current state of labor-management relations or it can be intended to influence the status of these relations in the future. For a variety of reasons, workers could report minor injuries that they might otherwise ignore. They might be attempting to protest against conditions in the workplace; they might be trying to get back at management or a particular manager for some disliked action or policy completely unrelated to safety and health; or they might be attempting to gain bargaining leverage for future negotiations with management.

By the same token, management, for its own reasons, can put pressure on the medical staff and the safety and health staff to screen carefully reported injuries. They might perceive workers as lazy and view reports of minor injuries as efforts to get out of work; they might simply be callous toward the safety and welfare of their workers; or they might also be trying to establish a negotiating position. In addition, they can discourage workers directly from reporting such injuries in both subtle and not-so-subtle ways.

The nature of labor-management relations at the national level can also affect injury reporting particularly in countries where there are high degrees of labor solidarity and/or managerial solidarity. Thus, coordinated efforts to report injuries or to discourage injury reporting can result from labor-management discord at the national level.

Industrial Composition and Ethnic Homogeneity

Two final factors confounding comparisons from country to country relate to national work forces. These are different distributions of the industrial composition and different degrees of homogeneity of national work forces.

Industrial Composition. One would expect countries with relatively many workers in high-risk industrial sectors, such as mining, construction, and manufacturing, to have higher injury rates than ones in which the low-risk service sector is relatively dominant. Moreover, there are significant differences in risk, even *within* industrial sectors. For example, according to the National Safety Council (1982), the work injury incidence rate for all U.S. manufacturing firms in 1981 was 7.37 cases per 100 full-time workers. However, incidence rates within the manufacturing sector ranged from 3.11 cases per 100 full-time workers in aircraft and parts manufacturing to 31.64 cases per 100 full-time workers in ship and boat building and repair. Such a great difference in injury rates almost certainly is due to ship and boat building and repair being an inherently more dangerous industry than aircraft and parts manufacturing. Thus, all other things being equal, the reported work injury rates in a country like the United States, which has a relatively large aircraft industry, would likely be lower than the injury rates in a country like Sweden, which has a relatively large shipbuilding industry.

Ethnic Homogeneity. The homogeneity of the national work force is also likely to distort comparisons. Where there are large numbers of foreign workers one might expect higher injury rates. In many cases, foreign workers are not likely to speak the national language, are less educated, and do not know their safety and health rights. Also, foreign workers may be reluctant to resist dangerous work for fear of job loss and deportation or other negative consequences. Lee and Wrench (1980) found that foreign workers in the United Kingdom had higher injury rates because they were disproportionately represented in more hazardous jobs. On the other hand, the same factors that would lead to more actual injuries would lead to the underreporting of them. The expected greater accuracy of serious injury reporting is a factor that will be used to advantage in this research.

There is considerable variation in the ethnic homogeneity of the countries considered in this study. Germany has a large population of guest workers, primarily from southern Europe, especially Turkey and Italy. It is estimated that in 1978, there were 1.9 million foreign workers, accounting for 7.4 percent of the 25.2-million-worker labor force in Germany (Römer, 1979). In the United States there is a large but unknown number of undocumented foreign workers. It seems reasonable to assume that many injuries among undocumented workers here go unreported due to the workers' fear of being deported or due to pressure from the employer.

The United Kingdom, Sweden, and Japan, in that order, range from many to very few foreign workers. The United Kingdom has attracted large numbers of immigrants from former colonies such as India, Pakistan, and the West Indies since World War II. As of 1986, the United Kingdom had 2.4 million ethnic minorities constituting 4.3 percent of the population. Many of these minorities do speak English, however, as reflected by the fact that approximately 1 million of them are British born (British Information Services, 1987). Sweden, although more homogeneous, has attracted large numbers of immigrants from southern Europe in recent years in addition to Scandinavian immigrants who have been attracted to jobs in Sweden over a great many years. Even more recent has been a large influx of political refugees from the Middle East, who have not been assimilated as easily as earlier immigrants. Japan has the most homogeneous population of any industrialized nation in the world due to the tight control on immigration throughout its history. There are relatively few foreigners who have been allowed into Japan to work. Also, there is only a tiny population of illegal immigrant workers in Japan.

The predicted relationships between homogeneity of population and injuries would not apply to Kenya. For years Kenya has had moderate-sized minority populations of Arabs, Indians, and Europeans, and more recently it has attracted refugees from Ethiopia and other African countries. However, very few of these minorities work as laborers in industrial settings. Jobs in these settings are too highly prized to be allotted to African minorities unless ethnic Kenyans cannot fill them. In addition, Arabs and Indians have traditionally constituted a large percentage of the merchant class in Kenya. Europeans are heavily represented in managerial and professional occupations and as large landowners. None of these occupations are particularly hazardous.

NATIONAL WORK INJURY EXPERIENCES

Several steps have been taken to reduce the difficulties in international work injury experience comparisons stemming from the above factors. First, longitudinal injury statistics are provided in Table 5-1 to permit consideration of the trends in injury rates within these different countries over time. Second, *fatal* work injuries are considered in Table 5-2, eliminating the duration of work incapacity as a complicating factor in comparisons between countries. It also eliminates much of the uncertainty regarding whether the incident really is work related. In contrast, it is often difficult to distinguish whether a back or shoulder injury for example, occurred at work or at home. Third, to facilitate international comparisons, only the manufacturing sector is considered in Table 5-2. Further steps to enhance the comparability of fatality statistics are discussed after consideration of historical trends in injury experience.

Trends in Occupational Injury Rates

Table 5-1 provides longitudinal statistics on the numbers and rates of occupational injuries in each of the industrialized countries considered in this study. Because of the aforementioned differences, it is not possible to make meaningful comparisons between countries on these injury statistics. However, these statistics do shed some light on long-term trends in injury experience within countries. Still, there have been changes in record keeping and reporting that distort even these comparisons. Also, there have been changes in industrial composition over time. For the industrialized countries for which the less hazardous service sector has become more important over time, looking at economy-wide injury statistics exaggerates the reported declines in rates. Unfortunately, time series injury data were not available for the manufacturing sectors of most of these countries. (For the United Kingdom they were not available for the economy as a whole, so only manufacturing-sector injuries are represented for the United Kingdom in Table 5-1.)

These data must be interpreted in light of differences in the methods of data collection used by various countries. The United States provides a good example of the complexity of the injury-reporting system. A system of data collection is mandated under the 1970 Occupational Safety and Health Act. The system developed subsequent to this legislation was created by OSHA and the Bureau of Labor Statistics (BLS). It requires employees to keep records using a specified format. The BLS also conducts annual surveys to compute injury, illness, and fatality rates and compiles data from some state workers' compensation agencies and from surveys of injured workers. Other federal systems provide additional injury data through household interviews and hospital emergency-room admissions records (Office of Technology Assessment, 1985). With the exception of farms, where only establishments with 11 or more employees are covered, OSHA injury statistics cover all private-sector employers with one or more employees. Lost-workday cases occur when a worker is injured and unable to work for a day beyond the day of the injury. Also included among lost-workday cases are cases of restricted work activity (i.e., a worker is unable to perform his/her own job and is assigned to another job; the worker is unable to work at his/her own job *full time*; or the worker is unable to perform all the normally assigned activities of his/her own job). OSHA-recordable injuries not involving lost workdays or restricted work activity include injuries involving loss of consciousness or medical treatment other than first aid (the definition of which is itself quite complex).

The U.S. injury statistics reported in Table 5-1 show an increase from 3.3 lost-workday injuries per 100 full-time workers in 1973 to 4.2 in 1979, followed by a decline to 3.4 in 1983 and then an increase to 3.6 in 1984 and 1985. The overall change from 1973 to 1984 was a 9 percent increase in reported injury rates.

As indicated in Chapter 3, earlier statistics than those from 1973 are not comparable due to changes in injury definition and record keeping requirements. It was also noted there that the apparent increase in injury rates that occurred during the 1970s may be spurious. This issue has come up repeatedly in debates about the effectiveness of OSHA. It is suggested by some supporters of OSHA that significant underrecording of injuries occurred during the early years after the establishment of OSHA due to confusion. As people

TABLE 5-1
OCCUPATIONAL INJURY EXPERIENCE IN SIX COUNTRIES

	United States[1]		West Germany[2]		Sweden[3]	
	Number of Injuries[7] (1,000s)	Injuries per 100 Full-Time Workers[7]	Number of Injuries[8] (1,000s)	Injuries per 100 Full-Time Workers[8]	Number of Injuries[9] (1,000s)	Injuries per Million Hours Worked[9]
1950	N.A.	N.A.	45.257	.411	N.A.	N.A.
1955	N.A.	N.A.	56.776	.367	120.833	23.1
1956	N.A.	N.A.	N.A.	N.A.	119.997	22.9
1957	N.A.	N.A.	N.A.	N.A.	113.373	21.9
1958	N.A.	N.A.	N.A.	N.A.	109.428	21.1
1959	N.A.	N.A.	N.A.	N.A.	111.169	21.3
1960	N.A.	N.A.	57.490	.322	115.525	21.3
1961	N.A.	N.A.	N.A.	N.A.	119.200	22.2
1962	N.A.	N.A.	N.A.	N.A.	114.012	21.1
1963	N.A.	N.A.	N.A.	N.A.	113.646	20.5
1964	N.A.	N.A.	N.A.	N.A.	117.352	21.3
1965	N.A.	N.A.	56.880	.290	116.029	20.5
1966	N.A.	N.A.	N.A.	N.A.	111.499	19.6
1967	N.A.	N.A.	53.410	.280	122.855	21.9
1968	N.A.	N.A.	48.414	.249	122.772	22.2
1969	N.A.	N.A.	48.902	.248	123.204	22.0
1970	N.A.	N.A.	51.496	.263	121.824	21.1
1971	N.A.	N.A.	51.499	.258	112.532	19.6
1972	N.A.	N.A.	49.326	.246	107.220	18.9
1973	1,830.7	3.3	47.267	.233	106.689	18.7
1974	1,941.0	3.4	46.238	.232	115.722	20.2
1975	1,772.6	3.2	42.025	.218	115.423	20.1
1976	1,918.1	3.4	39.459	.205	110.018	19.0
1977	2,146.8	3.7	40.009	.209	115.208	19.8
1978	2,438.5	4.0	38.827	.200	122.906	21.6
1979	2,701.4	4.2	40.796	.206	112.880	21.9
1980	2,491.0	3.9	40.051	.198	107.029	20.6
1981	2,408.9	3.7	40.056	.199	97.871	18.8
1982	2,141.3	3.4	39.478	.201	95.945	18.8
1983	2,140.3	3.4	35.119	.182	95.589*	18.8
1984	2,449.7	3.6	34.749	.176	97.728*	N.A.
1985	2,484.7	3.6	34.431	.169	N.A.	N.A.

TABLE 5-1 (Continued)

	United Kingdom[4]		Japan[5]		Kenya[6]	
	Number of Injuries[10] (1,000s)	Injuries per 100 Workers[10]	Number of Injuries[11] (1,000s)	Injuries per Million Hours Worked[12]	Number of Injuries[13] (1,000s)	Injuries per 100 Workers[13]
1950	N.A.	N.A.	N.A.	N.A.	N.A.	N.A.
1955	N.A.	N.A.	N.A.	N.A.	N.A.	N.A.
1956	N.A.	N.A.	N.A.	N.A.	N.A.	N.A.
1957	N.A.	N.A.	N.A.	N.A.	N.A.	N.A.
1958	N.A.	N.A.	401.760	N.A.	N.A.	N.A.
1959	N.A.	N.A.	435.017	N.A.	N.A.	N.A.
1960	N.A.	N.A.	468.139	N.A.	N.A.	N.A.
1961	N.A.	N.A.	481.686	N.A.	N.A.	N.A.
1962	N.A.	N.A.	466.126	N.A.	N.A.	N.A.
1963	N.A.	N.A.	440.547	N.A.	N.A.	N.A.
1964	N.A.	N.A.	408.331	N.A.	N.A.	N.A.
1965	N.A.	N.A.	428.558	N.A.	N.A.	N.A.
1966	N.A.	N.A.	406.361	N.A.	N.A.	N.A.
1967	N.A.	N.A.	394.627	N.A.	N.A.	N.A.
1968	N.A.	N.A.	386.443	11.08	N.A.	N.A.
1969	N.A.	N.A.	382.642	10.37	N.A.	N.A.
1970	N.A.	N.A.	364.444	9.20	N.A.	N.A.
1971	204.935	3.54	337.421	8.14	N.A.	N.A.
1972	194.579	3.52	324.435	7.25	N.A.	N.A.
1973	209.699	3.71	387.742	6.67	N.A.	N.A.
1974	199.090	3.52	347.407	5.11	N.A.	N.A.
1975	184.300	3.5	322.322	4.77	N.A.	N.A.
1976	181.000	3.5	333.311	4.37	N.A.	N.A.
1977	187.900	3.6	345.293	4.32	N.A.	N.A.
1978	186.600	3.6	348.826	3.91	N.A.	N.A.
1979	268.500	3.3*	340.731	3.65	N.A.	N.A.
1980	133.300	2.9*	335.706	3.59	N.A.	N.A.
1981	4.218	.0708	312.844	3.23	5.540	.541
1982	4.193	.0746	294.319	2.98	5.086	.490
1983	4.349	.0793	278.623	3.03	4.719	.432
1984	4.729	.0874	271.884	2.77	4.730	.422
1985	N.A.	N.A.	257.240	2.52	5.277	.449

* = provisional data
[1] Sources: U.S. Department of Labor, Bureau of Labor Statistics. *Handbook of Labor Statistics, 1977.* Washington, D.C.: U.S. Government Printing Office, 1977; U.S. Department of Labor, Bureau of Labor Statistics. *Occupational Injuries and Illnesses in the United States by Industry.* Washington, D.C.: U.S. Government Printing Office, successive years.

TABLE 5-1 (Continued)

[2] Sources: Hauptverband der gewerblichen Berufsgennossen-schaften. *Arbertunfallstatistik für die Praxis, 1986.* Berlin: 1986.

[3] Sources: National Board of Occupational Safety and Health. *Occupational Injuries 1983.* Stockholm: Statistics Sweden, 1986; National Board of Occupational Safety and Health. *Occupational Injuries, 1984 Preliminary Report.* Stockholm: Statistics Sweden, 1985b.

[4] Sources: Health and Safety Executive. *Health and Safety Statistics.* London: Her Majesty's Stationery Office, successive years.

[5] Sources: Japan Institute of Labour. *Japan Industrial Relations Series: Industrial Safety and Health*, Series 9. Tokyo, 1982; Japan Industrial Safety and Health Association. *1985/86 Annual Report.* Tokyo, 1986.

[6] Source: International Labour Organization. *1987 Yearbook of Labour Statistics*, Geneva, Switzerland, 1987.

[7] Reported injuries: lost-workday cases. Coverage: private sector employers with 1 or more employees (11 or more employees in the case of farms).

[8] Compensated injuries, excluding commuting injuries, involving 3 or more days absence from work. Coverage: all employers and employees covered by trade cooperative association workers' compensation.

[9] Compensated injuries, excluding commuting injuries, involving one or more days absence from work beyond the day of the accident. Coverage: all employers and employees. Injuries and injury rates after 1977 are not fully comparable with those before 1977.

[10] Reported injuries involving 3 or more days absence from work up to 1980 and "fatal and major injuries" for 1981-83. Coverage: manufacturing industries. Figures exclude Northern Ireland.

[11] Compensated injuries: deaths and injuries resting eight or more days until 1973 and four or more days after 1973. Coverage: all private sector establishments with 1 or more employees, excluding seamen.

[12] Reported injuries: injuries which are significantly serious that the employee is unable to work within 24 hours of the end of the shift on which he/she was injured. Coverage: private sector establishments with 100 or more employers.

[13] Lost-workday cases. Coverage: private and public sector employees, not including the self-employed.

learned more about the injury-recording requirements, the number of reported injuries increased due to greater accuracy.

The injury statistics for West Germany reflect compensated injuries that involve three or more days of incapacity to work. Commuting injuries, though compensated, are not included in the statistics reported here. All employers and employees in Germany are covered by industrial injury insurance, so they are all included in these statistics. Entrepreneurs and other self-employed individuals may contract for voluntary coverage. Government workers, including the military, are covered under a separate workers' compensation system. These workers and the voluntarily covered self-employed are covered in the injury statistics reported in Table 5-1.

The West German injury statistics show a steady decline in reported injury rates during the 1950-85 time period. These declined a total of 59 percent from .411 injuries per 100 workers in 1950 to .169 in 1985. Interestingly, the rates of reduction of injury rates before and after the passage of the *Arbeitsicherheitsgesetz* are about the same. In the nine years prior to its passage in 1974, injury rates declined 20 percent from .290 injuries per 100 workers to .232. In the nine years following 1974, there was a decline of 22 percent from .232 to .182. This lends credence to the argument of critics of the *Arbeitsicherheitsgesetz* that the reduction in injury rates following its passage could be attributed to a general long-term trend rather than to the law itself.

Swedish occupational injury statistics are also derived from compensation records. The workers' compensation system in Sweden is comprehensive both in terms of the coverage of injuries and the coverage of the labor force. All injuries involving incapacity to work one day after the date of the accident are compensated under the workers' compensation system. Commuting injuries are also compensated, but they have been factored out of the statistics reported in Table 5-1. Participation in the workers' compensation system is compulsory for all employers, employees, and trainees in Sweden, including foreigners. Even members of the armed forces are included in this system.

Longitudinal comparisons of injury rates are affected by changes in the workers' compensation system, including injury reporting changes that took place in the last few years. However, the National Board of Occupational Safety and Health (1986) reports that there were no substantial changes in the rate of injuries reported during that period. Due to the record keeping changes that occurred in 1977, it is more enlightening to consider separately trends in injury rates that occurred up to that time from changes that took place since then.

According to the statistics reported here, injury rates in Sweden increased 1 percent from 19.6 injuries per million hours worked in 1971 to 19.8 in 1977. From 1977 to 1983 there was a 5 percent decline from 19.8 to 18.8 injuries per million hours worked. These statistics confirm the observation of the National Board of Occupational Safety and

Health (1986) that there has been little change in injury rates in recent years.

The United Kingdom provides a classic case study of the influence of legislation and legislated changes on reported injuries and injury rates. Industrial injury statistics for the United Kingdom are derived from mandatory reporting requirements that are undergoing significant changes during the 1980s. Injuries up to the year 1980 were reported under the provisions of various safety and health laws covering different sectors of the economy including the Factories Act of 1961, the Explosives Act of 1875, the Mines and Quarries Act of 1954, the Agriculture Act of 1956, the Mineral Workings Act of 1971, and the Office, Shop and Railway Premises Act of 1963.

The coverage of businesses in the United Kingdom provided by these laws was incomplete. As an indication of this, the Health and Safety Executive (1982) reported that there were 139 industrial deaths *voluntarily* reported in 1980 in addition to the 440 that were mandatorily reported under existing legislation. Because of such problems, the Notification of Accidents and Dangerous Occurrences Act of 1980 was passed to provide more uniform and comprehensive reporting coverage of injuries. The new reporting requirements did not, however, take effect until 1986. Thus, there are several years for which an interim reporting scheme is used. Statistics under this scheme are not comparable with either earlier or later statistics.

The injury statistics for the 1977-80 time period refer to injuries requiring three or more days of absence from work. This same definition is used under the new reporting regulations that took effect in 1986. However, for the 1981-83 time period on Table 5-1, only fatal and major injuries are reported.

Table 5-1 indicates that there was a decline in reported injuries from 1971 to 1980. During this time period, reported injuries in manufacturing declined 18 percent, from 3.54 per 100 employees to 2.9. The Health and Safety Executive (1982) cautions against placing excessive emphasis on this decline because 1980 was a recession year in the United Kingdom. The 1981-83 statistics show a substantial (23%) increase from .0708 to .0874 fatal and major injuries per 100 employees in all industries. The time period is too short and this change is too small to indicate any significant trend.

The Japanese statistics of the *number* of injuries reported in Table 5-1 come from workers' compensation data. Because virtually all nongovernment employees are covered by the workers' compensation system in Japan, a broad coverage of workers is represented in these statistics. Only self-employed workers and seamen are not accounted for in these statistics. Injury *rate* statistics come from responses to an annual survey and cover private-sector establishments with 100 or more employees. Injury statistics deriving from these two systems are used in different places for different purposes.

The statistics on number of injuries here are based on an injury definition that was modified in 1973, complicating longitudinal study of work injury experience. Prior to that time, an accident resulting in the inability to work for eight or more days was considered a work injury. Since then, injuries involving the inability to work for four or more days have been included. There has been a sharp decline over time in the number of injuries despite the more inclusive definition of later years and the growth of the work force.

There has also been a very impressive long-term decline in the reported *rate* of injuries in Japan, which is derived using yet another injury definition. In 1968 there were 11.08 injuries per million hours worked. By 1972, the year of passage of the Industrial Safety and Health Law, this rate had declined to 7.25, a drop of 35 percent from 1968. By 1985 the rate had fallen to 2.52 injuries per million hours worked, representing a decline of 77 percent over the 1968-85 time period. Interestingly, there was a decline of 40 percent in the four years following the 1972 law and a decline of 35 percent in the four years preceding it.

Still, as noted in the last chapter, there appears to be significant underreporting of injuries in Japan. It is likely that this underreporting has increased in recent years as companies and workers have tried to improve upon previous years' performances and as the zero-accident campaigns took effect after 1973. It is also noteworthy that, unlike with the United States, these statistics do not include days of restricted work activity. Moreover, it is said that, due to very flexible job descriptions in Japan, it is easier to transfer an injured worker to a less demanding job than it is in the United States.

The Kenyan injury statistics in Table 5-1 are derived from the *1987 Year Book of Labour Statistics* (International Labour Office, 1987). Injuries listed are those that involve lost workdays. No indication is given in these statistics as to the minimum period of work incapacity for an incident to qualify as a lost-workday injury, just as there is no indication of whether these are reported or compensated injuries. The 100-worker basis for the injury rate computation includes both part-time and full-time workers. Because there are so many part-time workers in Kenya this has the effect of understating the injury rate. Explicitly noted by the International Labour Office (1987) is that small rural establishments are not included in the employment figures. They are likely also not included in the injury figures. The years listed are the only ones for which injury data are available.

The injury statistics indicate that there has been a moderate decline in injury rates over the time period covered. The injury rate declined from .541 injuries per 100 workers in 1981 to .422 injuries per 100 workers in 1984. It then increased to .449 in 1985. This represents a 17 percent injury rate reduction over the entire 1981-85 time period. The time period for which injury statistics are available is too short to draw much from. Also, unlike the other countries considered here, there is *a priori* as much reason to expect that injury rates would be rising in Kenya due to industrialization as there would be to expect that they would be falling due to improved safety and health conditions.

In summary, there have been clear-cut declines in injury rates in two countries, Japan and West Germany, in recent years. The results are more ambiguous for the other three industrialized countries. In each of these other countries there have been recent changes in record-keeping practices that create distortions. Still, there are certain indications of long-term declines in the injury rates of these industrialized countries. The results are less certain for Kenya due to the limited availability of data.

NATIONAL WORK FATALITY EXPERIENCES

Due to the aforementioned difficulties, it is not possible to compare work injury experiences across countries with the data in Table 5-1. To make such comparisons we consider here a type of injury for which there should be relatively few definitional discrepancies between countries and time periods--worker fatalities. Fatalities are considered just within the industrial sector most relevant to this study--manufacturing--to further enhance comparability.

The fatality injury statistics reported in Table 5-2 come from the *1987 Year Book of Labour Statistics* (International Labour Office, 1987). Fatality rates are reported by the International Labour Office (1987) but these are not comparable. Fatality rates in Germany are given in terms of the number of fatalities per 1,000 work-years of 300 days each. For Japan, Sweden, and the United States, the rates are given per 1 million hours worked. For the United Kingdom fatality rates are given per 1,000 wage earners. Kenya also reported fatality rates in terms of fatalities per 1,000 workers for several years in the 1970s, but it no longer reports fatality rates. To compare manufacturing-industry occupational fatality rates directly, these have been calculated using the number of fatalities and the number of employees in this sector.

A further step taken to facilitate international comparisons was to factor out commuting fatalities that are included in the German fatality statistics reported to the International Labour Organization. A different source, *Arbeitsunfallstatistik für die Praxis* (Hauptverband der gewerblichen Berufsgenossenschaften, 1983, 1986), which lists commuting and at-work injuries separately, was used in this disaggregation. The proportions of commuting fatalities, as reported in *Arbeitsunfallstatistik für die Praxis*, were calculated for each of the years from 1977 to 1985. The worker fatality totals reported in the *1987 Year Book of Labour Statistics* were then reduced by these proportions, and these calculated work fatality totals are reported in Table 5-2. *Arbeitsunfallstatistik für die Praxis* data could not be used by themselves because there is no breakdown for manufacturing fatalities.

Table 5-2 shows considerable differences in the fatal work injury rates of the six countries considered. The United Kingdom had the lowest manufacturing-industry fatality rate with 2.10 fatalities per 100,000 workers. It was followed by Sweden (3.58), Japan (3.79), the United States (4.62), Germany (7.97), and Kenya (23.90). The only exceptions within years to the cumulative rankings across the years are 1981 and 1983, when Sweden and Japan switched positions in the rankings.

In addition to the data limitations noted above, several additional factors should be borne in mind when considering these comparisons. There were several years of missing data for these countries; 1979 and 1980 for Kenya, and 1985 for Sweden. Still this factor should not affect the rankings. Because fatality rates tend to decline over time, the inclusion of these missing data would likely increase the Kenyan fatality rate (the missing Kenyan data are from early years). They would also probably increase the difference between Swedish and Japanese fatality rates because the most recent year of Swedish data is missing. A factor operating in the opposite direction with respect to Swedish-Japanese comparisons is the relatively high number of hours worked by the Japanese. One would expect a greater likelihood of injuries for the more hours one works. Because we are considering the number of fatalities relative to the number of workers, rather than to the number of hours worked, this makes Japanese fatality rates appear higher. In contrast, Kenya, where there are large numbers of part-time workers, has relatively lower fatality rates on this basis than if an hours-worked basis were used.

There can be no doubt that any international comparison of injury or fatality rates is tenuous at best. However, the results here are provocative. The consistency of the rankings across the years provides some confidence in the direction, if not the magnitude, of differences in national manufacturing fatality rates. With but few exceptions, these rankings also conform with all-industry fatality rate rankings calculated for these countries but not reported in detail here. These fatality rates were calculated on three different bases: fatalities per 100,000 persons at risk, fatalities per 100,000 workers employed, and fatalities per 100,000 population.

This ordering or ranking of fatality rates by countries contains both expected and unexpected results. Kenya's bottom ranking is not at all surprising given its early stage of industrialization and the government's haphazard approach to the regulation of safety and health. The United Kingdom's relatively low fatality rates are, however, unexpected due to that country's reputation for destructive conflict between labor and management. The relatively high fatality rates of Germany are equally surprising, as is the magnitude of Japanese fatality rates. The safety and health system in Germany is highly regarded by those who are involved with it and those who have studied it. Both Japan and Germany have attracted considerable attention in recent years because of the reputedly congenial and successful labor-management relations in those countries.

Clearly, these data raise questions about whether some commonly held assumptions or elements of conventional wisdom about safety are really valid. The first of these is embodied in the frequently espoused aphorism that "safety pays," that is, that it is in both labor's and management's economic interest to reduce the rate of injuries. The United Kingdom is often viewed as a classic example of a national industrial failure. On virtually any measure of national economic performance since World War II, the United Kingdom fares very poorly in comparison with other industrialized nations. It is frequently referred to in the popular press for what it can tell us about policy failures. This dismal economic performance, coupled with its relatively good fatality rate performance, seems at odds with the "safety pays" slogan.

In contrast to the United Kingdom, Japan and Germany have been the industrial miracles of the Western world since World War II. After having their economies virtually destroyed during the war, they now have the third and fourth largest gross national products, respectively, in the world. Japan and, to a lesser extent in recent years, Germany have been showcases of successful economic and industrial policies. The policies and practices of their managers, particularly the Japanese, have received worldwide attention. Given the assumption of a positive relationship between economic/financial performance and occupational safety and health, one would anticipate better performances on fatality measures than those indicated in these two countries. One must, therefore, question the validity of this conventional wisdom.

Doubt is also cast on the universality of this assumption by within-country differences in occupational safety and health. In Japan especially, but in other countries as well, the working conditions are far safer and healthier in large firms than in small firms. The large firms undoubtedly have certain expertise and resources that are not available in small firms, thereby accounting for some of this disparity. It is probably the case that safety and health expenditures are more likely to be profitable in large firms. Large employers generally have more invested in equipment and in the training of their workers. The return on these investments would be jeopardized by accidents. They are also likely to be able to achieve certain economies of scale relative to safety and health expenditures in the hiring of specialists, the training of workers, and the safeguarding of machinery. In addition, highly visible large firms could potentially suffer more from adverse publicity than small firms should serious accidents occur. Small firms would apparently not find the financial incentives for safety and health activities as compelling as do the large firms.

Another element of conventional wisdom called into question by this analysis is that higher levels of cooperation between labor and management will invariably result in more effective safety and health

TABLE 5-2
FATAL WORK INJURY EXPERIENCE
FOR SIX COUNTRIES (MANUFACTURING)

	Number of Fatal Injuries[1,2]	Employment[3] (thousands)	Fatal Injuries per 100,000 Workers
United States			
1979	1,150	22,458	5.12
1980	1,170	21,942	5.33
1981	1,050	21,817	4.81
1982	870	20,286	4.29
1983	840	19,946	4.21
1984	870	20,995	4.14
1985	920	20,879	4.41
Average	981	21,189	4.62
West Germany			
1979	848	8,793	9.64
1980	789	8,842	8.92
1981	733	8,597	8.53
1982	650	8,321	7.81
1983	505	8,006	7.43
1984	560	7,933	7.06
1985	512	8,007	6.39
Average	670	8,357	7.97
Sweden			
1979	37	1,026	3.61
1980	40	1,025	3.90
1981	45	984	4.57
1982	29	946	3.07
1983	33	941	3.51
1984	27	953	2.83
1985	N.A.	N.A.	N.A.
Average	35	979	3.58
United Kingdom[4]			
1979	180	7,395	2.43
1980	151	7,081	2.13
1981	111	6,365	1.74
1982	129	6,005	2.15
1983	114	5,664	2.01
1984	126	5,579	2.26
1985	111	5,578	1.99
Average	132	6,238	2.10

TABLE 5-2 (Continued)

Japan			
1979	580	13,330	4.35
1980	582	13,670	4.26
1981	577	13,850	4.17
1982	549	13,800	3.98
1983	455	14,060	3.24
1984	476	14,380	3.31
1985	465	14,530	3.20
Average	526	13,946	3.79
Kenya			
1981	48	146.3	32.81
1982	37	146.8	25.20
1983	38	148.8	25.54
1984	30	153.2	19.58
1985	26	158.8	16.37
Average	36	150.8	23.90

N.A. = not available

Sources: International Labor Office. *Year Book of Labour Statistics.* Geneva, Switzerland, successive editions; Hauptverband der gewerblichen Berufsgenossenschaften. *Arbeitsunfallstatistik für die Praxis.* Berlin, successive editions; Bureau of Labor Statistics, unpublished statistics; and personal calculations.

[1] Comprehensiveness of coverage of fatalities varies across countries. For example, these unpublished U.S. fatality statistics, which come from the U.S. Bureau of Labor Statistics, are for private sector establishments with one or more employees (published data pertain to private sector establishments with 11 or more employees). Japanese fatality statistics include all establishments with one or more employees. German fatality data pertain to all establishments covered by workers' compensation, which is all private sector establishments with one or more employees and self-employed individuals who elect to purchase coverage.

[2] Reported accidents: U.S. and Japan. Compensated accidents: Germany, Sweden, and the United Kingdom. Fatal accidents commuting enroute to and from work are excluded.

[3] Employment statistics for the U.S., Sweden, and Japan are derived from labor force sample surveys and general household sample surveys. Employment statistics for West Germany and the United Kingdom are official government estimates based on surveys and other sources. All these employment statistics come from the *Year Book of Labour Statistics*, successive editions.

[4] Statistics include Northern Ireland.

performance. Again, the United Kingdom has one of the worst, if not *the* worst, reputations for cooperation among these parties for an industrialized nation. As we saw in Table 1-1, the rate of industrial disputes in the United Kingdom was far higher than in other countries considered in this study. This is certainly an indication of lack of cooperation between labor and management. In addition, safety and health issues are often the focus of labor-management disputes. As we will see, the British automotive plant of Company Y clearly has an approach to safety and health that is high in assertiveness and confrontation and low in cooperation between labor and management. And we have every reason to believe that this approach is typical of British industrial relations in general. Nevertheless, the United Kingdom has a relatively good industrial safety record, at least on the measures referred to here. It may be that labor's inclination to protest managements' actions, including those that threaten safety and health, has some benefits with respect to safety and health.

Both Germany and Japan are recognized for predominantly cooperative relationships between labor and management. The German safety and health system in particular is noted for the cooperative arrangements between labor and management as mandated by codetermination legislation. The Japanese safety and health system is also characterized by cooperative labor-management relations as recommended by the government. In research that is still underway, this system has been found to be highly effective for major Japanese employers but far less effective for their subcontractors. This may help explain the relative performance of Japan in this fatality rate comparison, but the German performance remains surprising.

Consideration of the relationship between the existence of labor-management cooperation and the questionable validity of the assumption that safety pays provides further clarification of these findings. As noted in the introduction, cooperation occurs when there is a confluence or linking of goals. If under certain conditions there is a conflict between management's goal of improving company financial performance and labor's goal of improving safety and health conditions, then cooperative approaches to safety and health are not likely to take place or to be effective. A more assertive approach would be necessary to improve safety and health under such conditions.

One final element of conventional wisdom appears worth questioning given the data on national worker fatality rates. That is, that cooperation between industry and government, like cooperation between labor and management, promotes safety and health. The United Kingdom and Sweden do, in general, conform to the assumed pattern. Sweden and, to a somewhat lesser extent, the United Kingdom have cooperative approaches to government regulation of industry in the safety and health field. As expected, they performed relatively well on fatality rate comparisons. However, the United States, which has a tradition of adversarial relations between government regulators and industry regarding occupational safety and health, fared better than one might expect on these fatality rate comparisons. Moreover, Japan and Germany are particularly noted for predominantly cooperative government-industry relations. Much of their notable economic success has been attributed to this. Their safety and health systems also emphasize cooperation between employers and government regulatory bodies. Despite this, Germany fared poorly on the worker fatality rate comparisons and Japan fared less well than one might expect.

The above analysis suggests ambiguous relationships between government-industry-labor cooperation on safety and health and injury rate performance. The lack of financial incentives for the firm to promote safety and health beyond a certain point explains some of this ambiguity. Also, some clarification of these results can be provided by considering safety and health relations in Japan and the United Kingdom in light of the two-dimensional view of conflict behaviors (i.e., assertiveness and cooperativeness) presented in Figure 1-1. As noted in Chapter 4, the conflict-coping behaviors utilized by labor and government in Japan are different for large firms than small firms. Labor and government regulators engage in behavior bordering on collaboration (high cooperativeness, moderate assertiveness) vis-à-vis the management of large firms. In contrast, labor in small firms engages in accommodative behavior (high cooperativeness, low assertiveness) toward management. Government regulators engage in avoiding behavior (low cooperativeness, low assertiveness). This low assertiveness (for the small firms) by both labor and government is not appropriate behavior for an important issue like occupational safety and health.

One could postulate then that Japanese management (in small firms), in the absence of assertive behavior by labor or government, and in the absence of financial incentives to do more, cuts corners on safety and health activities. One might also postulate that the more assertive labor force and more assertive government regulators in the United Kingdom bring about better safety and health conditions, at least for the small firms. This would be reflected in the national fatality statistics for Japan and the United Kingdom. Thus, this suggests that it is necessary to have an assertive labor force and regulatory system to coerce certain firms, especially small firms, to undertake activities that are not profitable from management's perspective.

Increased levels of cooperation among labor, management, and government have been assumed to be vital ingredients of any attempt to revise the social contract in the United States. It appears, however, that increased cooperation is useful only up to a point in improving occupational safety and health. This analysis suggests that assertiveness by labor, government, and management are also necessary for effective safety and health systems. We will take up these points again in the final chapter where we propose a contingency theory of cooperation and conflict regarding occupational safety and health.

In the following chapters we consider the safety and health activities of several multinational automotive companies. These will provide two more levels of analysis (corporate-level analysis and plant-level analysis) for examining occupational safety and health systems. The corporate- and plant-level analyses viewed in light of and taken together with the national-level analyses (Chapters 2, 4, and 5) and the industry-level analysis (Chapter 3) should provide us with more confidence in the findings and recommendations we discuss in Chapter 9.

6

WORKER SAFETY AND HEALTH IN COMPANY X

Our analysis of occupational safety and health issues has so far focused on national-level and industry-level issues. Analysis at these levels is obviously essential for gaining an understanding of the similarities and differences in approaches to dealing with workplace safety and health across nations and across industries. It is also necessary for making some assessment of the relative effectiveness of these approaches. Nevertheless, consideration of workplace safety and health at the corporate and plant levels is important for gaining a more thorough understanding of these issues. It allows us to see the influences of nation-specific and industry-specific factors in far greater detail. It also allows us to assess the degree of discretion available to managers and workers for dealing with workplace safety and health. In other words, we can judge the extent to which the choices they make regarding occupational safety and health are determined or constrained by the national and industrial environment in which they operate (i.e., environmental determinism is supported) and/or the extent to which these choices do make a difference in performance (i.e., the strategic choice perspective is supported). With these aims in mind, we proceed with our analysis of safety and health activities in Company X.

Company X is a large U.S.-based multinational automotive company operating in numerous countries. Although automotive operations account for the majority of its business, it has various nonautomotive subsidiaries as well. Three plants of Company X were studied in site visits: one in a midwestern industrial state of the United States, one in West Germany, and one in a developing country, Kenya. All three of these plants are unionized. The handling of safety and health in each of these plants is described in this chapter. Comparisons are made regarding safety and health inputs, work injury experience, and labor-management-government cooperation and conflict. The injury experience comparisons are, however, severely hampered by data deficiencies and different national work injury definitions. These data problems are themselves noteworthy for the problems they create in the multinational management of safety and health.

Before considering the safety and health operations in the individual plants of Company X, it is instructive to consider the structure and functioning of the occupational safety and health operations at the corporate level.

CORPORATE SAFETY AND HEALTH OPERATIONS

The Corporate Occupational Safety and Health Department is a component of the Industrial Relations Division of Company X. Its functions encompass a broad spectrum of occupational safety and health activities, including training, conducting safety and health surveys, consulting with divisional and plant safety and health personnel, assisting in labor-management negotiations on safety and health, record keeping, conducting research, and coordinating OSHA compliance.

The Occupational Safety and Health Department serves essentially a staff function at the corporate level; it also supports the safety and health staffs within the various divisions and individual plants. As we will see, the interactions of these safety and health managers with line managers, whose safety and health activities they must supervise, lead to classic examples of line-staff disputes described in management literature (Longenecker and Pringle, 1981).

The plant and division safety and health experts operate within two organizational hierarchies. They report directly to their superiors in their plant and division personnel departments, but they also have certain reporting obligations to division and corporate safety and health managers with respect to the safety and health function. The plant or division hierarchy is far more important to the safety and health experts. The plant or division manager has much more power to promote or retard the career of a safety and health expert than does that individual's superior in the safety and health hierarchy. For example, the safety and health expert's direct superior within the plant or division would determine raises and could promote or fire the expert. The possibility exists for advancing within the division or corporate safety and health hierarchy; however, given the relatively few division-level and corporate-level positions in safety and health, job openings there are scarce. It is far more likely for there to be an opportunity for advancement within the plant or division personnel or labor relations departments.

An interesting development occurred several years ago in Company X that illustrates the difficulties of safety and health professionals operating in this dual hierarchy. It also illustrates the difficulty of accurately assessing injury experience of a firm even within a country. In an effort to increase safety consciousness and reduce accidents at the plant level, the Occupational Safety and Health Department sent letters to the five plant managers whose plants had the lowest injury rates commending them on their performance and encouraging them to keep up the good work. Letters were also sent to the five plant managers with the highest injury rates, pointing out their poor rankings and urging increased efforts in the safety area. Copies of these letters were also forwarded to top management.

These letters precipitated an unexpectedly strong negative reaction in the company. Plant managers who were cited as having poor performance on the injury experience dimension were deeply concerned that these letters would adversely affect their careers. Not surprisingly, they questioned the comparability of injury rates at different plants. They argued that various plants are engaged in different production processes, use equipment and physical plants of different ages, and employ workers with different experience levels. The plant managers who fared poorly in these rankings also blamed the safety/health and medical personnel at the plants. When reports filtered back to headquarters that some of these low-ranking plant managers were planning to fire their safety/health and medical professionals, the Corporate Safety and Health Department intervened on the behalf of these professionals with top management. Of equal or greater concern were reports that at least one of these plant managers had simply ordered the safety/health and medical staff to see to it that the plant's injury record improved even if it meant falsifying the data. It was feared that this practice, which admittedly has been a problem in both the firm and industry, would increase because of the greater emphasis on reported injury rates. This would reduce the accuracy and usefulness of injury statistics. (Like other major auto firms, Company X received OSHA fines for underrecording work injuries in the 1986-87 time period, several years after this controversy.) Because of the adverse and largely unanticipated reactions to these letters to the top-ranking and bottom-ranking plant managers, it was decided that they would be discontinued and, at the same time, the emphasis on injury statistics and plant rankings was downplayed.

The evaluation of plant-level safety performance is now less formal. The data necessary to compare the injury statistics are still available in the company's computer system. Managers at the division and plant levels, including safety and health managers, have access to these data to determine how an individual plant or division is doing relative to the rest of the company. One could also search at the plant level for injury patterns regarding the type of injury, the type of job on which the injury occurred, the supervisor under which the injury occurred, the time of injury, and so on. This information could then be disseminated to the relevant supervisory personnel. This, however, is not being done on a systematic company-wide basis, and it is uncertain how many managers make use of this database. The current injury-reporting system is conceded to be somewhat deficient, and efforts are being made to upgrade it. Line managers currently have far more complete data on other performance dimensions such as production, quality, and cost control. This disparity in information is likely to contribute to the placement of greater emphasis on these other areas of performance.

Another factor influencing how much emphasis line managers place on safety and health is the degree to which their performance in this area affects their overall evaluation. Plant managers are reportedly evaluated on their safety and health performance by headquarters' management. However, it was unclear how much importance was attached to this dimension in deciding on raises, bonuses, and promotions. The general feeling, however, was that safety and health performance was not very important in the overall evaluation of managerial performance. Both management and labor safety and health professionals contended that the slogan "Safety is number one" (i.e., the most important thing) is a cliché that does not reflect true corporate priorities. They maintained that conflicts with other organizational goals often do occur and when they do, production, quality, and cost control usually take precedence over safety.

Paralleling developments in the industry as a whole, the status of staff performing the safety and health function within Company X has been upgraded in recent years. This elevation can be attributed both to the institution of OSHA and to the greater emphasis placed on occupational safety and health by unions in recent years. Formerly, a safety and health position was viewed as a dead-end job. Oftentimes, managers who were regarded as "deadwood" and who did not have any safety and health training were assigned to these positions. The thinking was that this was a way to keep someone on in the company where they would not do too much damage. Over time, it became clear that this approach to safety and health was not effective. Moreover, increased government and union involvement in safety and health increased the likelihood that poor performance in this area would have negative financial repercussions. As a result, there has been an upgrading of the professionalism and qualifications of the safety and health staff in recent years. Still, the status of the safety and health professionals lags behind that of other line and staff personnel at comparable levels.

International Activities

The Occupational Safety and Health Department engages in a number of international activities, including record keeping, training, and sharing of information pertaining to safety and health practices. Injury data from plants outside of the United States and Canada are collected by this department. However, because the injury definitions differ so widely from one country to another, these data have not been put to any meaningful use. The Occupational Safety and Health Department directed overseas safety managers to begin reporting injuries to corporate headquarters using the OSHA injury definition. Implementation of this directive was expected to be difficult because it requires double record keeping at most plants outside of the United States. These plants would continue to be required to report injuries to their respective national governments using nation-specific injury definitions. Moreover, implementation started off slowly. By the time this new reporting system was a year old, the corporate safety staff had not yet met with overseas safety managers to discuss reporting procedures. The injury-reporting forms also had no specific definitions to clarify injury categories such as "injuries involving restricted work activity," "injuries involving days away from work," and "injuries without lost workdays." Thus, it is likely that there are significant differences in what data are being recorded in these different categories of injuries. A European office to coordinate injury recording for operations there was planned, but the idea was subsequently abandoned.

Until the 1979-83 recession, the company sponsored international safety and health conferences that brought together safety and health personnel from around the world. At these conferences, safety and health personnel shared information on common problems and potential solutions. There was hope among the safety and health staff that these conferences would be resumed, but continuing budgetary constraints make this unlikely.

The staff of the Occupational Safety and Health Department periodically travel to overseas facilities. In this way, they can provide advice to overseas managers regarding the handling of safety and health issues, and they can effect a certain degree of international coordination. Still, visits to a specific plant are likely to be several--maybe many--years apart. Thus, the utility of this practice is questionable. There are no occupational safety and health training programs specifically targeted to managers assigned to international operations. Managers newly assigned overseas would have to take the initiative for preparing themselves to handle any additional safety and health responsibilities in their new positions.

In sum, occupational safety and health are handled in Company X primarily on a national basis with relatively little international coordination by the corporate headquarters. Further discussion of this is provided in the sections dealing with the West German and Kenyan plants.

Corporate Level Cooperation on Safety and Health

As noted in Chapter 3, the 1973 agreements between the auto companies and the UAW stipulated the establishment of national joint labor-management committees to deal with safety and health matters. At Company X, this committee consists of two management representatives from the Occupational Safety and Health Department and two union representatives.

The functions of this committee are spelled out in the "Memorandum of Understanding: Health and Safety" attached to the 1973 contract and contracts that were subsequently negotiated. Specified activities are:

1. Meeting at least quarterly

2. Reviewing Company X's safety and health operations and making recommendations when appropriate

3. Developing and overseeing the implementation of a safety and health training program for union members of the plant safety and health committees

4. Developing guidelines regarding employee safety and health training

5. Reviewing and analyzing federal, state, and local safety and health regulations that may be relevant to safety and health programs in the corporation

6. Reviewing serious and unusual safety and health situations that occur in plants and recommending solutions

7. Reviewing data supplied to OSHA on safety and health operations at the plants

8. Handling safety and health matters referred to the committee by the plant committees

This committee eventually developed into a far more effective vehicle for promoting safety and health than most labor and management officials had anticipated. Still, it took several years for the labor and management representatives on this committee to develop a satisfactory working relationship. A management participant characterized the first few years of this committee's operation as being quite confrontational. After that, a more cooperative relationship developed between labor and management. This cooperative spirit within the committee has been credited with paving the way for subsequent agreements that have improved safety and health operations through other joint labor-management endeavors. One notable example of this is the committee's sponsoring of independent research to resolve disputes about safety and health.

The 1984 UAW agreement with Company X established a research program to fund scientific research on safety and health hazards by independent scientists. This research program was funded over three years by $4 million set aside by the company. An advisory board of independent scientists provides technical input and oversight. The labor-management safety and health committee uses this research program to resolve disputes about safety and health issues. By all accounts, this is a significant improvement over previous practices. Formerly, labor and management cited existing research or funded new research that supported their preconceived notions about an issue, thereby only heightening the controversy.

Other provisions of the 1984 agreement reflect new priorities that go beyond the traditional concern with reducing accidents and resulting injuries. These include establishing a pilot ergonomics project in one plant; strengthening plant-level hazardous-materials control committees; permitting plant safety and health committees to consider safety and health issues related to planned changes in production processes or equipment and to planned construction of new facilities; increasing emphasis on preventive and diagnostic medicine within the plants; improving communications between the company and the UAW on matters of safety and health by means of computer links; upgrading safety and health training throughout the corporation; and improving communication about hazardous substances in anticipation of the then impending Hazard Communication Rule. All these activities, with the exception of the research that is funded separately by the corporation, are funded out of a corporate contribution of four cents per hour worked in the company.

Injury Experience

Data on injury experience at Company X provide evidence of the effectiveness of labor's and management's efforts to improve occupational safety and health at Company X. Diagram 6-1 plots the lost-workday case incidence rate (number of lost-workday injuries per 200,000 hours worked) of Company X (U.S. and Canadian operations only) for the years 1975-84. In light of the subsequent OSHA penalties for underrecording injuries at Company X, these data must be viewed with great caution. Still, there is no reason to believe that there has been any change in the relative degree of underrecording for the period of time covered. Thus, reported *changes* in injury experience may be more valid than reports of injury *levels* or rates.

This incidence rate for Company X declined dramatically from 2.86 lost-workday cases per 100 employees in 1975 to a low of .71 in 1981. This represents a 75 percent reduction in injuries in six years. From 1981 to 1984 the incidence rate increased slightly to .79. Because statistics prior to 1975 were calculated on a different basis, comparisons with that period are not possible. More recent statistics are also not available, but it is known that they are far higher in the postfine era due to increased conscientiousness in recording practices and possibly even overrecording to avoid future penalties.

It is interesting to speculate about why the incidence rate in 1975 was so high relative to the other years considered. Perhaps the cooperative agreement of 1973 had not yet produced any results. Also, sources in the industry noted that there were certain start-up costs associated with the institution of OSHA that were blamed for an increase in injuries. Safety managers were spending so much time figuring out how to comply with OSHA requirements that they were not able to devote their full attention to work on safety and health matters with which they had been traditionally concerned. Also, Company X officials contend that safety and health officials at the plant level initially were recording incidents as injuries that did not fit OSHA injury definitions, resulting in overrecording.

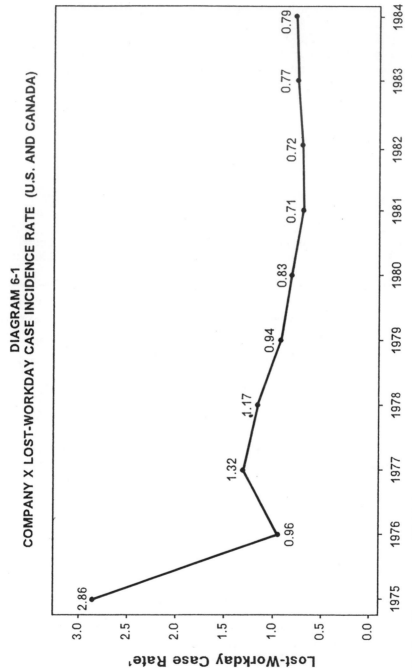

DIAGRAM 6-1
COMPANY X LOST-WORKDAY CASE INCIDENCE RATE (U.S. AND CANADA)

Lost-Workday Case Rate[1]

2.86
0.96
1.32
1.17
0.94
0.83
0.71
0.72
0.77
0.79

1975 1976 1977 1978 1979 1980 1981 1982 1983 1984

[1] Lost-workday cases per 100 full-time workers

Diagram 6-2 plots the lost-workday case incidence rate for the company for the years 1977-84 on the same graph with injury rates for the U.S. motor-vehicle industry and all U.S. industries. Internally collected Company X data are compared with National Safety Council data for these two sectors. (It should be noted that these injury data for all U.S. industries and for the motor-vehicle industry differ from the U.S. Bureau of Labor Statistics data considered in Chapter 3. The motor vehicle industry fares better in comparison with all industries using these data than it does if Bureau of Labor Statistics data are used.)

There are several trends worth noting in Diagram 6-2. First, Company X, like the motor-vehicle industry and the U.S. economy as a whole, experienced an overall decline in lost-workday cases, despite some fluctuations during this time period.

Second, Company X has improved its injury rate to a greater extent than the auto industry, which, in turn, has improved more than the economy as a whole. From 1977 to 1983, the lost-workday case rate for Company X declined 42 percent from 1.32 to .77. This compares quite favorably with the decline of 26 percent in the motor-vehicle industry (from 1.34 to .99) and the 11 percent decline for the U.S. economy (from 2.48 to 2.20) on this same measure during this time period.

Third, the fluctuations over time in the lost-workday injury rate at Company X follow expected patterns. There was a decline during the 1979-82 recession, followed by a rise since then. The U.S. economy as a whole also followed this general pattern. There was, however, a large increase in the lost-workday case incidence rate for the motor-vehicle industry in 1980. This may simply be a statistical aberration. The motor-vehicle industry and the all-industry data are based on responses to National Safety Council surveys. With the smaller sample of firms in the motor-vehicle industry than in the U.S. economy, results for a given year may be misleading. The motor-vehicle industry did have a lower injury rate than the U.S. economy as a whole for all the other years considered.

Further evidence of the long-term improvement in safety conditions at Company X is provided by examination of the company's experience with fatal injuries. Table 6-1 shows the number of fatalities for the years 1970-85 and the fatality rates for 1976-85. (Until 1980 these figures are for U.S. and Canadian operations combined; from 1980 onward, they are for U.S. operations only.) Although there have been significant fluctuations within this time period, it is evident that there has been a modest overall decline in the number of fatalities. From 1970 to 1979, during which time U.S. and Canadian statistics were combined, the number of fatalities decreased from 11 to 6. Still, in the year 1977, there was a high for the 1970-85 time period of 20 fatalities. From 1980 to 1985 the number of fatalities at U.S. plants declined from 9 to 4.

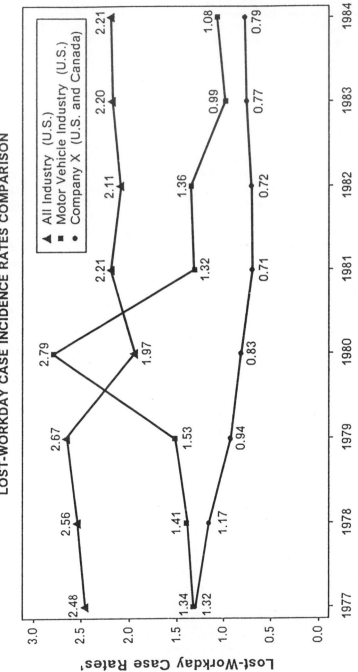

DIAGRAM 6-2
LOST-WORKDAY CASE INCIDENCE RATES COMPARISON

Source: Company X; "All Industry" data and "Motor Vehicle Industry" data come orginally from National Safety Council. *Work Injuries and Illness Rates.* Chicago, (successive editions).
[1] Lost-workday cases per 100 full-time workers

TABLE 6-1
COMPANY X FATALITIES AND FATALITY RATES

	Number of Fatalities	Fatality Rate Number of Fatalities per Million Hours Worked
1970	11 (U.S. & Canada)	N.A.
1971	8	N.A.
1972	10	N.A.
1973	11	N.A.
1974	13	N.A.
1975	3	N.A.
1976	7	0.006330 (U.S. & Canada)
1977	20	0.015955
1978	11	0.008555
1979	6	0.004720
1980	9 (U.S. only)[1]	0.009445 (U.S. only)[1]
1981	12	0.012120
1982	9	0.011185
1983	9	0.009725
1984	6	0.005860
1985	4	0.003675

N.A. = Not available
Source: Company X records
[1] From 1980 on, figures are for U.S. only. Prior to that, they are for U.S. and Canada combined.

There has also been great variability but a significant overall decline in the *rate* of fatal injuries. These can be seen even more clearly on Diagram 6-3. The fatality rate hit a peak of .015955 fatalities per million hours worked in 1977. The fatality rate reached a low of .003675 (for U.S. operations only) in 1985. Over the 1976-85 time period there was a decline in the fatality rate of 42 percent. It is interesting to note that the fatality rates did not follow the same pattern as the lost-workday injury rates, which fell during the recession and rose thereafter. This may be due to the fact that fatalities are such rare events that other factors may be more important than work pace in determining whether one or two more or less fatalities occur in a given year. Taken together, these data indicate a substantial safety improvement at Company X since 1975.

In the sections that follow, the safety and health operations of Company X plants located in three countries, the United States, West Germany, and Kenya, are considered. Descriptions of the plants themselves and broader issues in labor-management relations are provided to give a fuller context to the discussion.

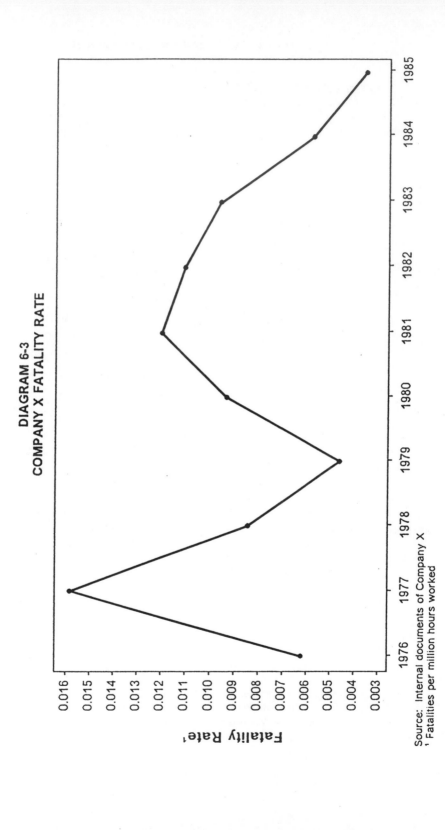

DIAGRAM 6-3
COMPANY X FATALITY RATE

Source: Internal documents of Company X
[1] Fatalities per million hours worked

COMPANY X: U.S. PLANT

The U.S. plant considered here is located in a midwestern industrial state, in the traditional heartland of the auto industry. It is old, built in 1945, and quite large. There are approximately 7,500 workers employed there--this was increased to 8,000 in 1985--assembling medium-weight multipurpose vehicles, pick-up trucks, and one-ton military vehicles, the design of which is based on that of the pick-up truck. There are two assembly lines operating for two shifts each. One line produces approximately 730 of the multipurpose vehicles per day and the other line produces approximately 900 of the pick-up trucks and military vehicles combined, for a total daily production of about 1,630 vehicles. The most recent quality audit at the plant for which we have data rated the assembled trucks at an average of 113 on a quality index in which 145 is a "perfect truck." Workers at this plant, like others in the U.S. auto industry, are well paid, earning about $13 an hour in wages (1985 figure).

This is an interesting plant in which to consider cooperation between labor and management on various issues, including safety and health, because the need for cooperation here is more acute than in most of the other plants visited. Because this plant is relatively old, it is not as efficient as newer plants, and it is also more hazardous. Many such plants have been closed by Company X in recent years, and such a development here is a concern of managers and workers alike. One of the lines will be discontinued because of a lack of competitiveness with similar models from other manufacturers. The plant is bidding, along with other Company X plants, for the right to build new vehicles that will enter production within the next few years. Winning one of these bids would likely mean maintaining current employment levels or even increasing employment; losing the bids could mean a substantial number of layoffs. The main criteria for assigning work on the new vehicles will be the productivity and quality records of the plants.

Labor-Management Relations

In many respects, the overall tone of the labor-management relations at this plant fits the confrontational stereotype to which the problems in the U.S. auto industry in recent years have been attributed. There are, however, some noteworthy exceptions.

This researcher heard accounts of serious tensions and even fist fights between and among workers and managers. Some disputes are, no doubt, unavoidable due to the large number of individuals at the plant, but these were more pronounced here than at any other automotive plant visited in this research. These disputes concerned various issues, such as personality differences, line-staff conflicts, and work practices, including those related to safety. Racial tension was also a factor in some conflicts--about 30 percent of the work force are minorities, most of whom are black.

Absenteeism. One indication of difficulty in labor-management relations is the high rate of absenteeism at the plant. Joint efforts by labor and management have, however, substantially reduced absenteeism and fostered general labor-management harmony. Nevertheless, absenteeism is still regarded as a serious problem. The handling of the absenteeism problem is representative of general labor-management relations at the plant, so this is considered in some detail.

Absenteeism rates for the years 1981-85 are provided in Table 6-2. Absenteeism data are broken down into three categories: total absenteeism, contractual absenteeism, and controllable absenteeism. Total absenteeism includes absenteeism for all reasons. Contractual absenteeism includes absenteeism for such reasons as vacations, jury duty, military leave, etc., which are allowable according to provisions in the company contract with the UAW. Controllable absenteeism refers to absenteeism from other causes, such as sickness, injury, or simply because a worker doesn't feel like working on a given day. As Table 6-2 indicates, both total absenteeism and total controllable absenteeism have been quite high at the plant. There was, however, a significant decline from 1981 to 1984. During this time period, controllable absenteeism went from a high of 17.4 percent in 1981 to a low of 8.9 percent in 1984. Total absenteeism, meanwhile, dropped from a high of 25.7 percent to a low of 14.0 percent in these same years. Both controllable and total absenteeism increased in 1985 to 10.5 percent and 16.2 percent, respectively.

TABLE 6-2
COMPANY X, U.S. PLANT ABSENTEEISM RATES
(HOURLY EMPLOYEES)

Year	1981	1982	1983	1984	1985
Total Contractual Absenteeism	8.3	6.4	4.8	5.1	5.7
Total Controllable Absenteeism	17.4	13.1	11.6	8.9	10.5
Total Absenteeism	25.7	19.5	16.4	14.0	16.2

Source: Company X, U.S. plant records

Workers who are absent for noncontractual reasons receive no wages for those days of absence. If certified sick or injured, they are usually eligible for sickness and accident benefits or workers' compensation, but workers absent without a valid excuse receive no direct payment whatsoever. Absent workers, however, traditionally have received benefits such as health-care coverage and vacations no matter how often they were absent. Benefits provided by the firm but unearned by the workers due to absenteeism cost the plant an estimated $20 million in 1984.

Several joint labor-management programs are responsible for at least some of the decrease in absenteeism during this 1980-85 time period. It is worth noting, though, that absenteeism decreased in all the plants studied during what was virtually a worldwide recession from 1980 to 1983. The 1985 increase in absenteeism reinforces the view that some of the previous decline was due to the recession. But the fact that 1985 absenteeism rates were still well below the 1981 levels is an indication that these programs have had an effect.

In 1982 a nationwide agreement was reached by Company X and the UAW to control absenteeism by focusing efforts on employees with excessive absenteeism. The thrust of the program is to provide benefits only to the extent that they are earned. Benefits covered include holidays, vacation pay, sickness and accident compensation, bereavement pay, and jury-duty pay. Employees with a 20 percent or greater absenteeism rate are subject to this benefit-reduction program.

A second approach to attendance control is an in-plant union-management program instituted in 1984 to work with excessively absent employees through a problem-solving orientation involving counseling and progressive discipline. This approach is based on the assumption that excessive absenteeism should be viewed as a symptom of some underlying problem rather than the problem itself. This underlying problem might be drug or alcohol abuse, marital or financial difficulties, or some other issue that must be dealt with before absenteeism can be meaningfully addressed. Such problems obviously have safety and health implications as well.

A third attendance-control program consists of a bonus system for rewarding workers with good attendance records. Workers earn a bonus of $50 for each quarter they have perfect attendance. Additional bonuses are provided if an employee has perfect attendance for three and for four consecutive quarters, such that an employee with a year's perfect attendance would receive a total of $500.

The efforts of labor and management to cooperate in reducing absenteeism are interesting in their own rights. They reflect a growing recognition by labor and management in the U.S. auto industry that cooperation is essential to meet the challenges of foreign competition. As such, this has a bearing on labor's and management's involvement in occupational safety and health.

Safety and Health Activities

The Safety Department at the plant consists of the safety manager and two safety and health representatives, one for each shift. Others involved with safety and health activities at the plant include various medical and clerical personnel, supervisors, foremen, union representatives, and the workers themselves. The duties of the Safety Department include training, record keeping, analyzing safety and health data, conducting safety inspections, providing safety and health reports to managers and workers, and conducting annual environmental surveys.

Supervisors are required to give five-minute safety talks monthly, but there is a very wide latitude and little supervision regarding how they conduct these. Some give regularly scheduled safety and health talks to all the workers under their jurisdiction. Most others are less structured in meeting this requirement. They may satisfy the requirement by walking around their department and talking with individual employees about relevant safety concerns. This could take just one or two minutes or significantly longer in unusual cases. Obviously, with such a flexible system, it is difficult to ensure compliance with this requirement.

Foremen and supervisors, in addition to labor representatives and the Safety Department staff, may inspect for hazards and receive complaints about hazards from workers. Upon learning about some hazardous condition, a foreman or supervisor can correct the problem him/herself or get someone from maintenance or another appropriate department to do the actual work. A union representative can go directly to the responsible foreman or supervisor and attempt to get the problem ironed out between them. As we will see below, what happens in practice is indicative of the status of the Safety Department.

Cooperation and Conflict

As in the rest of the industry, cooperative efforts to improve safety and health at this plant began with the 1973 UAW-auto industry contract. The operation of this agreement here provides some insight into how it has been implemented at the plant level.

The plant Safety Committee is comprised of two individuals--the plant safety manager and the union safety and health representative. The plant safety manager reports to the plant personnel director and his assistant directors. He is relatively young, and is professionally trained in the health and safety field, having taken college-level courses in this area. He was in his position for approximately 8 years as of 1985. The union safety and health representative has been with Company X for over 30 years and has been the representative to the Safety Committee since the committee was established in 1973. Prior to that time, he had worked on the assembly line and had been active in the UAW. As per the agreement, he was appointed to the safety and health representative position by the union and is paid by the company. When he was appointed, he did not have any expertise or experience in the safety and health field; since then he has received such training from both the company and the union. He participates in virtually all of the activities of the Safety Department through membership on the Safety Committee. Reflecting this, he is referred to as an "extra man" in the Safety Department.

Among the cooperative activities of the Safety Committee are a number of training programs. These include providing a one-hour safety and health orientation session for new employees formerly provided solely by management. The committee also provides lockout training, showing workers how to shut down malfunctioning machinery completely before they attempt to adjust or repair it. In accordance with the 1984 UAW agreement with Company X, the funds generated for safety and health training (i.e., the $.04 per hour provision) are being used initially to improve the training of foremen, supervisors, and other line personnel, along with union representatives, all of whom are in positions to influence the safety activities of other employees.

A basic problem underlying safety and health conflicts is that many line managers and workers apparently do not consider safety and health to be very important compared with their various other work concerns. In addition, they view safety and health as being principally the responsibility of union and management specialists. They see their own responsibilities in these areas as negligible. As an example of this, there is a tendency for line managers to refer any safety and health problem that arises to the Safety Committee rather than handling it themselves or calling the Maintenance Department as they are supposed to do. The Safety Committee reported receiving 2 to 3 work orders per day from supervisors requesting the correction of various safety/health problems. In addition, the committee reportedly receives between 8 and 12 informal requests to correct hazards each day. According to stated policy, the Safety Committee is supposed to be called in only when its special expertise is needed to advise how a problem should be solved; it should not be involved with routine problems.

Union representatives follow a similar pattern. There are over 30 union representatives in the plant and any of them should be able to handle all but the most technical safety and health problems. Still, they also tend to refer most safety and health matters to the union safety and health representative. A focus of safety and health training of line managers and union representatives is to encourage these individuals to take more responsibility for safety and health.

Other safety and health issues of concern at the plant include eye injuries and the use of safety glasses and other personal protective devices (discussed below), lockout procedures, the accumulation of potentially dangerous fumes from battery discharge, the rolling road test for assembled trucks, and the use by workers of small storage rooms underneath the assembly lines to take naps, play cards, or engage in other unauthorized activities. This last practice is dangerous because toxic fumes can collect in these enclosed spaces.

One concern that had been resolved was cited as an example of the cooperative orientation regarding safety. This was the practice of driving trucks before the primary brake was installed. The procedure for moving such vehicles was under negotiation for ten years before the agreement that they would only be pushed in order to reduce the risk of injury was finally reached. Although conceding that ten years was an excessively long time to resolve this issue, labor and management representatives to the Safety Committee were very pleased that an agreement had been reached, and they attributed this to the cooperative spirit in the committee.

The operation of the plant's Safety Committee is fascinating in terms of the degree of cooperation between the two committee members in the face of significant conflicts with others in the plant. The Safety Committee members occasionally find themselves in conflict with line managers/supervisors, workers, or even both groups at the same time. Conflicts with line managers and supervisors usually arise when there are disagreements over such factors as the appropriateness of certain work practices, the safety of certain equipment, or the enforcement of certain safety guidelines. Conflicts with workers often center on such practices as the use (or nonuse) of personal protective devices, including safety glasses and ear plugs. Various unsafe work practices can produce conflicts not only with the worker but also with his/her supervisor. These could occur if the supervisor either encourages or does not discourage such practices. Here again, the widespread abuse of the plant's policy on the use of safety glasses is an example. Also, in one department that has experienced an usually high incidence of lacerations, a policy of "no bare skin" is frequently ignored. Workers complain that the gloves they are supposed to wear are too hot, and supervisors, not wanting to "rock the boat" and possibly cause production problems, do not enforce the rules.

The management and union safety and health representatives have worked well together to promote safety and health in the plant in the face of these conflicts. They both noted that by working together as a team they had greater credibility and influence. Managers, for example, not only had to be concerned with the safety manager, but they also had to worry about potential problems with the union if they ignored a Safety Committee directive. Workers could, of course, also request an inspection from OSHA if a hazard were not corrected. Workers who ignored the Safety Committee faced the prospect of being disciplined by management, probably without support from the union.

Two specific examples were cited that indicate the tension that safety-related conflicts can produce. In one case, the union safety and health representative reported "punching out" a worker who was about to strike him with a six pack of beer cans because he resented being reprimanded for an unsafe act. In another case, the safety manager reported being accosted by the senior line manager in charge of the plant during a weekend. This occurred when the safety manager attempted to shut down some piece of machinery. This machinery had already caused one accident and he considered it to be unsafe. In this case, the line manager poked, pushed, and threatened the safety manager in an attempt to intimidate him from "red tagging" the machinery. The safety manager nevertheless shut down the machinery and dared the supervisor to remove the tag. The union safety and health representative in this case played a supportive and mediating role, walking the safety manager around the plant to give him a chance to cool down after this confrontation. In light of such conflicts, the safety manager and the union safety and health representative joked that training in karate would be useful for serving on the Safety Committee.

During an inspection undertaken for the benefit of this researcher and a senior manager in the Corporate Occupational Safety and Health Department, both the safety manager and the union safety and health representative alluded to being disliked by both production workers and managers: In their words, "Nobody wants to see us." They took turns dealing with distasteful tasks such as reprimanding workers for unsafe work practices, with the other playing a supportive role in case of trouble. In one instance, an employee was smoking a cigar while working in an area with combustible materials. Because the action was so stupid, as well as extremely dangerous, there was an element of black humor associated with it. The union safety and health representative convinced the safety manager to reprimand the individual, pleading, "I took care of the last one."

Despite the generally cooperative nature of the Safety Committee, both committee members have various constraints that limit how strongly they can promote safety and health within their own constituencies. As we have already pointed out, the safety manager operates in a dual hierarchy--within the plant and within the Corporate Safety and Health Department. The reward structure within the plant is likely to have more immediate and long-term bearing on the safety manager's career. Thus, the safety manager cannot afford to alienate the plant manager or his superiors within the Personnel Division in his efforts to further safety and health. He also has to be wary of fast-track upwardly mobile line managers.

The union safety and health representative is in a similar situation. He is appointed by the UAW, which has aggressively pursued improvements in occupational safety and health. Individual workers, however, often give priority to personal convenience over safety considerations, and they resent efforts to make them change their unsafe practices. The union safety and health representative is, no doubt, aware that if he pushed his fellow UAW members too hard and an excessive amount of criticism got back to UAW headquarters, the union leaders might feel forced to remove him from this position and send him back to work on the assembly line.

Workers have a right to union representation should they file a grievance regarding safety and health. Thus, the union safety and health representative must be available to help represent workers with a complaint about safety and health conditions in the plant or about their being disciplined on a safety and health matter. Clearly, supporting a worker who has violated some safety standard is a difficult task for the union safety and health representative. If, however, the discipline is arbitrary or inconsistent, there is justification for opposing it.

Injury Experience in the U.S. Plant

There was a dramatic decrease in the number and rate of injuries at the plant in the seven years for which data are available. This can be clearly seen in Diagrams 6-4 and 6-5. In 1977 there were almost 550 recordable injuries, resulting in an injury incidence rate of close to 6.5 recordable injuries per 100 employees. (Note that these figures cannot be compared directly with the lost-workday incidence rates for all of Company X reported in Diagrams 6-1 and 6-2, because recordable injuries include injuries not involving lost workdays.) The number of recordable injuries reached a low in 1980 of approximately 150, with a corresponding low rate of approximately 2.70 recordable injuries per 100 workers in 1982. Since these low points, there have been slight rises in the numbers and rates of injuries. By 1985 the number of recordable injuries had risen to 287 and the injury rate had risen to approximately 3.6 cases per 100 employees. These were still far below 1977 levels on both dimensions. There has been only one work fatality at this plant since 1970. Comparisons of fatality rates with those at the West German plant are contained at the end of this chapter.

These declines and subsequent rises in numbers and rates of injuries follow the same pattern as production rates during the recession and later recovery. Still, there are two reasons to believe that there has been a general long-term decline in both of these measures. First, the numbers and rates of injuries started declining substantially prior to the recession. And, second, since the recovery, these measures have not risen to anywhere near the pre-recession levels.

Safety officials and line managers at the plant believe that most of the attainable reduction in injury rates has already been achieved. Thus, the focus is now on maintaining the improved safety and health conditions at the plant and achieving incremental reductions in the numbers and rates of injuries. This aim is demonstrated in the goal-setting exercise in the safety area. The plant safety manager provided the department heads with data on the injury experience in

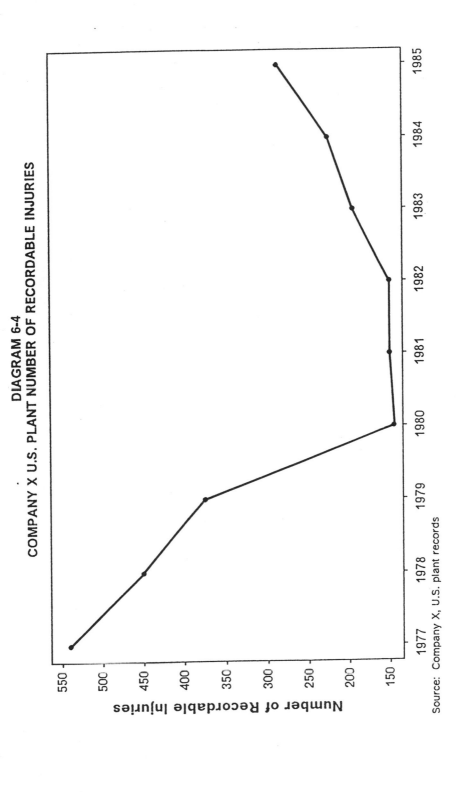

DIAGRAM 6-4
COMPANY X U.S. PLANT NUMBER OF RECORDABLE INJURIES

Number of Recordable Injuries

Source: Company X, U.S. plant records

DIAGRAM 6-5

COMPANY X U.S. PLANT RATE OF RECORDABLE INJURIES

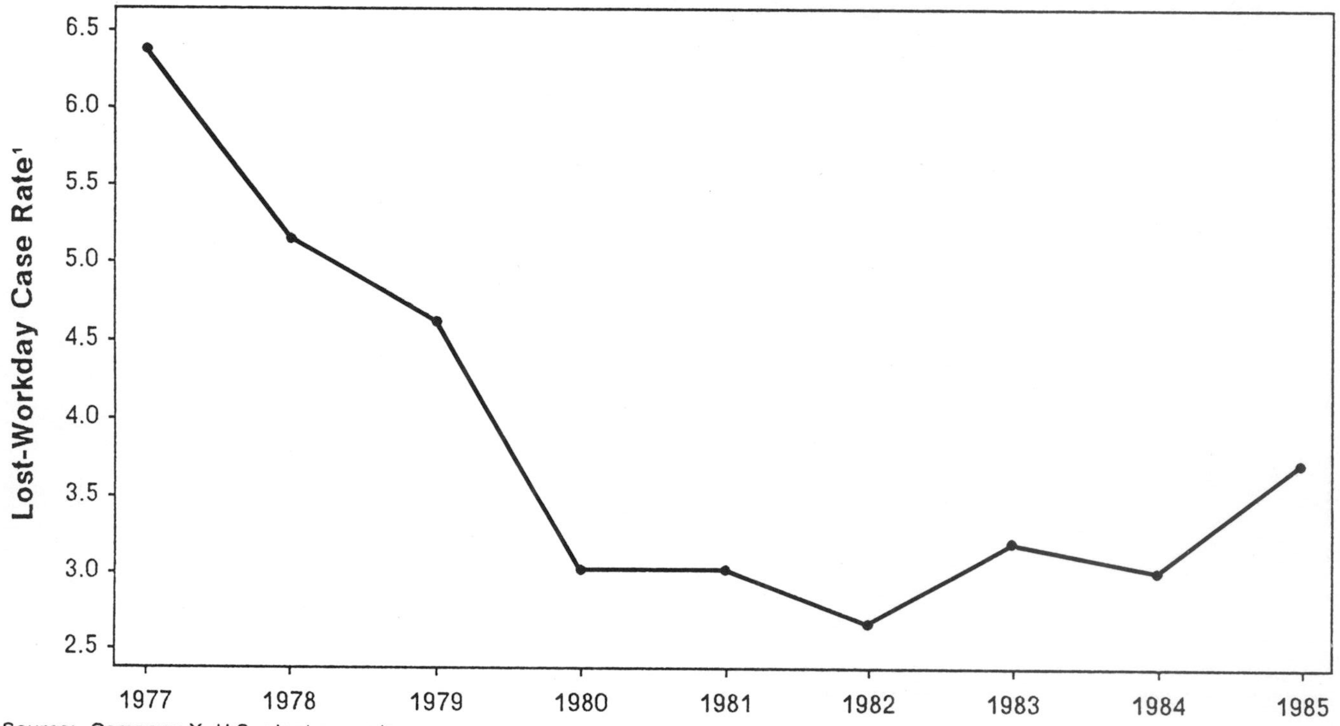

Source: Company X, U.S. plant records
[1] Lost-workday cases per 100 full-time employees

their respective departments and in the plant as a whole in 1984 and asked them to set a goal to equal or reduce the injury rate for their departments in 1985.

A report (Table 6-3) prepared by the Safety Department and circulated to supervisory and managerial personnel contains goal- and performance-related information for the plant. It shows the number of injuries in each department for 1984 and 1985. It also shows the departmental and plantwide goals for 1985, the difference between 1985 goals and performance, and 1986 predictions. The 1985 departmental "goals" were set by individual departmental supervisors and the overall plant goal was set by the plant safety manager. The 1986 "predictions" were also set by the plant safety manager.

For those departments that reported 1985 goals, the aggregate goal for 1985 represented a 32 percent reduction in the number of injuries compared with the 1984 performance. The plant-wide goal represented a 10 percent reduction. There was considerable variation in how ambitious the departmental supervisors were in setting goals. Some sought to match their 1984 performance and others sought to reduce injuries by more than 50 percent. With higher production levels and some problems adjusting to the addition of 500 new employees plantwide in 1985, few departments met their goals. Only 4 of 22 departments reporting had fewer or equal numbers of injuries than targeted by their goals; the remaining 18 had greater numbers of injuries. For the plant as a whole, the 287 injuries exceeded the goal level of 205 by 40 percent, causing some concern.

As mentioned above, one problem area at this plant is eye injuries. The number of eye injuries increased dramatically from 342 in 1980 to 1,056 in 1984, apparently because of worker resistance to wearing eye protection. The union had previously negotiated an agreement to allow workers to work without safety glasses in certain areas, but this agreement was nullified by OSHA. The approach to dealing with this problem now is to try to encourage supervisors to enforce rules requiring the use of protective devices more strictly. More recent statistics indicate this has had some success. The number of eye injuries declined by 12 percent (108 to 95) from January 1984 to January 1985. This occurred although there was an 11 percent increase in employment from 7,250 to 8,050. Despite these recent improvements, both the plant safety manager and the union safety and health representative expressed concern and some pessimism regarding eye injuries. The union safety and health representative was in a particularly difficult position because of the negative feelings of his fellow union members about wearing protective glasses. He could not afford to pursue worker reprimands for safety violations too vigorously nor could he refuse to assist disciplined workers in grievance procedures without risking loss of support from his union brothers and sisters and ultimately his position as safety and health representative.

Overall, it is obvious that much progress has been made in dealing with safety and health at this plant despite significant

TABLE 6-3
COMPANY X, U.S. PLANT INJURY PERFORMANCE 1984, 1985
AND GOALS/PREDICTIONS 1985, 1986

Dept.	Shift	Actual Injuries 1984	Actual Injuries 1985	1985 Goal	Diff.: 85 Actual vs. 85 Goal	1986 Prediction	
17-29	(1)	17	20	14	+6	(1)	15
	(2)	14	31	N.A.	---	(2)	20
18	(1)	5	6	2	+4	(1)	4
	(2)	7	9	3	+6	(2)	10
19	(1)	10	9	5	+4	(1)	6
	(2)	10	20	5	+15	(2)	12
7-28	(1)	16	18	12	+6	(1)	12
	(2)	17	26	N.A.	---	(2)	18
8	(1)	10	6	5	+1	(1)	4
	(2)	13	10	6	+4	(2)	8
9	(1)	12	20	8	+12	(1)	10
	(2)	17	20	8	+7	(2)	15
Paint Line 1	(1)	N.A.	5	N.A.	N.A.	(1)	4
Line 1	(2)	N.A.	8	N.A.	N.A.	(2)	6
Line 2	(1)	N.A.	2	N.A.	N.A.	(1)	4
Line 2	(2)	N.A.	5	N.A.	N.A.	(2)	4
Insp.	(1)	5	5	5	EVEN	(1)	3
	(2)	5	7	5	+2	(2)	5
Mater.	(1)	8	10	6	+4	(1)	6
	(2)	4	8	3	+5	(2)	4
Sanit.	(1)	2	2	1.8	-.2	(1)	1
	(2)	3	2	2.7	-.7	(2)	1
	(3)	3	4	2.7	+1.3	(3)	2
Maint.	(1)	11	11	9.9	+1.1	(1)	8
	(2)	4	6	3.6	+2.4	(2)	4
	(3)	9	5	8.1	-3.1	(3)	3
P. Eng.		1	4	1	+3		2
Powerhouse		1	3	0	+3		0
F.I.R.		N.A.	2	N.A.	N.A.		0
A.R.C.		N.A.	3	N.A.	N.A.		0
Total		228	287	205[1]	+82		191[2]

N.A. = Not available
Source: Company X, U.S. plant records
[1] This figure is a plant-wide goal. It is not the sum of the individual departmental goals.
[2] This figure is the sum of the departmental predictions.

obstacles. Most notable among these obstacles are ingrained attitudes and work practices of workers and managers that conflict with safety and health. These continue to make occupational safety and health a much more contentious issue at this plant than need be the case, and, in the process, safety and health performance is undermined. The improvements in conditions at the plant are largely attributable to the UAW-Company X agreements to cooperate on safety and health and the way in which they have been implemented at this plant.

COMPANY X: WEST GERMAN PLANT

The West German plant is the oldest and largest of the three Company X plants visited. It has been in operation for more than 50 years. Originally it was the flagship plant of a West German auto company that was acquired by Company X prior to World War II. Administrative headquarters of this German company adjoin this plant and now serve as the headquarters of Company X's West German operations. For the sake of brevity, we shall refer to this West German subsidiary of Company X as Company X_G.

The West German facility is extremely large. (The precise number of workers is withheld for the sake of confidentiality.) About 20 percent to 25 percent of the employees are foreign guest workers, largely from Turkey and Italy. The auto assembly operation at this facility has production of between 1,000 and 1,500 passenger cars per day. There is only one production shift, but there is a second shift that does maintenance work.

Workers at this plant are well paid. The 1983 wage for the production workers was between 18 and 20 Deutschemarks per hour (about $7 to $8) at existing exchange rates. This means that the workers here are much better paid than Company X workers in Kenya, but not quite so well paid as workers in the United States. Subsequent depreciation of the dollar relative to the Deutschemark substantially increased the dollar equivalent of the German workers' compensation to only slightly below that of U.S. workers. Also, fringe benefits typically are more generous in Germany than in the United States. Because the per capita income in Germany is somewhat lower than that in the United States, the relative standing of the German auto workers with respect to the distribution of income in their country is about the same as that for their U.S. counterparts.

The workers at this site are not all engaged in auto assembly operations. Some, for example, are engaged in foundry work that supports the auto assembly activities; others are headquarters personnel. The focus of our concern here, however, is on the auto assembly operations.

Labor-Management Relations

Labor-management relations at this plant are greatly influenced by the mandated codetermination framework described earlier. As required by this framework, there is worker participation at the national level through worker membership on the board of directors, at the plant level through membership on a works council, and at the shop-floor level through the activities of works-council members and safety stewards.

There is evidence that worker participation at this plant has both cooperative and conflictual aspects. This is apparent in the handling of absenteeism and worker safety and health at the plant. We will first consider absenteeism, an issue dominated by conflict, and then proceed to consider safety and health, which entails much more cooperation between labor and management.

Absenteeism. Absenteeism is considered a serious problem at the plant, and efforts to curb it have generated much controversy. Absenteeism rates for sickness and unknown causes over an 11-year period fluctuated considerably, following the strength of the national economy. This absenteeism rate was 10.8 percent in 1972; it declined to 6.4 percent in 1974, a recession year. It rose to 12.9 percent by 1979, declined again to 8.1 percent in 1980, another recession year, and rose again to 9.6 percent in 1983.

Several efforts by management to reduce absenteeism met with considerable resistance by labor in the works council and through legal challenges and adverse publicity in the media. Two early efforts to reduce absenteeism were neither controversial nor particularly effective. Supervisory and medical personnel were asked to determine if there were unpleasant or unhealthy conditions in the workplace that were causing absenteeism and that could be altered. Also, they were asked to talk with workers who had high rates of absenteeism. Because this latter approach was unsystematic, management proposed to tie in the time clocks to the plant computer system. This would then permit easy identification of workers with high absenteeism records or suspicious absenteeism patterns. The works council strongly objected to this proposal. It was viewed by workers as being dehumanizing. Allusions were made to the Orwellian specter of machines monitoring human behavior. Newspapers and periodicals picked up this theme, and the proposal was eventually dropped by management to end the controversy.

Another absenteeism control measure generated even more controversy. This was the practice of checking up at home on workers who called in sick. Workers who were found to be faking disability were subject to disciplinary action. Writers and editorial cartoonists had a field day commenting on this practice. It was portrayed in publications sympathetic to labor as a *Krankenjagd,* that is, a hunt of the sick. Employers were accused of hiring investigators to stalk and harass legitimately disabled employees. Publications sympathetic to management portrayed healthy workers faking illnesses or injuries to get excused from work and collect sickness or accident benefits. This practice of checking up on workers was challenged in the federal labor courts on the grounds that it was an invasion of privacy.

As this suggests, there was relatively little cooperation between labor and management on controlling absenteeism. Labor and management viewed this as a win/lose disagreement. Labor felt that efforts to reduce absenteeism were threatening the health of the workers and were dehumanizing. Management felt that labor representatives were obstructing progress on this issue. They referred to works-council members as "left wing" in their approach, and they believed their position would "kill the goose that lays the golden eggs."

Safety and Health Activities

The safety and health activities at the West German plant are largely structured to conform with regulatory requirements specified by the national government, the state government, and the trade cooperative association (TCA) for the metal-working industry. The program aspects influenced by these regulations include the number of safety engineers employed at the plant and their responsibilities, and the existence, composition, and responsibilities of a plant safety committee. The safety training required for employees in general and for safety specialists and line managers in particular are also dictated by these regulations.

The safety structure at this plant is unique due to its location in the same complex as Company X_G headquarters. The safety manager for Company X_G is also the safety director for this plant. Other safety directors in Company X_G report to him and to their immediate superiors, that is, plant personnel directors within their local plants. The safety manager reports to the plant personnel director, who also fills a dual role as Company X_G personnel director. The typical structure in Germany (and that specified by the ASiG) has the safety manager reporting directly to the plant manager. Company X_G's structure, which is modeled after Company X's structure in the United States, is common for German subsidiaries of U.S. firms. As dictated by national safety and health legislation, the works council is consulted regarding the appointment of the personnel directors and safety managers within Company X_G.

Safety regulations specify the number of safety engineers to be provided by the plant based on the number of employees and the hazardousness of their work. Workers at this plant are categorized into three different job hazard categories that require different amounts of safety-engineer time per employee. As a result of the large size of the plant, there are quite a few safety engineers here. Others who are involved with safety and health include the medical personnel, works-council members, and safety stewards, also called safety helpers.

The number of safety stewards is also dependent on the number of employees. Management is required to appoint one for every 70 employees, so there are numerous safety stewards at this plant. These safety stewards are described as providing extra sets of eyes and ears for the foremen in locating hazards. They are viewed as being particularly effective in communicating safety and health concerns to workers because they are at the same level of the organizational hierarchy. Additionally, they receive complaints from other employees that they direct to the respective foreman. If not satisfied with the foreman's response, they may direct complaints through the line management hierarchy and/or through the Safety Department hierarchy. Still dissatisfied employees can take their complaints to the plant Safety Committee and works council.

The ultimate authority and responsibility for safety and health within the plant was said to rest with line management; safety personnel work in a largely advisory capacity. Safety Department personnel function on three levels. The first level involves considering safety and health implications of new machinery and production processes and specifying how these should operate. The second level of activity involves analyzing injuries that occur to determine the cause(s) and recommending actions to prevent recurrence. The third level consists of involvement with various in-plant training and consulting activities and attendance at meetings in which safety and health matters are considered. Included on this level is conducting monthly safety inspections that take place at prearranged times and that also involve the relevant foremen and safety stewards. One aspect of training that is interesting from an international perspective is the practice of the Safety Department providing background material to foremen for monthly safety and health talks. The use of these monthly talks has been adopted from the U.S. operations of Company X; German safety and health legislation dictates that a minimum of only two talks per year be given. It is noteworthy that German supervisors are more faithful to meeting this monthly safety-talk requirement than are their American counterparts.

Another component of the plant safety and health operations dictated by safety and health regulations is the plant Safety and Health Committee. The composition of this committee conforms to the regulatory guidelines. It consists of four works-council members, a medical representative, four safety stewards, the safety manager, and the plant personnel director, who is the direct representative of management. Management maintains a majority on this committee. As required, this group meets four times a year to consider various safety and health issues. It reviews safety statistics and receives reports on both specific serious accidents and measures being taken to prevent their recurrence. Committee members also deliberate on various activities to be undertaken by the Safety Department.

Cooperation in Safety and Health

It is clear that safety and health is viewed and treated as a predominantly cooperative issue at this plant and in Company X_G in general. Labor-management cooperation on safety and health takes place through structures specified by law. These include the works council, the plant Safety Committee, and the participation of safety stewards and works-council representatives on safety inspections. These vehicles for eliciting labor-management cooperation on safety and health were viewed on the whole by both labor and management as being desirable and effective in promoting safety and health. Management felt that labor's participation in safety and health matters improved its understanding of the issues involved. In line with this, it promoted more compliance with safety and health guidelines and, in management's view, a more reasonable labor position regarding requests for safety and health expenditures. Labor felt gratified that it had some vehicle for pursuing its concerns relative to safety and health even if it did not always get everything it wanted.

The nature of the relationship between management and the quasi-governmental TCA representatives was also predominantly cooperative. There was a certain amount of flexibility in the enforcement of safety and health regulations and an informal avenue of communication between regulators and management. For example, although the plant had three safety engineers fewer than the number required according to the safety-engineer guidelines, this was not viewed as a problem. The safety manager explained that this was the result of changes in the work force during the preceding year. According to him, the TCA recognizes that it takes time to hire and/or train safety engineers. He felt that the TCA would be pleased if other employers under its jurisdiction were this close to compliance.

One factor in this plant's favor when compared with other employers is that all the safety engineers were employed in this position full time. A widely recognized problem with the safety system in Germany is the use of engineers with other responsibilities as part-time safety engineers. Although this is illegal, it is a common practice.

The Safety Department and the TCA cooperate in the training of new safety engineers. An individual who is hired as a safety engineer must have certification as an engineer or skilled craftsman. However, he/she most likely does not have any training directly related to safety. The new safety engineer then is enrolled in a six-week safety training program provided by the TCA. This training is coordinated with an internal training program conducted by the Safety Department of Company X_G.

There is reportedly good two-way informal communication between the safety manager and the TCA regulators. The safety manager feels comfortable calling in a TCA representative to get an informal opinion about some safety and health issue and need not fear receiving a citation if conditions are found to be at variance with regulations. The safety manager, in turn, is contacted by TCA representatives seeking information on how Company X_G is dealing with various safety or health issues that may be troubling other employers under their jurisdiction. This is because Company X_G is one of the largest employers in this TCA and can afford to develop state-of-the-art approaches to safety and health problems. The TCA then communicates these procedures to the other employers.

Intrafirm and Interfirm Cooperation. The safety structure of Company X_G is similar to that of Company X in the United States with respect to its facilitation of intrafirm cooperation. The Corporate Safety Department of Company X_G coordinates the safety and health activities at the various plants through record keeping activities, dissemination of accident reports, and training and consulting activities--essentially the same approach as that employed by the Corporate Safety and Health Department in the United States. This coordination is much easier for Company X_G because the number of plants operated by this subsidiary is far fewer than the total number of Company X plants. There is also less variation in the regulations governing the plants under the jurisdiction of the Safety Department of Company X_G. In one sense this is obvious because the plants of Company X_G are a subset of the plants of Company X. But there is even greater variation in the United States and Canada, where there are simply more states and provinces in which Company X plants are located than there are political jurisdictions affecting Company X_G. The Company X_G plants are located in three German *Länder* and one neighboring country.

Despite the effective systems for communication and cooperation within Company X's U.S./Canadian operations and within its Company X_G subsidiary, there is currently little communication or cooperation between corporate headquarters in the United States and this West German subsidiary regarding safety and health. There were only a few components of Company X_G's safety program that were adopted from its corporate parent. As noted, one was the five-minute safety talks given by foremen. Another, the adoption of the U.S. structure for safety and health, was actually a problem because it was at variance with German safety and health regulations. A vehicle capable of promoting greater corporate coordination of safety and health, the Company X international conferences, had been cancelled earlier.

Injury statistics for Company X_G are reported to the Corporate Occupational Safety and Health Department. However, due to different national definitions of injuries, these have not been of much use for evaluating safety performance cross-nationally. Several measures to standardize injury reporting in Europe were being considered at the time of this writing.

There is considerable communication and cooperation among competitor automotive firms in Europe on a variety of work issues, including occupational safety and health. The safety managers in the automotive industry in Germany occasionally get together to discuss such matters as common safety and health problems, pending safety and health regulations or legislation, and labor-management issues. Interestingly, one issue of labor-management conflict, the reporting of company and industry injury statistics, was dealt with by this group. This issue is discussed below.

Conflicts in Safety and Health

Despite the predominantly cooperative orientation of safety and health activities at Company X_G, there was a degree of conflict regarding specific issues. Disputes over the wearing of personal protection devices, for example, safety glasses, hard hats, and ear plugs, were common. This was the case despite the even greater reliance on engineering controls to eliminate hazards in German industry in general and in this plant in particular than in the United States. The safety manager complained of being constrained by the regulatory framework from disciplining workers who did not follow work rules. He also complained that the works-council members were of little help in obtaining compliance. He viewed them as too concerned with not offending anyone for fear of losing votes when they come up for reelection to the works council.

Several safety problems have a distinct national flavor to them. An example of this is the abuse of alcohol, which, like in the U.S. operations of Company X, pose hazards in X_G. Problematically, because beer is virtually the national drink in Germany, vending machines containing beer are present in employee cafeterias and lounges directly adjacent to the assembly line. Similarly, the German obsession with driving fast creates safety hazards on company grounds as workers arrive at and leave from work. These conflicts between safety and national traditions do not have easy solutions.

A point of conflict between labor and management is the practice of providing advanced warning to foremen and supervisors regarding the day and time that the monthly inspection will take place. The safety engineer conducts the interviews the first week of every month. He/she schedules with the supervisory personnel the day and exact time of the inspection several days or more in advance. This issue is occasionally raised at works-council meetings and it is a point of disagreement between labor and management. Labor representatives feel that this permits a foreman or supervisor to pay little attention to safety throughout most of the month and then to take corrective actions to eliminate any unsafe conditions just prior to an inspection. They feel there is a need for more uncertainty regarding the timing of an inspection so that foremen and supervisors will attempt to keep the work environment hazard-free at all times. For its part, management feels that the current system is effective because it achieves the desired result of eliminating hazards.

Priority of safety versus production concerns is another issue that is raised frequently at the works-council meetings. Labor representatives often complain that production takes precedence over safety in the decisions of supervisory personnel. The safety manager conceded that this complaint had validity, at least as far as some supervisors are concerned.

The availability and use of injury statistics is yet another point of disagreement and conflict. It was pointed out in Chapter 4 that injury statistics for the German automotive industry as a whole are not available to labor. This plant is typical in that regard. These data are apparently kept closely guarded by company safety directors to avoid comparisons between different employers. Whether the intent is to protect the managers of poor-performing firms, or, as the safety director of X_G contended, the works-council members of such firms, this practice is a source of conflict.

There are other examples of injury statistics not being used to their full potential. The Safety Department records and reports the injuries broken down by department for the plant, and an injury report summary is distributed monthly throughout the plant. Supervisory and managerial personnel are not, however, evaluated in any way on the basis of the injury experience in their areas of responsibility. The safety director indicated that there would be considerable resistance to any attempt to do so. In any event, he felt it would be unfair to supervisors of inherently more dangerous work areas.

Compared with the U.S. plant, there are relatively few conflicts between safety staff and line managers. The safety engineers have more authority and prestige than their counterparts in the United States. This is the case throughout Germany and perhaps it is due to the long tradition of regulating workplace safety and health there. Also, line managers may be less likely to challenge the authority of the safety engineers due to their legislative mandate and due to the additional leverage provided by the works-council members and safety helpers. The presence of the corporate X_G Safety Department at this location also provides added leverage for the safety engineers in potential conflicts with line managers.

Although the relations between the Safety Department and TCA regulators are quite cordial, there are some conflicts over the strictness of safety and health regulations. The safety manager claimed that certain regulations in Germany are even stricter than those in the United States, especially in the area of machinery guarding. It was felt that overprotecting workers erodes a sense of personal responsibility for their own safety.

Injury Experience in the West German Plant

The X_G plant has apparently become a somewhat safer place to work in recent years. This can be inferred from slight long-term reductions in its injury rates on several dimensions.[1] Moreover, the numbers of the most serious injuries--amputations and fatalities--have declined significantly.

The frequency of total recorded injuries declined from 33 recorded injuries per million hours of paid work in 1970 to 25 in 1974, a recession year. Then, with some fluctuations, this rate rose to 32 in 1981, only slightly lower than the 1970 figure (see Table 6-4). The method of computation for this injury frequency rate was changed in 1981 to the number of injuries per million hours *worked* from the number of injuries per million hours *paid*. The injury rate on the new basis should be higher, all other things being equal. This is because, with compensation for vacations, holidays, and such, employees' paid hours are greater than their hours worked. Because of this change, comparisons of injury rates between pre- and post-1981 are imprecise, but there does appear to be a decline in the injury frequency rates in 1982 and 1983.

The decline in the injury severity rate (not shown) over the years is more impressive than that of the injury frequency rate. In 1970 the rate of workdays lost due to recorded injuries per million hours paid stood at 460. This rate declined to a low of 320, again in 1974. Then, with some year-to-year fluctuations, it rose to 360 in 1981. The basis on which this injury severity rate is calculated also changed in 1981, so precise comparisons again are not possible. As with the injury frequency rate, there appears to be a significant subsequent decline in this rate.

Statistics also indicate a decline in the number of fatalities and amputations at the plant. During the 1970s there was an average of 1.4 fatalities per year, and as many as 4 fatalities in each of two years. During the first few years of the 1980s, there were no fatalities recorded at the plant. Not surprisingly, there were far more fatalities that occurred commuting to and from work than occurred in the plant. During the 1970s there was an average of 5.4 amputations per year. These are injuries involving the loss of a body limb, or even a portion of a finger. During the first few years of the 1980s, there was an average of 3.3 injuries per year of this type.

The safety manager indicated that the injury rate at this plant was about twice that of a competitor in Germany. He attributed this difference to underreporting by the competitor. He charged that the competitor transferred injured workers to very easy jobs so that their injuries would need not be recorded. It was not possible to verify this claim. Given the scarcity of data, we cannot say any more about the injury experience of X_G relative to other German automotive firms.

TABLE 6-4
INJURY AND FATALITY EXPERIENCES FOR U.S. AND WEST GERMAN PLANTS OF COMPANY X

| | U.S. Plant | | | | West German Plant | | |
	Number of Injuries	Injuries per Million Hours Worked[1]	Number of Fatal Injuries	Fatalities per Million Hours Worked	Number of Injuries	Injuries per Million Hours Paid/Worked	Number of Fatal Injuries	Fatalities per Million Hours Worked
1970	N.A.	N.A.	0	0	2,025	33	4	0.0651465
1971	N.A.	N.A.	0	0	2,019	34	1	0.0168350
1972	N.A.	N.A.	0	0	2,099	34	4	0.064830
1973	N.A.	N.A.	0	0	1,988	33	0	0
1974	N.A.	N.A.	0	0	1,041	25	1	0.0240385
1975	N.A.	N.A.	0	0	1,213	26	1	0.0214135
1976	N.A.	N.A.	0	0	1,846	31	1	0.0168065
1977	540	30	0	0	1,807	30	1	0.016115
1978	450	27	1	0.06	2,135	32	1	0.0154560
1979	375	24	0	0	2,225	32	0	0
1980	145	15	0	0	1,368	28 (35)[2]	0	0
1981	150	15	0	0	1,693	32 (40)[2]	0	0
1982	150	14	0	0	1,484	(35)[2]	0	0
1983	195	16	0	0	1,137	(28)[2,3]	0	0
1984	225	15	0	0	N.A.	N.A.	N.A.	N.A.
1985	287	N.A.	0	0	N.A.	N.A.	N.A.	N.A.

N.A. = Not available

Source: Company X documents. These figures are estimated from diagrams that plot injury rates over time.

[1] Company documents show injury rates per 100 employees. One hundred employees would work approximately 200,000 hours per year, so injuries per million hours worked is five times the rate of injuries per 100 employees.

[2] Calculations are based on hours actually worked rather than on hours paid. Figures not in parentheses are calculated on the basis of hours paid.

[3] For the first five months only.

However, the above evidence does indicate that, like the U.S. plant, the West German plant is becoming a safer place to work. Injury experience relative to the U.S. plant is considered at the end of this chapter.

COMPANY X: KENYAN PLANT

The Kenyan plant of Company X (X_K) began operations in 1977. Fifty-one percent ownership of this firm is held by the Kenyan national government, which purchased that percentage of the capital stock initially issued. The plant assembles a wide assortment of trucks and busses from components shipped from its parent firm. It also assembles vehicles from a Japanese firm partially owned by Company X. Assembled trucks range from 1-ton pick-ups to trucks weighing up to 13.5 tons. These trucks are designed to be extra heavy-duty to meet the demands placed on them by the treacherous local driving conditions. The plant has a capacity to produce 18 trucks per day, and it employs approximately 400 blue-collar and white-collar workers, of whom only 5 are foreign nationals (mostly Americans). The assembled trucks are sold within Kenya and in several East African countries. The plant has apparently been quite successful. According to published reports, the Kenyan government had recouped its initial investment within four years.

As is the case for most of the plants visited in other countries, the workers at this plant are among the best paid in their locality. Although the wages are very low by Western standards, approximately $200 per month, the standard of living afforded by such wages makes these workers quite well off compared with others in Kenya. Relatively speaking, the jobs these workers fill are viewed as being even more desirable and prestigious than the production jobs in the U.S. and West German plants. The workers' wages also place them higher within their country's income distribution than is the case for workers in the other countries. This can be seen by considering that $200 per month translates to $2,400 per year, or eight times the average per capita income of $300 per year in Kenya. Auto assembly workers in the United States would likely make no more than two times the U.S. average per capita income.

Labor-Management Relations

The work force at the plant is unionized, but it is not a closed shop; a number of workers do not belong to the union. The union does not have a great deal of influence in negotiations with management due to the generally weak position of labor in the country. This may be attributed to socio-economic and political/legal conditions.

As at other plants visited, productivity improvement and absenteeism control were considered for what they could indicate about labor-management relations in general. The contrast with other plants in the handling of these issues illustrates major socio-economic differences between this country and the others in the study. Productivity at the plant is thought of primarily in terms of quality. Although capacity at the plant is 18 trucks per day, production is usually scheduled at a lower rate than this to meet sales forecasts. At the time of the plant visit, scheduled production was only 10 trucks per day, and this target was usually not met. It takes the workers approximately three times as long to assemble a truck here as it takes workers in U.S. plants of the same company. However, because workers here are paid less than one-tenth that of their counterparts in the United States, this production rate was viewed favorably in Company X. Also, because of the unused capacity, the level of production is of less concern for management than at other plants visited. Management is easily able to meet current demand. At one time, the plant had an incentive program to increase output, but the program was discontinued. The factory manager of the plant simply exhorts the workers to work harder whenever they fall behind the production schedule. Temporary or "casual" workers are also used when the need for increased production arises. These workers are paid the minimum wage, which is considerably below the wage level of permanent workers, and they receive few benefits.

During downturns in demand, production workers may be laid off. However, in the preceding year, a number of redundant workers were kept on the payroll despite a demand decline. This was said to encourage worker loyalty and build political support in Kenya.

In contrast to the plant's low-key approach to quantity of output, there is considerable emphasis on quality. The plant uses a corporate index for measuring quality. Management reported that the plant has been averaging about 138 on the quality index, which is quite close to the 145 rating designated for a "perfect" vehicle. This was considerably better than the 113 rating achieved at the U.S. plant.

Quality is encouraged through a number of approaches, some of which are typical of Western plants and some of which are distinctive of the local culture. A quality-of-work-life program was instituted in the plant several years earlier. Quality circles meet every morning to discuss production issues, of which product quality is foremost. A more traditional notion of productivity, level of output as related to scheduled production, is also an important topic. The topic of worker safety was described as a "regular item of discussion." There is also a monthly quality contest in which work groups compete for a quality award. Along with being recognized at the monthly plant meeting, the winning team is awarded a local delicacy, a goat roast, for lunch one day. These are viewed as significant inducements for quality production, and the factory manager noted that there was considerable peer pressure within work groups to produce quality products.

Economic and cultural influences are also evident in the handling of absenteeism. There were a number of factors cited as contributing to the very low rate of total absenteeism, approximately .5 percent to 1 percent. This total absenteeism rate includes permitted and unpermitted absences but not vacation time or plant shutdowns. Workers are not paid when they are absent, and given the low level of income, there is a strong economic incentive to go to work every day possible. The plant has a progressive discipline system for absences, similar to the systems found in the other plants visited.

Because truck assembly jobs are so desirable relative to the limited number of other work opportunities in Kenya, the threat of losing one's job at this plant is taken very seriously. Company X_K also makes it easy and desirable to go to work. The company provides workers with free bus transportation to and from work. Because it is highly unlikely that workers could afford their own automobiles, and because public transportation is neither safe nor reliable, this is an important factor in getting people to work. In addition, workers are served a company-subsidized hot meal at lunch (the main meal of the day in Kenya) for the dollar-equivalent cost of approximately 16 cents. With massive starvation in neighboring Ethiopia and food shortages in parts of Kenya as well, this has significant appeal.

A final inducement for workers to come to work even when sick or injured is that free medical care is provided by two full-time nurses and a physician who is on call twice a week. For most Kenyans, visiting a private physician would be prohibitively expensive, and there are no free medical clinics. So, going to work when sick makes a great deal of sense. The medical-care program at this plant seems to be superior to that provided by most other employers in Kenya. Most workers in the wage economy pay into medical insurance plans, but when they get sick they must go to specific hospitals that typically are of poor quality with little medicine or treatment available. For example, at the time of this writing, the main hospital in Nairobi had run out of most antibiotics, and the families of patients had to bring in food and bed linens for them and provide most of the nursing care required.

Safety and Health Activities

There are both many similarities and distinctive differences in the handling of worker safety and health at this plant compared with other Company X plants. As in other locations, the safety program involves such elements as safety training, safety inspections, and supervising and motivating employees to work safely. There is a safety indoctrination for new employees before they start their jobs. This is particularly important here because new workers are generally unfamiliar with machinery and unaware of its potential hazards. There are also monthly fire drills and frequent training programs for fire fighting. Protective equipment, such as safety shoes, safety glasses, gloves, leggings, and coveralls, are provided to the workers free of charge. When injuries do occur, medical care is provided and the injury is recorded according to X_K's own injury criteria.

Safety and health, along with fire protection and plant security, are supervised by the factory manager. Plant security was said to be especially important because the trucks, tools, and materials are tempting targets for theft by workers and others. Theft is the primary reason for dismissal at the plant, accounting for most of the 10 percent annual turnover. Thus, considering these concerns, plant security received the greatest share of the factory manager's attention followed by fire protection and then safety and health.

The similarities between worker safety provisions in this plant and safety programs in U.S. plants can be attributed largely to the few American managers in the Kenyan plant. The factory manager of the plant noted that he had had considerable involvement with worker safety at his previous assignment in the United States. More than any corporate policy, this prior experience seemed to be a significant factor in modeling the safety program here after ones in the United States. The factory manager and his staff had not, however, received any special safety and health training prior to their assuming these positions. According to corporate policy, they could elect to attend safety and health training programs at corporate headquarters, but the expenses for this would need to be assumed by Company X_K.

Perhaps symbolic of a certain degree of isolation of the safety program from corporate influence was an old safety sign on the bulletin board in the plant. This sign detailed the corporate safety philosophy and general procedures that should be followed to enhance safety. The philosophy and procedures were still relevant, but the chief executive officer pictured on the sign had retired shortly after the plant had opened, years earlier. The factory manager conceded that it had been quite some time since he had read this sign, and he suspected that few, if any, employees bothered to read it. Also relevant to this sense of isolation is that no corporate safety and health official had ever visited this plant.

Compared with similar plants in the United States and other Western countries, this plant might appear somewhat more hazardous. For example, workers are not issued hard hats, which are common in other plants, or hearing protectors, although noise levels are quite high. A noise problem would not be surprising because there are no industrial noise regulations in Kenya. There was also a greater requirement for physical exertion because the shell of the truck being assembled and the major truck components were on rollers that the workers themselves pushed around the plant from work station to work station. In most other plants visited, the truck assemblies were moved by a conveyor belt, and as we shall see in Chapter 8, the Swedish plant of Company Z provided electric-powered carriers to move them around. Given the cost of labor versus capital in Kenya, the use of a labor intensive conveyor system would be a logical choice. It probably would also be considered desirable by the government and by the workers themselves. It entails the use of more workers and thus would contribute in a small way to reducing unemployment. Nonetheless, this choice increases the risk of certain types of injuries such as strains and sprains.

Another example of how less automation results in a greater risk of injury existed in the painting operations. Here, the truck was mechanically hoisted up by a chain so that the workers could paint the underbody. There were supposed to be safety chains in position to break the fall of the truck and prevent it from crushing the workers if the hoisting chain broke. However, during the plant tour, the factory manager had to instruct the workers to put up the safety chain because they had neglected to do so. By contrast, in the U.S., Western European, and Japanese plants, painting is more mechanized. In some cases, robotic painters are in use; in other cases vehicle parts are mechanically immersed in paint; in still other cases parts of the vehicle are painted while they move along an assembly line. Still, there are new risks created by automation. As noted, there have been cases of workers in other countries being injured and even killed by robots.

Several conditions and illnesses that have received more attention in recent years in industrialized nations as injuries have come under greater control are not matters of concern at X_K. Thus, noticeably lacking was any mention of psychological stress of workers, carpal tunnel syndrome, or any diseases related to the handling or breathing of toxic substances. The lack of concern with these issues is, in part, due to the focus of attention being placed on more obvious problems and, in part, due to the lack of any trained occupational safety and health professional at X_K.

Another interesting difference between X_K and auto plants in industrialized countries concerns government regulatory activities. Although Kenyan law stipulates that every factory facility must be inspected once a year, this plant had not been inspected for four years. This was attributed to a shortage of government inspectors. Still, given the way the law is written, having the plant inspected is the responsibility of management and, paradoxically, the company could be penalized for the plant not having been inspected despite the fact that inspections had been requested.

Injury Experience in the Kenyan Plant

Due to the lack of a standard injury definition in Kenya, any injury data would be suspect. According to the plant management, the only injuries that are reported to the government and entered into X_K records are those that entitle the employee to workers' compensation. Although no specific data were provided, the factory manager characterized the safety record at the plant as good, and better than those in most other factories in Kenya.

The observation that working conditions at this plant are more hazardous than at plants in industrialized countries should not be taken as evidence of poor management or of a lack of concern by management for worker safety. They simply are reflections of the socio-economic conditions in Kenya. Providing jobs, even jobs that are somewhat more dangerous than ones in industrialized countries, is considered more important than achieving increased production and safer working conditions through automation in a country with 35 percent to 40 percent unemployment. And when the cost of labor is as cheap as it is in Kenya, there is no incentive for the plant to automate and, by so doing, eliminate some of the more hazardous jobs.

Cooperation and Conflict in Safety and Health

The discussion of cooperation and conflict in safety and health provided in Chapter 4 for Kenya as a whole applies to this particular plant as well. That is, management's behavior toward labor could be characterized as dominating. It is essentially paternalistic, attempting to convince workers to do what is in their own safety and health interests, even if they don't realize it. Labor's behavior toward management could be described as appeasing. Labor does not have much knowledge or influence regarding safety and health either in negotiations or on the factory floor. Negotiators typically accept management's safety and health proposals without putting forth any of their own, and workers usually do not know what rights they have. Management's and government's behaviors toward each other could be characterized as neglecting.

The effectiveness of this reliance on management to promote worker safety and health is difficult to judge due to the questionable validity of national statistics on industrial injuries and diseases and the lack of such statistics for this plant. Thus, an evaluation of the worker safety and health system in this plant must be more impressionistic than the approach used in the other plants. Based on both observation of the plant and interviews with a wide range of individuals, it was clear that safety and health were not accorded quite the same emphasis in industrial sites in Kenya as in the other countries considered in this study. But, by the same token, there did not appear to be any major problems. Moreover, the contrast between safety and health conditions in the truck assembly plant visited versus conditions in jobs in the informal sector was much more striking than differences between safety and health conditions in this plant and conditions in plants in the industrialized countries. Most of the credit for the relatively safe work environment would have to be given to management by default. Clearly, neither the government nor the union has influenced safety and health conditions at this plant to any significant extent. The government does, however, have substantial *potential* influence on safety and health matters, but it has apparently chosen to abdicate this responsibility and to focus on other concerns.

Given the low level of formal education of most of the workers and their lack of experience in industrial settings, management has a more difficult job convincing workers to follow safe work practices than is the case in industrialized countries. During the tour, the factory manager corrected several workers who were engaged in unsafe activities. He also told of workers selling the safety boots they received from the company. This has resulted in a policy requiring such workers to buy the second pair of safety shoes for themselves.

In general, it seems that the safety and health activities at this plant are being carried out as well as could be expected given the backgrounds of its workers and the social, economic, political, and legal environments in which this plant operates.

PLANT COMPARISONS

As the above descriptions amply demonstrate, comparisons of safety and health activities of plants operating in different countries are fraught with difficulty. However, when certain precautions are taken, such comparisons can be enlightening. In the following sections the safety and health operations of the three Company X plants are compared on the following dimensions: inputs/resources devoted to safety and health activities, injury rates, and extent of labor-management-government cooperation.

Inputs

Data on resources available to the safety and health function at the three plants are sketchy. Nevertheless, what little data there are indicate that the German plant devotes the most resources to safety and health on a per employee basis of the three plants visited, and the Kenyan plant devotes the fewest.

The best indication of the disparity in resources devoted to safety and health is the number of safety and health professionals employed at the three plants. Although the German plant has fewer than the required number of safety engineers, it has proportionately more safety and health professionals than does the U.S. plant, which is not governed by detailed staffing regulations. At the German plant, there is one safety engineer for every 1,750 workers. Not even counting the numerous German safety stewards, this staffing level is one and a half times the level at the U.S. plant, where there are three professionals (the safety manager and two safety and health representatives) for 8,000 employees, or one for every 2,667 workers. Even this comparison understates the staffing disparity between the two plants because there are several other professionals in the Safety and Health Department of the German plant who handle administrative functions.

The safety manager and the safety and health representatives at the U.S. plant perform these functions themselves.

The Kenyan plant is much smaller than both of the other plants, and it does not have anyone assigned full time to safety and health. Thus, comparisons of staffing levels are difficult. However, given certain reasonable assumptions, it is apparent that there is less professional time devoted to safety and health on a per employee basis than at either of the other two plants. The factory manager, who handles the safety and health function along with numerous other managerial activities, probably spends no more than 10 percent of his time on safety and health, and it is unlikely that he spends even this much time. If he did, this would translate into one full-time safety and health professional for every 4,000 employees because there are 400 employees in the plant. This would represent a safety and health professional staffing level of two-thirds that of the U.S. plant and about two-fifths that of the German plant.

Injury Experience

The fragmentary evidence that is available indicates that the U.S. plant has improved from having a nearly equal injury rate with that of the German plant to having a considerably better injury rate. A comparison of available injury statistics is provided in Table 6-4. No statistics are available from the Kenyan plant. Given what has been said about the injury-reporting system in Kenya, meaningful comparisons of injury rates would not be possible even if these data were available. Still, it seems reasonable to speculate that there is probably a somewhat higher incidence of injuries in the Kenyan plant than in the U.S. or German plants. However, many of these are probably minor injuries that would not merit workers' compensation and thus would not be recorded.

Injury and fatality data for the U.S. and German plants are listed on Table 6-4 for the years they were available. Although injury frequency rates are calculated differently at these plants--injuries per 100 workers at the U.S. plant versus injuries per million hours at the German plant--they are compared by converting U.S. injury rates to the German basis. These plants also record injury severity rates but the approaches for measuring them vary to such an extent that meaningful comparisons are not possible. Thus, they are not reported here.

As noted earlier, there has been only one work fatality at the U.S. plant since 1970. In contrast, there were 14 fatalities at the West German plant between 1970 and mid 1983. In fairness, though, it should be noted that the German plant is much larger than the U.S. plant, and it includes some more dangerous operations, such as foundry work, that are not performed at the U.S. site. Thus, a more meaningful comparison is between the fatality rates at the German plant and the North American operations of Company X as a whole

(Table 6-1). There are only three years (1976-78) for which fatality data for both of these units are available, but these show a substantial disparity in favor of the North American operations. For these years the North American operations had a simple average of .01028 fatalities per million hours worked. This is 63 percent of the simple average rate of .01629 fatalities per million hours worked during these years at the West German plant. This actually understates the difference, because during the 1976-78 time period the German fatality and injury rates were calculated on the basis of hours *paid* rather than the lower basis of hours *worked*.

The nonfatal injury frequency data also suggest that the U.S. plant had safer operations than the German plant. In the first year for which injury frequency data were available from both plants--1977--the nominal rate of injuries in each of these was approximately 30 injuries per million hours. However, due to differences in injury definition in Germany and the United States, it can be surmised that the U.S. plant did much better on this dimension. This is because an injured German worker must be unable to work for three full days before the injury is recorded as a lost-work injury. In the United States a lost-work injury is defined as one in which the worker is unable to perform his/her own job for one full day. Thus, some less serious lost-work injuries are recorded in the U.S. plant that would go unrecorded in Germany. Moreover, OSHA-recordable injuries not involving lost workdays or restricted work activity are included in the work injury data for the U.S. plant. Therefore, one would expect a higher reported injury rate in the U.S. plant, all other things being equal.

The relative performance of the U.S. plant on the injury-rate dimension was even better by 1981. By 1981 the injury rate at the U.S. plant was 15 injuries per million hours or one-half of what it was in 1977. In contrast, the injury rate at the German plant had increased slightly to 32 injuries per million hours worked. It is noteworthy that this higher injury level occurred in the German plant despite the far higher staffing level of safety and health specialists.

Neither of these plants followed the decline in injury rates that corresponded with the 1979-83 recession that occurred in the United States and Germany. The injury rates at the U.S. plant started falling prior to the recession and then stabilized during it. The injury rates at the German plant remained essentially stable during the recession.

It is worth speculating about the reasons for the apparent improvement in the relative performance of the U.S. plant compared with that of the German plant. The data for the U.S. plant correspond roughly to the tenure of the current safety manager. Certainly some of the credit for the improvements during this time period must be given to him. Those involved with safety and health at the plant also give credit to the labor-management agreements on safety and health.

It is also possible that some of relatively good and improving performance of the U.S. plant could be attributed to statistical artifacts. Safety and health and medical personnel have a certain amount of discretion regarding the treatment of injured workers and their evaluation of employee fitness to work that has a bearing on the recorded injury statistics. This is the case in both the United States and Germany. The union representation in safety and health activities provides some control on arbitrary decision making in this arena for both countries and in both plants. Because of the codetermination system, the influence of labor regarding such arbitrary decisions is even greater in the German plant. Thus, one would expect management to be able to influence the reported injury rates to a greater extent in the U.S. plant than in the German plant.

There is probably also a greater financial incentive at the U.S. plant to keep the reported injury rates low. This is because the U.S. plant is self-insured for workers' compensation so that Company X pays the full cost of compensation to the injured employees. The German plant belongs to a TCA and the degree of correlation between injury rates and premiums paid by Company X_G is unclear, even to the management of the company.

There has been greater emphasis on reducing injury rates at a national corporate level in the United States than in Germany since the Corporate Safety and Health Department called attention to injury rates at U.S. plants several years ago. As noted, this had the unexpected effect of increasing the "gaming" of reported injury statistics. There was no evidence that this was occurring at the U.S. plant, but there was a greater incentive for it to occur there than at the German plant.

Cooperation and Conflict

From the preceding discussions of cooperation and conflict at these three Company X plants, it is clear that labor-management cooperation regarding safety and health is greatest at the German plant. It is also clear that conflict on this issue is most intense at the U.S. plant. Referring to the model presented in Figure 1-1, the cooperative/assertive behaviors of management in handling safety and health conflicts with labor in the U.S., German, and Kenyan plants are plotted in Figure 6-1.

The German management's conflict-coping behavior is moderately high on cooperativeness and moderate on assertiveness. This is close to the compromising position. The moderate assessment of cooperativeness is explained by the fact that there is more potential for cooperation than has been actualized. The structures and procedures to facilitate labor-management cooperation on safety and health have been in operation in one form or another at the German plant for most of the postwar period. They were established by the passage of codetermination legislation in the early 1950s. Despite this lengthy tradition, it is clear that these arrangements are not used to the extent that they could be. The fact that the Safety Department does not share available injury statistics with labor is at the least an indication of a lack of cooperation, if not conflict. Labor's cooperation with management is also lacking in part. Safety managers still complain of the inability or unwillingness of labor representatives to get workers to follow safety procedures such as wearing safety equipment. The level of conflict related to safety and health at the German plant is not as overt and harsh as at the U.S. plant, but it is evident nonetheless.

Management's (and labor's) behaviors at the U.S. plant for coping with safety and health conflicts could best be described as moderate on cooperativeness and high on assertiveness. The tradition of cooperation on safety and health is much shorter at the U.S. plant than at the German plant. Labor and management representatives are, however, making progress in dealing with these matters in a more cooperative manner than in the past. Formerly, they exhibited competing behavior, that is, low cooperativeness and high assertiveness. The level of conflict at the plant regarding safety and health is still quite high, but significant improvements in safety and health have been accomplished despite that.

FIGURE 6-1
MANAGEMENT'S CONFLICT-COPING BEHAVIORS
AT COMPANY X PLANTS

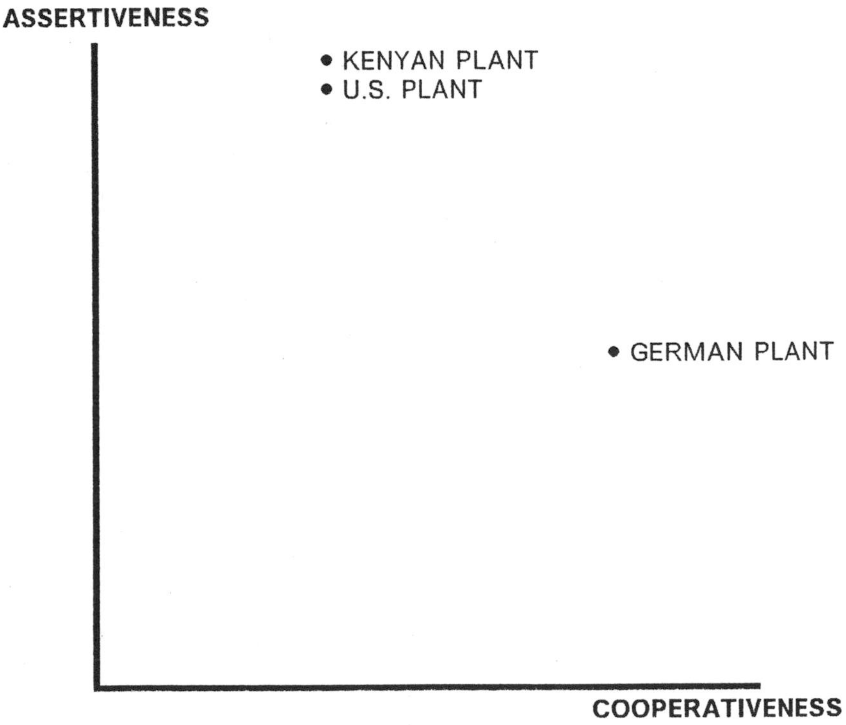

ASSERTIVENESS

• KENYAN PLANT
• U.S. PLANT

• GERMAN PLANT

COOPERATIVENESS

The conflict-coping behaviors at the Kenyan plant are different for management and labor. This is due to the dominant position of management vis-a-vis labor. Management's behavior entails a high level of assertiveness and a moderate level of cooperativeness. This description, however, is somewhat misleading. Management's cooperativeness (defined as looking out for the concerns of others) in the Kenyan plant could better be characterized as paternalistic. Also, there is relatively little conflict to cope with because labor is so weak relative to management. Labor's behavior in this situation is accommodating (appeasing), that is, high on cooperativeness, and low on assertiveness. Labor has so little bargaining power at the plant that it has no choice but to abide by management's decisions regarding safety and health.

It is instructive to consider the relations between management and government safety and health officials using this same model. The natures of these relationships at these three plants are typical for the respective countries. For each of these three cases, the conflict-coping behaviors between management and government are reciprocal. The German plant had the greatest amount of cooperativeness by both government officials and management in their conflict-coping behaviors, with moderately high assertiveness. The U.S. plant evidenced the greatest level of assertiveness in the relationships between management and government safety and health officials, with moderately low cooperativeness. The Kenyan plant exhibited low assertiveness and low cooperativeness in these relationships. This position is characterized by Thomas (1976) as avoidance (neglect) and is clearly inappropriate for an important issue like occupational safety and health.

It is apparent that the predominant factor explaining the differences between the approaches to safety and health at these three Company X plants is the various external environments in the three countries in which these plants operate. Most significant in comparing the U.S. and German plants is the different regulatory environments faced by the plants both in the safety and health field and in the broader field of labor-management relations. Company X has a highly developed safety and health program compared with other employers in each of the three countries considered. Nevertheless, in Germany, where the plant did not even technically meet the legislated safety-engineer requirements, there were far more resources devoted to safety and health than in either the U.S. or Kenyan plants. It is likely that the discrepancies in favor of a German plant compared with U.S. and Kenyan plants for other companies with less well developed safety and health programs would be even greater. This suggests that the laws dictating safety and health arrangements make a great deal of difference, at least with respect to inputs.

Labor participation in safety and health activities is guaranteed by the state in Germany through codetermination laws. This is a significant factor when considering labor's participation in these activities. Although workers have negotiated many of the same rights of participation in the U.S. auto industry as the law dictates for all industry in Germany, the legislative backing is significant. The legislated arrangements are more permanent, and less subject to even voluntary modification in times of difficulty, such as occurred at Chrysler during its financial crisis. The legislated codetermination system makes it possible for labor to have more influence in safety and health activities at the German plant. However, in spite of, or perhaps because of, these mandated participatory avenues, labor has not been as assertive in pursuing safety and health matters in negotiations and at the shop-floor level as in the U.S. plant. Perhaps this is because most of the current workers in the German auto industry did not have to work as hard to win rights of participation as did their counterparts in the United States. Moreover, because these rights to participate in safety and health activities are guaranteed to all workers in Germany, they may not be viewed as being as important as they are by U.S. auto workers.

The greater amount of potential labor influence on safety and health and the greater inputs devoted to safety and health in Germany have not been translated into better performance in this arena. In fact, it appears that the German plant has a considerably worse injury rate than the U.S. plant. Some of this is no doubt due to statistical distortions. Ironically, the greater influence of labor in the German plant probably contributes to the appearance of relatively poorer injury rate performance than is actually the case there. This is because more "borderline" injuries would likely be recorded.

In Kenya, the most important environmental factor is the assortment of socio-economic considerations associated with its developing-country status. This dictates the lesser emphasis placed on occupational safety and health at a national level compared with other more basic needs, such as job creation and economic development. The haphazard nature of the country's injury-reporting system seems to be a direct result of this. The nominal use of safety and health standards set in more developed countries and/or recommended by international agencies shows the symbolic and political importance of occupational safety and health. Yet it also highlights the difficulties for a developing country like Kenya to match safety and health standards of industrialized countries.

NOTE

1. The injuries referred to in this section are in-plant injuries only. Commuting injuries are not included. As noted in Chapter 4, an injury in Germany is recorded only if it results in more than three days of lost work. The statistics on days lost due to work injuries reported here include the first three days of incapacity when the length of incapacity exceeds three days. They do not include any days of work

incapacity when the total length of work incapacity is three days or less.

7

WORKER SAFETY AND HEALTH IN COMPANY Y

We continue our corporate- and plant-level analyses in this chapter with an examination of occupational safety and health activities in Company Y. Like Company X, Company Y is a large U.S.-based multinational automotive company with automotive and nonautomotive operations located throughout the world. Four automotive plants of Company Y were studied in this research. Two are in the United States, one is in the United Kingdom, and one is in Belgium. All four of these plants are unionized . The U.S. plants are located on the northern fringe of the Sun Belt, in the Southeast, and in the Midwest. The Belgian plant is located close to the West German border, and, in fact, is an operating unit of the West German subsidiary of Company Y. Both the British plant and the Belgian plant report to the European headquarters of Company Y. In this chapter primary attention is given to the British plant and the midwestern U.S. plant.

Like other domestic auto firms in the United States, Company Y suffered through serious financial difficulties during the auto industry upheavals of the 1970s and early 1980s. Significantly, its European operations (Company Y_E) were much healthier financially than its U.S. operations during most of this time period.

The organization of this chapter is as follows. There is an overview of (world) corporate safety and health operations in Company Y. The midwestern U.S. plant is then considered. Following this are sections dealing with safety and health at the British national subsidiary level of Company Y (Company Y_{UK}) and at the British plant. Finally, some comparisons between the British and U.S. plants are provided.

CORPORATE SAFETY AND HEALTH OPERATIONS

The Corporate Safety Department is housed in the Personnel Services Department at Company Y. It is separate from but works closely with the Corporate Health Department. The Corporate Safety Department performs a number of staff functions, including training, record keeping and reporting, disseminating information, advising top-level corporate management and lower-level safety managers (called safety engineers in company Y), assisting in labor negotiations, and investigating accidents. The training function includes providing programs for division- and plant-level safety engineers. In addition, some training programs are provided in conjunction with the UAW for company and union safety and health representatives.

As in the other companies considered, the corporate and division safety engineers do not have direct line authority over safety engineers at lower levels in the organizational hierarchy. Their role is more that of consultants or advisors. The division safety engineers and the plant safety engineers owe their primary allegiance to their superiors in the division and plant hierarchy, and they are usually housed in the plant and division personnel departments. Their division and plant superiors are primarily responsible for performance evaluations, salary increases, and promotions. Superiors within the safety hierarchy provide data that can be used by others for these evaluations, and occasionally they provide recommendations for promotions to a higher-grade classification within the safety structure of the plant or division. As in other companies, there are relatively few advancement opportunities within the safety field in Company Y. Thus, the typical road to advancement for members of the safety staff is out of safety and into other personnel functions.

The Safety Department of Company Y performs the usual record keeping/reporting functions. These include collecting injury and other related safety data from plants and divisions, and filing required reports with OSHA and state occupational safety and health departments. One additional record keeping/reporting activity merits some consideration. This department circulates a monthly report of injury experience for all Company Y operations in North America. This contains incidence rates, severity rates, and lost-workday case rates for North American operations as a whole and for each of the divisions and plants. The individual divisions and plants are also rank ordered from best to worst on the basis of a composite of these three injury experience dimensions. These reports are disseminated to Company Y vice-presidents, division managers, and plant managers and to corporate, division, and plant safety personnel. Significantly, the union also receives copies of these reports. Because these reports are a distinctive feature of the safety activities at Company Y, their use is considered in more detail below.

Many of the responsibilities for directly overseeing the safety and health activities in the plants are delegated to the divisions. These include goal setting, evaluating performance relative to safety and health, and the determining how that should be factored into the overall performance evaluations of managers and supervisors. The divisions carry out periodic inspections of plants to supplement injury statistics used in making such evaluations.

The Corporate Safety Department relies on injury reports from plants and divisions to help identify correctable hazards throughout the operating facilities of Company Y. Special attention is paid to reports filed for every work fatality occurring in the North American operations. Lost-time injury statistics are also analyzed for trends in the nature or source of injuries.

The injury experience reports noted above are provided by the Corporate Safety Department to division and plant managers for their use in goal setting and in evaluating performance of individual managers. The importance attached to the injury experience rankings varies from division to division and from plant to plant. However, there is a considerable amount of competition among plants and divisions to improve their rankings. Plant managers and division managers do not want to see their units in the bottom half of the rankings, and the notoriety associated with being ranked last is something to be avoided at all costs. Reflecting the emphasis placed on injury experience within the corporation, managers and supervisors are also evaluated on the safety and health dimension. In many units supervisors must receive at least a "satisfactory" rating on safety and health to earn a raise. In some cases only personnel receiving "excellent" ratings merited raises.

The U.S. plants of Company Y placed considerable emphasis on improving their relative standings in these rankings. Plant-level and corporate-level safety and health officials at Company Y indicated that these rankings catch peoples' attention and that they have increased the importance attached to safety and health considerations in the company.

It is interesting to note that these rankings of injury experience have been accepted and used with much less turmoil and controversy than was the case in Company X. Still, there are safety officials and plant managers at Company Y, not surprisingly those whose units are ranked low, who complain that the rankings are unfair. They contend that the rankings do not take account of differences in the ages of the facilities (e.g., one would expect older facilities to be less safe) and differences in the inherent dangers of the different operations undertaken at the various plants (e.g., forging and stamping are generally regarded as being among the more hazardous operations).

One might speculate about why these rankings have not produced the same degree of controversy at Company Y as in Company X. It appears to be due, in part, to the fact that no individual plant managers are singled out for praise or criticism in the reports. It is also attributable to the continuing nature of the reporting. That is, there is always next month for a given plant to improve upon its relative performance. Thus, any single report is not given the same significance as the letters at Company X, and the plant managers and safety managers need not feel as threatened. Still, they do have an incentive to reduce injuries.

Over the time period of this study, significant improvements in safety and health conditions have been achieved at Company Y as reflected in the injury statistics discussed below. These improvements can be attributed both to labor-management cooperation and technological improvements in machinery and work processes.

International Activities

As noted, the safety and health activities are organized on national and/or regional bases in Company Y. All the North American safety activities are coordinated at this office. For the company's European operations, there is a safety and fire coordinator for manufacturing operations in that region. His job is to "commonise" the approach to safety and health used in these plants. Within national operating units of Company Y_E, safety and health activities in manufacturing and other areas of operation (e.g., sales, finance, product development, etc.) are coordinated by a national safety engineer. These individuals report to safety and health superiors at headquarters of Company Y and Company Y_E. However, they are generally free to develop their own policies and strategies relative to safety and health. The organizational structure for coordinating medical activities within countries is separate but similar. The safety and health operations of Company Y_{UK} follow this general pattern.

The general decentralization of safety and health responsibilities is due, in large part, to the complex variations in national safety and health regulations. There is a need to rely on local knowledge of these regulations. Because of this decentralization, there is little corporate control over safety and health activities outside of North America. There are, however, two principal vehicles that are utilized to provide a modicum of international coordination. One of these is an international corporate safety and health conference. This provides a forum for safety and health representatives from corporate operations throughout the world to share ideas for coping with common problems. As an example of this, one of the corporate safety engineers cited British techniques of guarding machinery as useful information that had been shared at one conference. He noted that the British plants of Company Y were ahead of plants elsewhere in guarding technology due to the very strict (in his view, too strict) regulations imposed by the British Health and Safety Executive. Unfortunately, these conferences were suspended from 1980 until 1985 due to corporate financial difficulties.

Another vehicle for coordinating and sharing safety and health information is visits by corporate staff to international operations. It is unlikely, however, that much can be accomplished by these because the corporate safety manager visits plants in individual locations around the world only about once every four or five years.

The Corporate Safety Department receives injury data from Company Y operations worldwide, but, for the most part, these data are not comparable due to different injury definitions. From time to time the development of a corporatewide injury definition has been considered at Company Y. The same difficulties confronting other companies have discouraged serious efforts to develop such a definition for the entire company. In particular, the need for double record keeping in plants where the national injury definition differs from the corporate definition has been a major obstacle.

For several years, a standard injury definition in certain international components of Company Y had been utilized. However, this practice was discontinued for cost-cutting reasons. The Tractor Division of Company Y, for example, had been reporting injuries in its European operations using the U.S. injury definition. Also, Canadian operations of Company Y had been reporting their injuries to the Corporate Safety Department using the U.S. injury definition (these are included in Company Y's North American injury statistics reported below). In both cases, this required double record keeping. For the Tractor Division, this also required a considerable amount of travel to European tractor plants by a staff member from the Tractor Division headquarters in the United States to ensure uniform procedures in record keeping.

Some international operations do attempt, on their own, to record injuries using the U.S. injury definition. The British component of Company Y records injuries using both the British injury definition and the U.S. definition. There are, however, likely to be discrepancies in the British interpretation of the U.S. injury definition because there is no corporate control system for monitoring record keeping at the international level.

Corporate safety officials would like to see the establishment of a companywide injury definition and reporting system to facilitate better evaluation and control of safety and health activities worldwide. However, they are resigned to living with the current system given cost constraints and corporate trends away from uniform injury reporting.

Corporate-Level Cooperation on Safety and Health

Company Y's agreement with the UAW regarding cooperation on safety and health is essentially the same as that of Company X, so only a few highlights will be noted. As in Company X, there is a labor-management safety and health committee in Company Y that meets periodically to develop joint approaches to resolving safety and health issues of concern to both labor and management. Members of this committee also have input into labor and management positions taken on safety and health issues in contract negotiations.

Like in Company X, funds have been set aside for training union and management safety representatives and for research. This committee has responsibility for determining a research agenda to be supported by these funds. To date, studies on ergonomics and on mortality rates and cancer rates among certain classes of workers are among the research projects that have been funded by this committee.

As with other U.S. auto companies, the 1973 agreement with the UAW was a catalyst for labor-management cooperation on safety and health in Company Y. This same agreement specified a framework for more general labor-management cooperation in such areas as quality of work life, and productivity and quality improvement. Progress in realizing labor-management cooperation in these other areas, however, trailed that in safety and health. It was not until the serious recession of 1979 hit Company Y that significant steps were taken to enhance broader-based labor-management cooperation. By this time, labor-management cooperation on safety and health was already well established. Still, mechanisms to enhance this cooperation were upgraded at this time as well. Cooperation on safety and health in many ways served as a model for this broader cooperation. Moreover, cooperative efforts in safety and health are viewed as being complementary to employee involvement in these other areas. Occupational safety and health are described, at least in company rhetoric, as part of the overall productivity/quality/profit picture.

The experience with worker involvement in safety and health is regarded very favorably at Company Y. This cooperation was credited with having produced the significant reductions in injury rates discussed in the next section. The labor-management cooperation has also made occupational safety and health a less contentious issue in labor-management relations. Moreover, according to managers, occupational safety and health issues are less likely to be used by labor to pursue other issues. In the past, workers seeking to slow down work or to create trouble to get back at supervisors for some actual or perceived affront would occasionally raise spurious safety and health complaints. Such actions occur much less frequently now. The system in place for resolving disputes at the plant and corporate levels facilitates genuine problem solving.

Despite the overall satisfaction with the operation of safety and health activities at Company Y, a number of problems remain. These include the inability to achieve adequate ventilation and noise reduction in certain areas. Certain operations were also cited as still having difficulties in controlling injuries. Specifically mentioned were some stamping operations where workers were paid on an incentive basis. It was felt that the incentive pay caused workers to disregard their own safety in the pursuit of higher output. Assembly operations, where work pace is dictated by line speed, do not have this problem. Also, despite improvements resulting from labor-management cooperative agreements, there were still difficulties in achieving complete worker compliance with safe work-practice rules. In addition, and reflecting industrial trends, even as workplace injuries have come under greater control, occupational health issues have become more problematic. Finally, some conflicts related to efforts to improve productivity by cutting the work force and increasing the work pace have arisen. Whether or not there actually are safety and health risks associated with these productivity improvement measures is a matter of dispute.

From an outsider's perspective, one current organizational problem is the relatively low prestige awarded the safety and health professionals compared with other line and staff managers in

Company Y. This makes it more difficult for them to bring about improvements in safety and health in their areas of responsibility. That their complaints about safety and health problems and their own efforts to correct them are frequently ignored by other managers attest to this low prestige and thwarted improvement efforts.

Before proceeding with a review of injury experience at Company Y, it is interesting to consider opinions from Company Y personnel about OSHA and its recent emphasis on cooperation. These views coincide with the prevailing industrial view. Basically, this view is that OSHA formerly was very bothersome. Company Y safety officials complained that poorly trained and heavy-handed OSHA inspectors distracted them from their work during the agency's start-up phase. They blamed these distractions for an unusually high number of fatalities (15) in 1972. Since then OSHA has generally been regarded as only mildly bothersome but, for the most part, irrelevant. OSHA-sponsored programs aimed at fostering cooperation between labor and management were viewed as unnecessary. Moreover, the requirements for participating in these programs were not well understood, apparently because no one felt it was worth the effort to learn about them.

Like the other major U.S. auto firms, Company Y received substantial fines in the late 1980s for injury underrecording. These fines, no doubt, changed management's views on the irrelevance of OSHA. They also raised certain questions about the accuracy of the injury statistics reported below. Still, as was argued in the last chapter, it seems reasonable to give greater credence to *changes* in injury rates than to the actual *levels* of these rates.

Injury Experience

There has been a significant reduction over time in injury rates as reflected in several measures of injury experience in Company Y's North American operations. Tables 7-1 and 7-2 show historical injury rates for all of Company Y's North American operations and for Company Y's North American automotive operations. The rates considered are: the injury incidence rate (the number of recordable injuries per 100 employees, i.e., per 200,000 hours worked), the injury severity rate (the number of workdays lost due to injuries per 100 employees), and, for the most recent years, the lost-workday case rate (the number of injuries resulting in lost workdays per 100 employees).

The trends in the incidence rates for all of Company Y's North American operations and for Company Y's North American automotive operations follow the same basic patterns. During the time period 1977-85 there was an overall 51 percent decrease in the incidence rate, from 6.73 to 3.33 injuries per 100 employees for the entire North American operations of Company Y. There was also a 50 percent decrease in the incidence rate, from 6.67 to 3.36, for the North American automotive operations during this same time period.

TABLE 7-1
COMPANY Y INJURY EXPERIENCE
NORTH AMERICAN OPERATIONS

Year	Incidence Rate per 100 Employees	Severity Rate per 100 Employees	Lost-Workday Case Rate per 100 Employees
1977	6.73	42.68	N.A.
1978	5.99	27.13	N.A.
1979	6.78	53.90	N.A.
1980	4.60	32.63	N.A.
1981	3.69	19.88	N.A.
1982	3.10	6.53[1]	N.A.
1983	3.62	6.84[1]	1.82
1984	3.49	5.39[1]	1.45
1985	3.33	6.05[1]	1.23
Average	4.59	35.24 (1977-81) 6.20 (1982-85)	1.50

N.A. = Not available
Source: Company Y documents
[1] Different base for severity rate was used starting in 1982. Formerly, specific "charges" for certain types of injuries (e.g., fatalities and amputations) were added to the number of days lost due to injuries. Beginning in 1982, only the days lost due to lost-time injuries were contained in the severity rate.

The declines in the injury severity rates are of the same order of magnitude as those for the incidence rates, although the comparisons are complicated by record-keeping changes that took place in 1982. Prior to 1982, specific "charges" for certain types of serious injuries (e.g., death or amputation) were added to the number of days lost due to injuries to calculate the injury severity rate. Beginning in 1982, these charges were no longer added to the actual days lost due to lost-time injuries when computing this rate. Thus, it is necessary to consider the injury severity data from 1977-81 and 1982-85 separately. There was a 53 percent reduction in the severity rate, from 42.68 in 1977 to 19.88 in 1981, for the North American operations. Additionally, there was a 7 percent decline, from 6.53 in 1982 to 6.05 in 1985, using the new method of calculation of the severity rate.

The declines for the North American auto operations were very similar on these two injury severity rates. From 1977 to 1981, there was a decline of 51 percent, 30.69 to 15.01; and from 1982 to 1985, there was a decline of 14 percent, 6.56 to 5.64, using the new injury severity rate calculations.

TABLE 7-2
COMPANY Y INJURY EXPERIENCE
NORTH AMERICAN AUTO OPERATIONS

Year	Incidence Rate per 100 Employees	Severity Rate per 100 Employees	Lost-Workday Case Rate per 100 Employees
1977	6.67	30.69	N.A.
1978	6.14	25.53	N.A.
1979	7.42	51.59	N.A.
1980	4.79	20.42	N.A.
1981	3.68	15.01	N.A.
1982	3.12	6.56[1]	N.A.
1983	3.57	5.85[1]	N.A.
1984	3.59	4.96[1]	1.45
1985	3.36	5.64[1]	1.20
Average	4.70	28.65 (1977-81) 5.75 (1982-85)	1.33

N.A. = Not available
Source: Company Y documents
[1] A different method of calculation for severity rate is used as of 1982. Formerly, specific "charges" for certain types of injuries (e.g., fatalities and amputations) were added to the number of days lost due to injuries. Beginning in 1982, only the days lost due to lost-time injuries were contained in the severity rate.

As Table 7-3 indicates, there have also been declines in the numbers of the most serious injuries, those resulting in death or disability. For the North American operations as a whole, there is a clear downward trend in the number of fatalities, from 9 in 1977 to 4 in 1983. The number of permanent partial disabilities decreased from 68 to 24, and temporary total disabilities decreased from 1,688 to 442 during the same time period. These decreases in serious injuries are particularly significant in establishing the validity of injury reductions at Company Y because these injuries are much less subject to record keeping errors and intentional underrecording than less serious injuries that are more heavily represented in overall injury statistics.

On the whole, there is a great deal of satisfaction expressed by both labor and management involved with the North American operations regarding improvements in safety and health. Both the reductions in injury rates and the establishment of mechanisms for labor-management cooperation to bring about future improvements were praised. Nevertheless, there is recognition that safety and health problems do exist and that they will continue to present challenges.

TABLE 7-3
COMPANY Y SERIOUS INJURIES
NORTH AMERICAN OPERATIONS

Year	Total Serious Injuries	Fatalities	Permanent Total Disability	Permanent Partial Disability	Temporary Total Disability
1977	1,764	9	0	68	1,688
1978	856	5	0	76	775
1979	2,404	9	1	70	2,324
1980	905	4	0	39	862
1981	640	2	0	41	597
1982	467	2	0	14	451
1983	470	4	0	24	442
Average	1,072.3	5.0	0.14	47.4	1,019.9

Source: Company Y documents

The following sections describe safety and health operations at a Company Y plant in the midwestern United States and these operations in the United Kingdom, both at the national corporate subsidiary level and at an individual plant level.

MIDWESTERN U.S. PLANT

The midwestern plant of Company Y is located in a mid-sized city of a Sun Belt state. It is a relatively old plant, dating back to the early 1950s. Automobiles were assembled at this plant for most of the time since its start-up. The plant had been scheduled to be shut down in the early 1980s during the depths of the recession, but instead it was assigned production of two new pick-up trucks that turned out to be big hits with consumers. As a result, the plant has been portrayed as a model of industrial turnaround in favorable articles written about it in the popular press and in industrial publications. Because of the plant's ongoing success with these popular vehicles, there was a pervasive sense of accomplishment and achievement among both blue-collar and white-collar workers interviewed.

The accomplishments here are evident in objective measures. The plant was reportedly ranked first on Company Y ranking schemes for both productivity and quality. The quality index applies to all Company Y plants, but it was unclear whether the productivity ranking scheme applied to all plants, regardless of the vehicle produced, or only to the much smaller number of plants assembling small trucks. Workers and managers claimed that not only did this plant have the highest quality rating in Company Y, but that it produced the highest quality trucks in the world. This is obviously a subjective judgment, but it does reflect the confidence of the personnel at this plant.

Due to the brisk demand for the vehicles produced here, there is a heavy workload. Scheduled production is 75 vehicles per hour for two ten-hour shifts, for a total of 1,500 vehicles per day. This work pace of two hours overtime per day was in effect for the two years prior to the researcher's visit.

There are approximately 3,450 wage (production) and salaried workers combined. The production workers at the plant are organized by the UAW. The composition of the work force reflects local demographics. It is diverse with respect to race, age, and experience. In addition, there also are a significant number of women in the work force. Although the plant had been operating on overtime for the previous two years, there had not been any hiring of new employees.

Not surprisingly, the workers here are very well paid. The base wage is slightly over $13 per hour (1985 figure). With time and one-half pay for overtime, the lowest paid assembly workers made approximately $35,000 in each of the preceding two years. Some skilled craftsmen who made a higher base wage and who worked as much overtime as they could reportedly earned over $70,000 in each of these years.

Absenteeism at the plant declined significantly in relation to overall rates in the auto industry in recent years. The rate of absenteeism was reported to be the lowest in Company Y during the early 1980s. Workers attributed this decline to improved working conditions and employee morale. An attendance bonus program has also helped. The working conditions and morale had improved markedly along with productivity and quality in the last five or six years. Much of the credit for this was attributed to a new plant manager who took control at that time. He was described as being far more concerned about the workers than the previous plant manager, who was described as autocratic, dictatorial, and resistant to change.

One aspect of this different orientation of the new plant manager is a greater degree of employee involvement in decision making. This is most readily apparent in the employee involvement groups. There are 34 such groups in the plant, composed of 8 to 10 employees each. Both wage and salaried employees can participate in these groups, which meet for about 1.5 hours per week. Meetings take place both during working hours and after work and participants are paid for their time of involvement in both cases. They may consider any issues of concern that are not covered by contractual agreements. Issues that have been investigated by employee involvement groups include new health insurance arrangements, vendor relationships, philanthropic activities, and occupational safety and health issues. A new health insurance plan brought about by the initiative of these groups reportedly provides better coverage at a lower cost than the previous plan.

Occupational Safety and Health

There are two full-time safety engineers, one for each shift, who are in charge of occupational safety and health operations at the plant. The senior safety engineer has been in this position for 8 years. Prior to that time, he had been in the U.S. Air Force for 21 years, his final 14 of which were spent in bomb disposal operations. The junior safety engineer has 3 years experience in his current position. The safety engineers have responsibility for accident prevention, record keeping, some safety and health training, and any other safety and health activities or concerns that are not specifically delegated to someone else. These safety engineers report to a section supervisor who oversees safety, security, and fire protection. This section supervisor, in turn, reports to the plant industrial relations manager. The safety engineers and the section supervisor also report on their activities to the division safety engineer, who does not have any direct line authority over these plant-level officials. This organizational structure leads to occasional conflicts for plant safety officals, similar to those described in Company X. These occur when production or cost concerns conflict with safety concerns. Clearly the reward structure encourages greater attention to be paid to production and cost control.

Since the 1973 industrywide agreement with the UAW, there have been two union safety and health representatives in the plant. One of these is the regular representative; the other is an alternate who assumes the safety and health responsibilities when the regular representative is not at work. These representatives work with the safety engineers on the whole gamut of safety and health issues faced at the plant. Safety engineers and safety and health representatives have as an objective to conduct a joint safety and health inspection once a week. However, in practice, both the safety engineers and the union safety and health representatives typically perform their own independent inspections on an informal basis--observing for hazards as they pursue their other activities--rather than conducting formal joint inspections.

A number of other individuals in the plant are involved with various aspects of safety and health. Among these are the medical staff, which includes two full-time nurses and a full-time physician whose presence is somewhat unusual in a U.S. auto plant. There is also a salaried worker who has full-time responsibility for processing workers' compensation claims.

Operating staff also have certain safety and health responsibilities. First-line supervisors are required to give one five-minute safety and health talk per week. These talks may come from a manual of "canned" talks provided by an occupational safety and health consulting firm that is under contract with the plant for assistance in training. The talks may instead focus on some issue of special concern to the supervisor, such as a recent accident, the use of safety equipment, or safe/unsafe work practices. The first-line supervisors and the general foremen and department superintendents to whom they report are responsible for ensuring that the operating conditions in their areas of responsibility are safe.

In recent years the injury experience in the areas of responsibility of these supervisory personnel have been carefully reviewed weekly by a plant operating committee comprised of the upper-level managers at the plant. The senior safety engineer meets with this committee to report on the injury experience in the plant as a whole and within departments for the preceding week. Any supervisory personnel who have an unusual number of injuries in their jurisdictions during the week are also asked to attend the meeting to explain the reasons for these injuries. Needless to say, supervisory personnel do not look forward to such invitations.

Injury Experience

Historical data on the injury experience of this plant are provided in Table 7-4. This shows the incidence rate, the severity rate, and the injury experience ranking of this plant among all North American Company Y plants for 1977 through 1985. This ranking is based on an index derived by combining incidence rates and severity rates through a formula used by the Corporate Safety Department. Table 7-4 also provides data on the lost-workday case rates for 1984 and 1985. These data indicate that this plant has done somewhat worse than average for Company Y on these injury-rate dimensions over most of this time period.

During the time period considered, this plant has experienced a decrease in the injury incidence rate; however, it is not possible to judge the net change in the injury severity rate due to the change in its method of calculation. The incidence rate declined 47 percent from 9.77 injuries per 100 employees in 1977 to 5.15 in 1985. This decrease is only slightly less than the declines of 51 percent and 50 percent for the total North American operations of Company Y and the North American auto operations, respectively. Still, this plant started and ended this time period with injury incidence rates that were substantially higher than those of both North American operations groups.

The injury severity rate at this plant *increased* 76 percent from 1977 to 1981 (10.27 lost days per 100 employees to 18.07 lost days). This was followed by a decline of 59 percent (18.58 to 7.71) on the new injury severity measure for the period 1982-85. In contrast, the total North American operations of Company Y and the North American auto operations both experienced declines on these measures for both time periods.

As noted previously, all the U.S. plants of Company Y are ranked at corporate headquarters by their injury experience. This plant was in the middle of the rankings during the 1977-85 time period. It started the time period ranked 37th and ended it ranked 35th; during the period it was ranked as high as 26th and as low as 48th out of approximately 70 ranked plants. These rankings, which have introduced an element of competition among the plants, have caused the current plant manager to seek reduction of the plant's injury rates to improve its relative performance. He has emphasized this in dealings with the safety and health staff and supervisory personnel. As evidence of this, he instituted a system of evaluating supervisory personnel on their injury experience.

There are a number of goals of the plant with respect to safety and health. Plant officials would like to eliminate all OSHA-recordable injuries and become the top-ranked plant in the company. However, such targets were considered infeasible given the high level of production and the age of the plant. Thus, plant safety personnel have a more modest goal of reaching a ranking in the top ten plants of Company Y. There is also a goal to keep this rate of all injuries (including even first-aid injuries, which are not recordable according to OSHA criteria) under 2 percent of the work force per week for each department. Currently, some departments have been averaging over 4 percent.

TABLE 7-4
COMPANY Y MIDWESTERN ASSEMBLY PLANT
INJURY EXPERIENCE

Year	Ranking/ Number of Plants Ranked	Incidence Rate per 100 Employees	Severity Rate per 100 Employees	Lost-Workday Case Rate per 100 Employees
1977	37/72	9.77	10.27	N.A.
1978	48/74	10.72	8.23	N.A.
1979	40/74	4.76	42.84	N.A.
1980	36/73	2.14	37.33	N.A.
1981	26/70	2.11	18.07	N.A.
1982	43/56	1.91	18.58[1]	N.A.
1983	31/56	2.99	8.08[1]	N.A.
1984	44/62	6.03	9.07[1]	1.37
1985	35/62	5.15	7.71[1]	.81
Average	38/67	5.06	23.35 (1977-81) 10.86 (1982-85)	1.09

N.A. = Not available

Source: Company Y documents

[1] A different base for the severity rate is used as of 1982. Formerly, specific "charges" for certain types of injuries (e.g., fatalities and amputations) were added to the number of days lost due to injuries. Beginning in 1982, only the days lost due to lost-time injuries were contained in the severity rate.

Cooperation and Conflict

It is clear that occupational safety and health is a priority concern for both management and labor at this plant. The plant manager is keen on improving the injury experience ranking of the plant relative to other plants in Company Y. An additional concern is the cost of accidents and injuries. It was noted, for example, that in one week there had been 114 minor injuries. The senior safety engineer estimated that each of these injuries would result in a worker being away from his/her job for 20 to 25 minutes for medical attention. This would translate into a total of 38 to 48 hours of lost production time per week, costing the plant as much as $1,000 in wages and fringe benefits. Other employees who stopped working to help or just to watch would impose additional costs, as would equipment damage from the associated accident. This concern about accidents filtered down through management levels due to the emphasis placed on evaluation of supervisors on the injury experience in their areas of responsibility. The safety engineers also noted that there was considerable pressure placed on them to improve safety performance at the plant.

The employees are very concerned about safety and health issues at this plant. They actively pursue their safety and health concerns through a variety of channels, including contacts with the union safety and health representatives and the union negotiating team during plant-level contract negotiations and by filing safety and health grievances.

Typical of plants operating under the UAW safety and health agreements, there is a considerable amount of cooperation among labor and management safety and health representatives. These individuals reported highly supportive and effective working relationships with each other. The safety engineers and the union safety and health representatives can usually get an unsafe condition corrected without any formal consultation among themselves simply by talking directly with the workers and/or the supervisory personnel involved. In the cases where there is some disagreement over the appropriate course of action to take, the safety engineers and the union safety and health representatives can often work out an agreement informally among themselves and the other parties involved. Where this is not possible, the disagreement may lead to the filing of a grievance. On occasion when a supervisor has opposed a recommended solution, the safety engineers have taken what they refer to as a "back-door" approach, confidentially suggesting to the union representatives that a grievance be filed. Overall, though, supervisors are generally cooperative in resolving safety and health issues.

Joint training of union and management safety and health representatives was cited as a factor in promoting a spirit of cooperation among these individuals. Because they attend training programs together at corporate headquarters and at other locations away from the plant, this permits them to develop a certain degree of camaraderie in nonwork situations. For example, they mentioned that in such settings they would often go out together for dinner or a drink. They felt that this carried over into their work, allowing them to solve problems more amicably. They considered this to be a highly beneficial by-product of the training.

Both the safety engineers and the union safety and health representatives participate in plant-level contract negotiations regarding safety and health. They act as advisors to their respective negotiating teams. Negotiations regarding safety and health issues were reported to be relatively free of contentiousness. Most of the union's demands pertaining to safety and health conditions are generally conceded to by management.

This plant had the usual disagreements over the wearing of safety equipment and the following of safe work practices. Workers also occasionally contested whether the prescribed work method for a particular job was safe. In disputes where workers contest discipline they have received for not following safety rules, the union is obliged to defend them if requested to do so. However, the union usually undertakes the defense without much enthusiasm when it is clear that the employee is guilty as charged.

Another area in which there was evidence of substantial conflict on the safety and health dimension is in the frequent filing of grievances by production workers. For the most part, these grievances are filed over legitimate disagreements regarding safety and health conditions. A common complaint concerns the air quality in areas adjacent to work sites generating airborne pollutants (e.g., paint fumes or gasoline fumes). In a majority of these cases, complaints were filed with OSHA by individuals who had not raised the issue earlier with either a safety engineer or a union safety and health representative. This suggests a lack of confidence in the safety engineers and the union safety and health representatives that did not seem warranted. None of these complaint inspections resulted in OSHA citing the plant for a safety and health violation. In a few cases, it was evident that disgruntled workers requested inspections to harass or "get back at" supervisors for some issue not having to do with safety and health.

One issue that arose on the day of the researcher's visit to the plant was illustrative of both cooperation and conflict in the handling of safety and health matters. An OSHA inspector arrived during the day to investigate a safety and health complaint filed with the agency by a worker who had previously been dismissed. The worker had been dismissed for refusing to perform his job, which consisted of taking off two 25-pound metal rods from each vehicle that came down the assembly line. Because of the speed of the assembly line, this worker was lifting 150 of these rods (i.e., 3,750 pounds) per hour, and he felt that this constituted hazardous work. When the OSHA inspector arrived, one of the union safety and health representatives was called in for consultation. While everyone participating in these consultations conceded that this was not a particularly pleasant job, it did not violate any OSHA standards, and it was not viewed as being especially hazardous. Even the union safety and health representatives, who are obliged to represent the worker in such consultations, felt that the worker simply had a bad attitude. They did not consider this to be an issue worth pursuing.

The emphasis placed on injury statistics in plant comparisons and in staff evaluations, although beneficial in terms of increasing the attention devoted to safety, creates certain conflicts as well. Supervisors, on occasion, reportedly discourage the reporting of accidents or otherwise "fudge" on the injury statistics in an effort to improve the evaluations of their safety performance. The safety engineers, however, felt that there was more underrecording of injuries going on at other plants of Company Y and that this plant suffered in comparison. No doubt, this perception could be used as a justification for further fudging. It is likely that such attitudes contributed to the falsification of injury records (at a different Company Y plant) that led to the imposition of the OSHA fines.

The junior safety engineer indicated that a similar conflict developed between the safety and health staff and medical personnel pertaining to the effects on injury statistics of different possible medical treatments. Some injuries are defined by the type of medical treatment provided. For example, a laceration that is treated with a suture or a butterfly bandage is an OSHA-recordable injury. The same laceration that is, instead, dressed with a regular bandage is not an OSHA-recordable injury. The safety and health staff would naturally prefer a treatment that does not add to the number of recorded injuries due to the emphasis placed on reducing injury statistics by the plant manager. In situations requiring a close judgment call on the type of treatment, there are occasionally disagreements between what the safety and health engineers think is sufficient treatment and what the plant physician thinks is the preferred treatment. Of course, the plant physician has the final say.

Another related area of labor-management conflict is in the filing of claims for workers' compensation. Workers' compensation benefits are much more generous than are the benefits for nonwork-related disabilities. So it is in the interest of an employee to have a disability condition classified as work related. The plant, along with the rest of Company Y, is self-insured for injury compensation. Because of this, there is a strong financial incentive for the plant to treat a disability condition as nonwork related. Individual employees and the plant management have vigorously pursued their interests, and cases have ended up in court. Plant personnel attempt to sort out what they consider to be bogus claims and deny benefits to such individuals. Still, the workers' compensation administrator at the plant noted that there were cases where individuals received workers' compensation benefits to which she did not feel they were legitimately entitled. The administrator also conceded that there were a few cases in which workers were eligible for workers' compensation benefits but she deliberately misled the injured workers into believing that they were not entitled to them and benefits were withheld. These were injuries incurred in the company parking lot that the administrator considered to be the result of stupidity and/or horseplay. She did not feel that injuries suffered under such conditions deserved the more generous benefits that would come from workers' compensation. In other instances she saw to it that workers got more compensation that they were legally entitled to. This occurred in cases of partial amputations, for example, the worker losing part of a finger, which could be described in the workers' compensation claim as being more serious than it really was.

Interestingly, there were relatively few complaints about OSHA at this plant. There was some concern over "nit-picky" rules and regulations, but it was conceded that OSHA had made substantial progress in eliminating many of these. Still, it was felt that some of the OSHA standards that make sense for a small operation are not workable for an operation the size of this plant. Overall, however, OSHA was viewed as neither particularly troublesome nor particularly helpful at this plant. OSHA was judged to be more important for monitoring safety and health conditions in smaller operations that were less likely to have sophisticated safety and health programs such as existed at this plant and company. Safety and health personnel were, however, frustrated about the ease with which disgruntled workers could make spurious requests for inspections simply to harass management. Moreover, the OSHA fines imposed on Company Y after the visit to this plant made OSHA even more of a threat to be reckoned with by plant management.

BRITISH OPERATIONS

Company Y's operations in the United Kingdom are extensive. As of 1985 there were 23 factories or operating units there organized into 8 operational groups that employed over 50,000 workers.

The chief safety engineer for Company Y_{UK} has responsibilities similar to those of the safety engineering staff that oversees Company Y operations in North America. Reporting to him are group safety engineers, and, in some cases, (depending on plant size), plant safety engineers. The chief safety engineer's responsibilities include training, record keeping and reporting, disseminating information, advising top-level management and lower-level safety engineers, investigating accidents, and generally developing safety and health strategies and policies for Y_{UK}. One activity dictated by the HSW Act is the development, dissemination, and continual revision of a corporate health and safety policy manual that covers over 80 different topics.

Y_{UK} safety and health staff had recently conducted special safety and health training programs for 400 plant engineers. At these programs a topic of special interest was overseeing the safety and health activities of subcontractors who come onto company premises. Accidents involving subcontractor employees have been a serious and continuing problem at Company Y_{UK}.

Y_{UK} safety and health staff keeps injury records according to three different injury criteria. First, all injuries requiring any medical treatment are recorded. Second, all injuries involving lost work beyond the shift in which the injury occurred are recorded. These injuries, for the most part, correspond to the U.S. injury definition and are the ones reported back to U.S. headquarters.[1] Third, injuries involving four or more days away from work are reported to the British government.

Injury data conforming with these definitions/criteria are collected monthly. Injury reports and analyses focusing on lost-work injuries are made every six months. These reports are sent to key plant personnel (plant managers, industrial relations directors, and safety engineers). These individuals then circulate this information to plant safety and health committee members for appropriate action to be taken. Also, the injury reports are circulated to the top management of Company Y_E and of Company Y_{UK}; and they are sent to the safety and health staff at world headquarters. Injury experience Is also reported in the annual shareholders' report.

The injury reports are used primarily to compare current performance of operating units with the units' previous performance. Unlike the injury experience reports used by North American operations, these injury reports are not used to compare injury performance among operating units. (The rankings referred to below in the discussion of injury experience of the British plant were developed by this researcher.) It is felt by management that the various risks inherent in different plants would make such comparisons unfair. The safety and health goal for Company Y_{UK} is to decrease the injury rate (overall and for individual operating units) while increasing the production rate. In the past, the injury rate has risen and fallen with the production rate.

A joint labor-management safety and health committee exists at the national level for Company Y_{UK}. It meets twice a year to review safety and health conditions, to take remedial action when problems are discovered, to disseminate safety and health information, and to develop special safety and health campaigns.

Cooperation and Conflict

Labor-management cooperation on safety and health in Y_{UK} has improved in recent years. It was conceded that safety and health issues had been quite adversarial in the past. The corporate safety engineer of Y_{UK} contended that safety and health issues are still used by labor as a lever during contract negotiations to win concessions. However, this differs from the everyday interactions regarding safety and health between labor and management that are more cooperative. The increased cooperation was attributed to: (1) committees being run in a more participatory fashion than previously when the management chairmen often took dictatorial approaches; (2) committee members feeling more confident that management will be receptive to their ideas; and (3) the use in some instances of joint (worker-manager) chairmen of the committee. The increased cooperation on safety and health was even credited with improving industrial relations in general. The area of occupational safety and health is viewed as an excellent "ice breaker" for encouraging cooperation between labor and management on a broader range of issues.

Despite improvements in recent years, conflict regarding safety and health among labor, management, and government remains a problem. The refusal of workers to wear proper safety equipment was a common complaint. A company safety report complained of the "obduracy of persons" regarding the improper use of protective equipment. One approach used to address this problem is to have a labor-management committee write letters to the offending individuals. Obviously this is a cumbersome approach to work-rule compliance. Another problem in labor-management relations with respect to safety and health derives from the fragmented structure characteristic of unions in the United Kingdom. Different unions representing different classes of workers in a given plant have their own safety and health agendas.

Management had various complaints about government safety and health regulations and their enforcement, especially regarding ambiguity and confusion. Also, it was noted that inspectors were generally not available for informal consultation to eliminate this confusion. It is noteworthy that the company had been successfully prosecuted on several occasions by the Health and Safety Executive for safety and health violations.

Injury Experience

Some statistics on the injury experience of Company Y_{UK} are reported in Table 7-5. Although sketchy, these provide evidence that there have been improvements in injury rate performance over the years. The earliest year for which data are available is 1976, during which the lost-time injury frequency rate was 12.40 injuries per million hours worked. Thereafter, the frequency rate declined irregularly to 7.51 lost-time injuries per million hours worked in 1985. This represents a decline of 39 percent from 1976. This decline was somewhat less than the 51 percent decrease from 1977 to 1985 in the incidence rate for Company Y's North American operations. Still, the decreases in the injury rates for both of these corporate units were in the same general order of magnitude.

TABLE 7-5
COMPANY Y$_{UK}$
(GREAT BRITAIN)
INJURY EXPERIENCE

Year	Number Of Lost-Time Injuries	Lost-Time Injury Frequency Rate[1]	Lost-Workday Case Rate[2] per 100 Employees
1976	N.A.	12.40	2.48
1977	> 2,000	11.56[3]	2.31[3]
1978	1,610	10.10	2.02
1979	2,030	10.10	2.02
1980	1,659	8.30	1.66
1981	1,452	11.19	1.52
1982	1,219	9.85	1.97
1983	902	8.12	1.62
1984	784	7.75	1.55
1985	700	7.51	1.50
Average		9.69	1.87

N.A. = Not available
Source: Company Y$_{UK}$
[1] Number of lost-time injuries per million hours worked
[2] Number of lost-time injuries per 100 full-time employees. This was calculated by the researcher using the assumption that 100 full-time employees work 200,000 hours a year
[3] For first three quarters only

BRITISH PLANT

The British plant of Company Y$_{UK}$ is located on the outskirts of London in a rundown section of town. The plant is quite old, dating back at least to World War II, when it served as an aircraft manufacturing plant. The plant now manufactures and assembles medium- to heavy-duty trucks, with a capacity of 72 per shift. The overall operations at the plant are divided into Factory A and Factory B, which are located in different buildings and perform different functions.

There are approximately 1,700 hourly paid employees at the plant. There are also 280 managers and 300 supply workers and engineers, for a total of almost 2,300 workers. Virtually all the production workers are male; women were said not to like this type of work. Approximately 60 percent of the hourly paid workers are minorities, including West Indians, Indians, Africans, and Pakistanis. One reason that was cited for the high-minority representation in the work force was that the plant was located in an area that was heavily populated by minorities. Although there is high unemployment in the United Kingdom, and the jobs at this factory are quite attractive, white workers shunned them because of the location. Most of the salaried workers were white, and racial and even class distinctions were evident in labor-management relations.

Jobs at this plant are well paying in comparison with other job opportunities in the United Kingdom. Nevertheless, at prevailing exchange rates in 1983, the $4 to $5 per hour base pay of hourly workers in the United Kingdom was substantially less than the wages at the American plants and somewhat less than the wages at the Belgian plant ($5 to $6 per hour). Still, lower costs of living in Britain mean the disparity in the purchasing power between U.S. and U.K. workers of Company Y is less than the nominal wages would indicate.

Absenteeism at the plant is moderately high by U.S. standards but is considered to be under control by plant management. Total absenteeism, which includes all absenteeism except vacation absences during plant shutdowns was about 7.5 percent. Adjusted or unexcused absences ran about 5 percent to 5.5 percent. These figures were compared favorably by plant management with those at a Company Y plant in Amsterdam, Holland, which had, on average, an incredibly high total absenteeism rate of 40 percent. Also, it was noted that sick workers are eligible for compensation (paid by the employer who is reimbursed by the government) that replaces part of their lost income. Workers may certify themselves as sick and unable to work for up to a week. Considering these factors, management felt that the absenteeism rates were reasonable.

Several measures are used to control absenteeism at the plant. One of these is a system of progressive discipline such as is typically employed in U.S. plants. Another is making spot checks on employees at their homes to verify that those who claim to be sick are actually unable to work. This practice, which has generated so much controversy in Germany, was not particularly controversial in the United Kingdom. It certainly did, however, indicate a lack of trust in the workers.

One other measure for controlling absenteeism is the payment of attendance bonuses. The U.S. plant also provides attendance bonuses; however, what made the system at the British plant particularly interesting was that managers also receive such bonuses. Production workers were paid 7 to 9 pounds (1 £ $\simeq$ $1.50) per week for perfect attendance (1983 figure). Excused absences did not disqualify an individual from receiving the bonus. The salaried workers in the safety office were entitled to bonuses in the amount of 10 pounds per week for perfect attendance. This would be worth approximately $750 for one year's perfect attendance.

The labor-management relations at this plant and in Company Y_{UK} as a whole conformed with the stereotypic view of British labor-management relations. That is, there was considerable conflict and animosity, that was no doubt exacerbated by racial and class differences, between labor and management.   Moreover, the poor labor-management relations have led to lower levels of productivity at these operations.

An employee's letter to the editor and the response in the Company Y_{UK} newspaper highlighted several issues related to labor-management relations. The letter took exception to articles in previous editions of the newspaper that had unfavorably compared the British workers in Company Y_{UK} with German workers.   These articles had been written following a joint labor-management fact-finding tour of Company Y plants in Germany.   The letter suggested that German workers were more productive because they received higher wages, had more holidays, and received pay during layoffs (unlike British workers). The letter also placed blame for the relatively poor performance of British plants on management over-staffing and inefficiency.

The editor's response conceded only two of these points--that the German workers were paid slightly more than the British workers and that the German workers receive more holidays.   Both of these conditions, however, were attributed to excessive wage settlements achieved by British workers.   The editor contended that excessive wages for British labor in general had weakened the exchange rate of the pound considerably versus the German mark, leading to the higher value of the German workers' wages. The greater number of holidays enjoyed by the Germans was also attributed to the greater emphasis placed on negotiating wage increases by the British workers compared with more emphasis placed on holidays by the Germans.

The overall gist of the response was that none of these factors was adequate to explain the sizeable differences in productivity between the British and German workers and that British workers themselves must be blamed. Specifically mentioned were unofficial strikes and restrictive work practices that were charged with causing a loss of between 20 percent and 30 percent of production yearly.

This correspondence typified attitudes at this plant in general. Labor and management blamed each other for problems that existed. Safety managers also accused line managers of responsibility for problems that existed in the safety and health operations.

Safety and Health Operations

The safety and health activities within this plant followed dictates of national legislation and national collective bargaining agreements. There were three safety and health engineers at this plant who served principally in an advisory capacity and seven union safety representatives. One of the safety engineers served the entire plant, and there was one safety engineer assigned to Factory A and one assigned to Factory B.

There were also three labor-management safety and health committees at the plant corresponding to the jurisdictions of the safety engineers. These committees were formed several years before they were required by the Health and Safety at Work Act of 1974, and they meet monthly, exceeding the mandated four meetings per year.

A very detailed and potentially lengthy procedure to be followed when a worker has a safety grievance is spelled out in a pamphlet called "Agreement on Health and Safety for Hourly Paid Employees." According to this, a worker with a grievance is first supposed to discuss the grievance with his/her foreman. If the worker is not satisfied with the outcome of this discussion, the matter should be pursued with the shop steward, who will join the employee in discussions of the matter, in turn, with the foreman, the general foremen, and the union safety and health representative. The union safety and health representative may then bring unresolved disputes before the plant safety and health committee. If the matter is still not resolved after consideration at this level, labor or management may call in the Factory Inspectorate for an external resolution of the matter.

Cooperation and Conflict

There was some evidence of cooperation but much greater evidence of conflict between labor and management pertaining to safety and health at this plant. The safety committee structures were viewed as beneficial in promoting safety and health through labor-management cooperation. These committees were able to improve compliance with safety and health standards by both workers and supervisors. The functioning of these committees had improved over time and the involvement of workers in safety and health activities was viewed as a positive factor.

Evidence of conflict between labor and management regarding safety and health was easy to find. Workers not wearing proper safety equipment and the lodging of safety and health grievances were the two most obvious conflicts. Workers and union representatives who aggressively promote workers' safety and health rights created conflict but they improved working conditions at the same time. However, in some cases, workers made frivolous complaints that did not result in any hazard reduction but were merely attempts to harass management or simply to get a break from work. This clearly is a destructive form of conflict. Moreover, the situation was exacerbated by the multiple unions at the plant and the various concerns that they aggressively pursued.

Another type of conflict exists between safety engineers and line managers regarding the detection and the correction of workplace hazards. The safety engineers are supposed to carry out formal inspections of the plant on a quarterly basis. They admitted that they did not always adhere to this schedule but carried out informal inspections on a sporadic basis. When a hazard is found, the foreman responsible for the area is notified and directed to correct the situation. Follow-up inspections are usually conducted several weeks later. The safety engineers complained that the hazards are only rarely corrected by the time of the follow-up inspection. Usually they have more success in getting the hazard corrected after the second inspection, but they often are ignored again. Because of this, like their counterparts in the United States, they occasionally suggest to individual workers or union safety and health representatives that they file grievances about the condition. Due to the adversarial nature of the grievance procedure the condition is more likely to be corrected.

Safety engineers cited the tendency of line managers to ignore them as evidence of the lack of importance attached to safety and health at the plant. Production was given much higher priority. They also complained that they had difficulty convincing line managers of the need for safety training and education because this would take workers away from the production line. Related to the safety engineers' perception of the importance attached to safety and health is their perception of their own status in the organization. They complained that their low pay and small and crowded office confirmed to workers and managers alike that safety and health were not very important.

The complaints of the safety staff at this plant were both more numerous and more severe than at any other plant considered in this research. At other plants, safety personnel admitted to feeling a certain amount of animosity from individual workers and line managers. They also complained that some of these parties did not take safety and health seriously enough. However, these safety engineers felt that they weren't really taken seriously by anyone. The safety engineers must rely on persuasion to get things accomplished, and this is difficult given their perceived low status. Their role is largely advisory and they have only limited direct authority. For example, they typically are not involved in filing or reconciling safety and health grievances. They do have the authority to stop production if a hazardous situation is not corrected, but this is an extreme measure that would be viewed as a failure of their persuasive abilities.

Safety and health were viewed as being complementary to production and other economic goals of the plant only to a limited degree. This was evidenced by the slow response to requests to correct safety and health hazards. It was also evident in comments by the plant manager about the importance of safety and health. For example, he objected to the notion of evaluating individual managers on the safety and health dimension. He was afraid that managers might sacrifice production if safety and health performance were compensated. However, other plants considered in this research were both safer *and* more productive.

Because only one British plant was visited, it is uncertain how representative the safety and health relationships at this plant are of safety and health conditions throughout Company Y_{UK}. The corporate safety engineer of Company Y_{UK} felt that the problems described above were the fault of the plant safety engineers themselves. He indicated that where safety engineers establish their credibility in the plant through their technical expertise and persuasive abilities then such problems do not occur. Still, the injury experience at this plant was fairly typical of that of Company Y$_{UK}$ plants in Britain as a whole. It would appear that the assertiveness of workers and the union in promoting safety and health to a certain extent compensates for the lack of assertiveness by the safety and health staff.

Injury Experience

Table 7-6 shows the number of lost-time injuries and the lost-time injury frequency rate of this plant along with its ranking on this dimension among all Company Y$_{UK}$ plants. A ranking of "1" would mean the plant had the lowest injury rate. As this indicates, the plant started out the 1974-85 time period with 12.30 lost-time injuries per million hours worked. This increased to 22.10 in 1976. It reached an all-time low in 1983 of 7.07 and since then it has climbed back up to 7.95 (1985). The plant started out the time period ranked 15th out of 26 plants; it ended the time period ranked 12th out of 24. Its best ranking was 7th out of 26 in 1978 and its worst was 21st out of 26 in 1976.

TABLE 7-6
COMPANY Y$_{UK}$ BRITISH PLANT INJURY EXPERIENCE

Year	Number Of Lost-Time Injuries	Lost-Time Injury Frequency Rate[1]	Lost-Workday Case Rate[2]	Ranking/ Number of Ranked Plants[3]
1974	N.A.	12.30	N.A.	15/26
1975	N.A.	18.80	N.A.	15/26
1976	N.A.	22.10	N.A.	21/26
1977	N.A.	17.50	N.A.	15/26
1978	N.A.	9.86	N.A.	7/26
1979	110	N.A.	N.A.	N.A.
1980	116	N.A.	N.A.	N.A.
1981	64	12.67	N.A.	15/27
1982	43	9.90	N.A.	9/24
1983	24	7.07	N.A.	10/24
1984	26	7.84	1.57	12/24
1985	25	7.95	1.59	12/24
Average	58.29	12.60	1.58	13/25

Source: Company Y$_{UK}$
[1] Number of lost-time injuries per million hours worked
[2] Number of lost-time injuries per 100 full-time employees. This was calculated by the researcher using the assumption that 100 full-time employees work 200,000 hours a year.
[3] Ranking is based on injury frequency rates.

Looking at the 1976-85 time period, the plant went from much worse than average for Company Y_{UK} to only slightly worse than average. In 1976 the plant's lost-time injury frequency rate was 22.10 compared with 12.40 for all of Y_{UK}. By 1985 the difference was negligible on this dimension, 7.95 compared with 7.51. Thus, the plant had experienced a 64 percent decline in this rate during this time period compared with a 39 percent decline experienced by Y_{UK}.

Given the volatility in the lost-time injury rate at the plant it is perhaps more appropriate to compare the 1985 performance with an average of the 1974, 1975, and 1976 performances. The decline of 55 percent from this average of 17.73 is still greater than that of all Y_{UK} from 1976, thus indicating that relative performance has improved.

U.S./BRITISH COMPARISONS

It is only possible to make some very rough comparisons between the U.S. and British safety and health operations of Company Y. In the area of inputs, data are only available at the plant level. These indicate that the safety and health function at the British plant is much more heavily staffed than at the U.S. plant. There are three safety officials at this plant responsible for approximately 2,300 production and salaried workers combined. This converts to one safety official for every 767 workers. This is more than twice the ratio of safety staff to other workers in the U.S. plant, where there are two safety engineers for approximately 3,500 wage and salaried workers or one safety engineer for every 1,750 workers. Given the dubious effectiveness of these safety officials, it doesn't appear that this plant is gaining much from the relatively high level of staffing.

The U.S./U.K. differences in union safety and health representation are even greater. The seven British union safety and health representatives (from the various unions representing workers) at a plant of 2,300 workers converts to one union representative per 329 workers. This is more than five times the level at the U.S. plant where there is one union representative for every 1,750 workers.[2] This heavy representation of labor safety and health representatives allows the unions to pursue aggressively safety and health concerns, offsetting the lack of assertiveness by the safety and health staff.

Injury Experience

The relative performances of Company Y (North American operations) versus Company Y_{UK} are difficult to judge although the injury definitions used in these two areas of operation are similar. There are only three years (1983-85) for which comparable statistics are available. As can be seen by comparing Table 7-1 with Table 7-5, the lost-workday case rate for Company Y's North American operations was better than that of Company Y_{UK} for two of those three years (1985: 1.23 versus 1.50; 1984: 1.45 versus 1.55). It was worse in one year (1983: 1.82 versus 1.62). The three-year average on this measure for Company Y's North American operations is only slightly lower than that for Company Y_{UK} (1.50 versus 1.56). There is a somewhat greater disparity on this dimension between Company Y's North American auto operations and Company Y_{UK}. The North American auto operations had an average lost-workday case rate of 1.33 (per 100 employees) in 1984 and 1985. Still, the minimal differences in these comparisons do not allow us to draw any firm conclusions about the relative safety performances of these business units.

The U.S. plant of Company Y has a somewhat lower lost-workday case rate than the British plant. This rate averaged 1.09 in 1984 and 1985 for the U.S. plant compared with 1.58 for the British plant in these two years. In percentage terms this is a considerable difference. The British plant has a 45 percent higher lost-workday case rate than the U.S. plant. Still, the time period for which comparable data are available is short. Also, underrecording of injuries at the U.S. plant could account for much of the differences in injury rates, especially because in the United States the injury statistics are given greater weight in managerial evaluations. With additional data it would be fruitful to consider further possible underlying sources of bias, including other employer and employee incentives for having injuries recorded or not recorded.

Although the data are limited, again there is evidence of an inverse relationship between safety and health staffing levels and injury experience. The British plant had these higher injury rates despite having almost twice as many safety and health specialists per capita as the U.S. plant.

Cooperation and Conflict

In both of the plants, management's behavior for handling occupational safety and health conflicts with labor is highly assertive and only moderately cooperative. There have, however, been increases in cooperation in recent years, which have been more pronounced in the U.S. plant. It is thus judged that management at the U.S. plant has slightly more cooperative and slightly less assertive conflict-coping behaviors than the management of the British plant. Labor's conflict-coping behaviors at these two plants are reciprocal with those of management, with British labor somewhat less cooperative and somewhat more assertive than U.S. labor. British and U.S. labors' relative positionings on Figure 1-1 would be approximately the same as those for their respective managements.

NOTES

1. In addition to the length of time of work incapacity criterion, OSHA imposes certain injury or treatment criteria of injuries. Thus,

some incidents involving no lost workdays could be classified as injuries by OSHA. Due to the lack of any Company Y system for ensuring conformity in reporting injuries according to these criteria, there are certain differences in reporting practices between U.S. and British components of Company Y.

2. These figures include nonunion management personnel, so they should only be considered as general measures of plant size.

8

WORKER SAFETY AND HEALTH IN COMPANY Z

In this chapter, we bring to a close our examination of occupational safety and health at the corporate and plant levels. The focus of our analysis in this chapter is Company Z, an automotive firm based in Sweden with operations in several countries, including the United States. Although considerably smaller than Company X and Company Y, like them, Company Z has substantial nonautomotive activities. Company Z has been among the leaders of Swedish companies in pioneering efforts to promote occupational safety and health and more general quality-of-work-life improvements. Thus, it provides a useful perspective for this study to look at Company Z's safety and health activities in two truck plants, one in Sweden and one in the United States. Relevant dimensions considered in these plants for comparative purposes are: (1) basic organizational information, (2) the structure and functioning of the safety and health programs, including resources utilized and cooperative/conflictual aspects of labor-management relations regarding these programs, and (3) injury experience.

ORGANIZATIONAL STRUCTURES AND OPERATIONS

In Sweden, the Truck Division of Company Z operates as a separate company. Most of the operations of the Truck Division are located in the same general vicinity, close to one of the major cities in Sweden. There are just three plants of Company Z in the United States; these are located at great distances from one another and they each operate as separate divisions in the corporation.

Both of the plants under consideration are relatively new and comparable in size. The Swedish plant began operations in 1981. Featuring a dramatically new production process, it provides an experimental approach to quality-of-work-life improvement. The U.S. plant began operations in 1975 under different ownership. It was acquired by the present parent company several years later after being idled for a period of time due to the bankruptcy of its former corporate parent.

These plants are both quite small compared with most of the other automotive plants considered in this study. (The one exception is the Kenyan plant of Company X, which is even smaller.) The medium- to heavy-duty trucks assembled at these plants have a far greater labor content than do automobiles or light trucks because there is less opportunity for automation of production processes. Most of the trucks assembled have been ordered prior to assembly, and various options are specified on a manifest that accompanies the truck during assembly. These plants have much smaller production runs than automobile plants; each has a single shift production of about 20 to 25 trucks per day. Scheduled production at both plants is between 5,000 and 6,000 trucks per year. There are approximately 260 production workers at the Swedish plant and approximately 400 production and maintenance workers, combined, at the U.S. plant. (There are also about 260 salaried workers at the U.S. plant, for a total of approximately 660 employees.)[1]

The workers at the Swedish plant are not as inexperienced as the newness of the plant might suggest. Many of the workers at this facility were not newly hired but rather were transferred from other nearby facilities owned by the same company. There is, however, approximately a 20 percent yearly turnover at the plant and at the rest of Company Z in Sweden. This is extraordinarily high compared with auto firms in the United States. This means that there is a fairly large minority of inexperienced workers at any given time.

The high turnover rate at the Swedish plant was attributed by management to the generous benefits provided to unemployed workers by the Swedish social welfare system. There are also attractive alternative employment options in the area paying as much or more than work for Company Z. In contrast, jobs at the Company Z plant in the United States are highly prized. They are the best-paying production jobs in the area. In fact, in 1985 when this plant announced plans to start hiring new workers for increased production, the Personnel Department was overwhelmed with applicants. Some applicants had traveled hundreds of miles from throughout a multistate region in the hope of landing a job at this plant.

The organization of work is significantly different in the two plants. Trucks under construction in the U.S. plant are moved via a traditional assembly line. In the Swedish plant, trucks in progress are moved by individually controlled, battery-powered transporters. These transporters reduce noise levels and do not contribute to in-plant pollution levels. They were specially designed by the company in an experimental effort aimed at improving the quality of work life by eliminating the need for an assembly line. The work still flows in two lines, "flow 1" and "flow 2," but the transporters give the worker control over work speed. Workers can build up buffers and vary work speed throughout the day. This flexible production is intended to reduce the psychological stress of assembly work, a more important concern in Sweden than in the United States. In addition, the transporters can be raised or lowered to give the workers better access to the truck components on which they are working, thereby reducing injuries resulting from reaching or working in awkward positions.

Workers in the Swedish plant who reach their daily production quotas early are permitted to stop working. They can then use the balance of the workday to learn new jobs, for which there is a financial incentive, or, less constructively, to rest, to engage in recreational activities--table tennis is particularly popular--or even to take a nap.

Other Swedish truck plants in the vicinity use the more traditional assembly line approach to production. Even in these plants, however, the workers' jobs are more flexible than in the U.S. plant.

SAFETY AND HEALTH ACTIVITIES

The structure and operation of the occupational safety and health function of Company Z in Sweden are largely dictated by national safety and health legislation and national labor-management agreements. Because the Truck Division of Company Z operates as a separate company, a company-level labor-management safety and health committee is required. This committee oversees and coordinates the safety and health activities of all the Truck Division plants in Sweden. These plants are in close proximity to one another, thereby facilitating direct oversight of safety and health activities by the committee. There are approximately 4,000 employees in these plants. As required by Swedish law for a plant of this size, there are two professional safety engineers and two physicians at this plant. They are assisted in their activities by several clerks and auxiliary medical personnel.

The safety committee is headed by the vice-president of production of the Truck Division, and it is composed of eight labor representatives and seven management representatives (including the plant manager of the facility, which is the focus of this comparison). The composition of this committee conforms with the national Swedish labor agreement on working conditions, which stipulates that employees comprise a majority on the mandated labor-management safety committees. The plant physicians and safety engineers are not voting members of the committee, but they routinely attend as observers and technical specialists. The committee, which meets four times a year and at other times as the need arises, reviews accident reports and injury statistics, makes recommendations, funds various safety and health activities from a budget it administers, and, to a large extent, sets safety and health policy and goals. Safety goals typically are incremental yearly reductions of the numbers of injuries for each reporting area. Other functions of the safety committee are the same as those specified in the Working Environment Agreement negotiated among the Swedish Employers Confederation, the Swedish Confederation of Trade Unions, and the Swedish Federation of Salaried Employees in Industry and Service (see Chapter 4).

In addition to the company-level safety committee, there are safety committees at the plant level and at the department level. For example, there are plant-level safety committees at the focal assembly plant and at an older truck assembly plant nearby. There are safety committees for white-collar workers in the administrative offices and for production workers in various other departments. These committees meet once a month and administer small budgets available for safety and health expenditures. Safety delegates or stewards are appointed by their union for each of the work areas (consisting of about 30 to 40 workers each) within each plant or department.

Safety and health activities at the focal plant are typical for these other plants and departments as well. At the shop-floor level, foremen are responsible for conducting formal safety and health inspections once a month. The company safety committee (or one of its subcommittees) conducts inspections every six months. The safety delegates also conduct inspections as they see fit, but because they spend much of their time on the shop floor anyway these are not usually formal inspections; they simply look for hazards as they conduct their other work activities.

The safety delegates represent the employees in working for safety and health improvements within their specified work areas. An individual employee with a relevant concern is supposed to bring the issue first to the attention of his/her supervisor. If the supervisor is not available or fails to take action satisfactory to the employee, the employee then raises the matter with the safety delegate. The safety delegate represents the employee in discussions of the issue with the supervisor, with the plant safety committee, and/or with the company safety committee. An individual employee who is dissatisfied with the outcome of this process or the pace at which the appeal process takes place has a powerful trump card to play. He/she may demand a government inspection and force the safety steward to halt production until the inspector arrives. At this plant, this happens about once a year, usually when an employee gets frustrated over what appears to be foot dragging by management in responding to some safety or health complaint of the employee.

When an accident (or near accident) occurs, the relevant company and union personnel will investigate the circumstances. Typically included among the investigators are one of the safety engineers and the foreman and safety delegate responsible for the area in which the accident occurred.

In the U.S. plant, the safety and health organization and activities are much simpler and less dictated by government regulations and union agreements. Company Z's operations in the United States are not covered by the safety and health cooperation agreements the UAW negotiated with other auto firms in 1973. Safety and health operations at the plant are also largely autonomous from corporate control. The involvement of Company Z's U.S. headquarters in safety and health is restricted mainly to record keeping and reporting. The U.S. corporate manager of safety and health also has responsibility for security at the plants and equal employment opportunity compliance. His office collects injury statistics from the few U.S. plants and ranks the plants on their performance. It also serves as a conduit for this and other safety and health information flowing back to the plants.

Corporate involvement from Sweden in safety and health affairs at the U.S. plant is minimal and largely informal. There are frequent visits to the plant by corporate delegations from Sweden. They may, on occasion, discuss some safety and health matter with plant officials. For example, visiting corporate officials noted that the noise levels in the plant were relatively high compared with those in truck plants in Sweden. However, there has been no deliberate attempt to modify the U.S. safety and health operations to conform with those of Company Z's facilities in Sweden. Other issues pertaining to labor-management relations and personnel matters have been similarly unaffected by corporate headquarters, which appears willing to trust the judgment of U.S. managers.

At the U.S. plant, the safety administrator has primary responsibility for all facets of safety and health in the plant, including training, inspecting, and record keeping. During the course of this study, there was a change in personnel at this position. The first safety administrator was promoted to a more senior position in the Personnel Department that did not involve safety and health activities. Both of the safety administrators were young. Neither had formal educational training in the occupational safety and health field prior to this assignment; both were more generally trained in the personnel field. The safety and health field was not a career track for either of them; rather, this position was a step in their personnel careers.

The first safety administrator estimated that he spent approximately 70 percent of his time on safety and health, with the rest of it spent on other personnel-related issues. This, however, seems to be an exaggeration. The union representative estimated the time spent on safety and health by this safety administrator to be only 25 percent. In subsequent analyses we will use the midpoint of these two estimates, 47.5 percent. The safety administrator also has responsibilities in various other personnel areas, such as hiring, training and disciplining workers, and monitoring absenteeism. Earlier in the plant's existence, the safety administrator function had been a full-time position but additional responsibilities in other areas were assigned to it. The safety administrator reports to the plant personnel manager, who has oversight responsibility in this area.

Other personnel involved with safety and health are the plant nurse, her supervisor, who has record keeping responsibilities, and various clerical workers. Supervisory personnel are involved through training workers and supervising efforts to keep work areas hazard-free. Supervisors are required to give weekly five-minute safety talks that focus, for the most part, on what employees themselves can do to avoid accidents. Most of these are "canned lectures" that come from notes prepared by the safety administrator. The safety administrator and the relevant supervisory personnel investigate and report on accidents when they occur.

Several years earlier management formed an ad hoc committee to deal with the perceived problem of excessive noise at the plant.

This committee consists of most of the management-level safety personnel and several other line and staff managers. The comment by Swedish corporate officials about noise levels was not the sole cause for the formation of this committee but it probably gave it added impetus.

PLANT COMPARISONS

This section considers differences between the U.S. and Swedish plants on several dimensions: resources devoted to safety and health, cooperation and conflict orientations, and work injury experience.

Inputs

Data on resources devoted to the safety and health functions at these two plants are incomplete but nevertheless provide some insight into organizational commitment to this area. The amount of safety administrator/safety engineer time per employee appears to be somewhat greater at the Swedish plant. The estimated 47.5 percent of the safety administrator's time devoted to safety and health for 1,050 employees (1986 figure) works out to one full-time administrator for 2,211 employees. This is only a slightly lower safety and health staffing level than the one full-time safety engineer per 2,000 employees at the Swedish plant. (Two full-time safety engineers are employed for the 4,000 workers at the several truck plants clustered together in Sweden.) The actual disparity in safety and health staffing levels is, however, greater than this indicates. As noted in earlier chapters, when a safety administrator or safety engineer has other responsibilities, these can detract from the performance of the safety and health function. Thus, the safety administrator at the U.S. plant may, for periods of time, be devoting little or no attention to safety and health matters. There are also important qualitative differences regarding the safety and health functions at these two plants. At the Swedish plant the safety engineer position clearly is accorded greater prestige than the safety administrator position at the U.S. plant. Safety engineering is a viable and respected career track in the Swedish operations. In the U.S. operations, there are not even any higher full-time safety positions to which the safety administrator can aspire. The safety administrator position is viewed as a challenging but temporary assignment for upwardly mobile young managers in the Personnel Department. Other personnel duties that the safety administrator has assigned to him may be accorded weight equal to or greater than that accorded to safety and health in determining his advancement in the organization.

There are also important quantitative and qualitative differences in other employees' contributions to safety and health at these two locations. At the Swedish plant, employee and manager time devoted to safety and health in various committee meetings and other activities is significant. Moreover, there are other safety and health personnel at the Swedish plant, most notably two full-time plant physicians (compared with just one full-time nurse at the U.S. plant), who contribute substantially to the quality of the safety and health program.

Precise figures on other safety/health inputs were also not available, but it was clear that considerably more resources were devoted to safety and health at the Swedish plant than at the U.S. plant. This was evident in the attention paid to noise limitation through engineering controls and in the development of the electric truck movers. It was also evident in the existence of budgets available for discretionary expenditures by the safety committees in Sweden.

Cooperation and Conflict

Compared with workers in the Swedish plant, the U.S. workers have very little involvement in decision making regarding safety and health. Until only recently, workers did not participate in any formal way in the inspection procedures. They still do not participate in goal setting or in the evaluation of the plant's overall safety and health performance. The union does, however, periodically have safety and health programs at its biweekly meetings. These are completely independent of company safety efforts.

Workers at Company Z's U.S. plant won modest rights to participate in safety and health activities in a 1984 contract. This was more than ten years after the first landmark cooperative safety and health agreement in the auto industry. At the urging of the national UAW, the local bargaining unit at Company Z demanded in the 1984 contract negotiations that a union safety and health representative position be established. Despite management's initial resistance to this demand, it eventually conceded to it. The union safety and health representative now accompanies the safety administrator on the monthly inspections. He also receives and investigates safety and health complaints from workers and works with the safety administrator to resolve problems. This union involvement with safety and health activities, although a change from past practices, is still relatively modest compared with companies covered by the 1973 agreement.

Ironically, despite the relatively low level of employee participation in safety and health decision making at the U.S. plant, safety and health performance appears to be more dependent on employees' individual safety and health practices. Compared with the Swedish plant, the prevention of injuries and disabilities in the U.S. plant is more dependent on workers' protective equipment. This is particularly evident with respect to noise. Workers in a number of areas in the U.S. plant were required to wear hearing protection. In the Swedish plant, the loudest sounds on the shop floor came from the employees' radios that were blaring from individual work sites. The low level of production noise was due to engineering efforts such as the development of the transporters. In contrast, safety contests in the U.S. plant foster a sense of competition among workers regarding safety and housekeeping. U.S. workers, like Swedish workers, are responsible for keeping their own work areas safe and clean. In the U.S. plant, workers in the work area judged the safest and cleanest in the monthly inspection are rewarded with free coffee or milk and doughnuts. They also retain a trophy for the month.

Even before agreement on labor involvement in safety and health, workers in the U.S. plant could raise concerns about safety and health with their supervisors and with the safety administrator. They could also file grievances on these matters through their union steward. The union and management would then try to resolve the grievances, with the union having the right to strike over unresolved grievances. There were relatively few safety and health complaints that even reached the grievance stage and none that progressed to the strike stage. An individual worker also has the legal right to request an OSHA inspection should a condition persist that he/she believes to be hazardous. In almost all cases workers exhaust internal appeal procedures before seeking outside involvement.

The minimal employee involvement in safety and health decision making in the United States is consistent with the desires of management. Managerial personnel felt that they could do a better job of managing the safety program without employee involvement in decision making than with it. Thus, they felt that there was no need to concede a managerial prerogative. At one point, they even expressed concern that increased employee and union knowledge and involvement in safety and health could actually create problems, such as disputes over trivial, nondangerous OSHA violations. However, after the 1984 agreement, management personnel reconciled themselves to union participation in safety and health matters. This initial fear can be partially explained by an event several years earlier when a disgruntled employee called for an OSHA investigation over a minor housekeeping matter.

The above incident and the minimal employee involvement in safety decision making can best be understood in the context of the American tradition of adversarial relationships between labor (at least organized labor) and management. Many of the managers had previously worked in other parts of the auto industry (including with the previous parent firm) where they had become acculturated to adversarial relations, and they may have brought that orientation with them. Still, the labor-management relations at this plant were more cordial than in many other parts of the U.S. automotive industry. For example, there have been no strikes in the plant's 14-year history. Nevertheless, the labor-management relations clearly had more in common with the rest of the U.S. auto industry than with the Swedish operations of Company Z.

There was also a certain degree of paternalism in the labor-management relations at the U.S. plant. This perhaps may have seemed more obvious because the production workers lived primarily in the rural South and many of the managers had come from the midwestern center of the auto industry. Managers felt that they could represent the interests of the employees better than the union could. This feeling was commonly expressed by managers who said that they were not "anti-union" but "pro-employee." The union was viewed as a third party, that had to be lived with but that stood in the way of better management-employee relations.

Indicative of the status of labor-management relations, managers refused the researcher permission to meet with union officials to discuss safety and health issues on company premises. This was a courtesy that was extended at most of the other plants that were visited. A meeting was, however, arranged independently at the union headquarters to discuss these matters.

Managers at the Swedish plant and at the Swedish corporate headquarters complained about the large number of requirements placed upon them by government and by labor-management agreements. In their view, these limited their prerogatives in managing the work force in a broad range of activities, including those related to safety and health. Moreover, they felt that the government required them to undertake certain activities that caused them to sacrifice production for worker convenience. The view of some managers that government had "gone too far" regarding safety and health regulations was, however, disputed by safety and health professionals in the company.

The sharp contrast in the orientations of labor-management relations can be seen quite graphically by reference to Figure 1-1. Management's behavior toward labor regarding safety and health in the U.S. plant can be viewed as high in assertiveness and low in cooperativeness. This is in the competition (domination) region. Management's behavior toward labor in the Swedish plant can be viewed as low in assertiveness and high in cooperativeness. This is in the accommodation region. The dominating and accommodating relationships in these two plants would appear at opposite extremes in the cooperation/conflict matrix.

Labor's orientation in these two plants is different than that of management. In the U.S. plant, labor's behavior is moderate in assertiveness and moderate in cooperativeness. In the Swedish plant, labor's behavior is moderate in assertiveness and high in cooperativeness. Thus, there is not as great a disparity between these plants in labor's behavior toward management as there is in management's toward labor.

Injury Experience

Given the major differences in orientations of the safety and health programs at these two plants, it is interesting to consider differences in injury experience. As was noted previously, injury statistics are subject to a number of statistical distortions that make comparisons difficult. When viewed with appropriate caution, however, the comparison of injury rates at these two plants is quite interesting.

Table 8-1 shows work injury rates for the U.S. and Swedish operations on the following dimensions: injuries per million hours worked, lost hours (due to injuries) per million hours worked, and lost hours per injury. The statistics for the Swedish operations include the plant described above (since it began operations in 1981) and several company plants in the same general vicinity. The only time for which statistics for the focal plant are available separately--weeks 1 to 43 of 1983--was when the plant had a considerably higher injury rate than one older truck assembly plant nearby, 79.1 versus 41.8 injuries per million hours. This was attributed to high personnel turnover resulting in many new inexperienced workers and to many production changes occurring at the same time. The injury statistics were reported to be roughly comparable at the two plants after that period.

TABLE 8-1
INJURY RATES FOR THE
U.S. PLANT AND SWEDISH PLANTS OF COMPANY Z

	U.S. PLANT			SWEDISH PLANTS		
	Injuries per Million Hours Worked[1]	Lost Hours per Million Hours Worked	Lost Hours per Injury	Injuries per Million Hours Worked	Lost Hours per Million Hours Worked	Lost Hours per Injury
1975	15.20	3,069.15	201.90	N.A.	N.A.	N.A.
1976	3.20	377.30	117.90	N.A.	N.A.	N.A.
1977	2.79	384.39	137.80	48.2	5,135.88	106.6
1978	8.30	615.14	74.10	51.5	5,015.52	97.4
1979	17.34	3,103.09	178.90	36.8	3,815.78	103.7
1980	7.61	400.00	52.56	43.7	3,806.85	87.0
1981	3.98	406.30	102.10	39.0	4,798.10	123.0
1982	5.89	314.28	53.33	37.8	N.A.	N.A.
1983	7.24	327.99	45.33	43.4	N.A.	N.A.
Average	7.95	999.74	107.10	42.9	4,514.43	103.54

N.A. = Not available
Source: Company Z records
[1] Personal calculations based on the assumption that 100 full-time workers work 200,000 hours per year.

The differences in injury rates between the U.S. and Swedish operations are both striking and surprising. Statistics are available for both the U.S. plant and the Swedish plants for the years 1977-83. Only injuries per million hours worked are available for the Swedish plants in 1982 and 1983. For the years 1977-83, the U.S. plant had far fewer injuries per million hours worked. For each year in which comparable statistics are available (1977-81) the U.S. plant also had far fewer lost hours per million hours worked. The average number of injuries per million hours worked in the Swedish operations (42.9) was more than 5 times the average of 7.94 in the U.S. plant. Over the time period considered, the disparity varied considerably. In 1977 the Swedish operations had an injury rate 17 times as high as the U.S. plant; in 1979, the rate was only twice as high.

The disparity in lost hours due to injuries per million hours worked is almost as great as the disparity in the injury frequency rate. For the years 1977-81 there was an average of 4,514.43 lost hours per million hours worked in the Swedish operations. This is 4.5 times the average in the U.S. plant of 999.73 lost hours due to injuries per million hours worked from 1975-83. The seriousness of the injuries, as indicated by the lost hours per injuries, was roughly comparable in the two plants. In the U.S. plant there was an average of 107.10 hours lost per injury in the 1975-83 time period. In the Swedish operations there was an average of 103.54 hours lost per injury from 1977 to 1981. These statistics are especially puzzling given comments by safety and health personnel in the Swedish operations that injuries were not a problem. Their main concern was with stress, both the physical and psychological varieties.

As we saw for Company X and Company Y, again there is an inverse relationship between safety and health staffing levels and injury rates at Company Z. Still, the disparity in staffing levels between the Swedish and U.S. operations of Company Z is not that great, at least in terms of quantity of personnel.

The reasons for these enormous disparities in injury rates are worthy of speculation. The first source to consider naturally would be a difference in injury definition, but these are very similar. In both cases, the injured worker must not be able to work the day after the injury occurred for the incident to be counted as a lost-work injury.

A second factor to consider is whether or not the U.S. or Swedish operations have significantly different injury rates than similar firms in their respective countries. As a check on the representativeness of these two operations, comparisons were made with the national injury statistics of firms in the same industry.

Automotive manufacturers in Sweden for the years 1980, 1981, and 1982 averaged 39.4 injuries per million hours worked (National Board of Occupational Safety and Health, 1983, 1984, and 1985a). This is very close to the 40.2 injuries per million hours worked reported by the Swedish operations of Company Z for the same time period. In contrast, the motor vehicle and equipment industry in the United

States had far higher lost-work injury rates than Company Z's U.S. plant. This industry averaged 19 lost-work injuries per million hours worked for these three years compared with an average of 5.8 lost-work injuries for the U.S. plant over the same time period. This comparison indicates that the U.S. plant's better injury record compared with that of the Swedish operations can be attributed primarily to the U.S. plant's superior injury record relative to the U.S. motor vehicle and equipment industry rather than to a particularly poor injury record by the Swedish operations.

The organization of work at the focal Swedish plant, although designed to improve the quality of work life, including reducing injuries, probably accounts for some of the unfavorable disparity in injury rates. The Swedish workers have much more flexibility in how they perform their work tasks than do individuals who work on an assembly line. Although an attractive feature of the work environment in many respects, this flexibility gives the worker more opportunities to do something that will injure himself/herself.

Another apparently favorable aspect of the work flexibility is that workers can work at their own pace rather than having to work at the speed of an assembly line. This has the potential safety benefit of not *forcing* workers to rush their work and, by so doing, to take certain risks. However, it does *allow* the worker to act in these ways. Moreover, there do appear to be real incentives for the workers to hurry because they are permitted to engage in various desirable activities once their daily work quota is reached. This incentive factor is similar in certain respects to that in piece rate or incentive pay work, which are associated with higher injury rates than straight wage work.

The differences in production technology, however, clearly do not explain all the disparity in injury statistics. The other Swedish truck plants that have production technology more similar to that in the United States also have injury rates far higher than those at the U.S. plant.

Two other explanations appear to account for some of this injury rate disparity. First, in Sweden, workers can receive sickness and injury compensation for work-related and nonwork-related disabilities for several years before becoming eligible for an early retirement pension. Thus, a few workers with long-term work-related disabilities can greatly inflate the injury severity rates and absenteeism rates, because they could be counted everyday for several years among those absent due to work illnesses or injuries. In the U.S. plant, a worker with a nonwork-related disability would only be included in the absenteeism statistics for one year. For work-related injuries, the length of time a worker would be included in the injury statistics would vary from case to case; however, there have not been any cases when an injury has been counted for a long period of time.

Second, there may be a better (or at least a more inclusive) injury-reporting system in Sweden. The medical staff there believe that improvements in safety and health over time are not fully reflected in the statistics. Some injuries and illnesses that previously went unreported are now being recorded. In addition, it is very likely that workers are counting as injuries and missing work for incidents that would not be certified as injuries and cause loss of work in the U.S. plant. This seems likely to be the case for several reasons.

Of primary importance is the fact that workers in Sweden have the final say in determining what is and what is not counted as a work injury. Physicians may encourage employees to initiate reporting procedures when they believe employees have been injured on the job. But it is the duty of the company to report to the government every incident in which an employee claims to have incurred a work injury, regardless of the view of the doctor or of management. Thus, it would be a simple matter for a worker to fake (or to exaggerate) an injury and to have it recorded in the statistics. The likelihood that at least the exaggeration of injuries occurs is high due to the nature of the injuries recorded at the Swedish operations. Although there is no direct financial incentive for an individual to report an injury, there is an indirect incentive. Higher reported work injury rates provide labor unions with certain bargaining leverage in their efforts to win greater control over work. Because of this, unions in Sweden encourage workers to report all injuries.

As previously mentioned, safety personnel stated that strains were more of a concern than other injuries, which they contended were not a problem. It seems likely, then, that the injury statistics would contain a large proportion of physical strains, such as a pulled muscle in the back or in an arm. (The Swedish operations' injury statistics indicate only the location of the injury, not the nature of the injury.) Although strains might cause a loss of work, they are obviously not as serious as a major injury like a broken bone, a severe laceration, or an amputation. There is also less concrete evidence of the actual existence of such an injury.

Strains are certainly viewed differently by medical and safety and health personnel at the U.S. plant. They were never mentioned as a concern there. Medical and safety and health personnel in the United States typically insist on some evidence of an injury rather than simply taking the worker's word that the injury occurred, as is the case with strains at the Swedish plant. The screening out of bogus claims is considered an important function of company medical and safety personnel in the United States. It is also likely that in the U.S. plant, medical staff and safety and health personnel and even the employees themselves would think that a strain would need to be more severe to be considered incapacitating than would be the case in Sweden. Moreover, because U.S. safety personnel are evaluated, in part, on the plant's safety record, they will have an incentive not to record borderline cases as work injuries.

The greater reliance in Sweden on the individual's judgment concerning incapacity to work is also reflected in the country's absenteeism policies. As previously noted, workers can certify themselves as unable to work for physical or even mental or emotional reasons (e.g., depression or psychological stress) for up to seven days before a doctor must certify that they are unable to work. During this time period, the workers receive 90 percent of their salary. Self-certified illnesses account for about 3 percentage points of the 13 percent absenteeism rate due to work-related and nonwork-related injuries and illnesses. This is about equal to the total absenteeism rate due to work-related and nonwork-related injuries and illnesses at the U.S. plant.

The U.S. plant requires a doctor's certification of illness for three days' absence. Hourly workers are eligible for sickness and accident benefits at about 60 percent of salary after they are absent due to illness for seven days. Prior to that, they receive no benefits except in cases of injuries and/or hospitalization. When an attendance control program was first initiated in 1979, workers were required to submit a doctor's excuse for one day's absence. This met with worker resentment and was changed. There is now no longer a distinction made between excused and unexcused absences. Workers are still encouraged to submit doctors' excuses for less than three days' absence. Because workers are disciplined for excessive absenteeism, such documentation could benefit the worker.

The attendance control program has a progressive discipline system. The first step is informal counseling, followed by written reprimands and progressively longer suspensions before the final step of termination. Not surprisingly, absenteeism rates are much higher in the Swedish plant--19 percent to 22 percent versus 3.5 percent to 6 percent in the U.S. plant.[2]

There are also different incentives for the employer and the employees in the United States and Sweden to claim that an incapacity to work is due to a work-related or nonwork-related injury/illness. In Sweden, there is a slight incentive for a worker to get the incapacity certified as due to a work-related injury or illness. Although the compensation for the first 90 days of incapacity is the same--90 percent of wages, regardless of the reason for the incapacity--after 90 days, workers with a work injury or illness receive somewhat more generous benefits than this 90 percent. Those with a nonwork-related incapacity continue to receive this 90 percent of wages. From the employer's perspective, there does not seem to be much of a difference, because both work-related and nonwork-related incapacities are compensated by the government.

In the United States, there is likely to be a strong incentive for workers to have an incapacity to work classified as work related, and a strong incentive among employers to have it classified as nonwork related. For a nonwork-related incapacity in the United States, the employer will typically pay the employee for a limited time period, after which the employee may simply be discharged. In the case of the U.S. plant, workers receive sickness and accident insurance benefits that provide 60 percent of their wages for 52 weeks. After that, they would go on long-term disability for the length of time they had been employed with the company, after which they would be discharged. They might then qualify for a social security disability pension (supplemental security income, SSI) if the condition is severe enough. Workers' compensation for a work-related disability is typically more generous, with the precise terms of compensation determined by the individual state's workers' compensation laws. In the U.S. plant, workers receive about the same *amount* of money under workers' compensation as under sickness and accident insurance. Workers' compensation provides 66.66 percent of wages, but there is a dollar limit to this. This has resulted in some workers actually receiving higher payments from sickness and accident coverage than they would receive from workers' compensation. However, the duration of coverage is more favorable to workers under workers' compensation than sickness and accident insurance. Thus, because workers can stay on workers' compensation longer than they can receive sickness and accident benefits, there is an incentive to get a disability classified as work related, particularly if it is serious.

The states also differ in the methods by which employers finance compensation to workers injured on the job. This might take place through mandatory contributions to state insurance funds, self-insurance, or payments to private insurance funds, which is the method in use at the U.S. plant. With each of these methods it is likely that costs to the employer will rise to some extent as compensation to disabled workers rises.

Sickness and accident insurance is also typically provided by private insurance carriers, as it is at this plant. However, indirect evidence suggests that company sickness and accident insurance premiums are not as sensitive to injury rates as are workers' compensation premiums. According to the union safety and health representative, injured workers receiving workers' compensation are brought back to work as soon as possible. If they are not fully recovered, they are given light work to perform. In contrast, injured workers receiving sickness and accident compensation are not permitted to return to work until they are completely healed. Thus, in general, and at this plant in particular, it appears that the employers have a financial incentive to have disabilities of questionable origin classified as nonwork related, whereas workers are motivated to have them classified as work related.

In addition to the differences in wage replacement compensation, U.S. workers disabled at work generally receive better health insurance coverage than do U.S. workers disabled off the job. If a worker is released due to a nonwork-related disability, health insurance will also be terminated, although the worker might eventually qualify for Medicaid. In Sweden, everyone is covered by the national health insurance system, so this is not a factor.

Given these conflicting financial incentives one should view cautiously the reported injury rates at the plant. More specifically, in light of management's greater control over the designation of work-relatedness of injuries (compared with workers), one would expect a downward bias in the reported injury rates. However, there was no evidence of denial of legitimate claims. In fact, the union safety and health representative noted that some workers have actually been reprimanded for not immediately reporting injuries when they occurred. Still, bringing employees back to work before they are completely healed and assigning them to light work would reduce the injury severity rate (lost hours per million hours worked) if not the injury incidence rate.

Thus, it would be reasonable to conclude that at least some of the difference in injury rates between the two plants could be ascribed to differences in national policies and practices concerning what is considered an injury and how it is certified as such. Depending upon one's point of view, this difference could be characterized in a variety of ways. One might characterize the Swedish operation as being more worker oriented in what it regards as a work injury. One could otherwise characterize it as having a loose control system. However, given the degree of disparity in work injury statistics, it is unlikely that these differences in policies and practices, no matter how they are characterized, could account for all of the difference. Some of this difference must be attributed to some real disparities in injury experience. The evidence of a safer work environment in the U.S. plant is surprising given the cooperative nature of the Swedish operation's approach to safety and the commonly held assumption that labor-management cooperation promotes workplace safety. Workers in the U.S. plant apparently are forced to take certain safety precautions that Swedish workers who have more autonomy do not take on their own. In other words, the Swedish workers are allowed to take more risks. Thus, the higher level of managerial assertiveness regarding safety and health in the U.S. plant is beneficial in getting workers to do what is in their own best interest. We will take up this point again in the next chapter when we propose a contingency theory for cooperation and conflict in occupational safety and health relations.

NOTES

1. Production and employment levels at the U.S. plant increased substantially after these data were collected. In 1986 there were approximately 1,050 salaried and hourly workers, combined, and production was about 39 trucks per day. The staffing level of the safety function, discussed later, remained basically the same.

2. All these figures are unadjusted, that is, they include sickness and injury absences, leaves of absence, disciplinary layoffs, and, for the U.S. plant, personal vacation days. They do not include any vacation absences in the Swedish plant or vacation absences occurring during shutdowns of the U.S. plant. As noted in Chapter 4,

all Swedes have access to various types of leave (e.g., child-care leave, paternity leave, and educational leave) seldom offered by U.S. companies.

9

CONCLUSIONS/RECOMMENDATIONS

This study has attempted to explore the regulation and management of occupational safety and health in the automotive industries of several countries. The occupational safety and health activities of several companies that operate in two or more of these countries were studied in detail. The broad economic, social, political, and legal environments in these countries were also considered as they affect occupational safety and health activities at national, industrial, corporate, and plant levels. Particular emphasis was placed on considering the role of cooperation and conflict among labor, management, and government in the occupational safety and health systems of these countries. One important aim in this undertaking was to ascertain if there are certain approaches to the handling of occupational safety and health activities in certain countries and companies that are more effective than other approaches, and, if so, whether these more effective approaches are transferable between companies and across countries.

Occupational safety and health is an intriguing issue to consider in an international context for a number of reasons. It is an issue for which labor, management, and government would appear to share a common interest in promoting better performance. Yet, despite these shared interests, occupational safety and health have been at the center of numerous controversies in the nations considered in this study. Understanding the nature of these controversies demanded an understanding of the environmental contexts in which these national occupational safety and health systems operate.

Occupational safety and health have become higher priority concerns and have had greater resources devoted to them during the time period covered in the study for the countries considered. This increased concern is certainly more evident in the industrialized countries, where significant revisions of occupational safety and health laws and regulations have taken place in recent years. No doubt this can be largely attributed to economic progress and increased standards of living.

This increased concern for occupational safety and health can also be attributed to technological factors. These include the greatly improved scientific ability to detect and measure hazards in the workplace and the far more rapid worldwide dissemination of information about safety and health issues. Scientists have found evidence of adverse health effects of more and more substances in the environment in recent years. Scientific instruments have also become more sensitive, allowing for detection of harmful substances in ever smaller quantities. These technological changes have for the first time made explicit certain trade-offs between worker protection and various financial and production considerations. Thus, there has been increased pressure in the legislative/regulatory arena and in collective bargaining to eliminate hazards or potential hazards in the work environment that were not detectable or even known to exist just a few years ago.

As we have seen there has been a shift in emphasis toward greater concern with occupational illnesses. Although no one would claim that occupational injuries are under control, a certain degree of success in this regard has allowed this shift in focus to occur. Technological innovations in production processes have also played a role in this development. As more workers sit in offices in front of video display terminals or at the controls of robots or numerically controlled machines and fewer workers actually work on assembly lines, this is a natural outcome. Old hazards are reduced but new ones are created.

There currently exist important mechanisms for international dissemination of information about work hazards and methods of coping with them. The news media, scientific exchanges, international organizations such as the International Labour Office, the Organization for Economic Cooperation and Development (OECD), international unions, and multinational corporations all play a role in this dissemination of information. News about disasters such as that in Bhopal, India is quickly communicated throughout the world. Even in developing countries like Kenya, a large percentage of the population is likely to hear about a disaster within a matter of hours. Political and industrial leaders recognize the dire implications if such a similar catastrophe should occur in their own spheres of influence. Thus, pressure exists to utilize the very best available hazard prevention technologies, which are often also the most expensive, even in countries where these are not always appropriate.

One implication of this for U.S. employers is that there will be continuing pressure by labor to match certain rights viewed as desirable that have been attained by workers in other countries. One example of this is the right to stop work perceived to be dangerous. Currently, only Swedish workers, of those considered here, have this right, but labor efforts to achieve comparable rights in the United States will, no doubt, prove contentious.

The issue of occupational safety and health is important enough by itself, but this study has implications beyond this particular issue. The regulation and management of occupational safety and health in various countries can serve as a prism through which we can view important differences in the economic, social, political, and legal environments of these countries. Moreover, the nature of the relationships among labor, management, and government with respect to safety and health are indicative of the overall status of labor-management-government relations in these countries. Success in dealing with occupational safety and health issues is encouraging for the prospects for dealing with other even more contentious issues in labor-management-government relations. Conversely, the inability to handle them constructively has ominous implications.

The focus on cooperation and conflict in this research is important in this regard. It is related to a common prescription for U.S. industrial ills. A frequently prescribed tonic for lagging U.S. economic performance is the replacement of the traditional contentious relations among labor, management, and government with more cooperative relations modeled after those of our more successful trading partners. This study allows us to look at cooperation and conflict relative to a specific work issue and to assess the viability of this conventional wisdom.

Based upon this study, this prescription is found to be a simplistic solution. The cooperativeness and assertiveness of labor, management, and government relative to occupational safety and health and other work issues are rooted in the particular national environments. It is not realistic to expect that such relations simply could be taken from one national context and grafted onto another. Although certain aspects of labor-management-government relations that are effective in one environment are transferable to other environments, this is the exception rather than the rule. Moreover, the fundamental conventional-wisdom assumption that conflict is undesirable is not in all cases valid, at least with respect to occupational safety and health.

The automotive industry, which provides the industrial context for this study, is extremely important. In the countries considered, with the exception of Kenya, the auto industry is the most important manufacturing industry on a number of dimensions. The auto industry is one of the largest, if not *the* largest, employer in these countries. Automobiles and trucks are also very important in terms of international trade. The relative success of domestic auto industries of the various countries has an important bearing on their balance of payments. In addition, in recent years, the automotive industry has become an increasingly important customer for high technology supplier firms. It is the chief customer for robots for use in production. Also, computers and computer components are used extensively in production and increasingly in the vehicles themselves.

The automotive industry is on the leading edge of industrial developments in these countries. It has frequently been the first industry within these countries to deal with important issues that have implications for the entire economy. The approaches used to deal with these issues have also been used as models by other industries confronting the same or similar problems. This has been the case with respect to quality-of-work-life issues, productivity and quality improvement, and absenteeism control. Auto industry efforts in these areas have been carefully studied and widely reported. There has been less attention given to precedent-setting activities and agreements related to occupational safety and health issues in the auto industry, but important lessons can be drawn in this area as well.

Increasing international and domestic competition in the auto industry is placing great pressure on U.S. producers to improve the productivity and quality of their operations. This pressure is coming from both traditional Japanese and European producers and new competitors operating in low-wage countries such as Korea, Yugoslavia, and Mexico. Japanese firms now beginning production in the United States also pose a major challenge.

As these competitive pressures increase, two diametrically opposed responses relative to the regulation and management of safety and health are possible. One is to attempt to downgrade safety and health concerns in the pursuit of high productivity and quality goals. The other is to attempt to integrate safety and health performance with other operating goals in a mutually reinforcing manner. This research indicates that either of these two responses could occur. The first, which is the path of least resistance, is both the most likely and the least desirable response.

FINDINGS

Several important findings or conclusions drawn from this study are considered below. Implications of these findings, along with recommendations for labor, management, and government, are considered in the next section.

1. *Safety needs pertaining to occupational safety and health are (in Maslow's terminology) predominantly satisfied, nonmotivating needs for typical workers and managers in the industrial settings considered in this study.*

This does not mean to suggest that there are no longer hazards in the work environment. It does mean that those hazards that do exist are not significant motivators of behavior for individual workers. Maslow (1968) described safety as a lower-level need following physiological needs in his postulated hierarchy of needs. These lower-level needs must be satisfied before higher-level needs, such as love needs, esteem needs, and the need for self-actualization, become motivators of behavior. Only immediate and obvious hazards act as significant motivators to most workers and managers, and these are relatively rare in industrial settings, even in developing countries such as Kenya.

At the same time, though, it is clear that a great many less immediate and less obvious hazards do exist in the workplace. In the industrialized countries of this study, management, labor, and government safety and health experts clearly recognize the existence of these hazards, and they attempt to either eliminate them or protect workers from them. Their task, which at times is quite difficult, is to convince others in the work force and in management to recognize these hazards and to take appropriate precautionary measures.

The difficulty of this task is, in large measure, dependent on the degree of satisfaction of lower-level physical needs. The industrialized countries considered have been able to satisfy basic needs to a great extent due to the relatively high standards of living enjoyed by their populations. This satisfaction of basic needs has allowed them to focus greater attention on the less immediate safety and health hazards that have also accompanied industrialization. Still, the relative importance of concern about these less immediate safety and health needs varies over time and between companies. In general, the greater the satisfaction with economic conditions in the society as a whole, and/or with the financial conditions of an individual company, the greater will be the concern about these hazards.

The regulatory revolution initiated by the Carter administration and intensified under the Reagan administration is exemplary of this. This was intended to reduce the "burden of regulation" to stimulate economic growth. "Regulatory relief" was provided in the area of occupational safety and health and in other areas of social regulation (e.g., environmental regulation, energy usage, consumer product safety regulation) and in the regulation of specific industries (e.g., airlines, telecommunications, banking, and broadcasting). This deregulation reflected a feeling within these administrations and significant sectors of the U.S. electorate that economic growth had suffered due to excessive and unnecessary government regulation. It is not surprising that these efforts to reduce the costs of regulation took place during a time when the United States was confronted by significant economic difficulties, not the least of which was the deepest recession since the Great Depression. Efforts to tighten up on OSHA regulation at the end of Reagan's tenure in office could, in this sense, be taken as a measure of satisfaction with the economic recovery.

This view of the relative importance of safety and health is supported by events within the U.S. auto industry. In particular, evidence of this is provided by the agreement by the UAW to exempt Chrysler from changes in safety and health provisions of the contracts they negotiated with other auto employers in the early 1980s because of Chrysler's financial difficulties. These changes were widely hailed as improving safety and health conditions in the industry. However, it was conceded that they came at a cost to the industry. Chrysler workers did not want to impose such additional costs on the firm because of its precarious financial position at that time. There was a fear that any significant additional costs could push the firm to bankruptcy and result in the loss of their jobs.

The occupational safety and health conditions in Kenya also provide confirmation of this view of the relative priority of safety and health concerns. Kenya is an exceptionally poor country compared with the industrialized countries considered in this study, and the occupational safety and health conditions in the country as a whole reflect this. There are, however, pockets of industrialization in Kenya where enterprises, particularly multinational corporations, provide considerably higher standards of living for their employees than are available for the majority of Kenyans. In such enterprises the occupational safety and health standards and practices more closely resemble those in the industrialized countries than they do the standards and practices in other sectors of the Kenyan economy. This research suggests that the multinational corporations, or, more specifically, the expatriate managers from industrialized countries employed by these MNCs are largely responsible for these similarities. The government regulatory system is largely ineffective and there is relatively little demand from the workers for workplace safety and health protection. In fact, considerable effort needs to be expended to educate and motivate the Kenyan workers to exhibit a minimum level of concern for safety and health. Thus, in such countries, MNCs must assert their influence to fill this vacuum left by labor and government in the safety and health field.

2. *The financial incentives to the firm for performance in the area of occupational safety and health are unclear and vary depending on the circumstances.*

There are various costs of injuries and illnesses to the firm and to individuals. It is, however, difficult to judge the precise magnitude of the organizational costs resulting from injuries and illnesses just as it is difficult to judge the precise costs of measures undertaken to reduce injuries and illnesses. Thus, the cost effectiveness of many of these measures is indeterminate. This is the case despite the "safety pays" rhetoric and considerable efforts by labor and management safety and health specialists to show the financial benefits of these activities.

Management and labor safety and health professionals believe that occupational safety and health activities are, to a great extent, cost effective. These parties feel that there are many safety and health concerns on which joint labor and management gains can be achieved. However, there are aspects of safety and health where the gain of one party is viewed as at the other's expense. In game-theory terminology, occupational safety and health is viewed as a plus-sum game, but only up to a point, after which it is considered a zero-sum game. Participants' perceptions of the type of game they are involved in have a bearing on their behavior. Cooperation is an appropriate strategy in plus-sum games, whereas assertiveness is more effective in zero-sum games.

There are differences among plants, firms, industries, and countries regarding the extent to which joint gains in the safety and health field are believed by labor and management to be possible. Moreover, these beliefs change over time. Reflecting such differences in these beliefs, there is much greater cooperation on occupational safety and health issues in Sweden, Germany, and certain sectors of the Japanese economy than in the United States. In the U.S. auto industry the domain in which joint gains are perceived to be possible has increased substantially in recent years. In the United Kingdom occupational safety and health are viewed predominantly in zero-sum terms at the factory level by labor and management. This contrasts with the views on safety and health regulation at the national level, where considerable labor-management-government cooperation takes place. Within Japan the differences in perception of the nature of the "game" are also significant. Among master employers, large areas of mutual gain are perceived, and safety and health are viewed almost completely in plus-sum terms. In no other country do corporations see the improvement of safety and health performance as such an important element of competitive behavior as do the master-employer firms in Japan. In stark contrast, however, occupational safety and health are viewed predominantly in zero-sum terms by smaller subcontractors. These beliefs about the possibility of joint gains, coupled with various environmental limitations imposed by national conditions, largely determine the mix of cooperative/assertive behavior in the handling of occupational safety and health.

Early evidence in research that is still underway suggests that Japanese automotive firms operating in the United States have laid the groundwork to deal with safety and health in largely plus-sum terms. Their experience in the United States suggests that the domain for joint gains is greater than has been previously recognized by the U.S. auto firms.

3. *While cooperation on occupational safety and health is desirable, so too is assertiveness. A certain amount of conflict is inevitable and assertiveness by parties dealing with this conflict can be beneficial. This implies a contingency theory regarding the benefits of cooperation and conflict (i.e., assertiveness) in occupational safety and health relationships.*

In discussions of ways to improve the occupational safety and health system in the United States, most of the attention has been focused on the benefits of increased cooperation among labor, management, and government. Often overlooked are the benefits of assertiveness. Although there is no one ideal of assertive/cooperative behavior, it is clear that at least moderate levels of both of these are needed. The benefits of cooperation have been well documented in this study. Benefits of labor-management cooperation are clearly evident in the U.S. auto industry. The benefits of broader-based labor-management-government cooperation are also readily apparent in the European countries and in Japan among master employers.

This study has also provided evidence that a certain level of conflict (or, more precisely, assertiveness in conflictual situations) is also beneficial. Company Z's operations in the United States, which had high levels of managerial assertiveness regarding safety and health, had much lower injury rates than the Swedish operations, which were characterized by cooperative/nonassertive relations. The disparity in safety and health conditions between master-employer firms and small subcontractors in Japan also testifies to the benefits of both government and employee assertiveness. Because these small firms do not see it in their self-interest to aggressively promote occupational safety and health (as the major employers do), workers there suffer due to the lack of worker and government assertiveness in forcing management action.

The benefits of assertiveness are also supported by the worker fatality data. Surprisingly, the United Kingdom, which has notoriously poor labor-management relations, had the lowest worker fatality rates for the countries considered in this study. Still, regulatory efforts pertaining to occupational safety and health in the United Kingdom have a strong cooperative orientation. Also, the United States, which has a tradition of labor-management-government conflict and highly assertive behavior by these parties, has lower worker fatality rates than Germany, which has a tradition of harmonious relations among these parties. Moreover, Kenya, in which there were no obvious labor-management-government conflicts pertaining to occupational safety and health, had, by far, the highest worker fatality rates of the countries considered.

If, as suggested above, occupational safety and health is a zero-sum issue beyond a certain point, then improvements in safety and health performance beyond that point will result in a net cost to the firm. This inevitably leads to conflict situations that provoke varying degrees of assertiveness by labor and government in different contexts. It also results in adversarial relations among labor, management, and government of various intensities. The adversarial nature of the conflict-coping behavior in the United States is the result of labor and government forcing firms to undertake safety and health measures that are costly to them or that stymie efforts to increase production at the expense of safety and health. Labor's assertiveness and the adversarial relations between labor and management at the factory level are even more evident in the United Kingdom, with apparently even more favorable results, at least in respect to fatality avoidance.

Conflict arises on another level regarding occupational safety and health. This is the conflict between individuals' freedom in an organization and the need for workers and managers to follow and promote safe work practices. Individuals often choose less safe alternatives for personal convenience (e.g., not wearing safety glasses) or because they are more concerned with production. They do this, among other reasons, because they think the risk of injury is acceptably small. This places these individuals in conflict with the safety and health professionals and line managers whose job it is to ensure that individuals follow safe work practices. This latter factor is relevant in explaining the higher injury rates in Company Z's Swedish plant and the higher fatality rates in Germany. Great emphasis is given in Sweden and Germany on protecting workers' rights and on maintaining labor-management harmony, even to the point of allowing some unsafe work practices to exist. In contrast, there is far more assertiveness among American safety and health professionals regarding safe work practices.

What is suggested by this research, then, is a contingency theory of the benefits of labor-management-government cooperativeness and assertiveness regarding occupational safety and health. This means that cooperation among these parties will produce optimal results if and only if each of these parties has a certain minimum degree of power or assertiveness. Without such minimal assertiveness, difficulties like those that have arisen in Kenya, Sweden, and Japan (in small subcontractor firms) are bound to occur. By the same token, minimum levels of cooperativeness are necessary for the full benefits of assertiveness to accrue.

4. *There is little evidence to support the view of OSHA critics that the international competitiveness of U.S. firms has been compromised by overly protective safety and health regulations.*

First of all, countries with which U.S. economic/financial performance is unfavorably compared have, in some respects, more--not less--protective safety and health regulations. Secondly, for every example, such as the United Kingdom, where there seems to be an inverse relationship between economic/financial performance and injury experience, there is a counter example, such as the master-employer firms in Japan that have derived financial benefits from low injury rates owing to the high priority placed on promoting safety and health in regulatory and managerial practices.

The relationship between occupational safety and health experience and financial performance of firms is more complex than either the OSHA bashers or "safety pays" advocates would have the public believe. Suggestions for how occupational safety and health can be handled more effectively *and* with financial/economic benefits are provided below.

5. *The institutional context in which the firm operates is the primary determinant of what can and cannot be done regarding occupational safety and health.*

This institutional context pertains to the national social, economic, political, and legal environments and traditions in labor-management relations. Notable among these environmental determinants are the codetermination systems in Sweden and Germany; the tripartite systems of government in the United Kingdom, Sweden, and Germany; the highly cooperative relations among labor, management, and government in Japan; the adversarial collective bargaining traditions in the United States and the United Kingdom; the tradition of adversarial regulatory relations in the United States; and the single-party political system in Kenya. This environmental determinism also pertains to other work issues, such as absenteeism control and, to a lesser extent, productivity and quality improvement. This limits the amount of cross-national transferability of approaches for handling these issues that can occur even within corporations. Nevertheless, there is much greater opportunity for this transferability than is currently being utilized.

The legal and regulatory framework of most of the countries considered here dictate, to a great extent, the structure and functioning of occupational safety and health activities in the various plants and companies. There is, however, little direction given on these issues to firms in Kenya and to small companies in Japan. Compared with the European countries and the major employers in Japan, occupational safety and health mechanisms are also more flexible in the United States. In European countries with traditions of codetermination, labor's rights to involvement in decision making on issues of occupational safety and health place severe constraints on managerial prerogatives. This is the case despite the fact that labor has not taken full advantage of the safety and health codetermination rights afforded it in these countries.

The legal and regulatory frameworks in the various countries are not, however, immutable. They have developed from specific national circumstances that, in many cases, have changed over time. And these frameworks themselves are influenced by the new national circumstances. One need only look at the effect on labor policies of the U.S. occupations of Germany and Japan to see dramatic evidence of this. Moreover, the ability of labor and management to influence the national contexts is amply demonstrated by recent U.S. regulatory history involving dramatic swings in the nature of OSHA regulatory intervention.

Another result of the national influences on occupational safety and health activities is the variety of national work injury definitions. Differences in these national injury definitions, with their varying criteria and time requirements for work incapacity, do not come about by chance. They reflect an amalgam of national influences. These definitions and the provisions of injury and sickness compensation programs tell us a great deal about the political situations in these countries, especially in regard to the relative power of labor and management. As seen in Chapter 5 the differences in national injury definitions make international comparisons of injury experiences of countries difficult and imprecise.

6. *There is a lack of congruence about safety and health goals within organizations. Control systems for measuring performance and for rewarding or punishing goal attainment/nonattainment were also found to be lacking.*

Managers and workers at different levels of the organizations considered have different views of what the organization's safety and health goals are and how goal attainment is measured. The rewards and penalties for better or worse safety and health performance are similarly unclear, leading to uncertainty regarding how important safety and health are. This is plain bad management. Because goals, performance measures, and rewards and penalties are more clear-cut for other performance dimensions, such as productivity, cost control, and quality, these are likely to receive greater attention. In addition to bringing about inferior safety and health performance, this situation fosters cynicism as workers and managers alike see discrepancies between organizational rhetoric and actual commitment to safety and health.

7. *International coordination of occupational safety and health activities within most MNCs is weak.*
    The problems of measurement and control of occupational safety and health performance are difficult enough for companies operating in only one country, but they are much more complex when international operations are involved. Notable among the problems confronted by MNCs is the lack of comparable measures of performance for the various countries of operation. In the face of confusing nation-specific regulations regarding safety and health, responsibilities in these areas are typically delegated to national subsidiaries or operating units of the corporations. Usually only superficial effort is made to promote a corporatewide safety and health policy. The safety and health manager of the subsidiary is usually a national of the country of operation, regardless of the home country of the multinational corporation. This was the case in six of the seven plants operating outside of the home countries of the MNCs considered in this study.[1] As a result of the typical patterns for staffing the safety and health position, there is very little cross-national sharing of information that would naturally occur by transferring safety and health specialists within a company from country to country. International coordination of safety and health is further hampered by the lack of corporatewide injury definitions.
    The absence of corporatewide injury definitions also attests to the actual importance placed on occupational safety and health in the companies considered. It indicates that it is not nearly as great as the safety rhetoric implies. A maxim of management is that one must first be able to measure that which one wishes to control. Certainly the area of occupational safety and health is not unique with respect to corporate difficulties in measuring performance across countries. National differences in accounting and record-keeping requirements mean that dual record keeping is necessary to satisfy national and corporate reporting requirements in such areas of performance as cost control and productivity. Sufficiently detailed records are kept in these other areas of performance despite the costs involved because of the importance attached to them. Obviously, occupational safety and health have not been accorded the same importance by any of the companies considered.

8. *The evaluation of occupational safety and health performance is a highly political exercise that, if not handled properly, can be counterproductive.*

This pertains to evaluations at various levels within both companies and countries. The high potential for a "fudge factor" in work injury data appears to be largely responsible for this. Decisions made by workers, supervisors, and safety and health and medical personnel can greatly influence the reported injury rates. The greater the emphasis placed on reported injury rates for the evaluation of individuals and groups, the greater the temptation to cheat. This may involve not reporting or recording gray-area injuries. It may also involve physicians being urged to consider the reporting implications of different diagnoses and prescribed treatments for various injuries and illnesses. The reassignment of injured workers to light work to avoid recording a lost-time injury is a common practice. In some cases this is perfectly legal and it seems quite reasonable. In other situations it is illegal and poses a danger to those who are injured.

The motivations to cheat on injury data at the individual level reflect incentives at the organizational level. The fact that accidents and injuries cost money has long been noted by organizations although the precise amounts of these costs have been difficult to measure. Various incentives for low reported injury rates deriving from national workers' compensation systems are discussed in Chapter 5. As a result of these various individual and organizational incentives, the accuracy of injury data at plant, corporate, industrial, and national levels must always be suspect. The suspicions, however, can be allayed to a degree when there exist certain countervailing forces that provide crosschecks on the accuracy of the data. Such a function may be filled by safety and health and medical staff, and union representatives and workers themselves at plant and corporate levels; and by government safety and health regulators, academicians, and minority political parties within countries. The recent OSHA penalties for the underrecording of injuries by U.S. firms will have beneficial effects in this regard. Still, they will make longitudinal comparisons of injury experiences more difficult because of the need to compare more precise postfine data with less precise prefine data. (At least before the fines one could assume that the level of cheating was relatively constant.)

9. *Contrary to what one might expect, higher staffing levels of the safety and health function are not associated with lower injury rates.*

In fact, for Company X (U.S. and German operations), Company Y (U.S. and British operations) and Company Z (U.S. and Swedish operations), the operations with the higher staffing levels also had the higher work injury rates. There are at least two possible explanations for this counterintuitive finding. First, operations that have fewer safety and health specialists may rely more heavily on line managers rather than staff to manage the safety and health function, resulting in improved performance. Second, the lower reported injury level may be specious. It is possible that where the safety and health function is more generously staffed more accurate (and inclusive) injury records are kept. Still, given the small sample size of plants considered for these comparisons, more research is obviously needed on the relationship between safety and health staffing levels and injury experience.

10. *In the U.S. auto industry, effective labor-management cooperation on safety and health preceded and served as a model for cooperation on other issues of mutual concern to labor and management.*

The precedent-setting nature of the cooperative agreements on occupational safety and health is not widely recognized, even within the U.S. auto industry. However, safety and health proved to be an area in which cooperation was easier to achieve than in other areas due to the obvious confluence of interest. Satisfaction with the agreement and structures for labor-management cooperation on safety and health influenced the subsequent cooperative efforts in the areas of productivity improvement, quality improvement, and absenteeism control.

There is evidence from other countries, although it is somewhat more limited than that for the United States, that cooperation on occupational safety and health also paved the way for broader labor-management cooperation. No doubt, the ease with which the common interests of labor and management regarding safety and health can be enunciated makes this area a logical first step in labor-management cooperation.

11. *The regulation of occupational safety and health is, in part, inherently adversarial, although it need not be as destructively contentious as it has been in the United States.*

It has been argued that promoting safe and healthy working conditions is, to a great extent, profitable. Well-managed firms will enhance workplace safety and health out of a sense of enlightened self-interest. Still, there are certain safety and health activities or expenditures that will improve working conditions but that will not profit the firm. It is unlikely that more than a few corporations will act altruistically and incur many of these expenses voluntarily. Government agencies regulating safety and health, oftentimes at the prodding of labor, require firms to undertake some such unprofitable measures. This is a type of coercion whether the regulations are meekly accepted by industry, only grudgingly accepted, or in some way resisted. The lobbying by labor for such regulations, and government imposition and enforcement of these regulations, are reflective of the adversarial nature of safety and health regulation.

In the United States adversarial safety and health relations are readily apparent. There are certainly some beneficial results of this, but there are a great many negative ones as well. The starts and stops in government safety and health regulatory policies and activities and the feuding among labor, management, and government regarding these policies result in a considerable waste of time, energy, and financial resources for all the parties involved.

OSHA has received such tremendous amounts of criticism over the years from both labor and management that it is hard to envision the agency as noncontroversial. However, the great range of issues on which joint gains in the occupational safety and health arena are possible belies the need for conflict among OSHA, labor, and management, at least on these issues. The nature of safety and health regulation in Germany, Sweden, Japan, and the United Kingdom suggests that the controversy about occupational safety and health is more nation-specific than issue-specific. In these countries the coercive nature of safety and health regulations is handled with far less controversy than in the United States.

Still, various national characteristics, including more heavily centralized governments, better respected civil services, and national traditions of tripartite cooperation that are responsible for the more constructive regulatory relations, are not easily duplicated in the United States. Safety and health regulation in the United States will, no doubt, continue to be contentious for the foreseeable future.

12. *Occupational safety and health is both a symbolic and substantive issue in labor-management-government relations.*

The handling of occupational safety and health issues is viewed by some as a litmus test of management's concern for labor. From an outside observer's standpoint, the handling of safety and health issues can also be viewed as a bellwether of management's and labor's clout within companies, industries, and political systems of countries. Clearly, labor's position relative to management is stronger in Sweden and Germany than in the United States on a wide range of issues relevant to both parties. The legislative and regulatory guarantees of labor's rights in the safety and health arena and worker participation in general are evidence of this. In the United Kingdom, the passage and subsequent rescinding of numerous labor laws, including those related to safety and health, marked the rise and fall of labor's (and the Labour party's) influence. The cooperative and effective handling of occupational safety and health issues in the master-employer firms by labor, management, and government reflects the privileged position of these firms and their employees in Japanese society. The more hazardous working conditions in smaller subcontractor firms and the greater degree of controversy over these conditions are also reflective of these firms' positions in society. In Kenya, the nonenforcement of safety and health regulations and the absence of any organized labor opposition to this are symptomatic of labor's powerlessness both in relations with management and with government.

In the United States, labor's influence over occupational safety and health regulatory activities has risen and fallen with labor's influence in general. Because the Reagan administration was considered hostile to labor's interest, strong unions placed greater emphasis on labor-management safety and health agreements rather than on regulatory changes.

The symbolic nature of occupational safety and health is also evidenced by the common usage of slogans and platitudes about safety. Automotive industry managers frequently use such phrases as "safety is number one," "our concern for our workers is our first priority," or "there can be no production without safety" in talking to a wide range of audiences. Despite the frequent use of such platitudes, the only labor or management personnel directly involved in safety and health who claimed that these slogans actually represented reality were the Japanese. Even in the major Japanese firms, where safety and health are accorded a high priority, operating decisions often conflict with this rhetoric. In other companies and countries the exaggerated importance of safety and health suggested by these platitudes was generally acknowledged by labor and management alike. Virtually everyone agreed that production received a higher priority, although there was disagreement over whether this was a desirable state of affairs.

Another example of the symbolic aspect of safety and health is the tendency for concerns voiced by labor or management over safety and health issues to mask concerns about other issues. Thus, labor may complain about the safety and health implications of a work speed-up even if its primary concern is simply the added effort that must be expended. An individual disgruntled worker may also file a complaint with regulators about an alleged work hazard when that person is, in fact, upset about some other issue. Even in Japan, where workers are usually very loyal to the company, spurious complaints about safety and health conditions are lodged, oftentimes for political reasons. Managers may emphasize the safety benefits of housekeeping around the work area even if their prime motivation is to encourage attention to detail in the hope of improving product quality. The reason for the use of safety and health to achieve other ends is that it is a "motherhood" type of issue. Poor safety and health conditions are universally regarded as undesirable and it is hard to justify rhetorically opposition to improving poor conditions.

The symbolic character of occupational safety and health issues dictates that they take on added importance in the international activities of multinational corporations. MNCs are often viewed as mixed blessings by host countries, and they typically receive close scrutiny by the government, organized labor, the media, and the general public. This is especially the case when the MNC is a highly visible major employer as automotive plants invariably are. There is little an MNC could do to wear out its welcome in a host country faster than to conduct its operations with disregard for the well-being of its workers.

The symbolic nature of occupational safety and health has both positive and negative consequences. This symbolism explains why labor-management cooperation on safety and health preceded and served as a model for cooperation on other issues of mutual concern in the U.S. auto industry. It simply was easier to get started on cooperative ventures in safety and health. Still, the symbolic nature of safety and health at times interferes with genuine problem-solving efforts in these areas. This is particularly problematic when safety and health controversies become proxy battles for control of the work environment.

RECOMMENDATIONS

Having come this far in the discussion, it seems incumbent upon the author to point out certain implications of this study regarding how occupational safety and health might be better managed and regu-lated. Recommendations are offered pertaining to corporate, labor, and government involvement in occupational safety and health. The government recommendations concern the regulation of safety and health in the United States. Although some of these recommendations may appear obvious, experience with safety and health controversies indicates that what is obvious to one party is not always obvious to another.

Corporations

1. *Responsibility and accountability for safety and health should be delegated to line managers; staff support should be provided by full-time safety and health specialists.*

Only line managers can integrate safety and health concerns with other production decisions. It is clear that only they have the authority to reconcile the frequent conflicts between safety and health and other operating goals. Some mechanism for incorporating the safety and health dimension into overall performance evaluations must be used to make this delegation of responsibility more than a rhetorical exercise.

The ease with which individual workers and managers can relegate safety and health considerations to secondary or tertiary concern necessitates that one or more individuals have full-time safety and health responsibilities whenever possible. Unlike workers and managers with divided responsibilities, full-time specialists are not likely to view safety and health as "satisfied needs" and to let other tasks take precedence over their safety and health responsibilities. These safety and health specialists also have an important role to fill in showing top management the competitive advantages that can be derived from superior safety and health performance.

2. *Greater international coordination and control of occupational safety and health are essential for both practical and symbolic reasons.*

The lack of control may not result in a disaster like the one in Bhopal, India for a given corporation, although it could. Still, the cumulative costs associated with higher than necessary rates of injuries and illnesses incurred year after year throughout a large corporation may be even more substantial than those involved in a major catastrophe. Thus, it may very well be in the firm's long-term, enlightened self-interest to undertake the suggested activities. The increased concern about occupational safety and health issues worldwide makes this an increasingly important motivation. Moreover, the lack of accountability to world headquarters for safety and health sends the wrong signal. Juxtaposed with the close control and extensive reporting requirements for other performance dimensions, the message is that safety and health are not important.

3. *The most logical place for a corporation to begin international coordination of safety and health activities is with the promulgation of a corporate injury definition.*

To repeat, one must first be able to measure that which one hopes to manage. Not only will an international injury definition facilitate evaluation and control of safety and health activities but activities necessary to promote the use of this definition will also encourage the international exchange of safety and health information and practices. Such exchanges can significantly contribute to enhanced safety and health performance.

The activities of Company X in their promulgation of a corporate injury definition (at least for use in North America and Europe) are exemplary of what needs to be done in implementing this recommendation. They have coupled this introduction of the corporate injury definition with training and ongoing consultation for those required to record injuries under a new format.

The development of corporatewide injury definitions would permit the use of injury data for managerial evaluations as is done by Company Y in the United States. It is obvious that managers respond to those issues upon which they are evaluated. The weight given to performance in the safety and health area vis-á-vis such factors as product quality, productivity, and cost control in performance evaluations should be made explicit and communicated to managers. The process of explicitly weighting the importance of safety and health would be beneficial in and of itself. Top executives would be forced to go beyond platitudes in deciding the real importance of occupational safety and health. Where injury experience is used in performance evaluations, it should be done on a continuing basis as in Company Y, rather than on a one-shot basis as in Company X.

4. *Greater efforts must be made by management to ensure the validity of injury data and to develop other measures of safety performance.*

Without controls on the validity of the injury experience data, efforts to utilize them to improve performance will prove counterproductive. On a positive note, both government and labor can play a role in ensuring the credibility of company-generated injury data. The recent OSHA penalties on automotive companies for injury-reporting violations sent a strong message to industry that there is a high price to pay for such actions. To avoid such penalties in the future, companies must do a better job of ensuring the integrity of the injury data. It should be recognized that this task will become even more difficult the greater the emphasis placed on injury records in performance evaluations, despite the merits of this. Individuals involved in safety and health activities, including medical personnel, should be shielded from pressure by superiors to cheat on the data. Direct lines of communication from plant-level to division-level to corporate-level safety and health staff and from there to top management of the company should be kept open to provide protection should such pressure be applied. Actions such as the establishment of a corporate ombudsman office that can be used to protect such workers should be actively explored. Penalties within the companies for cheating or pressuring subordinates to cheat should be established, communicated, and imposed where appropriate.

The utilization of other measures of safety performance can reduce the temptation to fudge injury statistics. These measures might include performance of safety-enhancing activities such as training or involving employees in the safety program in various ways (e.g., suggestion programs, goal setting, monitoring safety performance, etc.). They might also include results of in-house inspections or external safety/health audits performed by consultants. The use of such measures would also convey the message that safety is more than the absence of injuries and that proactive measures to improve the work environment are valued.

5. *Both traditional and innovative approaches to the international coordination of safety and health should be pursued.*

Established activities, such as international conferences, training, and consultation, are valuable. The corporate safety and health conferences that were discontinued during the last recession served an important function. In the absence of more substantial exchanges they promoted the international exchange of ideas to improve occupational safety and health within companies to a degree surpassing other existing measures.

Training of safety and health staff assigned to operations in developing countries is especially important. Although multinational companies are usually able to hire safety and health professionals within host countries, this is not likely to be the case in developing countries. In addition, there is likely to be inadequate safety and health regulation provided by the host country government if Kenya is at all representative. The training provided will allow the companies to achieve a certain degree of uniformity in safety and health practices while at the same time allowing local managers to adapt and tailor these to suit local conditions.

It is also clear that there is a need for regular within-company consultation by safety and health specialists for problems that safety and health personnel at a plant are unable to handle effectively. Such consultation is typically available within company operations in the United States, Europe, and Japan. It should also be made more readily available for personnel in relatively isolated locations such as Kenya. Long-distance communication through phones and facsimiles can easily extend the expertise of company specialists. An international corporate safety and health "hot line" could be quite cost effective. Such practices are likely to be far more beneficial than a visit by corporate safety and health staff every few years. U.S. companies might well take some lessons from the Japanese firms beginning production in the United States for the types of innovative measures that can be utilized. In some cases, virtually all of the managerial and supervisory personnel have been taken to Japan for intensive multiweek training programs. Indoctrination in the company's safety and health philosophy and activities were key components of these training programs.

Other procedures they have pursued are also worth consideration. These include the permanent assignment of a Japanese safety and health advisor to work with the safety and health manager of the new American subsidiary. Another approach is the pairing of the new facility with a "mother factory" in Japan. Managers from the established facility provide advice on the full range of concerns, including those related to safety and health, at the new facility.

6. *Efforts should be made to pursue greater cooperation with labor in the safety and health arena and to explore opportunities for cooperation with government and even other firms, including competitors.*

Managers in the U.S. auto industry have been pleasantly surprised by the results of cooperative efforts with labor to promote safety and health, and these should be continued. It is likely that cooperation with state and federal safety and health regulators is also feasible. Cooperation between industry and government has been achieved in other countries in this study and it has produced beneficial results in many places. A good first step for management in the United States would be to tone down the oftentimes politically inspired criticism of OSHA and state OSHA plans.

Cooperation among firms through industrial associations, national organizations (such as the National Safety Council), and informal contacts is highly desirable. Firms can share information about common problems and effective methods of dealing with them. It is perhaps another reflection of the "motherhood" nature of safety and health that such cooperation occurs. Managers are much more secretive about other dimensions of corporate performance, although injury statistics are still a sensitive issue, especially in the aftermath of the OSHA fines. Still, greater interfirm cooperation on safety and health issues occurs in other industrialized countries than in the United States.

Despite the benefits of cooperation among these various parties, it should be recognized that there will always be some adversarial component to labor-management-government relations with respect to safety and health and that this is desirable.

Labor

1. *Labor should deal with safety and health issues in a substantive rather than a symbolic or political fashion.*

As noted, labor has occasionally used safety and health as a proxy issue to pursue other concerns, both in negotiations with management and in political activities. In the long run this is counterproductive. It undermines the trust that is necessary among these parties for real gains on safety and health to be achieved. Focusing on legitimate safety and health issues in a problem-solving manner is desirable. The UAW, in its relations with the auto industry employers regarding safety and health issues, would serve as a good model for other unions. In the political arena, labor should also resist the temptation to exaggerate deficiencies in safety and health regulation as part of its political strategy. Such exaggeration only further politicizes occupational safety and health and exacerbates the costly and inefficient swings in the cycle of regulation, deregulation, and reregulation.

2. *There is a need for labor to strongly encourage compliance with safe work practice rules by their members and to continue to demand safe working conditions from management.*

There is a tendency for individuals to ignore safety and health standards and rules when it is inconvenient to follow them. Managers who discipline workers for legitimate infractions should have the support, or at least the tacit approval, of the unions. This will do a great deal to ensure compliance with established work practices. Labor safety and health representatives must be protected from reprisals from their union colleagues for unpopular but necessary safety and health activities, just as management safety and health personnel must be protected within the corporation. Union safety and health representatives should also expect support from company safety and health officials when they protest hazardous conditions. Auto industry experience indicates that such mutual support can be very effective.

3. *Labor must help monitor the credibility of company safety and health statistics.*

Credible statistics are necessary for improvement in evaluation, control, and ultimately performance in the safety and health area. Theoretically at least, workers are in a better position than government regulators to discover cheating in injury reporting. Workers are in every plant throughout the year, whereas OSHA inspectors can conduct inspections of limited duration in only a fraction of the nation's businesses each year. The OSHA findings of injury underrecording by auto firms, however, suggest that additional efforts by labor to verify company injury data are required. If keeping separate records of injuries is impractical, labor unions could periodically survey their members regarding injury experience at randomly selected plants to compare results with company records. In countries such as Germany where access to injury statistics is limited, gaining greater access should be a priority concern in negotiations.

4. *Labor can increase its efforts to promote international exchanges of information on occupational safety and health within and between unions.*

Labor unions already promote such exchanges through international conferences and research, occasional international exchanges of workers, and other personal contacts. These existing forums for exchanges can be extended further. Conducting and sponsoring research on safety and health issues, and working to develop the unions' own international databases on injuries and illnesses along with ensuring the credibility of others' databases, are especially useful. These various activities will not only generate additional helpful information on safety and health, but, moreover, they will pressure corporations to improve their own international efforts as a matter of self-defense.

5. *Safety and health concerns must not be sacrificed at the bargaining table or in the political arena during periodic economic downturns.*

This, again, sends the wrong message to employers and to the government that gains by labor in safety and health come exclusively at a cost to business. It is precisely during these times when greater efforts should be made to identify areas of mutual gain for labor and business through cost-effective safety and health initiatives.

Government

1. *Efforts must be made to depoliticize occupational safety and health regulation.*

While it would be naive to expect political considerations ever to be removed from policy-making and enforcement activities, it is feasible to tone down the rancor of the political controversy surrounding them. Excessive swings in regulatory activities by OSHA have undermined the credibility of the agency with both labor and management. This has benefitted no one. Greater reliance on career civil servants at OSHA, selection of less controversial political appointees, and resistance by politicians to the temptation to use OSHA for political advantage would accomplish much in this regard. Nevertheless, it is highly unlikely that OSHA will ever achieve the political support and public acceptance of its regulatory counterparts in the other industrialized countries of this study.

2. *State and federal safety and health regulators should engage in highly assertive behavior in their function of monitoring compliance with regulations.*

This external policing of compliance with safety and health regulations increases the attention paid to safety and health by individuals and companies. This is important because, as we have seen, safety and health are easily forgotten. Contrary to the platitudes, safety and health activities are not always profitable to companies from an operational standpoint. Additionally, when unions are weak or nonexistent, labor is not in a good position to demand protective safety and health policies. Thus, there must be some external motivation to encourage or force firms to undertake activities that they would not do otherwise. Moreover, compliance monitoring provides external legitimation for union and management safety and health officials and increases their effectiveness. A certain degree of randomness in selecting firms for inspections and uncertainty (by firms) regarding whether or not they will be inspected is desirable. Also desirable is providing as little advance notification of inspections as possible. The notion of completely exempting any firms from inspections based on injury rates or any other criteria should be permanently abandoned. To put this in perspective, one could imagine the taxpayer behavior and public uproar in the United States if certain individuals were told that they would be exempt from audits by the Internal Revenue Service.

Other countries such as Japan and Sweden with highly cooperative government-industry relations might follow our example here. Random, unannounced inspections with a realistic threat of penalties for violations are inherently adversarial components of our regulatory system that can keep all parties "on their toes."

3. *In spite of the need for continued assertiveness, increased cooperativeness with both labor and industry is desirable.*

It has already been shown that there are areas for joint gains between labor and management in the safety and health area. The experience of the UAW and the auto industry testifies to this. So too do the experiences of other countries. Joint gains are also possible in government-labor and government-management relations. Greater efforts must be made to seek out these potential areas of joint gain and to convince *both* labor and management that government can be a trustworthy partner in safety and health activities. Currently, neither labor nor management believe this to be the case and all three parties suffer as a result. It is highly unlikely and not even desirable that government safety and health regulators would rely predominantly on cooperative efforts with these parties, abandoning adversarial or assertive behavior. Still, current relations are unnecessarily confrontational, resulting in lower than achievable levels of safety and health performance.

4. *U.S. safety and health regulators, following the lead of MNCs and unions, should intensify their international orientation.*

The increases in foreign trade, overseas investment by domestic firms, and investment by foreign firms in the United States make an international orientation by regulators increasingly important. Work practices and regulations in one country increasingly have international implications. Still, this international orientation is often lacking. Greater efforts should be made by OSHA and state-level regulators to pursue dialogue with their European and Japanese counterparts. In addition, foreign-owned factories that are being erected in increasing numbers in the United States provide convenient vehicles for U.S. regulators to learn about overseas safety and health practices. These can be compared with existing standards and practices in the United States to see which ones make the most sense. Providing technical assistance to regulators in developing countries could help prevent future disasters like that in Bhopal, which, along with other more obvious harm, do serious damage to U.S. national interests in the international arena.

RESEARCH LIMITATIONS

This research should be considered exploratory in nature. There are a number of limitations of this study that must be recognized when considering the results. The majority of these limitations stems from two primary sources: the imprecision and biases associated with occupational safety and health data, and the complexity of international research in general. Various problems with the injury and illness data are discussed in detail in the text. Measurement and recording problems within countries are not likely to disappear because of the conflicting self-interests of parties involved with safety and health. These conflicting self-interests lead to competing views on whether or not given conditions should be recognized as work-related injuries or illnesses. Actions consistent with these views are undertaken by these parties, which impart biases on injury statistics. Interestingly, the systems in place within countries to monitor injury reporting actually benefit from the mutual distrust among labor, management, and government that exists to varying degrees in different countries. Over time, it is possible that monitoring systems, supported by this mutual distrust, can increase the confidence in these statistics. Still, it is is reasonable to assume that occupational illness data will remain even more ambiguous than occupational injury data.

The difficulties associated with studying occupational safety and health within a country are minor compared with those involved with studying them across countries. Some problems are intrinsic to any international research effort, but others seem particularly acute for the study of occupational safety and health. Among the latter are the difficulties associated with different national definitions of injuries and illnesses and the different systems of reporting, recording, and compensating these.

Among the former problems is the culture-boundedness of any researcher. We all tend to view phenomena in other countries from our own cultural perspective. This is why one might find it odd to learn that the prize for the work group at the Kenyan auto plant with the best quality record is a goat roast. It makes sense within the culture although it seems strange by American standards. There, no doubt, are other features of occupational safety and health systems in the various countries considered, the significance of which escaped the notice of this researcher despite attempts to immerse himself in the local cultures to understand the contexts of occupational safety and health.

One problem endemic to any research utilizing interviews is exacerbated when the research is international. That is, the tendency for respondents to give socially acceptable answers. One element of this is national pride that tempts individuals to try to impress a foreign researcher in their descriptions of conditions in their country. Problems are downplayed, if acknowledged at all, and strengths are exaggerated. Another example of this is the tendency for safety and health managers of transnational subsidiaries to claim that safety and health systems were developed locally, no matter how great the similarity is to safety and health operations of the parent firm overseas. Only by cross-checking such assertions with as many people as possible and with any available archival data can one decide who and what to believe.

One advantage of international research associated with this international pride issue is that, in many cases, foreign corporate, labor, and governmental officials are more readily accessible to an international researcher than are comparable level officials in one's own country. For this researcher, access to such individuals was, in general, inversely related to the distance from home.

Because of the difficulties with the available data on occupational safety and health, a variety of research approaches were used. These included structured interviews, on-site visits, and reference to company and plant injury and illness data and various published data. This varied approach constitutes the multiple operationism recommended by Webb et al. (1966). The rationale behind this is that there are biases inherent in any research. However, the biases of any one research approach are likely to be different from those of another. The same reasoning dictated our analysis of safety and health on several levels: the national level, industrial level, corporate level, and plant level. Conclusions derived from the use of several approaches and levels of analysis are likely to merit a greater degree of confidence than those derived from a single research approach or single level of analysis. Despite the multiple operationism employed here, the findings of this study must be viewed as tentative. It is the hope of this researcher that questions raised by this study will provide some motivation for other researchers to explore the issues of this research in other contexts and with other research approaches. Also, a continuation of this study, focusing specifically on comparing the regulation and management of safety and health in the United States and Japan, promises to shed further light on the issues raised here.

NOTE

1. The only exception was the Kenyan plant of Company X in which the American factory manager filled the safety manager role. Apparently, it was felt that the expertise this individual had outweighed any disadvantages he might have had in understanding Kenyan laws and customs. No doubt, the lax enforcement of safety and health laws in Kenya made this a reasonable trade-off.

BIBLIOGRAPHY

Abegglen, J. C. *The Strategy of Japanese Business.* Cambridge, MA: Ballinger, 1984.

Abrahamsson, B. and Broström, A. *The Rights of Labor.* Beverly Hills, CA: Sage, 1980.

Africa Report. "Africa: A Statistical Profile." September-October 1983, pp. 58-60.

Aguren, S., Hansson, R., and Karlsson, K. G. *The Volvo Kalmar Plant.* Stockholm: Kugel Tryckeri A B, 1976.

Altshuler, A., Anderson, M., Jones, D., Roos, D., and Womack, J. *The Future of the Automobile.* Cambridge, MA: The MIT Press, 1984.

Ambrose, B. G. "Provisions of the Health and Safety at Work, etc., Act 1974." In *Report of Proceedings, Health and Safety at Work Act: Its Effects on Public Health Engineering.* Guildford, England: University of Surrey, April 1979, pp. A-1-A-11.

American Textile Manufacturers Institute v. Donovan. 101 Sup. CT 2478, June 17, 1981.

Andre, A., and Burchardt, K. *Employment and Social Security in the Federal Republic of Germany.* Sankt Augustin, West Germany: Asgard-Verlag Hippe, 1980.

Arthur Andersen and Company. *Cost of Government Regulation Study of the Business Roundtable.* Chicago: 1979.

Åsard, E. "Employee Participation in Sweden 1971-1979: The Issue of Economic Democracy." *Economic and Industrial Democracy* 1:3 (1980) pp. 371-393.

Ashford, N. A. *Crisis in the Workplace: Occupational Disease and Injury: A Report to the Ford Foundation.* Cambridge, MA: The MIT Press, 1976.

Auchter, T. G., Assistant Secretary of Labor for Occupational Safety and Health. "Statement Before the Manpower and Housing

Subcommittee of the House Committee on Government Operations." November 9, 1983.

Auer, P., Penth, B., and Tergeist, P. "Humanization of Work Between Labor Unions and the State--A Survey of Seven Countries." Working paper. Berlin: Science Center Berlin, 1980.

Axelsson, J. "Employees on Company Boards." In *Labor Market Reforms in Sweden: Facts and Employee Views,* edited by A. Larsson. Uddevalla, Sweden: The Swedish Institute, 1979, pp. 38-43.

Bacow, L. S. *Bargaining for Job Safety and Health.* Cambridge, MA: The MIT Press, 1980.

Badaracco, J. L. *Loading the Dice: A Five Country Study of Vinyl Chloride Regulation.* Boston: Harvard Business School Press, 1985.

Barstow, A. Personal correspondence. April 29, 1983.

Barth, P. S., with Hunt, H. A. *Workers' Compensation and Work-Related Illnesses and Diseases.* Cambridge, MA: The MIT Press, 1980.

Bennett, J. W., and Levine, S. B. "Industrialization and Social Deprivation: Welfare, Environment and the Postindustrial Society in Japan." In *Japanese Industrialization and Its Social Consequences,* edited by H. Patrick. Los Angeles: University of California Press, 1976, pp. 439-492.

Berghahn, V. R., and Karsten, D. *Industrial Relations in West Germany.* Hamburg: Berg, 1987.

Berman, D. M. *Death on the Job: Occupational Safety and Health Struggles in the United States.* New York: Monthly Review Press, 1978.

Blake, D. H., Frederick, W. C., and Myers, M. S. *Social Auditing: A Management Guide.* New York: Praeger, 1976.

Bodström, L. *Democracy at Work and Productivity.* Stockholm: Lindingö Tryckeri, 1977.

Booth, R. "What's New in Health and Safety Management." *Personnel Management* 17:4 (April 1985) pp. 36-39.

Brickman, R., Jasanoff, S., and Ilgen, T. *Controlling Chemicals: The Politics of Regulation in Europe and the United States.* London: Cornell University Press, 1985.

British Information Services. "Ethnic Minorities in Great Britain." *Survey of Current Affairs* 17:2 (1987) pp. 75-76.

Bundesministerium für Arbeit und Sozialordnung. *Bericht der Bundesregierung über den Stand der Unfallverhutung und das Unfallgeschehen in der Bundesrepublik Deutschland* (Accident Prevention Report). Bonn, West Germany: 1980, 1981.

Bundesverband der Betriebskrankenkassen. *Krankheitsarten und Arbeitsunfallstatistik.* Essen, West Germany: 1982.

Bundesvereinigung der Deutschen Arbeitgeberverbande. *Structure and Functions of the Confederation of German Employers' Associations.* Cologne, West Germany: n.d.

Business Week. "Can America Compete?" April 20, 1987, pp. 45-47.

_____. "The Reindustrialization of America." June 30, 1980, pp. 55-138.

_____. "The Revival of Productivity." February 13, 1984, pp. 92-100.

Chang, C. S. *The Japanese Auto Industry and the U.S. Market.* New York: Praeger, 1981.

Chelius, J. R. *Workplace Safety and Health: The Role of Workers' Compensation.* Washington, D.C.: American Enterprise Institute, 1977.

Chicken, J. C. *Hazard Control Policy in Britain.* New York: Pergamon, 1975.

Child, J. "Organization Structure, Environments and Performance: The Role of Strategic Choice." *Sociology* 6 (1972) pp. 1-22.

Clack, G. *Industrial Relations in a British Car Factory.* London: Cambridge University Press, 1967.

Cockar, S. R. *The Kenya Industrial Court: Origin, Development and Practice.* Nairobi, Kenya: Longman, 1981.

Cohen, S. D. *Uneasy Partnership: Competition and Conflict in U.S.-Japanese Trade Relations.* Cambridge, MA: Ballinger, 1985.

Confederation of Japan Automobile Worker's Unions. *Guideline for Coping with Introduction of New Technology.* Tokyo: October 1984.

Craig, G. A. *The Germans.* New York: New American Library, 1983.

Dawson, S., Pointer, P., and Stevens, D. "Resolving the Health and Safety Conflict." *Management Today* (April 1984) pp. 33-34, 36.

Deutsch, M. *The Resolution of Conflict: Constructive and Destructive Processes.* New Haven, CT: Yale University Press, 1973.

Di Pietro, A. "An Analysis of the OSHA Inspection Program in Manufacturing Industries 1972-1973." Draft Technical Analysis Paper. Office of the Assistant Secretary for Policy, Evaluation, and Research, U.S. Department of Labor, 1976.

Dore, R. P. *British Factory, Japanese Factory: The Origins of National Diversity in Industrial Relations.* Berkeley, CA: University of California Press, 1973.

Drake, C. D., and Wright, F. B. *The Law of Health and Safety at Work: The New Approach.* London: Sweet and Maxwell, 1983.

Earley, P. "What's a Life Worth?" *Washington Post Magazine.* June 9, 1985, pp. 11-13+.

Economist Intelligence Unit. *Trade Unions and the Law: Special Report No. 198 by Helen Rogers.* London: 1985.

_____. *Country Profile, Japan.* London: 1987a.

_____. *Country Profile, Kenya.* London: 1987b.

_____. *Country Profile, Sweden.* London: 1987c.

_____. *Country Profile, United Kingdom.* London: 1987d.

_____. *Country Profile, West Germany.* London: 1987e.

Edwardes, M. *Back from the Brink.* London: Collins, 1983.

Einhorn, E., and Logue, J. *Democracy on the Shop Floor?* Kent, OH: Kent Popular Press, 1982.

Enström, P., and Levinson, K. "Industrial Relations in the Swedish Auto Industry--Developments in the Seventies." In *Industrial Relations in the World Automobile Industry--The Experiences of the 1970s,* edited by W. Streeck and A. Hoff. Working paper. Berlin: Science Center Berlin, 1982, pp. 231-275.

Federal Minister of Labour and Social Affairs. *Co-determination in the Federal Republic of Germany.* Geneva: International Labour Organisation, 1976.

Federation of Professional and Trade Associations. *Information Leaflet on Statutory Accident Insurance.* Bonn, West Germany: 1977.

Fink, C. F. "Some Conceptual Difficulties in the Theory of Social Conflict." *Journal of Conflict Resolution* 12:4 (1968) pp. 412-460.

Frankel, G. "Kenya Struggles to Break Africa's Cycle of Hopelessness." *Washington Post.* November 18, 1984, pp. 1, 30-31.

Freund, W. C., and Epstein, E. *People and Productivity.* Homewood, IL: Dow Jones-Irwin, 1984.

Frick, K. "Little and Unsystematic Safety Activity in Small Enterprises." Paper presented at ILO Colloquium. Amsterdam, May 1980. *Working Papers.* Arbetslivscentrum, Stockholm, n.d.

Fujimoto, T. "A Short History of Occupational Accidents in Japanese Industries." *Report of the Institute for Science of Labour.* Kawasaki, Japan: No. 67, 1967.

Fujita, Y. *Employee Benefits and Industrial Relations.* Japanese Industrial Relations Series 12. Tokyo: Japan Institute of Labour, 1984.

Furlong, J. *Labour in the Boardroom.* Princeton, NJ: Dow Jones Books, 1977.

Gardell, B. "Scandinavian Research on Stress in Working Life." *Working Papers,* Stockholm: Arbetslivscentrum, 1980.

Gersuny, C. *Work Hazards and Industrial Conflict.* Hanover, NH: University Press of New England, 1981.

Glueck, W. F. *Personnel: A Diagnostic Approach.* Dallas: Business Publications, 1982.

Goldmann, R. "Six Automobile Workers in Sweden." In *American Workers Abroad,* edited by Robert Schrank. Cambridge, MA: The MIT Press, 1979, pp. 15-55.

Goldsworthy, D. *Tom Mboya: The Man Kenya Wanted to Forget.* New York: Africana Publishing, 1982.

Griffiths, R. F., ed. *Dealing with Risk: The Planning, Management and Acceptability of Technological Risk.* New York: John Wiley and Sons, Halsted Press, 1981.

Grunberg, L. "The Effects of the Social Relations of Production on Productivity and Workers' Safety: An Ignored Set of Relationships." *International Journal of Health Services* 13:4 (1983) pp. 621-634.

Grunberg, L., Everard, J., and O'Toole, M. "Productivity and Safety in Worker Cooperatives and Conventional Firms." *International Journal of Health Services* 14:3 (1984) pp. 412-432.

Hauptverband der gewerblichen Berufsgenossenschaften. *Arbeitsunfallstatistik für die Praxis.* Bonn, West Germany: 1983.

_____. *Arbeitsunfallstatistik für die Praxis.* Sankt Augustin, West Germany: 1986.

_____. *The "Berufsgenossenschaften"* [Trade Co-operative Associations]. Bonn, West Germany: n.d.

Hauss, F., and Rosenbrock, R. "Occupational Safety and Health in the Federal Republic of Germany--A Case Study on Co-determination and Health Politics." Working paper. Berlin: Science Center Berlin, 1982.

Hauss, F., and Rosenbrock, R. Interview. Berlin: Science Center Berlin, July 13, 1983.

Health and Safety Commission. *Newsletter.* London (various editions).

_____. *Time Off for the Training of Safety Representatives.* London: Her Majesty's Stationery Office, 1978.

_____. *Health and Safety Commission Report 1981/82.* London: Delco Printing, 1981.

_____. *Health and Safety at Work etc. Act 1974: Advice to Employers.* England: Linneys of Mansfield Ltd., 1983.

_____. *Health and Safety at Work: Safety Representatives and Safety Committees.* London: Her Majesty's Stationery Office, 8, 1984a.

_____. *Health and Safety Commission Report 1983-1984.* London: Her Majesty's Stationery Office, 1984b.

Health and Safety Executive. *Safety Committees.* London: Her Majesty's Stationery Office, 1978.

_____. *A Guide to the HSW Act.* London: Her Majesty's Stationery Office, 1980.

_____. *Health and Safety Statistics 1980.* London: Her Majesty's Stationery Office, 1982.

_____. *Manufacturing and Service Industries: Health and Safety 1981.* London: Her Majesty's Stationery Office, 1983.

_____. *Manufacturing and Service Industries: Health and Safety 1983 Report.* London: Her Majesty's Stationery Office, 1984.

_____. *Health and Safety Statistics 1983.* London: Her Majesty's Stationery Office, 1986.

Hoover, J. J. "Workers Have New Rights to Safety." *Personnel Administrator* 28:4 (April 1983) pp. 47-51.

Institution of Public Health Engineers. *Health and Safety at Work Act: Its Effect on Public Health Engineering.* Guilford, England: University of Surrey, April 1979.

International Labour Office. *International Recommendations on Labour Statistics.* Geneva, Switzerland: 1976.

_____. *1982 Year Book of Labour Statistics.* Geneva, Switzerland: 1982.

_____. *Encyclopedia of Occupational Health and Safety.* Vol. 1, 3rd (Revised) ed. (L. Parmeggiani, Ed.) Geneva, Switzerland: 1983.

_____. *1984 Year Book of Labour Statistics.* Geneva, Switzerland: 1984a.

_____. "The Human Condition in the World of Work." *ILO Information* 12:2 (May 1984) pp. 1, 6.

_____. *Safety and Health Practices of Multinational Enterprises.* Geneva, Switzerland: 1984b.

_____. *1985 Year Book of Labour Statistics.* Geneva, Switzerland: 1985.

_____. *1986 Year Book of Labour Statistics.* Geneva, Switzerland: 1986.

_____. Private Correspondence. April 5, 1985, August 4, 1986.

_____. *1987 Year Book of Labour Statistics.* Geneva, Switzerland: 1987.

Iwuji, E. C. "Industrial Relations in Kenya," In *Industrial Relations in Africa,* edited by U. G. Damachi, H. D. Seibel, and L. Trachtman. London: Macmillan Press, 1979, pp. 201-239.

Japan External Trade Organization. *Japan Handbook: JETRO's Desktop Economic Encyclopedia.* Tokyo: 1985.

Japan Industrial Safety and Health Association. *VDT Work and Occupational Health.* Tokyo: February 1984.

_____. *Guidelines to Occupational Health in VDT Operation.* Tokyo: December 20, 1985.

_____. *1985/1986 Annual Report.* Tokyo: 1986.

Japan Institute of Labour. *Industrial Safety and Health.* Japanese Industrial Relations Series 9, 1982.

_____. *Labor Unions and Labor-Management Relations.* Japanese Industrial Relations Series 2, 1983.

Kamata, S. *Japan in the Passing Lane.* Translated and edited by T. Abimoto. New York: Pantheon, 1982.

Kelman, S. *Regulating America, Regulating Sweden: A Comparative Study of Occupational Safety and Health Policy.* Cambridge, MA: The MIT Press, 1981.

Kochan, T. A., Dyer, L., and Lipsky, D. B. *The Effectiveness of Union-Management Safety and Health Committees.* Kalamazoo, MI: W. E. Upjohn Institute for Employment Research, 1977.

Kochan, T. A., Katz, H. C., and McKersie, R. B. *The Transformation of American Industrial Relations.* New York: Basic Books, 1986.

Kronlund, J. "Organizing for Safety." *Newscientist* 32:1159 (June 1979) pp. 899-901.

Larsson, A., ed. *Labor Market Reforms in Sweden: Facts and Employee Views.* Uddevalla, Sweden: The Swedish Institute, 1979.

Ledvinka, J. *Federal Regulation of Personnel and Human Resource Management.* Boston: Kent, 1982.

Lee, G. L. and Wrench, J. "'Accident-Prone Immigrants': An Assumption Challenged." *Sociology* 14:4 (November 1980) pp. 551-556.

Lee, S. M., and Schwendiman, G. *Japanese Management: Cultural and Environmental Considerations.* New York: Praeger, 1982.

Levi, L. "Quality of the Working Environment: Protection and Promotion of Occupational Mental Health." *Working Life in Sweden* 8 (1978).

Lichty, M. E. "A Prescription for Improving the Work Environment." *Employee Relations Law Journal* 8:1 (Summer 1982) pp. 73-91.

Lindholm, R., and Norstedt, J. P. *The Volvo Report.* Stockholm: The Swedish Employers' Confederation, 1975.

Linsemayer, T. "Foreign Labor Developments: ILO Examines Impact of Technology on Worker Safety and Health." *Monthly Labor Review* 108:8 (August 1985) pp. 46-47.

Litchmarsh, D. "Health and Safety at Work etc in Perspective." *Personnel Management* 16:5 (May, 1984) pp. 35-37.

Longenecker, J. G., and Pringle, C. D. *Management.* 5th ed. Columbus, OH: Charles E. Merrill, 1981.

Lundberg, L. "From Legislation to Work Environment: A Study on the Implementation of Occupational Safety and Health Rules." Unpublished manuscript. Uppsala University, Uppsala, Sweden, 1981.

Magaziner, I., and Reich, R. *Minding America's Business: The Decline and Rise of the American Economy.* New York: Vintage Books, 1983.

Mallory, M., and Bradford, H. "An Invisible Workplace Hazard Gets Harder to Ignore." *Business Week.* January 30, 1989, pp. 92-93.

Martineau, H. *History of England: From the Commencement of the XIXth Century to the Crimean War.* Philadelphia: Porter and Coates, 1864.

Maslow, A. H. "A Theory of Human Motivation: The Basic Needs." In *Organizational Behavior and The Practice of Management,* edited by D. R. Hampton, C. E. Summer, and R. A. Webber. Glenview, IL: Scott Foresman, 1968, pp. 27-39. Abridged from "A Theory of Human Motivation," *Psychological Review* 50 (1943) pp. 370-396.

McCall, B. "How West Germany Protects Its Workers." *Job Safety and Health* 5:7 (July 1977) pp. 21-25.

Mendeloff, J. "An Evaluation of the OSHA Program's Effect on Workplace Injury Rates: Evidence from California Through 1974." U.S. Department of Labor, Contract B-9-M-5-2399, 1976.

_____. *Regulating Safety: An Economic and Political Analysis of Occupational Safety and Health Policy.* Cambridge, MA: The MIT Press, 1979.

Mertens, A. *Occupational Safety and Health in the Federal Republic of Germany.* Dortmund, West Germany: Federal Institute for Occupational Safety and Accident Research, 1979.

Ministry of Labour, Labour Standards Bureau. *General Guidebook on Industrial Safety.* Tokyo: Japan Industrial Safety and Health Association, 1985.

Ministry of Labour, Labour Standards Bureau, Industrial Safety and Health Department, Industrial Health Division. *Working Environment Measurement System In Japan.* Tokyo: Japan Association for Working Environment Measurement, 1986.

Mirer, F. E. "Challenge and Opportunities in Union-Management Cooperation in the Health and Safety Field." *American Industrial Hygienist Association Journal* 44:12, (1983) pp. A-13-A-17.

Moore, S. D. "Sweden, in an Ideological About-Face, Begins Selling Off Some State-Run Firms." *Wall Street Journal.* March 20, 1984, p. 37.

Nader, R. *Unsafe at Any Speed.* New York: Grossman, 1965.

Naschold, F. "On the Prospects and Strategy of a Labour-Oriented Health Policy." Working paper. Berlin: Science Center Berlin, 1977a.

_____. "Problems of a Worker-Oriented Health Policy." Working paper. Berlin: Science Center Berlin, 1977b.

National Board of Occupational Safety and Health. *Occupational Injuries 1980*. Stockholm: Statistics Sweden, 1983.

_____. *Occupational Injuries 1981*. Stockholm: Statistics Sweden, 1984.

_____. *Occupational Injuries 1982*. Stockholm: Statistics Sweden, 1985a.

_____. *Occupational Injuries 1984, Preliminary Report*. Stockholm: Statistics Sweden, 1985b.

_____. *Occupational Injuries 1983*. Stockholm: Statistics Sweden, 1986.

National Commission on State Workmen's Compensation Laws. *The Report of the National Commission on State Workmen's Compensation Laws*. Washington, D.C.: 1972.

National Research Council. *The Competitive Status of the U.S. Auto Industry: A Study of the Influences of Technology in Determining International Industrial Competitive Advantage*. Washington, D.C.: National Academy Press, 1982.

National Safety Council. *Accident Facts, 1982 Edition*. Chicago, 1982.

National Safety Council. *Accident Facts, 1987 Edition*. Chicago, 1987.

_____. *Work Injury and Illness Rates*. Chicago, successive editions.

Neef, A. "International Trends in Productivity and Unit Labor Costs in Manufacturing." *Monthly Labor Review*. U.S. Department of Labor, Bureau of Labor Statistics. December 1986, pp. 12-17.

Nippon Steel Corporation, Personnel Development Division. *Nippon: The Land and Its People*. Tokyo, 1984.

Office of Technology Assessment. *Preventing Illness and Injury in the Workplace*. Washington, D.C.: April 1985.

Otsubo, M. "A Guide to Japanese Business Practices." *California Management Review* 28:3 (Spring 1986) pp. 28-42.

Ouchi, W. *Theory Z: How Americans Can Meet the Japanese Challenge*. Reading, MA: Addison-Wesley, 1981.

Page, J. A., and O'Brien, M. *Bitter Wages: Ralph Nader's Study Group Report on Disease and Injury on the Job.* New York: Grossman, 1973.

Pascale, R. T., and Athos, A. J. *The Art of Japanese Management: Applications for American Executives.* New York: Warner Books, 1981.

Patrick, H., ed. *Japanese Industrialization and Its Social Consequences.* Los Angeles: University of California Press, 1976.

Perl, P. "Major Work Stoppages Reach a Postwar Low." *Washington Post.* March 7, 1985a, p. A9.

_____. "Foreign Competition Blamed for 1st Ford Strike in 8 Years: Ohio Workers Cite 'Speed-Up' Pressures." *Washington Post.* September 13, 1985b, pp. 1, 8.

Pondy, L. R. "Organizational Conflict: Concepts and Models." *Adminstrative Science Quarterly* 12 (September, 1967) pp. 296-320.

President. *President's Report on Occupational Safety and Health.* Washington, D.C.: U.S. Government Printing Office, 1972.

_____. *Report of the President to the Congress on Occupational Safety and Health for Calender Year 1987.* Washington, D.C.: U.S. Department of Labor, Occupational Safety and Health Administration, 1988.

Prosser, W. L. *Law of Torts,* 4th ed. St. Paul MN: West Publishing, 1971, pp. 525-540.

Rake, A. "World Bank Report: Fun with Figures." *New African* (September 1983) p. 31.

Rinefort, F. "A New Look at Occupational Safety." *Personnel Administrator* 22:9 (November, 1977) pp. 29-36.

Rivlin, A. M. "Overview." In *The Swedish Economy,* edited by A. M. Rivlin, and B. P. Bosworth. Washington, D.C.: The Brookings Institution, 1987.

Roanoke Times and World News. "Worker Compensation Claims Mounting." April 5, 1985, p. B-6.

_____. "Alleged Robot Killings Being Investigated." May 22, 1987, p. A-8.

Römer, K., ed. *Facts About Germany.* Gutersloh, Germany: Lexikon-Institut Bertelsmann, 1979.

Rosenbrock, R. Interview. Berlin: Science Center Berlin, April 7, 1983.

Ruble, T. L. and Thomas, K. W. "Support for a Two-Dimensional Model of Conflict Behavior." *Organizational Behavior and Human Performance* 16:1 (1976) pp. 143-155.

SAF, LO, PTK. *Working Environment Agreeement.* Stockholm: Pogo Print, 1979.

Samuels, S., Director of Occupational Safety, Health and Environment AFL-CIO. Comments on an earlier draft of this manuscript. January 10, 1986.

Schick, A. G., Wokutch, R. E., and Conners, S. B. "An Integrating Framework for the Teaching and Researching of Corporate Social Responsibility." *Business and Society* 24:1 (Spring 1985) pp. 32-39.

Schmidt, F. *Law and Industrial Relations in Sweden.* Stockholm: Almquist and Wiksell International, 1977.

Schmidt, S. A. and Kochan, T. A. "Conflict: Toward Conceptual Clarity." *Administrative Science Quarterly* 17:3 (1972) pp. 359-370.

Schonberger, R. J., *Japanese Manufacturing Techniques.* New York: Free Press, 1982.

Schrank, R., ed. *American Workers Abroad.* Cambridge, MA: The MIT Press, 1979.

Simon, P. J. *Reagan in the Workplace: Unraveling the Health and Safety Net.* Washington, D.C.: Center for the Study of Responsive Law, 1983.

Smith, J. M. "Arbitrating Safety Grievances: Contract or Congress?" *Labor Law Journal* 33:4 (April 1982) pp. 238-246.

Smith, R. "The Estimated Impact on Injuries of OSHA's Target Industry Program." New York: Cornell University, n.d.

Smith, R. B. "Remarks of Roger B. Smith, Chairman, General Motors Corporation." *Program Summary of a Conference on Worksite Health Promotion and Human Resources: A Hard Look at the Data.* Washington, D.C.: October 11, 1983, pp. 3-5.

Steiner, G. A., and Steiner, J. F. *Business, Government, and Society: A Managerial Perspective.* 3rd ed. New York: Random House, 1980.

Stone, D. A. *The Disabled State.* Philadelphia: Temple University Press, 1984.

Streeck, W. *Co-determination: The Forth Decade.* Working paper. Berlin: Science Center Berlin, 1983.

Streeck, W., and Hoff, A. "Industrial Relations in the German Automobile Industry: Developments in the 1970s." In *Industrial Relations in the World Automobile Industry--The Experiences of the 1970s,* edited by W. Streeck and A. Hoff. Working paper. Berlin: Science Center Berlin, 1982, pp. 307-369.

Swedish Ministry of Labour. *New Labour Laws.* NY: Swedish Information Service, n.d.

Swedish Trade Union Confederation. *Working Hours and Employment.* Stockholm: February 1983.

Taira, K. "Japan's Law Unemployment: Economic Miracle or Statistical Artifact?" *Monthly Labor Review* 106:7 (July 1983) pp. 3-10.

Taylor, B. "Planning for the 1980s: Corporate Planning with Government and Unions." Paper presented at the Academy of Management Meetings. Atlanta, GA: August 1979.

Teplow, L. "Comprehensive Safety and Health Measures in the Workplace." In *Federal Policies and Worker Status Since the Thirties,* edited by J. P. Goldberg, et. al. Madison, WI: Industrial Relations Research Association, 1976, pp. 209-242.

Thimm, A. L. *The False Promise of Codetermination.* Lexington, MA: Heath, 1980.

Thomas, K. W. "Conflict and Conflict Management," In *Handbook of Industrial and Organizational Psychology,* edited by M. Dunnette. Chicago: Rand McNally, 1976, pp. 889-935.

_____. "Organizational Conflict," In *Organizational Behavior,* edited by S. Kerr. Columbus, OH: Grid, 1979.

Time. "How Japan Does It." March 30, 1981, pp. 54-63.

Trost, C. "OSHA to Check Safety at More Firms in an Expansion of Inspection Policy." *Wall Street Journal.* January 8, 1986, p. 56.

Tsurumi, Y. *Japanese Business: A Research Guide with Annotated Bibliography.* New York: Praeger, 1978.

UAW, International Union. *What Every UAW Representative Should Know About Health and Safety.* Detroit: UAW Social Security Department, 1979.

_____. *Occupational Fatalities Among UAW Members: A 14 Year Study.* Detroit: UAW Health and Safety Department, 1987.

U.S. Department of Labor, Bureau of International Labor Affairs. *Country Labor Profile--Federal Republic of Germany.* Washington, D.C.: 1979a.

_____. *Country Labor Profile--Sweden.* Washington, D.C.: 1979b.

_____. *Country Labor Profile--Kenya.* Washington, D.C.: 1980a.

_____. *Country Labor Profile--United Kingdom.* Washington, D.C.: 1980b.

_____. *Foreign Labor Trends--Japan.* Washington, D.C.: 1984.

_____. *Foreign Labor Trends--Federal Republic of Germany.* Washington, D.C.: 1986.

_____. *Foreign Labor Trends--Sweden.* Washington, D.C.: 1987a.

_____. *Foreign Labor Trends--United Kingdom.* Washington, D.C.: 1987b.

U.S. Department of Labor, Bureau of Labor Statistics. *Major Collective Bargaining Agreements: Safety and Health Provisions.* Washington, D.C.: U.S. Government Printing Office, 1976.

_____. *Handbook of Labor Statistics, 1977.* Washington, D.C.: U.S. Government Printing Office, 1977.

_____. *Occupational Injuries and Illnesses in the United States by Industry, 1975.* Washington, D.C.: U.S. Government Printing Office, 1978.

_____. *Occupational Injuries and Illnesses in the United States by Industry, 1976.* Washington, D.C.: U.S. Government Printing Office, 1979.

_____. *Occupational Injuries and Illnesses in the United States by Industry, 1977.* Washington, D.C.: U.S. Government Printing Office, 1980a.

_____. *Occupational Injuries and Illnesses in the United States by Industry, 1978.* Washington, D.C.: U.S. Government Printing Office, 1980b.

_____. *Occupational Injuries and Illnesses in 1979: Summary.* Washington, D.C.: U.S. Government Printing Office, 1981.

_____. *Occupational Injuries and Illnesses in the United States by Industry, 1980.* Washington, D.C.: U.S. Government Printing Office, 1982.

_____. *Occupational Injuries and Illnesses in the United States by Industry, 1981.* Washington, D.C.: U.S. Government Printing Office, 1983.

_____. *Employment and Earnings.* Vol. 31, No. 3. Washington, D.C.: U.S. Government Printing Office, March 1984.

_____. *Occupational Injuries and Illnesses in the United States by Industry, 1982.* Washington, D.C.: U.S. Government Printing Office, 1984.

_____. *Handbook of Labor Statistics 1984.* Washington, D.C.: U.S. Government Printing Office, 1985a.

_____. *Occupational Injuries and Illnesses in the United States by Industry, 1983.* Washington, D.C.: U.S. Government Printing Office, 1985b.

_____. *Occupational Injuries and Illnesses in the United States by Industry, 1984.* Washington, D.C.: U.S. Government Printing Office, 1986

_____. *Occupational Injuries and Illnesses in the United States by Industry, 1985.* Washington, D.C.: U.S. Government Printing Office, 1987.

_____. *Occupational Injuries and Illnesses in the United States by Industry, 1986.* Washington, D.C.: U.S. Government Printing Office, 1988.

U.S. Department of Labor, Occupational Safety and Health Administration. *All About OSHA.* Washington, D.C.: 1982.

U.S. Office of Management and Budget. *Budget of the United States Government* (department edition). Washington, D.C.: Executive Office of the President, Office of Management and Budget, U.S. Government Printing Office, successive editions.

Viscusi, W. K. "The Impact of Occupational Safety and Health Regulation." *Bell Journal of Economics* 10:1 (1979) pp. 117-140.

_____. *Risk by Choice.* Cambridge, MA: Harvard University Press, 1983.

Vogel, D. "Cooperative Regulation: Environmental Protection in Great Britain." *Public Interest* 72 (Summer 1983) pp. 88-106.

_____. *National Styles of Regulation: Environmental Policy in Great Britain and the United States.* Ithaca, NY: Cornell University Press, 1986.

Wallick, F. *The American Worker: An Endangered Species.* New York: Ballantine, 1972.

Walsh, K., and King, A. *Handbook of International Manpower Market Comparisons.* New York: New York University Press, 1986.

Watermann, F. *Die Berufsgenossenschaften.* Bonn, West Germany: The Central Association of Industrial Injuries Insurance Institutes, 1980.

Weaver, R. K. "Political Foundations of Swedish Economic Policy." In *The Swedish Economy,* edited by A. M. Rivlin and B. P. Bosworth. Washington, D.C.: The Brookings Institution, 1987.

Webb, E. J., Campbell, D. T., Schwartz, R. D., and Sechrest, L. *Unobtrusive Measures: Nonreactive Research in the Social Sciences.* Chicago: Rand McNally, 1966.

Weidenbaum, M. L. *Business, Government and the Public.* 2nd ed., Englewood Cliffs, NJ: Prentice-Hall, 1981.

WGBH. *Frontline.* January 23, 1984, "We Are Driven." Boston, MA. Television program.

Williams, R. "Government Regulation of the Occupational and General Environments in the United Kingdom, the United States, and Sweden." *Science Council of Canada Background Study* 40 (1977).

Willman, P. and Winch, G., with Francis, A., and Snell, M. *Innovation and Management Control: Labor Relations at BL Cars.* New York: Cambridge University Press, 1985.

Wokutch, R. E. "Measuring Corporate Social Performance: The Problem of Values." *Evaluation and Program Planning* 2:1 (1979) pp. 17-24.

Wokutch, R. E., and McLaughlin, J. "The Socio-Political Context of Occupational Injuries." In *Research on Corporate Social Performance and Policy,* edited by L. E. Preston. Greenwich, CN: JAI Press, 1988, pp. 113-137.

World Bank. *World Development Report 1987.* New York: Oxford University Press, 1987.

Yakabe, K. *Labor Relations In Japan: Fundamental Characteristics.* Tokyo: Ministry of Foreign Affairs, 1977.

Yanaga, C. *Big Business in Japanese Politics.* New Haven, CT: Yale University Press, 1968.

INDEX

92-94, 114, 131; worker participation and, 52; workers' compensation and, 156
Japan Industrial Safety and
Health Association, 48, 114
Japan National Railway, privatization of, 94
job tenure, injury rates and, 64

Kenya, 79; automation and,
204-5; Company X case and,
201-7; conflict and, 134-35, 206;
cooperation and, 133-35, 201,
206-9, 212; disability compensation, 144; fatality rates, 159;
foreign workers in, 150; government system, 96-97, 99;
health insurance, 203; industrial disputes, 6; injury rates,
146, 157-58, 205-6, 208; injury
reports, 204; labor legislation,
97-98; labor-management relations, 94-99, 201-3; per capita
GNP, 95; political influences,
147; priority of safety in,
267-68; regulatory activities,
133-35, 205; safety and health
legislation, 103-4, 115-16;
safety professionals in, 208;
unions and, 96, 97-99, 133, 201;
wages in, 201; workers' compensation, 146, 205
Kenyatta, Jomo, 97
keyboard operators, carpal tunnel syndrome and, 67
Kohl, Helmut, 86

labor: cooperation and, 76-77;
new social contract and, 15;
OSHA and, 27, 41-44, 46-47,
70-71, 74; safety and health
cooperation agreements and,
52-56; safety recommen-
dations for, 282-83; West Germany and, 85-87. See also
unions
labor legislation. See specific
countries

labor-management-government
relations, 2, 264-65; contingency theory of, 271; in Japan,
130-33; in Kenya, 97-99, 133-35;
national environments and,
265; recommendations for,
281-82, 284-85; in Sweden, 109,
126; symbolic issues and,
276-78; in U.K., 84, 106, 116-21;
in West Germany, 195
labor-management relations,
68-70; absenteeism and, 181;
injury reports and, 148; in Japan, 94; in Kenya, 201-3; new
social contract and, 15;
OSHA-sponsored programs,
71; safety committees and,
53-54, 171-72; in Sweden,
87-90, 126-30, 252-53; in U.K.,
105-6, 233-34, 236-37; in U.S.,
4, 179-81, 229-31, 252-53, 275;
in West Germany, 87, 121-25,
192-93, 195. See also conflict;
cooperation
Labor Standards Bureau, Japan,
113, 132
Landrum-Griffin Act (1959), 48
lawsuits, negligence and, 20-21
lead, 69
legislation. See specific countries
liability awards, 21
lifting, 69
line managers: accountability
and, 278; career-oriented, 185;
conflicts and, 183, 184; performance evaluations of,
169-70; safety and health managers and, 168; in U.K., 238-39;
in West Germany, 198
line-staff disputes, 168
lost-workday injuries, 151, 173,
175, 186, 209, 227

management, 26; conflict-coping
behaviors, 119-20; OSHA and,
27, 71; performance evaluations of, 169-70; strategic

ABOUT THE AUTHOR

RICHARD E. WOKUTCH is a Professor of Management in The R.B. Pamplin College of Business at Virginia Polytechnic Institute and State University (Virginia Tech) where he teaches in the areas of social issues in management, business ethics, and strategic management. He received his B.S. in mathematics and economics and his Ph.D. in business administration from the University of Pittsburgh. He has previously held positions as Visiting Fulbright Research Professor at the Science Center Berlin, West Germany and Visiting Fulbright Research Professor at Hiroshima Institute of Technology, Hiroshima, Japan.

Professor Wokutch has published articles in the *Academy of Management EXECUTIVE, California Management Review, Journal of Accounting and Public Policy, Journal of Public Policy and Marketing,* the *Labor Law Journal,* the *Journal of Business Ethics,* and *Research in Corporate Social Performance and Policy* on various topics related to the social, legal, and ethical environment of business.